THE IMPROVEMENT OF CORPORATE FINANCIAL PERFORMANCE

Recent Titles from Quorum Books

The Improvement of Corporate Financial Performance

A MANAGER'S GUIDE TO EVALUATING SELECTED OPPORTUNITIES

Sherman L. Lewis

Q

QUORUM BOOKS
New York • Westport, Connecticut • London

Library of Congress Cataloging-in-Publication Data

Lewis, Sherman L.
    The improvement of corporate financial performance.

    Includes index.
    1. Corporations—Finance.   I. Title.
HG4026.L623   1989   658.1′5   88-35684
ISBN 0-89930-432-X (lib. bdg. : alk. paper)

British Library Cataloguing in Publication Data is available.

Library of Congress Catalog Card Number: 88-35684
ISBN: 0-89930-432-X

First published in 1989 by Quorum Books

Greenwood Press, Inc.
88 Post Road West, Westport, Connecticut 06881

Printed in the United States of America

The paper used in this book complies with the
Permanent Paper Standard issued by the National
Information Standards Organization (Z39.48-1984).

10 9 8 7 6 5 4 3 2 1

The author extends his appreciation to Barbara Porter McCann of Darien Secretarial Service for professional dedication and cheerful cooperation in word-processing the text.

Contents

PART 2 CONTROLLING CURRENT PERFORMANCE:
WHO NEEDS TO KNOW WHAT, AND WHEN?

Preface

This book provides managers with clear exposition and detailed examples of practical decision making for planning and controlling operations. The material presented is based on extensive experience in management, consulting, and teaching.

The goal is sustainable sales and profit growth within acceptable limits of risk for both profitability and liquidity. Decisions must be guided by information that is timely, clear, and relevant. Upside potential must be weighed against downside risk. Benefits for the long term must be weighed against short-term realities. The financing of profit and growth plans must be supported by a planned capital structure that provides sufficient liquidity. The discount rate used for investments, called variously the investment rate, cut-off rate, cost of capital, or hurdle rate, should be at the minimum that provides positive financial leverage. A higher rate distorts the present value of cash flows thus precluding logical risk analysis. Intangibles must also be incorporated into the decision process. The company's reputation in the financial markets needs to be cultivated. Employee morale must be nurtured.

The book is divided into three parts, each of which emphasizes a particular viewpoint. Part 1 deals with the future--the choices made among the available courses of action that continually shape the future. Part 2 deals with the realities of daily events and the use of operating and financial data to concentrate on vital areas and critical factors. Control can be exercised only before or at the time of occurrence. The financial reports for longer periods and higher management levels are described as historical summaries that do not provide operating control. With an effective control system these reports should contain no surprises. The information network should provide current information on what needs to be known to those who need to know. Separate analyses are given for the evaluation of individual performance and for economic units. The problem of translating foreign currency into dollars to measure subsidiary operations is explored. Part 3 supplies the basics of the accounting "black box" to enable management to communicate effectively with accountants and others. Good managers are able to grasp the purpose of accounting and know how to get from it what they need. They direct the accounting process and keep accountants from reverting to a bookkeeping level or hiding behind jargon. Part 3 also provides the basis for information systems. All transactions must be coded and recorded in a manner that supports and facilitates both internal and external analyses and reporting. No system can possibly capture all the data that is needed or may be needed. The best approach is a "building block" system that encodes data in units that are adaptable to various uses.

The presentation focuses on the manager and the situation, not on techniques per se. Certain topics appear in two or all three parts in order to direct attention to: (1) evaluating choices for the future; (2) dealing with the current situation; or (3) using the information system.

The principal academic fields drawn on are:

Finance-- principally corporate finance but with some related macro and personal finance

Accounting-- principally managerial but with relevant cost and financial accounting

Economics-- managerial economics including micro (pricing) and some macro

Management-- as to goals and policies, and in terms of individual and economic entities

Mathematics-- common formulations

Systems-- information and control systems at the management level

The contribution from each field is brought to bear on each topic to the extent that it is relevant and practical in terms of decision making and control. A serious neglect of this approach in the literature is a primary motivation for undertaking this project.

A sharp distinction is preserved throughout between published information, as directed by outside authority, and internal information that is collected in building blocks to serve management needs. Topics not included in this book include data processing, telecommunications, management science, statistical analysis, human resource accounting, procedures and forms, and office methods. Ample material on these topics is readily available. Their proper use depends on the framework provided in this book. Hackneyed and imprecise terms such as "the bottom line," "return on investment," "management information systems," "management by objective," "participative management," "zero defects," "optimum results," and "suboptimal decisions" are avoided.

There is an unfortunate tendency to make the accountant a scapegoat, blaming bad news on the bearer. The job of accounting is to record and report transactions. But transactions are frequently complex, voluminous, and difficult to define. Moreover, the content of reports needed in the future is conjectural. Hence management must be responsible for the design and functioning of the accounting system. Accountants can advise and assist but no more. Just as war is said to be too important to leave to the generals, systems are too important to be left to the specialists. Systems capability ranks in significance with the capability of management, marketing, manufacturing, and finance-- weakness in one undermines the whole.

The efficiency of systems depends on the clarity of communications-- oral and written; superior and subordinate; one function with another; specialist and generalist. Technical people tend to become preoccupied with their expertise while managers tend to shy away from the topic to avoid exposing their ignorance. This problem is too often present with accountants--the "bean counters." Controllers carry a heavy load in meeting all requirements for published information. Records must be kept in compliance with all regulations and reports must be prepared to meet all externally imposed demands. Emphasis is on the total entity and past performance. In contrast, management needs data to help plan the future, to analyze investment decisions, to control current revenues and expenses, and to analyze performance by segments. This need is met to an extent by functional subdivisions within the controller's staff--budgets, costs, systems, audit, billing, payables, payroll, fixed assets, general accounting, tax, and data processing. The communication problem is further compounded by the natural tendency of many accountants to be reclusive, literal, inarticulate, technical, and defensive. Too often they are isolated--organizationally, socially, physically--limiting their acceptance and understanding of operations. There is a concomitant tendency for some managers to operate without significant input from accounting, and to develop homespun systems, often dangerous and expensive.

> Accounting graduates do not know how to communicate, do not reason logically, are deficient in interpersonal skills, and cannot think creatively and responsibly...The accounting profession is expanding, entering a new era with new functions within organizations... (Norton M. Bedford and William G. Shenkir, "Reorienting Accounting Education," Journal of Accounting [August 1987]: 86)

A constructive way to alleviate this handicap has been applied successfully in several organizations. An individual or staff--qualified in problem solving, analysis, systems, finance, and accounting--is an integral part of each operating group--marketing, manufacturing, engineering--and reports directly to the top position, such as vice president or general manager. These technical staffs are involved in all activities and learn the operations in detail. They take the initiative in developing systems, reports, and analyses that best serve the operating people and develop a close working relationship with the managers. They are the interface with other company staff, both providing any cooperation needed and interpreting information supplied. They insure the timely and accurate flow of information needed by accounting, interpret accounting reports to their departments, and contribute to the design of company systems. By understanding the accounting process they contribute to more effective and efficient systems, and to better reports and analyses. Proposals to top management can be better prepared, encouraging acceptance. Qualifications for this staff include communication skills, inquisitiveness, initiative, social orientation, operating experience, and degrees such as M.B.A., C.M.A., C.P.A., or industrial engineering.

This organizational proposal, as well as those made throughout the book, are directed toward overcoming failures in control that are cited regularly in periodicals and by the press. Several such statements are paraphrased to underscore the nature and degree of the shortcomings observed:

. Outmoded accounting systems may be responsible for the failure of
many companies to update their factories.
. Existing financial controls have inhibited the modernization of
manufacturers.
. Shortcomings of management accounting are delaying the introduction
of vitally needed new technology.
. Companies are being held hostage by the inadequacies and
inappropriateness of old management accounting practices.
. U.S. companies are being hamstrung by obsolete cost accounting and
management control systems.
. Updating outmoded accounting techniques may be imperative to
survival. Major changes in cost accounting must be developed.
. Accounting has failed to recognize the effect of intangibles such
as better quality and more flexible scheduling.
. Investments in new machinery and systems are necessary to improve
quality, leaving accountants with the challenge of measuring such
benefits as increased consumer satisfaction, faster delivery time, and
flexible production scheduling.
. Management focus on share prices and short term profitability
undermines programs that are needed for long-term competitiveness and
profitability.

These adumbrations cloud the issue. The shortcomings stated are
management failures that can be overcome by using the proposals made in
this book. Many companies have excellent systems by virtue of management
direction, organizational effort, ingenuity, perseverence, and continual
updating. Neglected systems fall into disuse and ersatz procedures grow
like weeds to meet new developments. Business dynamics compel constant
study and revision.
This book is addressed to those who recognize a need for better
information and are perceptive enough to know that improvement is not
only possible but essential. The material is presented in a manner
suitable for all managers--at all levels and in all functions. The
target audience includes all aspiring managers, consultants, accountants,
systems staff, auditors, analysts, business writers, students, and
teachers.

PART 1

ANALYZING ALTERNATIVES FOR GROWTH AND PROFIT: SHAPING THE FUTURE BY TODAY'S CHOICES

Introduction: Elements of the Decision Process

Certain fundamentals that underlie the decision-making process are broadly applicable and require continual attention. They are described briefly in this introduction and developed more fully in the examination of topics throughout the text:

Time
Volume
Costs
Opportunity Cost
Inflation
The Discount Rate
Risk
Liquidity
Measurement
Organization

Time

Each decision must be clearly defined in terms of its relevant length of time. In the long run all costs are variable: fixed assets can reach zero (or negative) value over time--the approach used for capital expenditure analysis. In the short run all costs are fixed: expenses cannot be reduced for brief periods such as power outages, fire drills, or storms. Arbitrary assumptions about time can be dangerous. A common error is the use of flexible annual expense budgets, developed for use in expense control, for situations with shorter or longer time spans. The breakout of variable and fixed expense elements based on time and volume assumptions is necessarily arbitrary and unlikely to be relevant to other situations. "There is a widespread and unfortunate notion that financial accounting costs are universally applicable for all kinds of business decisions" (Joel Dean, Managerial Economics, [Englewood Cliffs, N.J.: Prentice-Hall, 1951], p. 257).

Volume

The quantity to be produced must be specified for each decision and related to scheduled available capacity. A decision to increase production beyond planned capacity can entail substantial extra costs--overtime, subcontracting, delayed shipments, and capital expenditures. A decision to reduce output may lower some expenses but not necessarily as expressed in the flexible budgets. Budgets for expense control are based on plans for one year and expected output ranges within the year--the relevant range. Budgets for production outside the relevant range require separate determination.

Costs

"The word 'cost' has many meanings in many different settings" (Dean, Managerial Economics, p. 257).

Recorded product costs are historical costs based on GAAP (generally accepted accounting principles). Decisions must be based on future costs. Several concepts apply in addition to the elements of time and volume described above. Incremental costs are the added costs attributable to the decision, equivalent to marginal costs used in economics. Costs not changed by a decision are called sunk costs and can be omitted from analysis. Incremental costs may be out-of-pocket, requiring current outlay, or costs on the books that are applicable. Decisions to reduce activity involve determination of costs that can be eliminated--escapable costs--and those that are unavoidable.

All costs are controllable by someone. The determination of individual responsibilities for income and expense is called "responsibility accounting." What is controllable by one is not controllable by another but the term uncontrollable costs should be avoided. Costs that have full identity with a cost object (product, department, work order) are direct costs. All other costs are indirect for that cost object. Common costs are related to several cost objects and may be traceable in varying degrees, or allocated arbitrarily on some selected basis. Joint costs refer only to costs incurred in processing a single product to a split-off point where several end products emerge (paper, chemical, petroleum, meat processing). Joint costs can be related to end products only by arbitrary allocation. Costs incurred after the split-off point are measured directly to each product.

Opportunity Cost

This economic concept may be of central importance. For any decision that necessitates giving up some alternative, the lost gain of the best alternative is the opportunity cost. It is a profit or benefit foregone. It is zero if there is no alternative or if the best alternative has no value. It could equal the gain of the chosen alternative, such as may be the case for mutually exclusive choices, with subjective factors tipping the scale. Opportunity costs do not appear in the records but may be the controlling element; an overlooked opportunity cost can be significant even if intangible. For example, decisions to use management time in one endeavor rather than another can be critical, an important point in evaluating capital expenditure programs. Also some products and markets may be selected for more cultivation than others, involving both cash outlays and the time of salespeople. Available extra warehouse space used for convenience has an opportunity cost equal to its outside rental value, which may be zero or a large amount.

Inflation

Prices are constantly changing in response to market dynamics and government regulation. Price movements in general, as measured by some index, are also changing constantly--inflation and deflation. The study and prediction of prices requires recognition of both factors. Extensive and intensive efforts to adjust financial statements for inflation have produced no definable benefit for the public or for management. The two principal adjustment methods have the same goal but are opposite in concept. The "constant dollar" method uses a general price index such as the CPI (consumer price index) to adjust historical book amounts to present dollars. The "current cost" method disregards book amounts and restates balance sheet items (assets and debt) at current amounts, such as replacement cost. The two results may be similar or disparate.

Management concern is primarily with future cash flow. Estimation involves both changing price relationships and inflation, which are difficult to predict but can have a major impact. Assumptions used should be clearly stated and incorporated in the range of probable outcomes used for risk analysis. Current prices reflect current inflation and require no adjustment. Future cash flows can be adjusted in a range for both inflation and price relationships. The discount rate (net current borrowing rate) used to express future cash flows as present value requires no inflation adjustment; the future cost of debt is not relevant. The evaluation of current performance for past investments is aided by reference to the project cash flow ranges and assumptions.

Sales for a number of years may be adjusted for inflation if practial and desirable. For instance, if sales have doubled in nine years, the annual rate is 8 percent. If prices also doubled, the quantity is unchanged. Analysis may also be made relative to the industry for comparison of quantities as well as dollars. Sales reports for management should include both quantities and prices at the specific product level. At higher levels of summarization, total sales divided by total quantities yield only a statistical quotient that is not useful. Product prices are generally related to the prices of competitors. The relationship to general price levels is academic.

Excerpts from a speech by Paul A. Volker are relevant here.

So-called inflation accounting is at best an inadequate response to the increasing complexities of financial reporting...We recently went through a period when...inflation came close to making nonsense of standard accounting reports of profits...It may be misleading even to suggest that there is any single measure of profits or capital that is uniquely correct...There is a compelling need to innovate...to more closely reflect the nature of business results and the range of uncertainty.

(Paul A. Volcker, speech at the centennial meeting of the American Institute of CPAs in New York City, Journal of Accounting [November 1987]: p 4)

The Discount Rate

Investments are made to achieve growth and profit in line with goals and policies. A question fundamental to survival and prosperity is how to specify and measure the required profit for an investment. A discount rate that is too high chokes off good proposals and stunts growth. The spurious appeal of a high rate of return lowers the amount invested and can lead to an uncompetitive position. A discount rate that is too low may stimulate rapid growth but cause a poor return on investment. A return on assets lower than the borrowing rate reduces return on equity--negative financial leverage--and impairs liquidity.

The most constructive and practical rate is the borrowing rate net of taxes, kept up to date for both interest and tax changes. The rate should be based on substantial sums for long periods, consonant with the plans for both capital structure and capital expenditures. If a point is reached where new equity is needed to finance additional capital expenditure, a new investment rate should be determined to evaluate the incremental outlays. Equity rates exceed debt rates by a significant

margin because of risk. The new rate would be a weighted average of the
new equity rate and the debt rate for the added borrowing enabled by the
new equity according to the planned capital structure. For example: borrowing rate equals interest 10% minus tax (40%) = 6%. New equity rate =
15%. Capital structure = debt to equity ratio 50% (debt to capital 33
1/3%).

	Capital	Rate	Average	
Debt	$50	6%	$ 3	
Equity	100	15%	15	
	$150		$18	18/150 = 12%

Proposals to be financed with new equity would be evaluated with
the 12% rate as compared with the current 6% rate.   Continued use of 6%
is not correct because it assumes an excessive amount of debt that would
threaten solvency. Use of the 15% equity rate alone is not correct
because it disregards the added availability of debt.

Risk

Investment proposals may involve risk for both current outlays and
future cash flows. Risk refers to cash flow ranges that can be expressed
as probabilities.   Uncertainty relates to future events that cannot
reasonably be anticipated.   A single estimate of cash flows is a point
estimate. The chance for better results is "upside potential" and for
worse results "downside risk." Cash flows must be estimated in specific
amounts for each period with a probability expressed for each outcome.
The projections should include consideration of both changing price
relationships and inflation.   The use of probabilities facilitates
communication by putting subjective attitudes toward risk into concrete
form.   Individual risk attitudes are highly diverse, vary over time,
differ relative to the situation at hand, and are not necessarily
transitive.   Evaluation of proposals for both the gains and losses
related to their chance of occurrence is clearer, and agreement to
accept, reject, or re-examine is fostered.   The review of performance
after projects become operational is also aided by reference to the range
of outcomes.

A risk-free rate must be used to discount future cash flows to
present values so that risk can be separately and objectively appraised.
A higher discount rate distorts present values in disguised amounts. The
degree of bias is both unknown and varies among proposals according to
the rate used and the cash flow timing and amounts. The nature and
degree of risk must be assessed for both current and future cash flows by
period based on amounts not tainted by a random risk factor. Treasury
bond rates best meet the risk-free criterion but the practical alternative is the company's current net borrowing rate. The difference is
small in terms of capital expenditure evaluation and each company can use
a rate that is designed to avoid negative leverage. Few projects are
risk-free and a clear reading on downside risk for both amount and
probability is important.   There is a natural antipathy to the risk of
loss, tempered to some degree by greed for great gain.   Utility theory
describes the relationship between dollars and their "value" relative to
risk. To expect high return with low risk is unrealistic and self-
defeating.

Liquidity

Liquidity is the availability of cash over time to meet all obligations, with a reserve to handle contingencies and unexpected opportunities. If liquidity is threatened, management choices become limited to preserving cash at the expense of profits. The cost of insolvency is severe: forced sales, liquidation, reorganization, bankruptcy. Long-term liquidity, or solvency, relates to capital structure--debt and equity. Debt entails interest and repayment of principal. If profits fall off the reduced cash flows impair liquidity. Borrowing involves a degree of financial risk that is heightened by the operating risk attaching to investments. The combined risk is a policy question. Risk positions vary widely among industries and companies.

Liquidity is managed by cash flow projections in days, weeks, months--based on every source of cash flow in and out. Cash plans must be monitored daily and adjusted quickly for changing circumstances. The foundation for cash planning is the financial projection expressed in the balance sheet, income statement, and funds statement. Extra cash is planned to meet unforeseen needs and may be invested temporarily in marketable securities.

It is essential to have a clear understanding of the meaning of "funds" and "cash," terms too often used interchangeably. Cash is currency, on hand and in banks, available to spend and pay bills--legal tender. Funds are amounts determined by accrual accounting as expressed in the balance sheet. The funds statement sets out changes for the period in all balances. It is officially titled "Statement of Changes in Financial Position." Cash forecasts are essential but a history of cash receipts and disbursements has little or no management value, although it could aid cash planning. Funds statements are published but not records of cash. Investor concern with liquidity is legitimate but published forecasts are not required and are unlikely to be volunteered. The distinction between funds and cash is significant and should be carefully observed.

Measurement

Financial. The financial profitability of investments in assets is measured by cash flows for the economic life, expressed both as a rate of return and as net present value based on the discount rate. The rate of return, or yield, is implicitly the same for each period. No depreciation is expressed because depreciable assets are consumed within the economic life, either in full or down to net recoverable value in cash. No interest cost is expressed because it is part of the yield or discount rate. This financial method--cash to cash--is a true profitability measure not based on accrual accounting the primary purpose of which is to measure profit for interim periods. However, the cash impact of taxes must be included based on tax regulations and related accounting practices.

Accounting. Accounting profitability is based on accrual accounting according to GAAP and includes both cash and economic events and transactions. Periodic financial statements are prepared by "closing the books" at the time of "cut-off." Both completed and uncompleted transactions are measured and significant assumptions about the future must be made. Accounting rates of return used to measure performance and financial yields computed to make investment decisions differ, often to a marked degree, and must be evaluated separately.

Economic. The approach of economics is based on market values. The decline in market value for an asset is depreciation; an increase in market value is appreciation. The value of an asset in use is its ability to generate future cash flows, discounted to present value at the "appropriate" discount rate.

The value of holding an asset can be compared with its disposal value; this approach is used in capital expenditure analysis. Economic profit in theory does not exist in the long run because of competition. Revenue equals the cost of the factors of production--labor, rent, interest. Profit is regarded as an excess return arising from sources such as monopoly, innovation, and market disruptions.

Taxes. Taxes are constantly changing and are complex. They must be computed meticulously. They are a central part of both financial and accounting computations. The possible effect of taxes on future cash flows requires careful estimation.

Learning Curve. A particularly challenging problem is recognition of the learning curve and its effect on investment decisions, performance measurement, and record keeping and reporting.

Foreign Exchange. Operations in foreign countries involve both transaction costs for currency movements and translation adjustments when consolidated statements are prepared. The recognition of income taxes requires special attention. Decisions to invest abroad call for the particular evaluation of the risk factors for both asset profitability and currency exchange rates and regulations.

Organization

All decisions are guided by the company's goals, strategies, and policies. In turn, supporting objectives, plans, programs, and projects are formulated. These provide the basis for budgets and projected financial statements. Actual performance is then evaluated and future prospects weighed. The process is circular and ongoing.

Budgets embrace all activities and are stated for specific periods and individual responsibilities--"responsibility accounting"--reflecting organization structure and delegation. Prior to acceptance exploratory analyses are made as forecasts and projections, and pro forma statements may be prepared to demonstrate the effect of alternatives.

Published financial statements are regulated by GAAP and management policy on disclosure. Internal information can be generated in any form useful to management; it is not bound by accounting, either as a function or a definition. Management information and management control systems are much too important to be left to accountants and systems experts. Publicity to the effect that accounting fails to meet management needs is misguided.

1

Evaluation of Projected Financial Statements

FINANCIAL STATEMENTS

The end results of planning can be summarized in three projected financial statements:

> Balance Sheet--or Statement of Financial Position
> Income Statement--or Statement of Profit and Loss
> Funds Statement--or Statement of Changes in Financial Position

These projections are reviewed and evaluated for profitability, growth, liquidity, and risk relative to goals and policies. After any needed revision, they are restated as budgets to guide and coordinate all decisions and for comparison with actual results. The reporting formats presented are designed for internal use only; the niceties obligatory for published statements are disregarded.

Projected Balance Sheet

Net Current Assets:			
Current Assets			
Cash	$200		
Receivables	300		
Inventory	500	$1,000	
Current Liabilities			
Payables	150		
Accruals	100		
Taxes	50	300	$ 700
Net Fixed Assets:			
Land	100		
Buildings	600		
Machinery	900		
In Process	200	1,800	
Accumulated Depreciation		900	900
Deferred Charges			100
Deferred Taxes Payable			(200)
Net Assets			$1,500

```
Debt:
    Due in one year
        Bank Loan (15%)                          $  100
        Bond Payment (13%)                          100
                                                    200

    Long-Term Bond (13%)                            400     $  600

Equity:
    Capital Stock (100 shares)                      300
    Retained Earnings                               600          900

    Capital                                                  $1,500
```

This projection shows the result of all underlying plans for operations, investments, and financing stated in terms of assets, liabilities, and capital.

The capital structure is debt $600 and equity $900--a debt to equity (D-E) ratio of 67%. Debt is also 40% of total capital at $1,500, but this ratio is less useful because the total contains the amount to be measured. Published ratios are often not clear as to what is included in debt or even what is included in the denominator. Another measurement of dubious value includes all current liabilities in capital. This composition of capital is called "financial structure." Preferred stock that is considered part of equity because repayment is not obligatory is excluded from this example. However, for financial and management purposes, preferred stock is a distinct source of capital that must be analyzed separately. Dividends are usually fixed in amount and cumulative over time with preference over common dividends. Payment requires authorization by the board of directors but financially the effect is the equivalent of interest, a fixed charge that must be met to maintain good standing.

The current portion of debt--$200--is part of total debt--$600--to show the true picture of capital, contrary to the usual practice of inclusion with current liabilities. The timing of debt payment is relevant to liquidity but secondary to the contractual obligation to repay principal with interest. All debt must be included to measure financial leverage correctly, the effect that borrowing has on return to equity.

Capital stock--$300--is the total paid in by shareholders. There is no need to break out the amount based on state legal requirements such as par, stated value, no par, or excess amounts paid in, customarily shown in published statements as evidence of compliance with legal capital stipulation. Retained earnings of $600 include net income to date less declared dividends. Omitted here but considered later is the cumulative amount of translation adjustments for foreign subsidiaries, often a large debit. The total capital of $1,500 supports the net assets used to operate the business.

Current assets of $1,000 are offset by current liabilities of $300, and the $700 net is provided by capital. The current liabilities arise in the natural course of business and have no explicit cost. For liquidity measurement the current debt of $200 may be added to the $300 to show a current ratio of 2 to 1 ($1,000/$500) but this is not useful to management. This ratio is one of many prepared from published reports because better information is not available, and to provide comparability among companies and industries for general credit purposes. Management may need to be aware of analyses used by outsiders for purposes of public relations. Net fixed assets of $900 show planned acquisitions and disposals, less depreciation on buildings and machinery. The $200 in process includes projects in the capital expenditure program. Deferred charges of $100 are expenditures applicable to future operations for better matching of income and expense. Examples include relocation expenses, sales promotion material, and consulting charges. The $200 tax liability is deferred because of timing differences between total taxes based on accrual accounting and taxes currently payable based on the tax return. Payment is expected to be made in the future but the amounts and timing are conjectural.

Projected Income Statement

Sales		$4,000	100%
Cost of Sales		2,400	60
Gross Profit		1,600	40
Expenses:			
Marketing	$600		
Administrative	500		
Research	100	1,200	30
Operating Profit		400	10
Interest:			
Bank Loan (15%)	15		
Bonds (13%)	65	80	2
Profit Before Tax		320	8
Taxes (37.5%)			
Tax Return	80		
Deferred	40	120	3
Net Income		200	5
Retained Earnings:			
Opening Balance		400	
Ending Balance		$ 600	

The operating plans are projected to produce a $400 operating profit, 10% of sales. Interest is planned at $80, leaving $320 subject to taxes for which a rate of 37.5% is projected. It is expected that $80 will be currently taxable and $40 deferred to the future. The net income of $200 is added to the opening balance of retained earnings to arrive at the $600 shown on the balance sheet. No dividends are planned.

Projected Funds Statement
                Financing

Equity:
    Net income $200
    Add nonfund charges:
        Depreciation   110
        Deferred taxes   40
    Funds provided by operations $350

Debt:
    Bank loan   100
    Bonds   (100)   0
                Financing total $350

                Investing

Net current assets $100

Fixed assets:
    Buildings $100
    Machinery   150   250
                Investing total $350

The planned increases in net current assets and fixed assets are scheduled to be financed from earnings with no net change in debt or capital stock. No dividends are planned. The $100 increase in net current assets is supported by the individual amounts (not shown). The $250 increase in fixed assets is supported by the capital expenditure program. No retirements are planned. A supporting statement of cash flows could also be prepared based on these projections. All cash receipts and disbursements would be itemized for each period. The net changes in cash flow would be added to the present cash balance to project future cash balances by period. This cash flow analysis would show the degree of liquidity and indicate any need for change in the financing plan. The cash flow projection is based on the funds statement, which reflects all balance sheet changes on an accrual (funds) basis. This distinction between "funds" and "cash" is critical. Only cash pays the bills. The cash balance tomorrow depends on the cash received and paid out tomorrow.

Control of Net Assets

Asset control must be exercised separately for each account. The subject is briefly reviewed here. Chapters 2, 3, and 4 contain detailed expositions. Asset control rests basically on trade-offs between profit, risk, and liquidity in a wide variety of combinations reflective of management's aggressiveness and courage to take risks. The publicized ratios commonly used by credit grantors are of little use to management.

Cash. Cash balances change constantly and are controlled by the cash plan derived from the funds statement. Large cash balances strengthen liquidity but reduce return on assets (ROA), largely a subjective choice. The effect is illustrated for operation profit of $400 less $150 tax, or $250 net before interest:

	Balance Sheet	$150 Less Cash	$150 More Cash
Cash	$ 200	$ 50	$ 350
Assets	1500	1350	1650
Profit	250	250	250
ROA	16.7%	18.5%	15.1%
Cash to Assets	13.3	3.7	21.2

Effective cash management is receiving increased attention from both management and the financial community.

Receivables. Receivables can be expressed in number of days for comparison with credit terms.   For example, using financial statement amounts:

Receivables	$ 300	
Total Sales	$4000	= 7.5% of 360 days = 27 days

The receivables balance is current if terms are for 25 days and all sales are on credit. However, many factors must be considered, such as cash sales, terms of credit sales, seasonality, nontrade accounts, credit balances, and bad debt allowance. For example:

Net receivables	$300
Credit balances	50
	350
Bad debt allowance	30
	380
Nontrade accounts	20
Trade receivables	$360
Cash sales	$400
Credit sales	3600
Total sales	$4000

The revised calculation is:

Trade Receivables	$ 360	
Credit Sales	3600	10% of 360 days = 36 days

This answer is substantially higher than 27 days and indicates a serious condition if terms are for 25 days. Receivables should be:

```
Credit Sales        $3600
Days                 360    = $10 x 25 days     $250 plan
                                                 360 actual
                                                $110 excess--44%
```

If sales include two sets of terms--10 days and 60 days--each must be analyzed separately:

		Total		10 Days		60 Days
Credit Sales		$3600		$2520		$1080
Per Day (360 Days)		$ 10		$ 7		$ 3
Plan	25d	$ 250	10d	$ 70	60d	$ 180
Actual	36d	360	24d	168	64d	192
Excess	11d	$ 110	14d	$ 98	4d	$ 12
		44%		140%		7%

This breakout is essential but further data is needed: customer names, balances, dates, and collection status.

   Inventory. Inventory control is primarily a function of the production process and is a major factor in both productivity and expense control. Inventories are based on production plans and vendor relations, plus calculations of economic order quantity and safety stocks (described later). As a point of general reference, overall inventory turnover can be expressed as:

```
                   Cost of Sales  $2400
                   Inventory      $ 500   = 4.8 times or 75 days
```

Effective control rests on carefully defined categories and subdivisions.
   Payables to vendors are current liabilities deducted from current assets. The inventory balances can be offset by a range of payable credits from zero to the full amount billed. Inventory may be shipped and billed before vendor payment is due, giving rise to a credit balance. The net inventory balance is in a constant state of flux with varying patterns of usage and payment.
   Current Liabilities. Current liabilities include vendor balances, payroll accruals, taxes, utility bills, and other items arising in the ordinary course of business. This spontaneous credit has no explicit cost. The total offsets are deducted from current assets and the net amount is supported by the capital structure. The term working capital in common use is objectionable. Published reports include currently payable debt as a current liability, all of which appears in the liability section of the balance sheet, and current liabilities and debt are often subtotaled. These ingrained practices are contrary to logical analysis.

The goal is to achieve 30% ROA.

		Profit %		ROA

Higher turnover:

$$\frac{S\ 1000}{A\ 333} \quad \times \quad \frac{P\ 100}{S\ 1000} \quad = \quad \frac{P\ 100}{A\ 333}$$
$$3 \quad \times \quad 10\% \quad = \quad 30\%$$

$$\frac{S\ 1200}{A\ 400} \quad \times \quad \frac{P\ 120}{S\ 1200} \quad = \quad \frac{P\ 120}{A\ 400}$$
$$3 \quad \times \quad 10\% \quad = \quad 30\%$$

$$\frac{S\ 1200}{A\ 333} \quad \times \quad \frac{P\ 100}{S\ 1200} \quad = \quad \frac{P\ 100}{A\ 333}$$
$$3.6 \quad \times \quad 8.3\% \quad = \quad 30\%$$

Same turnover:

$$\frac{S\ 1200}{A\ 480} \quad \times \quad \frac{P\ 144}{S\ 1200} \quad = \quad \frac{P\ 144}{A\ 480}$$
$$2.5 \quad \times \quad 12\% \quad = \quad 30\%$$

$$\frac{S\ 833}{A\ 333} \quad \times \quad \frac{P\ 100}{S\ 833} \quad = \quad \frac{P\ 100}{A\ 333}$$
$$2.5 \quad \times \quad 12\% \quad = \quad 30\%$$

Lower turnover:

$$\frac{S\ 920}{A\ 400} \quad \times \quad \frac{P\ 120}{S\ 920} \quad = \quad \frac{P\ 120}{A\ 400}$$
$$2.3 \quad \times \quad 13\% \quad = \quad 30\%$$

$$\frac{S\ 920}{A\ 460} \quad \times \quad \frac{P\ 138}{S\ 920} \quad = \quad \frac{P\ 138}{A\ 460}$$
$$2 \quad \times \quad 15\% \quad = \quad 30\%$$

If both ratios are higher:

$$\frac{S\ 1100}{A\ 333} \quad \times \quad \frac{P\ 121}{S\ 1100} \quad = \quad \frac{P\ 121}{A\ 333}$$
$$3.3 \quad \times \quad 11\% \quad = \quad 36.3\%$$

If both ratios are lower:

$$\frac{S\ 900}{A\ 450} \quad \times \quad \frac{P\ 81}{S\ 900} \quad = \quad \frac{P\ 81}{A\ 450}$$
$$2 \quad \times \quad 9\% \quad = \quad 18\%$$

These examples show the need for asset control relative to sales, both in terms of turnover ratio and to avoid expenses attaching to excess assets. The sales profit percent relates to pricing, volume, and expense control.

When a company has divisions responsible for both profits and assets, the ROA equation can be used for each. For example, a company consists of three divisions and a home office, as follows:

	Company	Home Office	Division Total	A	B	C
Sales	$4000	$ 0	$4000	$2800	$400	$800
Expenses	3750	30	3720	2660	356	704
Profit	250	(30)	280	140	44	96
Assets	$1500	$100	$1400	$ 700	$400	$300
ROA %	16.67		20.00	20.00	11.00	32.00
Turnover	2.67		2.86	4.00	1.00	2.67
Profit %	6.25		7.00	5.00	11.00	12.00

The company goal of 16.67% ROA requires the divisions to realize 20% collectively. Division A has a 20% ROA based on high turnover. Division B has an 11% ROA, with a low turnover. Division C has a 32% ROA with a high rate of profit on sales. Each division must be judged independently. The division totals are for reference but not for control.

ROA analyses are made from records based primarily on costs according to GAAP. Depreciable assets are reduced by periodic depreciation charges. Equipment, for example, with a 10-year life purchased 8 years ago has a smaller balance than equivalent equipment acquired 2 years ago. Both the depreciation method and any change in price for the equipment purchased 6 years later affect the balances. Price changes reflect, but are not limited to, inflation. In six years equipment prices may increase, decrease, or remain the same.

Examples are given to illustrate the effects of time using depreciation by SL (straight line) and SYD (sum-of-the-years digits), first with no change in the price of the equipment and then assuming that the price doubles in 6 years--an annual rate of 12.2%. It is assumed that Division East was started 8 years ago with equipment costing $55,000 and a 10-year life, and that Division West was established 6 years later, 2 years ago, with identical equipment and a 10-year life. In the first example, the equipment cost is unchanged at $55,000 and in the second example the cost doubles to $110,000. SL depreciation is 10% a year. SYD is 55, the sum of 1 to 10, divided by 10 for year 1, by 9 for year 2, by 2 for year 9, by 1 for year 10.

	West (2 yrs. ago)		East (8 yrs. ago)	
Cost unchanged:				
Cost		$55,000		$55,000
SL	20%	11,000	80%	44,000
Balance - SL	80%	44,000	20%	11,000
SYD	19/55	19,000	52/55	52,000
Balance - SYD	36/55	36,000	3/55	3,000
Cost doubles:				
Cost		$110,000		$55,000
SL		22,000		44,000
Balance - SL		88,000		11,000
SYD		38,000		52,000
Balance - SYD		72,000		3,000

The impact on ROA can be great, first illustrated with an example assuming the case of cost increase to $110,000 and SYD depreciation shown above. ROA is compared for both East and West with income statements differing only for depreciation and balance sheets differing only for fixed assets.

Assets		West End of Year 2		East End of Year 8	
Above:					
Equipment cost		$110,000		$ 55,000	
SYD depreciation	19/55	38,000	52/55	52,000	
Balance	36/55	72,000	3/55	3,000	
Plus:					
Other assets		128,000		128,000	
Total		$200,000 B		$131,000 B	

Income Statement		Year 3		Year 9	
Sales		$150,000		$150,000	
SYD depreciation	8/55	16,000	2/55	2,000	
Other expenses		84,000		84,000	
		100,000		86,000	
Operating profit		50,000		64,000	
Tax at 40%		20,000		25,600	
Profit after tax		$ 30,000 A		$ 38,400 A	
ROA	A/B	15.0%		29.3%	

The East appears to be almost twice as profitable as the West. The example is reworked with SL depreciation.

Assets		West	East	
Equipment net-above		$ 88,000	$ 11,000	
Other assets		128,000	128,000	
Total		$216,000 B	$139,000 B	
Sales		$150,000	$150,000	
SL depreciation		11,000	5,500	
Other expenses		84,000	84,000	
		95,000	89,500	
Operating profit		55,000	60,500	
Tax at 40%		22,000	24,200	
Profit after tax		33,000 A	36,300 A	
ROA	A/B	15.3%	26.1%	

ROA for the West is now 15.3% (was 15.0%) and ROA for the East is now 26.1% (was 29.3%).

ROA may also be computed without depreciation as follows:

		West		East	
Total assets (depreciation added back)		$238,000 B		$183,000 B	
Operating profit (without depreciation		66,000		66,000	
Tax at 40%		26,400		26,400	
Profit after tax		39,600 A		39,600 A	
ROA	A/B	16.6%	A/B	21.6%	

Profits are now equal at $39,600. The higher equipment cost for West increases total assets by $55,000 and lowers ROA compared with East by 5 points. West ROA has increased by 1.6 (15.0 to 16.6) and East ROA has decreased by 7.7 (29.3 to 21.6). ROA can also be computed with inflation adjustments based on "current cost" or "constant dollar" methods.

In practice, experience with a variety of alternatives has led to no clear preference: consensus lies with amounts as recorded and reported for clarity and consistency. The cures seem to be worse than the disease.

The problem is more apparent than real. Each company division must plan and budget to achieve the best results attainable by asset utilization and profit rate on sales. Results are compared with budget, and new plans are made. Comparison among divisions should be limited to achievement compared with budget, interpreted in the light of circumstances. In terms of ROA, if the West budget is 15% and it achieves 18%, it outperforms the East with a budget of 30% and results of 28%. Each division, or segment, should be evaluated only in terms of its ability to contribute to profit over the company discount rate. In practice, conditions differ markedly among divisions--even those producing the same products with similar assets. The examples given are highly simplified to clarify the situation.

Assets are acquired by capital expenditure analysis using NPV (net present value), which is not constrained by GAAP because it is based on cash flows and the discount rate. Assets are held or sold using the opportunity cost approach, and these decisions are also part of the capital expenditure program. Undue concern with the limitations of book ROA because of "accounting" is sterile.

Leverage Ratios

Operating leverage is the effect of fixed operating expenses, as defined for a given time and volume, on operating profit for _changes_ in sales, expressed as a ratio--degree of operating leverage (DOL).

Financial leverage is the effect of fixed financial expenses, such as interest, on profit for _changes_ in sales, expressed as a ratio--degree of financial leverage (DFL).

The product of DOL and DFL is the degree of combined leverage (DCL).

The following four examples illustrate the method with 40% variable expenses (VE) and 60% variable margin (VM).

	No Leverage	High DOL	High DFL	High DCL
Sales	$1000	$1000	$1000	$1000
Variable expenses (VE)	400	400	400	400
A Variable margin (VM)	600	600	600	600
Fixed expenses	0	300	0	300
B Operating profit	600	300	600	300
Interest	0	0	400	200
C Profit	$ 600	$ 300	$ 200	$ 100
% to sales	60%	30%	20%	10%

DOL A/B	600/600 = 1	600/300 = 2	600/600 = 1	600/300 = 2
DFL B/C	600/600 = 1	300/300 = 1	600/200 = 3	300/100 = 3
DCL A/C	600/600 = 1	600/300 = 2	600/200 = 3	600/100 = 6

Assuming a 50% sales increase the effect on profit is calculated:
No Leverage: Profit $600 plus 50% (50% DCL1) = $300 = $900
High DOL: Profit $300 plus 100% (50% DCL2) = 300 = $600
High DFL: Profit $200 plus 150% (50% DCL3) = 300 = $500
High DCL: Profit $100 plus 300% (50% DCL6) = 300 = $400

The formula answers are supported by the full schedule:

	No Leverage	High DOL	High DFL	High DCL
Sales--up 50%	$1500	$1500	$1500	$1500
VE--40%	600	600	600	600
A VM--60%	900	900	900	900
Fixed expenses	0	300	0	300
B Operating profit	900	600	900	600
Interest	0	0	400	200
C Profit	$ 900	$ 600	$ 500	$ 400
% to Sales	60%	40%	33-1/3%	26-2/3%
Sales increase	50%	50%	50%	50%
New profit	$ 900	$ 600	$ 500	$ 400
Old profit	- 600	- 300	- 200	- 100
Profit increase	$ 300	$ 300	$ 300	$ 300
	50%	100%	150%	300%
DCL	1	2	3	6

Leverage is negative with lower sales. For high DCL if sales drop 10% to $900, profit drops 60% to $40. With no leverage, profit drops only 10% to $540.
The new leverage ratios are:

DOL	A/B	900/900 = 1.0	900/600 = 1.5	900/900 = 1.0	900/600 = 1.5
DFL	B/C	900/900 = 1.0	600/600 = 1.0	900/500 = 1.8	600/400 = 1.5
DCL	A/C	900/900 = 1.0	900/600 = 1.5	900/500 = 1.8	900/400 = 2.25

Leverage ratios change for every change in sales, becoming progressively smaller as sales increase. It is questionable whether the use of the multiplier is desirable; the incremental analysis for each sales level is simpler, clearer, and less prone to error. The principle of leverage is significant but must be used judiciously and within prescribed parameters of time and volume.

DISCOUNT RATE

The discount rate used to determine the present value of future cash flows for investment analysis can be used advantageously in conjunction with ROA. The discount rate is the minimum acceptable rate of profit and ROA is the average rate of profit; the distinction between a marginal rate and a weighted average is critical. Any investment with a positive NPV is acceptable for profit regardless of the effect on ROA. A positive NPV restated as ROA may lower or raise the overall ROA, which necessarily is a reflection of the profit on all assets acquired by investment decisions. It is worth noting that a company can have only one discount rate because it alone can borrow money, sell stock, and pay dividends; thus only one rate is applicable for all segments. Also, only one rate is applicable for all investments; all assets enter the ROA calculation. Differentials for investment by company segments or type of asset are relevant only to risk analysis.

Using a 10% discount rate as a separate step applied to the division profit analysis made above:

	Company	Home Office	Division Total	A	B	C
Sales	$4000	$ 0	$4000	$2800	$400	$800
Expenses	3750	30	3720	2660	356	704
Profit	250	(30)	280	140	44	96
Assets	$1500	$100	$1400	$ 700	$400	$300
ROA	16.7%	x	20%	20%	11%	32%
10% on assets	$ 150	$ 10	$ 140	$ 70	$ 40	$ 30
Gain (Loss)	$ 100	($40)	$ 140	$ 70	$ 4	$ 66

The added dimension is dollar gain, important by itself. For A, the 20% ROA is $70 gain and $70 at the 10% discount rate. For B, the 11% ROA is $4 gain and $40 at the discount rate. In C, the 32% ROA is $66 gain and $30 at the discount rate. The dollar gains are positive contributions to company wealth, raising the 10% rate to the weighted average ROA. C has a high 32% ROA compared with A's 20% ROA but the dollar gain at $66 is less than the $70 for A. The low 11% ROA for B contains a positive $4 gain.

With a 5% discount rate, the result is:

	Company	Home Office	Division Total	A	B	C
Profit	$ 250	$(30)	$ 280	$ 140	$ 44	$ 96
Assets	1500	100	1400	700	400	300
ROA	16.7%	x	20%	20%	11%	32%
5% on assets	$ 75	$ 5	$ 70	$ 35	$ 20	$ 15
Gain (Loss)	$ 175	($35)	$ 210	$ 105	$ 24	$ 81

The dollar gain relationships change but not the ROAs. Percents stated above are inadequate and may be misleading. The dollar gains are recapped:

	At 10%	%	At 5%	%	Increase	
A	$ 70	50	$105	50	$35	50%
B	4	3	24	11	20	500%
C	66	47	81	39	15	23%
	$140		$210		$70	50%

There is an instinctive aversion to investment proposals that lower ROA even though NPV is positive. The higher the gap between the discount rate and ROA, the greater the danger. Rejection of proposals with positive NPV can seriously impede growth and profitability.
For example:

	Investment Proposal	Current Total	Combined
Assets	A $500	$1000	$1500
10% Rate	50	100	150
Profit	B 60	240	300
Gain	$ 10	$ 140	$ 150
ROA	B/A 12%	24%	20%

The proposal shows a gain of $10 but ROA drops from 24% to 20%. A proposal with an ROA over 24% would raise the current ROA. The current 24% ROA might be composed of past investments as follows:

	Assets	Profit	ROA
	$ 100	$ 50	50%
	150	60	40%
	200	50	25%
	250	50	20%
	300	30	10%
Current	1000	240	24%
Add	500	60	12%
Combined	1500	300	20%

Assets of $300 are at the discount rate of 10%. The book ROA is often below the discount rate. For example:

	Assets	Profit	ROA
	$ 400	$180	45%
	300	42	14%
	300	18	6%
Current	1000	240	24%
Add	500	60	12%
Combined	1500	300	20%

ROAs are based on accrued accounting. Investments are analyzed for profitability with a discount rate to determine NPV using cash flows. (The reconcilement of the two measures is explained in chapter 3.)

STOCKHOLDER EQUITY

Book and Market

The projected equity total of $900 indicates $300 paid in by investors with 100 shares outstanding, called "capital stock." It is "common stock" when "preferred shares" are issued, a distinction little observed in practice. The $300 is not subdivided into the legal components specified by state law such as par, no-par, stated value, or excess amounts paid in. These archaic distinctions persist in published statements but have no value to management. Retained earnings of $600 include all net income to date less declared dividends. Net income of $200 divided by $900 equity equals 22.2% ROE.

Book value per share is $9.00--$900 equity divided by 100 shares. Earnings per share are $200 net income divided by 100 equals $2.00 EPS. EPS $2 divided by $9 book value also equals 22.2% ROE. The projections made exclude dividends but the ratio of dividends to net income is the pay-out ratio and the remainder is the retention ratio.

Assuming that a share of the stock is selling in the market at $15, it is at 167% of the $9 book value. Dividend yield is the rate of dividends to market value, stated on an annualized basis. The ratio of EPS to price is $2 to $15 = 13.3%. The reciprocal is $15 to $2, or 7.5 times, the price-earnings (P-E) ratio. The P-E is often called the "multiple."

Stock market prices are constantly in a state of flux and reflect expectations for changing combinations of company prospects, the industry outlook, and the economic climate. The company component is often in the minority. Market prices follow the efficient market concept of quickly embodying all new information: how "quickly" and how "all" is not fully determinable. Some degree of insider trading--a gray area--must be presumed to exist. Stock trading reflects investor preferences for combinations of profit and risk--portfolio theory. Risk can be progressively reduced by spreading investments over more industries and companies but profit potential is also limited. The risk reduction is for "unsystematic" or company risk. The risk of the market as a whole-- "systematic risk"--cannot be avoided. Because an investor can minimize the risk attaching to a single stock by diversification, market prices are said to include no premium for company risk. A major change in risk posture by a company can be accommodated by portfolio shifts but at some expense to investors. Managers can adjust investments in assets only over time and at considerable cost and risk. Managers are held responsible for serving the stockholders' financial interests, a combination of dividends and market price appreciation. As a practical matter, managers make decisions in the light of their own best interests because they cannot know stockholder preferences. Stockholders vote by decisions to sell, hold, or buy stock.

ROE and EPS

The single most accurate measure of company performance is ROE--net income divided by stockholder equity. Earnings per share--EPS--are widely used, particularly to compute the P-E ratio, a common denominator for all companies. EPS and market price separately are not comparable among companies because they are based on number of shares. EPS comparability for a company requires adjustment retroactively for shares outstanding.

The use of EPS to measure performance can be misleading. For example, if ROE remains constant at 20% for several years and there are no dividends, EPS shows a 20% annual gain:

		Equity	EPS Increase 20%
ROE:		$1000	
20%		200	$2.00
		1200	
20%		240	2.40
		1440	
20%		288	2.88
		1728	
20%		346	3.46

The effect on market price with constant 20% ROE is conjectural but it is informative to consider these possibilities:

		1		2		3	
ROE	EPS	Price	P-E	Price	P-E	Price	P-E
20%	$2.00	$50	25	$50	25	$50	25
20%	2.40	48	20	60	25	72	30
20%	2.88	46	16	72	25	104	36
20%	3.46	45	13	86	25	149	43

1 - P-E falls at a 20% rate and the price drifts down.
2 - P-E is constant and price rises at a 20% rate.
3 - P-E increases at a 20% rate and price at a 44% rate (120% of 120%)--a "growth" stock.
This table shows a range of stock prices from $45 to $149. The P-E ranges are from 13 to 43.
    When all earnings are paid out in dividends, equity and net income remain unchanged and ROE and EPS are constant. With no earnings retention, signalling a lack of investment opportunity, growth is limited and there is a probable negative market reaction. Even with constant ROE and EPS it is likely that the P-E and price will fall.
    With EPS constant at $2 and no dividends, ROE declines:

	Equity	EPS
ROE constant at:	$1000	
20%	200	$2.00
	1200	
16.2%	200	2.00
	1400	
14.3%	200	2.00
	1600	
12.5%	200	2.00

    ROE is a combination of ROA and financial leverage. The drop in ROE from 20% to 12.5% could arise from a drop in ROA from 11% to 8% with no change in financial leverage:

		Start			End		
Assets	ROA	$100	$11	11%	$100	$8	8.0%
Debt	Rate	60	3	5%	60	3	5.0%
Equity	ROE	40	8	20%	40	5	12.5%

The same drop in ROE can occur with no change in ROA but with reduced debt. The D-E ratio is reduced from 150% to 25%, with the interest rate unchanged:

		Start			End		
Assets	ROA	$100	$11	11%	$100	$11	11.0%
Debt	Rate	60	3	5%	20	1	5.0%
Equity	ROE	40	8	20%	80	10	12.5%

Also, a drop in ROA can be offset by higher financial leverage.

These examples demonstrate the significance of separate analysis of ROA and ROE and the evaluation risk and reward for both assets and financing.

"Sustainable Earnings Growth Rate"

There is a persistent and unfortunate tendency for direct and logical methods of analysis to be embellished and revealed as automatic problem solvers. An example is a formulation dubbed the "sustainable earnings growth rate"--SGR. Actually, the SGR is a truism developed directly from ROA as follows:

Profit after tax	$1500
Net assets	$\overline{10000}$ = 15% ROA
Interest less tax	$ 300
Debt	$\overline{5000}$ = 6% rate
Net income	$1200
Equity	$\overline{5000}$ = 24% ROE

Restated as an SGR calculation:
ROA   15%

Multiply by debt factor:
   Net assets $10,000 divided by
   debt $5,000 =   2   30%

Multiply by interest factor:

   Net interest $300 divided by
   profit after tax 1,500 =   -20% of 30%   -6

SGR (= ROE)   24%

An alternate and more complex method is: 15% ROA x 1.6 = 24% SGR, where 1.6 is the ratio of net assets $10,000 to debt $5,000 = 2 multiplied by .8 which is 1.0 less .2 above (300/1,500). All such methods simply adjust ROA for leverage and produce the same answer. SGR is always ROE before dividends. If dividends equal net income, SGR is zero and ROE is unchanged. With no earnings retention there is no growth. These assumptions are fallacious. It cannot be assumed that the invest-ment of earnings will yield the existing ROA, or that ROA will remain unchanged with no earnings reinvested. The question of investment and financing are fundamental and complex, and they do not lend themselves to simple formulations.

ECONOMIC MEASURES

Managerial economics contributes to the subjects of pricing, costs, profits, and capital expenditures and is included throughout the book. Omitted are the macroeconomic subjects of market structure--pure competition, monopoly, oligopoly, monopolistic competition, and product differentiation. Price theory, or microeconomics, reviewed here briefly, is difficult to apply in practice because relevant data are difficult to isolate. Pricing is pragmatic. Incremental analysis and break-even calculations exemplify the economics approach in practice. The eminent Joel Dean noted many years ago: "the mainstream of economic writing ... is too simple in its assumptions and too complicated in its logical development to be managerially useful" - (Joel Dean, Managerial Economics Englewood Cliffs, N.J.: [Prentice-Hall, 1951], p. vii).

Demand Schedules

The effect of price on demand is shown with all other factors held constant:

Quantity	Price	Total Revenue	Marginal Revenue	Selected Point Elasticities	Ref.
0	$200	$ 0	--	--	
1	180	180	$180	--	
2	160	320	140	4	A
3	140	420	100	--	
4	120	480	60	1-1/2	B
5	100	500	20	1	C
6	80	480	-20	2/3	D
7	60	420	-60	--	
8	40	320	-100	1/4	E
9	20	180	-140	--	
10	0	0	-180	-	

Elasticity assumes that quantity responds to price only, and point elasticity is a measure of change in quantity relative to change in price at a given quantity. For Point A: Q1 P$180 - Q2 P $160 = $20 and 160/20 = 8.Q2 - Q1 = 1 and 2/1 = 2. 8/2 = 4. This answer can be arrived at as follows with quantities only based on Q10:

    Point A = Q10 - Q2 = 8 and 8/2 = 4
    Point B = Q10 - Q4 = 6 and 6/4 = 1-1/2
    Point C = Q10 - Q5 = 5 and 5/5 = 1
    Point D = Q10 - Q6 = 4 and 4/6 = 2/3
    Point E = Q10 - Q8 = 2 and 2/8 = 1/4

When total revenue increases, elasticity is over 1 and positive; for decreases, it is under 1 and negative. For Q5, elasticity is unitary or 1.

Elasticity can also be expressed for a quantity range as arc elasticity:

A to B: Q4 - Q2 = 2
          Q4 + Q2 = $\overline{6}$ = 1/3

          P4 $120 - P2 $160 = $\underline{\$\ 40}$
          P4 $120 + P2 $160 = 280 = 1/7

          1/3   1/7 = 7/3 = 2-1/3 (A4 and B 1-1/2)

B to D: Q6 - Q4 = $\underline{\ 2}$
          Q6 + Q4 = 10 = 1/5

          P6 $80 - P4 $120 = $\underline{\$\ 40}$
          P6 $80 + P4 $120 = 200 = 1/5

          1/5   1/5 = 1/5 x 5/1 = 1 (B 1-1/2 and D 2/3)

Production Schedules

Increases in production quantities entail constantly higher total costs.   At low volumes of output average unit costs are high because of fixed costs; they are also high at high volumes because of bottleneck costs that occur when planned capacity is exceeded.   Marginal costs decline and then rise with increased output.

Quantity	Total Costs	Marginal Cost	Average Cost	Unit Costs Fixed	Variable
0	$145 LOW	--	$ 0	$145	$ 0
1	175	30	175	145	30
2	200	25	100	72	28
3	220	20 LOW	73	48	25 LOW
4	250	30	62	36	26
5	300	50	60 LOW	29	31
6	370	70	62	24	38
7	460	90	66	21	45
8	570	110	71	18	53
9	720	150	80	16	64
10	900	180	90	15 LOW	75

Total fixed cost remains unchanged at $145.   Marginal cost is the increase in total cost for each change in quantity. Average cost is total cost divided by quantity. It is composed of the fixed cost per unit--$145 divided by quantity and the variable cost per unit--average cost minus fixed cost per unit, or cumulative marginal cost divided by quantity.

Profit Schedules

The demand and production schedules are combined to determine profits for Q1 through Q8:

Quantity	Total Revenue	Total Cost	Profit	Marginal Revenue	Marginal Cost	Net Change
1	$180	$175	$ 5	$180	$ 30	$+150
2	320	200	120	140	25	+115
3	420	220	200	100	20	+ 80
4	480	250	230 A	60 D	30 E	+ 30 B
5	500	300	200	20 D	50 E	- 30 C
6	480	370	110	- 20	70	- 90
7	420	460	- 40	- 60	90	-150
8	320	570	-250	-100	110	-210

A   Q4 = maximum profit $230
B   Q3 to Q4 = net change + $30
C   Q4 to Q5 = net change - $30
D   Q4 = marginal revenue 60 plus Q5 marginal revenue 20 = 80
E   Q4 = marginal cost   30 plus Q5 marginal cost   50 = 80

Maximum profit is reached when marginal cost rises to equal marginal revenue, somewhere between Q4 and Q5. For example, if Q4 revenue is $495 and if cost is $263, profit is $232.

Fixed Market Price

When price is fixed solely by the market (pure competition), output rises to the point where marginal cost equals marginal revenue (price) to attain maximum profit. For example:

Quantity	Constant Price	Total Revenue	Total Cost	Total Profit	Per Unit Marg. Cost	Per Unit Marg. Revenue	Per Unit Avg. Cost	Profit
0	$40	$ 0	$400	$-400	$--	$--	$--	$--
10	40	400	1000	-600	60	40	100.00	-60.00
20	40	800	1150	-350	15	40	57.50	-17.50
30	40	1200	1200	0	5	40	40.00	0
40	40	1600	1260	+340	6	40	31.50	+ 8.50
50	40	2000	1390	+610	13	40	27.80	+12.20
60	40	2400	1600	+800	21	40	26.67	+13.33
70	40	2800	2000	+800	40	40	28.57	+11.43
80	40	3200	3200	0	120	40	40.00	0
90	40	3600	4500	-900	130	40	50.00	-10.00

Profit is zero at both Q30 and Q80--marginal revenue and marginal cost are equal at $40 per unit. Maximum profit is reached at Q70 where marginal cost rises to $40 to equal marginal revenue. For higher quantities marginal cost rises rapidly with the break-even point at Q80 and loss at Q90. Losses also occur at quantities below Q30.

A current comment on microeconomics by three professors is worth noting. "Strategic planning . . . the single most important application of microeconomics . . . not only gets at the heart of the firm's long-term resource allocation problem, it represents the life blood of the firm's future." (Thomas H. Naylor, John M. Vernon, and Kenneth L. Wertz, Management Economics [McGraw Hill: New York, 1983] p. 17.)

2

Current Assets: Investments to Support Operating Plans

The acquisition of all assets, and their retention, requires evaluation of both profitability and risk. Assets are used to earn operating profits, and all assets are subject to the same method of analysis and evaluation. Profitability analysis is based on the current discount rate (the borrowing rate less tax), and the estimated periodic cash flows expressed as both NPV and rate of return. Risk must be separately evaluated for each asset and for all assets combined. Finally, liquidity must be evaluated relative to all operating and investment plans translated into cash flows.

Current assets are partially offset by spontaneous credit--payables and accruals--to arrive at net current assets financed by the capital structure. Receivables and inventory are analyzed in this chapter for profitability only; risk evaluation is deferred to a later chapter. Tax factors must be considered for all decisions but can be omitted when they do not affect the analysis of and choice among alternatives. Taxes are introduced when the selected alternatives are assembled into plans and budgets. Also, there is no need to discount future cash flows to the present because increases in receivables and inventories are considered to have indefinite life. The increases are usually readily reversible so salvage value need not be considered. For example, a current asset of $1,000 providing a profit of $100 has a yield of 10%. This could be in perpetuity or for a limited life, say 10 years. If the $1,000 is recouped at the end of 10 years, the yield remains at 10% as follows by present value calculations:

profit $100 f6.14450 = $614.45
asset $1000 f.38555 = 385.55/1,000

The annual profit of a $100 for 10 years has a present value of $614.45. The asset value of $1,000 in 10 years has a present value of $385.55. The $1,000 asset thus has a 10% yield for any period.

Risk evaluation weighs the probabilities of variations in profits, investment, and economic life, described in a separate chapter. Cash and current liabilities are discussed briefly at the end of this chapter.

INVENTORIES

Inventory balances are maintained to help assure continuous production and timely customer shipments. Interruptions are costly but so are excess balances of stock. Inventory control endeavors to balance these costs as part of the purchase-produce-distribute cycle. The principal factors are sales forecasting, vendor delivery, and production methods, all major topics. The presentation is limited to three techniques that can contribute to an efficient and effective inventory control system: inventory classifications, order size, and safety stocks. Their appropriate application can often make a significant difference.

Inventory Classifications

The complexity of inventory control requires the use of categories designed to provide pinpoint definitions. Factors to be considered include location, physical nature, ownership, cost per unit, total cost, dependability of supply, demand predictability, susceptibility to theft, loss, or obsolescence, significance to sustained production or to timely shipment, and degree of replacement support for products in use. These factors apply to inventory control accounts such as raw materials, parts, supplies, work-in-process, and finished goods.

A particularly useful scheme is the ABC method of inventory classification which is well established in practice. A items are the most critical because of a combination of factors such as high unit cost, perishability, significance to production, dependability of supply, and variability of demand. C items at the other end of the scale are cheap and readily available. B items fall in between. After initial classification and use, items can be reclassified to suit changing needs. The classifications by number of items and dollars in inventory might be as follows, expressed as percents:

	Number of Items	Dollar Balance	Ratio
A	8	72	1:9
B	20	20	1:1
C	72	8	9:1
	100	100	

The A items are 72% of total cost but only 8% of the total number of items - a ratio of 1 to 9. These items are monitored closely. Single source vendors might be cultivated to provide assured and flexible delivery scheduled to hourly or daily needs. The goal would be to approach zero balances and zero defects, eliminating incoming inspection. C items are only 8% of total cost but are 72% of the total number of items - a ratio of 9 to 1, a relationship to A of 81 times. For these items control might be exercised monthly or quarterly with larger stocks carried to buffer possible shortages. B items can be controlled at some level between A and C.

The ABC method focuses attention where it matters most with the goal of effective results and efficient performance. The classifications should be reviewed regularly to preserve the benefits of the system. The percents in each category are not inherently significant. Four categories might be desirable in some cases, as for example, in percents:

	Number of Items	Dollar Balance	Ratio
A	5	50	1:10
B	15	30	1:2
C	30	15	2:1
D	50	5	10:1
	100	100	

Order Size

If one order is placed for a one-year supply, the order cost is low but the cost of carrying inventory is high. If an order is placed every day for a one-day supply, the order cost is high but the carrying cost is low. An optimum point can be derived by formula -- the economic order quantity or EOQ. To illustrate:

S - quantity needed for one year
C - incremental cost of one purchase order
P - purchase price per unit
H - incremental inventory carrrying cost percent

The square-root formula is:

$$\frac{2 \times S\ C}{P\ H} = EOQ$$

Example: S - 1800 units

C - $22.50

P - $40

H - 25%

$$\frac{2 \times 1800 \times \$22.50}{\$40 \times 25\%} = \frac{81,000}{10} = 8100 = 90\ EOQ$$

90 EOQ x $40 = $3600 purchase order amount

Dollar formula:

$$\frac{2 \times 72,000 \times \$22.50}{25\%} = 12,960,000 = \$3600\ EOQ$$

Proof:

$3600/$40 = 90 EOQ

S1800/90 = 20 orders per year

20 orders at $22.50 = order cost total $450

EOQ $\frac{90}{2}$ = 45 average inventory at $10 = carrying $450
                                            cost total $900

The formula derivation is: Order cost = carrying cost

$$\frac{SC}{Q} = \frac{QPH}{2}$$

$$2SC = Q^2PH$$

$$\frac{2SC}{PH} = Q^2$$

$$\sqrt{\frac{2SC}{PH}} = Q = EOQ$$

The effect of using different order quantities is shown in the following table:

Order Cost				EOQ		
Order quantity	10	30	60	90	150	900
No. of orders	180	60	30	20	12	2
Cost at $22.50	$4,050	$1,350	$675	$450	$270	$45
Carrying Cost						
Average inventory	5	15	30	45	75	450
Cost at $10	$50	$150	$300	$450	$750	$4500
Total cost	$4,100	$1,500	$975	$900	$1,020	$4545
Total cost over EOQ 90 total cost	$+3,200	$+ 600	$+ 75	$ 0	$+ 120	$+3645

Order quantities higher and lower than EOQ raise the cost totals, as shown, because one cost increases more than the other decreases. A change in order quantity from 30 to 60 units reduces total cost by $525 ($1,500 minus $975) but an equal change from 60 to 90 units lowers total cost by only $75 ($975 - $900). A change of 60 units from 30 to 90 saves $600 ($1,500 - $900) but from 150 to 90 units the saving is only $120 ($1,020 - $900). The high costs for the smallest and largest order quantities underscore the need for careful analysis of order sizes. However, the total cost differences are minor for small changes in quantities. For example, for order sizes of 75, 100, and 160:

Order quantity	75	100	110
No. of orders	24	18	16+
at $22.50	$540	$405	$368
Average inventory	38	50	55
at $10	$380	$500	$550
Total	$920	$905	$918

When a quantity discount is offered for larger orders, the analysis is as follows:

Price $40 with 5% discount ($2.00) for orders of 900 units. P $38 at H 25% = $9.50. Total discount 1800 units at $2 = $3600.

```
S 1800/Q 900 = 2 orders @ $22.50 =    $45
900/2 = 450 x $9.50                  4275
Total cost                           4320
EOQ cost for 90 units - above         900
Extra cost                           3420
Quantity discount - 1800 @ $2        3600
Net gain                            $180
```

This relatively small gain is questionable because the order is enough for 180 days, rather than the EOQ of 90 units for 18 days. There is a question of available storage space and increased risk of spoilage and obsolescence. The incremental holding cost could be higher than $9.50 per unit. With a $10 per unit cost the total is 450 x $10 = $4,500, compared with $4,275 and the increase of $225 exceeds the $180 gain. The quantity discount of $3,600 is attractive but requires careful analysis.

It is essential to develop reasonable incremental costs for ordering and carrying inventory. Full costs and averages are not relevant. Incremental costs can be developed by analysis and by trial and error. The effect on EOQ with lower ordering and higher carrying costs is illustrated for comparison with EOQ 90:

```
S 1800 units
C $16 (not $22.50)
P $40
H 40% (not 25%)
```

$$\frac{2 \times 1800 \times \$16}{\$40 \times 40\%} = \frac{57,600}{16} = 3600 = 60 \text{ EOQ}$$

$$S \quad \frac{1800}{EOQ \quad 60} = 30 \times \$16 = \$480$$

$$EOQ \quad \frac{60}{2} = 30 \times \$16 = \underline{\$480} \quad \$960$$

$$EOQ \quad 90 \qquad\qquad\qquad\qquad \underline{900}$$

Extra Cost   60

This small change occurs despite relatively large changes in opposite directions for ordering and carrying costs. If carrying costs had decreased to 18% together with the C at $16, EOQ remains at 90:

$$\frac{2 \times 1800 \times \$16}{\$40 \times 18\%} = \frac{5760}{7.20} = 8000 = 89.44 \text{ EOQ} = 90 \text{ EOQ}$$

To illustrate the effect of higher ordering and lower carrying costs:
```
S - 1800
C - $32 (not $22.50)
P - $40
H - 20% (not 25%)
```

$$\frac{2 \times 1800 \times \$32}{\$40 \times 20\%} = \frac{115,200}{8} = 14,400 = 120 \text{ EOQ}$$

$$\text{S} \quad \frac{1800}{120} = 15 \times \$32 = \$480$$

$$\text{Q} \quad \frac{120}{2} = 60 \times \$8 = \underline{480} \qquad \$960$$

EOQ 90   900

Extra Cost   60

If C was reduced to $18:

$$\frac{2 \times 1800 \times \$18}{\$40 \times 20\%} = \frac{64,800}{8} = 8100 = 90 \text{ EOQ}$$

These examples demonstrate the trial-and-error approach and the nature and range of the relationships. Approximations can provide valuable information.

The cost of ordering inventory is found by tracing all the steps taken such as stock record requisition, purchase order, receiving, inspection, storage, records, and payment. The expenses of each department and the number of transactions handled are found using records and budgets. The effect of an estimated change in the number of transactions on each expense provides approximate incremental costs. The process follows that used for preparing the departmental expense at different activity levels. A purchasing department is used for illustration:

No. of Orders	Expenses	Average
2,000	$100,000	$50

A change of only one order would change expense by $2 (not $50) about the cost of one form.

Number of orders plus or minus 10%:
Reduction:

- 200	- $3,000	+$15
1,800	97,000	

Increase:

+ 200	+ $3,000	$+15
2,200	103,000	

The incremental cost is $15, not $50.
Number of orders plus or minus 20%:
Reduction:

- 400	- $8,000	+$20
1,600	92,000	

Increase:

+ 400	+ $8,000	$+20
2,400	108,000	

The incremental cost is $20, not $50. Using this approach should produce a reasonable incremental ordering cost for use in analysis. The calculations should be reviewed periodically.

The cost of carrying inventory is generally in a range of 30% to 50% of inventory cost. The relevant expenses must be defined and analyzed such as interest, insurance, taxes, record keeping, spoilage, theft, obsolescence, space charges, and labor. The incremental rate is based on assumed changes in purchase levels and related changes in the expenses, similar to the procedure for ordering costs. Some expenses are fully variable with inventory and some are fixed within a narrow range. If the full carrying cost is 45%, the incremental rate for some assumed levels might be in a range of 15% to 25%. Interest should be included as an implicit cost independent of the company's debt position.

These incremental amounts can be used on a trial-and-error basis, as described, to discover possible significant savings. The accounting records are a source of information but do not provide the incremental data needed.

EOQ refers to orders placed with vendors. Economic lot size - ELS - refers to orders placed with the factory by the production control office. The calculations are identical but the incremental expenses differ.

To illustrate:

S - annual production needed
C - incremental cost to place an order with the factory, plus the factory setup cost
P - inventory cost per unit
H - incremental carrying cost percent

The square root formula is:

$$\frac{2 \times S \times C}{PH} = ELS$$

Example:

$$
\begin{aligned}
S &- 1800 \text{ units} \\
C &- \$22.50 \\
P &- \$40 \\
H &- 25\%
\end{aligned}
$$

$$\frac{2 \times 1800 \times \$22.50}{\$40 \times 25\%} = \frac{81,000}{10} = 8100 = 90 \text{ ELS}$$

This example repeats the example for EOQ 90:

$$\frac{S}{Q} \quad \frac{1800}{90} = 20 \times \$22.50 = \$450$$

$$\frac{Q}{2} \quad \frac{90}{2} = 45 \times \$10 = \underline{450} \quad \$900$$

The critical factor in ELS is the setup cost. To illustrate, assume that $\underline{C}$ is only $1.11, not $22.50:

$$\frac{2 \times 1800 \times \$1.11}{\$40 \times 25\%} \quad = \quad \frac{4,000}{10} \quad = \quad 400 \quad = \quad 20 \text{ ELS}$$

$$\frac{S}{Q} \quad \frac{1800}{20} = 90 \times \$1.11 = \$100$$

$$Q \quad \frac{20}{2} = 10 \times \$10 = \quad \underline{100} \quad \$200$$

ELS 90   900

Gain   700

The number of setups rises from 20 (1,800/90) to 90 (1,800/20). More frequent setups provide greater production flexibility and faster response to changed conditions, thus contributing to both cost efficiency and marketing effectiveness.

If the setup cost can be reduced only to $10, rather than $1.11, the result is:

$$\frac{2 \times 1800 \times \$10}{10} = 3,600 = 60 \text{ ELS}$$

$$S \frac{1800}{Q \quad 60} = 30 \times \$10 = \$300$$

$$Q \quad \frac{60}{2} = 30 \times \$10 = \underline{\$300} \quad \$600$$

ELS 90 $900

Gain $300

The saving is $300 compared with ELS 90 but far short of the saving for ELS 20. The examples show the importance of low setup costs.

Recap:

ELS	Total Cost	Setup Cost	No. of Setups
90	$900	$22.50	20
60	600	10.00	30
30	300	2.50	60
20	200	1.11	90
10	100	.28	180

Safety Stocks

Inventory carrying costs are usually computed on the basis of linear usage--the order quantity divided by two multiplied by the carrying cost per unit. In the example for 90 EOQ: 90/2 = 45 units x $10 = $450. This calculation of average inventory assumes that a new order is received when inventory reaches zero. If usage runs higher than expected, or if delivery is delayed, there is a stockout (SO). Production is delayed or must be rescheduled. Customer shipments are delayed. Both conditions are expensive. Protection is provided by carrying extra balances, or safety stocks (SS). Example:

S - 1800 units per year
EOQ - 90 units = 20 orders
1800/360 days = 5 units per day
EOQ 90/5 = 18 days usage
Delivery time 14 days:

EOQ	90
4 days usage	- 20
Inventory balance	70 order date

If it is estimated that protection against occasional delivery delays or extra usage can be provided by carrying an extra 50 units (ten-day delivery delay or higher daily shipments), the cost of this SS (safety stock) is 50 units x $10 = $500. This is an insurance cost that must be weighed against the loss probability of being out of stock (SO). The cost of being out of stock is difficult to estimate but approximation can be useful in avoiding high and low extremes of SS. Production staff prefers the comfort of large SS to assume continuous output. Marketing staffs prefer the assurance of prompt shipments to meet shifting demand. But management needs to keep a reasonable balance between the insurance cost of SS and the cost of SO.

Each possible SO condition requires individual evaluation as to its incremental cost and the probability of occurrence. Each inventory category must be analyzed separately and renewed periodically. Raw materials, parts, and supplies that are SO cause production delays, rescheduling, extra setups, expenses to expedite delivery, use of substitute materials, and impaired morale. Finished goods out of stock can cause lost orders, lost customers, customer dissatisfaction, substituted items at higher cost, expenses to expedite delivery, and impaired morale. Estimating stockout costs calls for a scenario of the likely response and possible consequences. Individuals may have widely ranging opinions that must be reviewed and revised, not unlike the Delphic technique, to reach a tenable middle ground.

The method is illustrated for an item of finished goods:

Annual sales   80,000 units
Incremental cost to order $40
Carrying cost per unit $40

$$\frac{2 \times 80,000 \times \$40}{\$40} = 160,000 = 400 \text{ EOQ}$$

$$\frac{S}{EOQ} \quad \frac{80,000}{400} = 200 \text{ orders per year}$$

The incremental cost of a SO is estimated for a trial analysis at $15 per occurrence. The following table lists SS units and the related SO probability as derived from experience and expectations--a difficult exercise. Statistical methods are also applicable. As the table shows, with no SS the SO probability (P) is 90%. It requires 60 SS to reduce the SO probability (SO-P) to zero.

1 SS units	2 SO-P	3 # of Orders	4 # of SO (2 x 3)	5 Cost per SO	6 SO Cost (4 x 5)
0	90%	200	180	$15	$2700
10	60	200	120	$15	$1800
20	40	200	80	$15	$1200
30	25	200	50	$15	$ 750
40	15	200	30	$15	$ 450
50	5	200	10	$15	$ 150
60	0	200	0	$15	0

The next table shows the carrying cost for the SS units:

SS Units	Cost per Unit	Total
0	$40	$ 0
10	$40	$ 400
20	$40	$ 800
30	$40	$1200
40	$40	$1600
50	$40	$2000
60	$40	$2400

SO cost declines with higher SS but carrying cost rises. The tables are combined:

SS Units	SO Cost	Carrying Cost	Combined	Change from SS 30
0	$2700	$ 0	$2700	$ +750
10	1800	400	2200	+150
20	1200	800	2000	+ 50
30	750	1200	1950	0
40	450	1600	2050	+100
50	150	2000	2150	+200
60	0	2400	2400	+450

The cost minimum is reached at $1,950 for 30 units, with a narrow cost range from 20 to 40 units. Costs are significantly higher for the extremes. The effect on profit could be substantial. Trial-and-error computations with ranges for SO and SS costs can help establish acceptable SS levels as well as direct attention to the significance of sales forecasting and vendor delivery.

For a SS of zero to show the minimum total cost, the carrying cost would have to be $95 rather than $40:

SS Units	(Above) SO Cost at $15	Carrying Cost at $95	Combined	Incremental Cost
0	$2700	$ 0	$2700	$
10	1800	950	2750	50
20	1200	1900	3100	320
30	750	2850	3600	500
40	450	3800	4250	650
50	150	4750	4900	650
60	0	5700	5700	800
				3000

The incremental cost column shows the premium required to provide lower SO and thus greater assurance of timely shipment. Carrying costs rise faster than SO cost falls.

A similar analysis develops a SO cost of $45 rather than $15 to justify SS 60 and zero SO. SO cost is multiplied by three.

SS Units	SO Cost at $45	Carrying Cost at $40	Combined	Incremental Cost
0	$8100	$ 0	$8100	$2300
10	5400	400	5800	1400
20	3600	800	4400	950
30	2250	1200	3450	500
40	1300	1600	2950	500
50	450	2000	2450	50
60	0	2400	2400	0
				5700

The increments occur with higher SS because SO cost falls faster than carrying cost rises. The SO probabilities are also subject to review as well as the number of orders per year. These estimates and calculations must be made separately for each pertinent category--a task that has the potential for a good pay-off.

The points described--inventory classifications, order size, safety stocks--contribute to the goal of effective inventory control. The primary factors are sales forecasting, production flexibility, vendor reliability, tight scheduling, zero defects, and participative management. Actual performance must be tracked closely and systems should be monitored and evaluated regularly. Physical counts should be maintained on a perpetual basis, obviating any shut down of operations. All stocks should be promptly purged of damaged, obsolete, and surplus items. The resulting balances will then reflect a practical optimum balance.

RECEIVABLES

Receivables are assets that require analysis for profitability and risk in the manner applicable to all investments. Customer balances are related to credit policies, payment terms, and collection practices. Industry practices vary widely but less so for companies within an industry. Credit can be an effective competitive factor but calls for close evaluation to avoid excess balances and reduced ROA. Incremental analysis of alternatives relates profit change to asset change to determine incremental ROA for comparison with the discount rate. Risk and liquidity must also be considered. The selected alternative becomes the budgeted receivable balance for comparison with actual results. Publicized ratios such as those that relate receivables to sales for turnover or number of days are superficial and can be misleading.

Examples

The following examples cover a variety of situations. A discount rate of 12% before tax is used, based on the company's borrowing position. Taxes are omitted because they do not affect the outcome. Taxes are introduced when the plans are put into budget form.

<u>Example 1</u>.   Change from cash sales to sales with 30 days credit; no bad
debts, 36 days outstanding balance; 360 days per year:

Sales increase	$10,000
Variable cost (VC)	8,000
Variable margin (VM)	2,000
Credit expenses (CE)	1,600
Profit (PR)	400
Asset increase:	
Receivables - 36 days	
or 10% of $10,000	1,000
Inventory (net of payables)	1,400
	$2,400
ROA: $400/2,400 =	16.7%
Discount rate	12.0%

<u>Safety factors</u>: (1) 12% of $2400 = $288 or $112 less than $400, a
28% margin; (2) $400/12% = $3,333 assets, $933 more than $2,400, a
39% increase; (3) any combination of lower profit and higher assets
that provides 12% or more
    Safety factor estimates help define the degree of risk. Liquidity
relates to carrying more assets and the related cash flows, but the
evaluation can only be made for all plans in total, both investing and
financing.
    The analysis is presented on a book basis, the customary practice,
for financial ratios. Strictly speaking the analysis should be made on a
cost basis--the difference is the profit in receivables:

Receivables	$1,000
less VM 20%	200
Cost basis	800
Inventory - net	1,400
	$2,200
ROA: $400/2,200 =	18.2%
ROA book basis	16.7%
Discount rate	12.0%

    This alternative method can be used when ROA is close to the discount
rate.   For example, to illustrate with receivables of $2,600 and 60% VC
(40% VM), the cost basis is $1,560 (2,600 - 1,040):

	Book Basis	Cost Basis
Profit gain	$400	$400
Asset increase:		
Receivables	$2,600	$1,560
Inventory - net	1,400	1,400
	4,000	2,960
ROA:	$400/4000 = 10%	400/2960 = 13.5%

    The book basis ROA at 10% is well below the 12% minimum but the cost
basis adds 3.5 points to exceed the 12% rate. The governing factor is
the percent of VC.

Example 2. Example 1 is repeated with the addition of a bad debt loss
provision of 1.2%:

```
              Sales increase            $10,000
              VC                          8,000
              VM                          2,000
              CE                          1,600
                                           400
              Bad debts at 1.2%           120
              PR                          280
              Asset increase:
                Receivables   $ 1,000
                less 1.2%          12     $   988
                Inventory - net          1,400
                                         $ 2,388

          ROA:  $280/2388 = 11.7%
```

Bad debts reduce profit and also receivables, and ROA drops below 12%.
On a cost basis ROA is over the discount rate:

```
              Receivables      $   988
              less VM 20%          198
                                   790
              Inventory - net    1,400
                               $ 2,190
              ROA:  $280/2190 = 12.8%
              ROA book basis = 11.7%
              Discount rate  = 12.0%
```

Example 3. Increase credit terms from 30 days to 60 days, and bad debts
from 2% to 3% of sales:

	30 d	60 d	Increase	
Sales	$36,000	$42,000	$6,000	
70% VC	25,200	29,400	4,200	
30% VM 10,800		12,600	1,800	
Bad debts:				
at 2%	720			
at 3%		1,260	540	
PR	10,080	11,340	1,260	
Asset increase:				
Receivables (1/12)	3,000	(1/6) 7,000	4,000	
less bad debts	- 60	- 210	- 150	
	2,940	6,790	3,850	
Inventory - net			3,150	
			7,000	

```
ROA:  $1260/7000 = 18.0%
On a cost basis:
  Receivables           $ 3,850
  at 70% VC     2,695
  Inventory - net         3,150       $5,845
ROA:  $1260/5845 = 21.6%
```

ROA is well above 12%. For questionable plans every estimate should be expressed in ranges with probabilities to test for the possibility of returns below 12%. For example, there could be a 10% chance of 20% VM thus reducing VM by $600 (10% of $6,000) and PR to $660 (1,260 - 600), and with assets increasing by $500 to $7,500 = ROA $660/7,500 = 8.8%. Such probing can clarify communication and strengthen analysis.

Example 4.   Sell to a new class of high-risk customers with a plan to realize 24% ROA. Three alternatives to the plan are also analyzed:

	Plan	A	B	C
Sales	$10,000	$10,000	$10,000	$10,000
VC	5,000	6,000	5,000	5,000
VM	5,000	4,000	5,000	5,000
CE	1,800	1,800	1,800	1,800
	3,200	2,200	3,200	3,200
BD (20%)	2,000	(20%) 2,000	(25%) 2,500	(20%) 2,000
PR	1,200	200	700	1,200
Receivables:	(72d = 20% of 360d and 144d = 40% of 360d)			
72 d =	2,000	2,000	2,000	(144 d) 4,000
less BD	400	400	500	800
	1,600	1,600	1,500	3,200
Inventory	3,400	3,400	3,400	6,800
Assets	5,000	5,000	4,900	10,000
ROA:	1,200	200	700	1,200
	5,000	5,000	4,900	10,000
	24.0%	4.0%	14.3%	12.0%

A - VM is 40%, not 50%. The loss of $1,000 from VM drops ROA to only 4%.

B - BD at 25%, not 20%. ROA is 14.3%.
C - Receivables and inventory double with no change in PR--ROA 12%.

This venturesome project defies close analysis but some reasonable ranges of outcome can be usefully explored. To test the risk exposure, arbitrarily assume that only these four analyses are made and that each is given an equal chance:

ROA %	Probability
4.0	25%
12.0	25%
14.3	25%
24.0	25%

There is one chance in four of making only 4% and also one chance in four of realizing double the 12% discount rate. There are three chances in four of realizing or bettering the discount rate. Individual reactions to such odds vary widely, a subjective process. The four ROAs total 54.3 with an average of 13.6%, well over the 12% minimum. However, this obscures the skew distribution and is statistically valid only for a large number of similar events, a situation seldom found in business. The decision hinges primarily on the downside risk of one chance in four of the 4% rate, a matter of risk attitude only partially offset by the upside potential.

3

Capital Expenditures: Investments to Support Operating and Strategic Goals

The continuing investment in assets (and disinvestment) is the mainspring of progress. With continuing operations and no investment a company is in the process of liquidation. Failure to abandon unproductive assets enervates the entity. Ill-considered ventures can spell disaster. "Planning and control of capital expenditures is the basic executive function....Capital budgeting is conceptually, at least, the universal business problem, encompassing all others...." (Joel Dean, Managerial Economics [Englewood Cliffs, N.J.: Prentice Hall, 1951] pp. 552, 553).

Capital expenditures are guided by goals, strategies, and policies, embracing growth, profitability, risk, and liquidity. Capital expenditure projects relate to objectives, plans, and programs and are incorporated into the financial plan and budgets. Evaluation of projects is judgmental but relevant analysis is essential. Many strategic decisions are beyond quantitative expression. Some projects provide only intangible benefits. Others are mandated by law or contract. As a speculation, constructive analysis applies to something over half of the dollar total and well over half the total number of proposals, depending largely on the level of strategic outlays. Use of estimates and approximations for dollars, timing, and risk is unavoidable. Analysis, however broad, that is relevant and raises pertinent questions is well worthwhile.

Many factors relate to the capital expenditure program:

> Outlays for fixed assets, current assets, expenses
> Gains from expense reduction and income increase
> Use of management time and existing facilities--
>   opportunity cost
> Competitive reaction
> Effect on employees, managers, stockholders, customers,
>   and vendors
> Relations with the financial markets, the public,
>   and government
> Operating and financial risk

Capital expenditures require large sums for long periods and risk may be high. Once started projects are difficult to stop or alter without large loss. There is extensive literature available but much of it is theoretical, lacking in relevance, or simply erroneous. There is a pressing need for a sound, practical demonstration of project analysis that relates both financial and accounting profitability with risk and the discount rate. The total amount of approved projects must be evaluated for operating risk relative to assets now held, for financial risk relative to liquidity and capital structure, and for the combined risk.

Each proposal should be fully identified and carefully described. Quantitative data includes:

> Cash outlays--amounts and timing
> Cash inflows--amounts and timing
> Disposal value for assets to be sold or replaced
> Future terminal value (salvage) of new assets
> Future prices by item and period, including inflation
> Tax rates and their application
> Discount rate to determine present value of future cash flows

Calculations are made for:

> Net present value (NPV)
> Yield--financial rate of return
> Accounting rate of return
> Cash payback period
> Risk ranges

The discount rate used must be a risk-free rate--the current borrowing rate less tax--so that all cash flows are expressed as comparable present dollars. A higher rate that includes a risk premium distorts the present values in disguised amounts and precludes logical risk evaluation. Risk evaluation and the discount rate are intertwined. Cash flows must be estimated in ranges with probabilities to determine a risk profile. Evaluation is made (a subjective process) of the profit probabilities relative to the discount rate. Popular terms such as "hurdle rate", "cut-off rate", and "investment rate" are not used because they are not definitive and can be misleading. The so-called "cost of capital" is not relevant. (These major subjects are explored in separate chapters.)

Overall judgmental review is also particularly important. An attractive proposal may relate to a market being dropped or to products being redesigned or phased out. Proposals may be for facilities scheduled for shut down or for conversion to automation. There may be a combined effect on the capacity of limited facilities such as power generation, storage, land, and transport. Finally, the impact on management time and ability should be considered, together with an eye on internal politics.

EXAMPLE FOR FIXED ASSETS

This example presents in detail the analysis needed for all projects but in simple form for clarity. Added factors appear in later examples. The subject is unavoidably complex but the presentation is designed for management guidance rather than skill in calculation. Engineering and financial staff can supply the requisite technical ability. But as with all professionals, managers are well advised to understand their methods, assumptions, and modus operandi.

The following data are used throughout this example:

> Acquire a machine for $30,000. No salvage value. Economic life 5 years. Depreciation $6,000 a year (30,000/5) = straight line (SL). Saving $9,000 a year. Tax rate 40%. Discount rate 6% net (interest 10% less tax).

Cash Flows

The effect of taxes on savings is computed to determine annual cash flows:

	Books	Cash
Saving	$9,000	$9,000
Depreciation	-6,000	
Taxable income	3,000	
Tax at 40%	-1,200	1,200
Net income	1,800	
Depreciation	+6,000	
Cash	7,800	7,800

The cash gain is $7,800 a year for five years. The tax liability is a cash item that must be deducted from the $9,000 saving to determine the net cash--otherwise the saving would be seriously overstated. If the tax is applied to $9,000 there is a failure to recognize the depreciation deduction--the tax is overstated by $2,400 (40% of $6,000) and cash is seriously understated. The parallel columns clarify the difference between accrual accounting and cash results, which are pertinent to financial analysis. Net income is also disclosed, a necessary accounting measurement.

Cash flows are central to financial analysis and must always be identified as before or after tax. Savings include both cost reduction and income increase. All items of cash flow must be individually estimated for each period, recognizing possible price changes and inflation. Estimated cash flow ranges and their probability of occurrence also need to be expressed as the basis for risk evaluation.

Net Present Value (NPV)

The present amount of future cash flows is present value (PV). When the present cash outlay is deducted the balance is NPV--positive or negative. Positive NPV is the gain in present dollars. DCF refers to discounted cash flow, or PV.

The effect of the discount rate on PV is illustrated for an annuity of $7,800 for five years with several rates. The discount factor for an annuity of $1 is designated f. At zero interest present value and future value are equal: 5 x $7,800 = $39,000.

Rate	Factor	PV	Percent
0%	f5.000	$39,000	100.0
6%	f4.212	32,854	84.2
12%	f3.605	28,119	72.1
18%	f3.127	24,391	62.5
24%	f2.745	21,411	54.9
30%	f2.436	19,001	48.7

The discount factors appear in the present value tables in the appendix. Computations are readily made with hand-held calculators. All cash flows are assumed to be made at year-end with taxes paid currently. Timing refinements are not needed.

The NPV calculation for the example is:

Cash flow	$ 7,800
6% discount f	4.212
PV	32,854
Cash outlay	30,000
NPV	2,854

The gain of $2,854 is subject to realization over five years. Positive NPV is requisite for profit approval, but may be subject to risk evaluation. With a 10% discount rate:

Cash flow	$ 7,800
10% discount f	3.791
PV	29,570
Cash outlay	30,000
NPV--negative	- 430

The project fails to earn 10% by $430 present value.

Discount Rate

The borrowing rate should be based on available loans of substantial sums for periods consistent with the capital expenditure program and capital structure. Rates are often pegged to the prime rate but some companies are able to borrow at a lesser rate. Most companies pay prime plus a premium based on credit strength. Interest rates, the nominal rates, can be decomposed into three factors: risk, inflation, and the "real" rate, a matter for economic analysis.

The tax rate should be based on current and expected rates and their application to the company's situation. Both cash flows and the discount rate must be expressed on an after-tax basis for consistency. Taxes have a major impact on cash flows and the effect is highly variable. The tax code is complex and constantly changing. Expert tax counsel should be used. The examples presented reflect the method for tax recognition without any attempt to express tax realities.

The discount rate should be kept current with changing interest rates and taxes. The following table illustrates some possible ranges:

Interest Rate	Discount Rate After Tax Rates of			
	20%	30%	40%	50%
5%	4.0	3.5	3.0	2.5
10%	8.0	7.0	6.0	5.0
15%	12.0	10.5	9.0	7.5
20%	16.0	14.0	12.0	10.0

The range is from 2.5% to 16.0%. The discount rate used should be changed for a difference of 1.0% or more. If the rate used is too low, some projects will show positive NPV that should be negative and their approval could create negative leverage and reduce ROE. With a rate that is too high, some projects that should be approved will show negative NPV and positive leverage will be missed. A simple example with no taxes or time discounting clarifies this central point. A merchant borrows $10,000 and buys goods. One year later he has received $11,500 for the goods and has a $1,500 margin. If the interest is 10% he pays $11,000 to the bank and gains $500--positive leverage. If the loan rate was 18%, the payment is $11,800 and the loss is $300--negative leverage. If the merchant uses his own money, the opportunity cost is the borrowing rate. If the merchant prefers not to borrow for a profitable investment, the profit foregone is the opportunity cost--the price of avoiding operating risk or financial risk.

Yield

Yield is a financial rate of return used universally to measure profits based on cash flows. For the example, yield is:

Outlay	$30,000	=	f 3.846 for 5 years
Cash gain	$ 7,800		

By calculator the yield is 9.435% compared with the 6% discount rate. The excess of 3.435% (9.435 - 6.000) represents the $2,854 NPV calculated above. By definition, NPV is zero when the yield and discount rate are equal--$7,800 x f3.846 (9.435%) $30,000. With a 10% discount rate NPV is negative $430, as above. The yield is still 9.435%, slightly below 10%.

Rates can be derived by interpolation from the present value tables:

10%	f3.791	3.791
?		3.846
8%	f3.993	
2%	.202	———
?		.055

Ratio:	.055/.202 = 27.23% x 2%	=	.5446%
			10,000%
	Yield--interpolation		9.4554%
	Yield--calculation		9.4349%
	Difference		.0205%

The small difference arises because the tables are logarithmic and the interpolation is linear. The measurement can also be made from 8%:

        f3.993 - f3.846 = f.147
        .147/.202 = 72.77% x 2% = 1.4554%
                                  8.0000%
                                  9.4554%

NPV is a dollar result and yield is the equivalent percent. Yields are more readily understood and permit comparative rankings. NPV analysis is always mathematically correct, as is the derived yield. Initial analysis for yield can sometimes produce anomalous answers, as demonstrated later. Yield is also referred to as an internal rate of return. The expression is superfluous and not true--it is in no way internal. All cash from all sources flows into the cash pool and all cash flows out of the cash pool. The source of the $30,000 has no relevance to the analysis. The $7,800 annual cash gain flows into the cash pool. Cash flows are the subject of cash management and liquidity.

If the cash flows are uneven each year--not an annuity--each year must be calculated separately. Using the 6% rate for varying annual cash gains totaling $39,000:

Year	f6%	Cash	PV	Cash	PV	Change
1	.943	$5,000	$4,715	$10,000	$9,430	+$4,715
2	.890	7,000	6,230	9,000	8,010	+ 1,780
3	.840	8,000	6,720	8,000	6,720	0
4	.792	9,000	7,128	7,000	5,544	- 1,584
5	.747	10,000	7,470	5,000	3,735	- 3,735
	(4.212)	39,000	32,263	39,000	33,439	+ 1,176
	Outlay		30,000		30,000	
	NPV		2,263		3,439	+ 1,176

For the annuity of $7,800 the NPV is $2,854. Most projects have uneven cash flows and their amounts and timing are significant to PV.

The discount rate should be established by top management, kept up-to-date, and used for all investment proposals throughout the organization. Both NPV and yield should be computed. Positive NPV is a current financial gain regardless of the nature or location of the project, or its organizational provenance.

If NPV is positive, yield is always more than the discount rate, and vice versa. Some NPV and yield relationships are illustrated using f4.212--6% for five years.

Cash Gain	$7,800	$7,123	$6,000	$5,500
PV--f.4212	32,854	30,000	25,272	23,166
Outlay	30,000	30,000	30,000	30,000
NPV	$2,854	$ 0	-$4,728	-$6,834
Yield	9.435%	6.000%	0%	-2.832%

NPV and yield relationships are not consonant because of scale. Projects with the same NPV may have different yields. For example, projects with different outlays but all with $4,000 NPV, have the following yields--6% for 5 years:

Outlay	Cash Gain	(f4.212)	NPV	Yield	
$1,000,000	$238,367	$1,004,000	$4,000	6.15%	(f4.195)
500,000	119,658	504,000	4,000	6.30%	(f4.179)
200,000	48,433	204,000	4,000	6.74%	(f4.129)
20,000	5,698	24,000	4,000	13.08%	(f3.510)
10,000	3,324	14,000	4,000	19.73%	(f3.008)
5,000	2,137	9,000	4,000	32.12%	(f2.340)
2,000	1,425	6,000	4,000	65.51%	(f1.404)
1,000	1,188	5,000	4,000	116.29%	(f0.842)

NPV is a true absolute measure--$4,000. All proposals make an equal contribution to profit. Yields are relationships--6% to 116% above-- that can be misleading. Projects can be ranked by yield but NPV must also be given. Ranking by NPV, with yield, is also useful. Yield approaches but never reaches 6% because of positive NPV.

Projects may also have the same yield but different NPVs. For example, projects with different outlays but all with 10% yield have the following NPVs--6% for 5 years:

Outlay	Cash Gain	(f4.212)	Yield	NPV	
$1,000,000	$263,780	$1,111,105	10%	$111,105	(f3.791)
500,000	131,890	555,525	10%	55,525	(f3.791)
200,000	52,759	222,220	10%	22,220	(f3.791)
20,000	5,276	22,222	10%	2,222	(f3.791)
10,000	2,638	11,111	10%	1,111	(f3.791)
5,000	1,319	5,556	10%	556	(f3.791)
2,000	528	2,222	10%	222	(f3.791)
1,000	264	1,111	10%	111	(f3.791)

A ranking by NPV is essential to show the real gain. With higher cash gains for the same outlays both NPV and yield increase but the relationship is not intuitive. An example is based on $20,000 outlay and increasing gains at 6% for 5 years:

Outlay	Cash Gain	(f4.212)	NPV	Yield
$20,000	$4,000	$16,848	$-3,152	0%
20,000	4,619	19,455	- 545	5.0%
20,000	4,748	20,000	0	6.0%
20,000	5,276	22,220	2,222	10.0%
20,000	5,966	25,129	5,129	15.0%
20,000	6,687	28,166	8,166	20.0%

NPV rises at a higher rate than yield.

With equal cash gains and decreasing outlays both NPV and yield increase. Assuming $4,000 cash gain at 6% for 5 years, and lower outlays:

Outlay	Cash Gain	(f4.212)	NPV	Yield
$20,000	$4,000	$16,848	$-3,152	0%
17,318	4,000	16,848	- 470	5.0%
16,848	4,000	16,848	0	6.0%
15,164	4,000	16,848	1,684	10.0%
13,408	4,000	16,848	3,440	15.0%
11,964	4,000	16,848	4,884	20.0%

This example preserves the yields found in the preceding table but the NPVs diverge after the first line.

These examples underscore the need for both NPV and yield and bring out their complex interrelationship.

Accounting Rate of Return

Records are kept by accrual accounting on which ROA and ROE are based. Profitability for financial analysis is based on cash flow--NPV and yield. The two measures are the same for total life, which is used for project analysis, but the need for interim accounting reports dictates arbitrary time cut-offs. The yield (cash) determined for a project necessarily differs from the accounting rate of return (accrual), and the differences can be large and extend over the project life. A project with a high yield often shows accounting losses in the early stages. These discrepancies need to be spelled out for both project approval and interpretation of results.

Continuing with the example:

> Outlay $30,000. Life 5 years. SL $6,000. Saving $9,000.
> Cash gain $7,800. Discount rate 6% net. Tax rate 40%.
> Net income $1,800 (gain $7,800 minus SL $6,000).
> Financial yield $30,000/$7,800 = f3.846 = 9.435%.

The accounting rate of return is based on the annual net income of $1,800 and the asset balance at the beginning of the year, or on the asset average:

Year	Net Income	Opening Balance Asset	Opening Balance ROA	Average Balance Asset	Average Balance ROA
1	$1,800	30,000	6.0%	$27,000	6.7%
2	1,800	24,000	7.5	21,000	8.6
3	1,800	18,000	10.0	15,000	12.0
4	1,800	12,000	15.0	9,000	20.0
5	1,800	6,000	30.0	3,000	60.0

The five-year average asset balance of $15,000 divided by $1,800 is 12% but this does not occur in practice and the formulation is not useful.

A comparable schedule for financial yield shows a constant return each year starting with 9.435% of $30,000 or $2,830 deducted from the cash gain to arrive at the principal reduction:

Year	Cash Gain	Yield 9.435%	Principal Reduction	Principal Balance
1	$7,800	$2,830	$4,970	$25,030
2	7,800	2,361	5,439	19,591
3	7,800	1,849	5,951	13,640
4	7,800	1,287	6,513	7,127
5	7,800	673	7,127	0
	$39,000	$9,000	$30,000	

This schedule is the same as for a level-payment mortgage, with a decreasing interest component and an increasing principal component. The principal reduction column is the equivalent of depreciation, known as the annuity method, and compares with SL $6,000 each year.

ROA is lower than yield in the first two years and much higher in the last two years. The discrepancy is more pronounced using the asset average, the common practice. Because of the depressing effect of new investments on accounting profitability in the early years, management may be deterred from launching profitable new projects that depress net income, EPS, ROA, and ROE.

When some outlays are expensed at once rather than depreciated, true for most projects, the difference between ROA and yield is greater. For example:

```
Outlay:  Asset            $20,000  5-year life  SL $4,000
         Expense          $10,000  tax rate 40%
         Saving           $ 9,000 a year  Discount rate 6%  f4.212
                                          Books           Cash
         Saving                          $ 9,000         $ 9,000
         Depreciation                    - 4,000
         Taxable income                    5,000
         Tax--40%                        - 2,000         - 2,000
         Net income                        3,000
         Depreciation                    + 4,000
         Cash gain                       $ 7,000         $ 7,000

Outlay:  Asset                           $20,000
         Expense          $10,000
         less tax         $ 4,000         6,000          $26,000
Cash gain  $ 7,000  f4.212                               29,484
         NPV                                             $ 3,484
         Yield $26,000/$7,000 = f3.714 = 10.803% yield.
```

The shift of $10,000 outlay from asset to expenses increases yield to 10.803% from 9.435%, reflecting the advantage of the earlier tax deduction. NPV increases by $630 from $2,854. However, the impact on ROA is severe. Because $10,000 is expensed, profit is lower by $6,000 after tax in year 1, but ROA is higher in later years because net income is higher and the asset base is lower:

Year	Net Income	Opening Balance Asset	Opening Balance ROA	Average Balance Asset	Average Balance ROA
1	$3,000				
Expense	6,000				
	-3,000	$20,000	-15.0%	$18,000	-16.7%
2	3,000	16,000	+18.8%	14,000	+21.4%
3	3,000	12,000	+25.0%	10,000	+30.0%
4	3,000	8,000	+37.5%	6,000	+50.0%
5	3,000	4,000	+75.0%	2,000	+150.0%

These results are highly skewed. The financial analysis includes the outlays for both the asset and expense as investments in calculating the

10.8% yield. Accrual accounting requires the net expense of $6,000 to be
deducted from income for the first period. This $6,000 could be added
back to assets in the schedule above for comparability but this is not
done in practice.   It would moderate the skew. This example shows that
the 10.8% yield requires a first year loss of $3,000 and negative ROA.
Old plants operating with long-depreciated assets tend to show inflated
ROAs compared with new plants acquired at higher price levels.
  The handling of depreciation and interest needs   to   be   clearly
understood.
  Depreciation is simply an allocation of cost over economic life so that
the use of depreciable assets can be charged to periodic (annual) income
on a planned, rational basis--an allocation. Financial analysis deals
with the economic life as a single period (five years), hence the asset
cost is expensed without allocation.   Total cash gain is $39,000-- 5 x
$7,800--covering the asset cost of $30,000 and leaving $9,000 excess --or
5 x $1,800.

           The PV of $1,800 x f4.212 = $ 7,581.60 plus
           the PV of $6,000 x f4.212 = $25,272.00 equals
           the PV of $7,800 x f4.212 = $32,853.60

  Cash flow can be arrived at by adding depreciation back to net income
as shown by the analysis of cash flows:

Net income	$1,800	Saving	$9,000
Depreciation	+6,000	less tax	-1,200
Cash	$7,800	Cash	$7,800

  It is necessary to point out that depreciation is not a source of
cash, a persistent but misleading notion. Cash arises from two sources
only: collecting more revenue (in cash)--an income gain--or paying less
expense (in cash)--a cost reduction.   Depreciation is only a cost
allocation. It can affect taxes (in cash) by the timing of the deduction.
  The discount rate used is the current borrowing rate less tax.   If a
higher rate is used to recognize the cost of equity for project
evaluation, it includes the interest rate.   No other recognition of
interest is applicable.   ROA is computed after tax but before interest
expense; ROE is computed after interest expense and after tax.

Cash Payback

  Cash payback expresses the time required for cash inflows to equal
cash outlays. From the example:

           Outlay $30,000   Cash Gain   7,800
                                          =   3.846 years (as a decimal)

When a single outlay is recouped by an annuity, the payback period equals
the annuity factor used to find yield.   Cash payback is a liquidity
measure and enters into cash planning. It is not a profitability
measure; cash gain is limited to outlay so the return by definition is
zero.

The long form of computation is:

Year	Cash Gain	Cum
1	$7,800	$ 7,800
2	7,800	15,000
3	7,800	23,400
4	6,600	30,000
	$30,000	

Year 4 is 6,600/7,800 = .846. Payback = 3.846 years.
Cash payback disregards the cash flow pattern within the payback period. For example, the payback period is three years in all the following cases:

Outlay	$30,000	$30,000	$30,000	$30,000
Cash Gain:				
Year 1	$10,000	$20,000	$ 1,000	$ 0
Year 2	$10,000	$ 9,000	$ 9,000	$ 0
Year 3	$10,000	$ 1,000	$20,000	$30,000

These differences can have a major effect on cash management but all have a 3-year payback period. Cash payback also disregards the cash flow pattern beyond the payback period. For example:

Outlay	$30,000	$30,000	$30,000	$30,000
Cash Gain:				
Year 1	$ 9,000	$ 9,000	$ 9,000	$ 9,000
Year 2	$ 9,000	$ 9,000	$ 9,000	$ 9,000
Year 3	$ 9,000	$ 9,000	$ 9,000	$ 9,000
Year 4	$ 0	$ 9,000	$ 9,000·	$ 9,000
Year 5	$ 0	$ 0	$ 9,000	$ 9,000
Year 6	$ 0	$ 0	$ 0	$ 9,000
Total	$27,000	$36,000	$45,000	$54,000
Payback	Minus	3-1/3	3-1/3	3-1/3
Yield (f3.333)	-5.1%	7.7%	15.2%	19.1%

Cash payback can be considered a guide to uncertainty if two projects are otherwise equally attractive but only one can be chosen (mutually exclusive) and one has a shorter payback period. Also in periods of acute cash shortage, the payback period may be relevant. But payback is not a guide to risk. Long payback periods may invoke little risk such as the special case of bond refunding explained later, or for machinery with predictable performance. In turn, short paybacks may be highly risky such as for novelties, toys, and styles. Years ago, and now largely forgotten, separate payback periods were established for different classes of assets. Use of a short payback period to reduce risk may well have the opposite effect with the approval of risky projects and rejection of safer ones with longer payback periods. Profitability could be severely impaired.

The use of discounting applies solely to NPV--a profitability measure --and not to cash flow--a liquidity ratio. Use of PV for cash payback is misguided.

Profitability Index

This measurement is derived from the NPV computation:

PV $32,854
Outlay $30,000   = 1.095 PI

For positive NPV the PI is always over 1.0. This index either agrees with the NPV or it is in error and should be avoided.

One source of error is the classification of cash flows as to outlay and cash gain. There is no effect on NPV but PI is changed. There are no rules governing the classification of cash flows by period--it is a pragmatic choice. A common practice is to deduct the salvage value PV from the outlay rather than include it as a cash flow in the terminal year. For example:

```
Outlay                                                            $40,000
Cash gain--$10,000 for 5 years at 10% = f3.791        $37,910
Salvage year 5:  $15,000 at 10% = f.621                  9,315    47,225
NPV                                                                7,225
            $47,225/40,000 = 1.18 PI   Yield 15.9%
Outlay                                                   $40,000
Less salvage 15,000 at 10% =f.621                         9,315    30,685
Cash gain--$10,000 for 5 years at 10% = f3.791                    37,910
NPV                                                                7,225
            $37,910/30,685 = 1.24 PI   Yield 18.8%
```

Nothing is learned from either PI. NPV and yield are sufficient. In the first example yield is 15.9% and in the alternative net method it is 18.8% because the outlay is artificially reduced by the salvage PV.

Also, outlays and gains by year may be dealt with gross or net, as follows:

Year	Outlay	Cash Gain	Net	f10% 5 yrs.	PV
0	$25,000	$ 0	-$25,000	1.000	-$25,000
1	10,000	10,000	0	.909	0
2	5,000	20,000	+ 15,000	.826	+ 12,390
3	0	30,000	+ 30,000	.751	+ 22,530
	$40,000	$60,000	$20,000		+$34,920 PV
					$ 9,920 NPV

$34,920/25,000 = 1.40 PI

Restated gross:

Year	Outlay	f	PV	Cash Gain	PV
0	$25,000	1.000	$25,000	$ 0	$ 0
1	10,000	.909	9,090	10,000	9,090
2	5,000	.826	4,130	20,000	16,520
3	0	.751	0	30,000	22,530
	$40,000		$38,220	$60,000	$48,140 PV
					$38,220 Outlay PV
					$ 9,920 NPV (same)

$48,140/38,220 = 1.26 PI - lower

Project size is also a source of error: three projects with 10-year lives and 10% rate - f6.145:

	A	B	C
Outlay	$15,000	$90,000	$90,000
Cash gain	3,000	18,000	15,205
PV (f6.145)	18,435	110,610	93,435
NPV	$ 3,435	$20,610	$ 3,435
PI	1.229	1.229	1.038
Yield	15.1%	15.1%	10.9%

A and B: same PI and yield but NPV far apart
A and C: same NPV but PI and yield far apart
B and C: NPV, PI, and yield far apart

A higher NPV is always more profitable regardless of PI or yield. A combination of higher NPV and lower PI can occur but is not illustrated.

EXAMPLE FOR CURRENT ASSETS

The first example was limited to depreciable fixed assets and expensed items. Many projects also require cash, receivables, and inventories, expressed as cash flows. There is no tax effect when the current assets are acquired or when they are recouped within the project life. To illustrate, it is assumed that all outlays occur at the start of the project and are fully recovered at the end:

Outlay:
        Asset cost $30,000 = 5 years = SL $6,000
        Net current assets $10,000 (Net CA)
Savings $9,000 a year. Tax rate 40%.
Discount rate 6% net   f4.212   f.747
Cash flow:

Savings	$9,000
Depreciation	-6,000
	$3,000
Tax (40%)	-1,200
Net income	1,800
Depreciation	+6,000
Cash gain	7,800

NPV:
  Outlay

Asset--depreciated	30,000	
Net CA--recovered	+10,000	
		$40,000

  Recovery

Cash gain: $7,800 f4.212 = 32,854		
Net CA: $10,000 f.747 = 7,470		40,324
NPV		324

The small NPV indicates a yield over 6% (6.29% by calculation). The effect of net CA is:

```
Outlay                              $10,000
Recovered                          - 7,470
Reduction                            2,530
NPV first example                    2,854
New NPV                            $   324
```

Failure to recognize the "cost" ($2,530) of using $10,000 for 5 years seriously overstates NPV. A project may also reduce net CA such as for a new process requiring less inventory, an increase in NPV:

```
Outlay
  Asset--depreciated $30,000
  Net CA--reacquired               -10,000        $20,000
Recovery
  Cash gain $7,800 f4.212           32,854
  Net CA $10,000 f.747            - 7,470
  PV                                               25,384
  NPV                                               5,384
```

The effect of Net CA is to increase NPV by $2,530.

ROA can be expressed by relating annual net income to the opening asset balances--fixed assets less depreciation and net CA for the full amount. For example:

	Net Income	Asset Balances (000)	ROA
Year 1	$1,800	30 + 10 = 40	4.5%
2	1,800	24 + 10 = 34	5.3%
3	1,800	18 + 10 = 28	6.4%
4	1,800	12 + 10 = 22	8.2%
5	1,800	6 + 10 = 16	11.2%

Recovery of $10,000 net CA at the end of year 5 is omitted. One purpose of such a schedule is to advise management of the probable effect of the project on profits and ROA, particularly in the early years. This schedule cannot be obtained from the records unless specific procedures are set up. ROA without net CA would be misleading. Some projects consist solely of current assets, as illustrated earlier. Some projects consist solely of expensed items such as R&D projects and plant rearrangements.

Cash Payback:

```
Outlay--Asset              $30,000
         Net CA             10,000
                           $40,000
                           Cash Gain
Year 1                       7,800
     2                       7,800
     3                       7,800
     4                       7,800
     5                       7,800
Total                       39,000
```

The annual cash gain total is less than the outlay so $1,000 is needed from net CA recovery at the end of year 5. In this case project life and payback period are equal but there is $324 NPV and yield over 6%.

It must be remembered that for financial analysis the changes in net CA are cash flows only, not accrual entries on the books. In particular, any increase in inventory must be net of outstanding liabilities; inventory increases only when it is paid for.

SALVAGE VALUE

Depreciable assets may have some recoverable value at the end of their economic lives that can be estimated, with an increase in NPV. The example given above for fixed assets assumed no recovery. The example used for current assets assumed full recovery of outlays. In the case of land some estimate of future values is necessary.

Land

If land is purchased for $80,000 and held for possible future use without cash gain the PV at 10 percent for $80,000 terminal value is as follows:

Years		PV	NPV
10	f.386	$30,880	-$49,120
17	f.198	15,840	- 64,160
25	f.092	7,360	- 72,640
50	f.009	720	- 79,280

Land purchased for $80,000, held for 10 years, and sold for $80,000 shows no profit, but at 10%, $80,000 has PV of only $30,880 and NPV is minus $49,120. At 100 years, PV is six dollars; at 150 years it is five cents.

If the land produces a net cash gain of $10,000 the rate is 12.5%--a perpetuity--$10,000/80,000. The PV is: $10,000 f8.0 (80/10) = $80,000, less $80,000 cost = zero NPV. At 10% and zero salvage value for the same years in the schedule above:

Years	f10%	Annuity $10,000	NPV
10	f6.145	$61,450	-$18,550
17	f8.022	80,220	+ 220
25	f9.077	90,770	+ 10,770
50	f9.915	99,150	+ 19,150

A practical assumption is that land value will remain unchanged--full cost can be recovered at any time. This approach is illustrated by combining the two schedules given above:

Years	PV Cash Gain	PV Land	PV Total	Outlay	NPV
10	$61,450	$30,880	$92,330	$80,000	$12,330
17	80,220	15,840	96,060	80,000	16,060
25	90,770	7,360	98,130	80,000	18,130
50	99,150	720	99,870	80,000	19,870

The cash gain PV increases faster than the land PV declines for a net gain in total PV over time. The yield remains constant at 12.5%-- $10,000/$80,000. A break-even for NPV at 10 years is: land PV of $30,880 minus NPV of $12,330 = $18,550 PV - divided by f.386 = $48,057 terminal value rather than $80,000. Or: $48,057 f.386 = 18,500 + 61,450 = 80,000. At 17 years with no terminal value NPV is $220--NPV 16,060 less PV land 15,840.

Depreciable Assets

For depreciable assets the amount of future disposal value is speculative in varying degrees according to the asset class. Both the future condition of the equipment and the market need estimation, including expenses for removal, conditioning, transport, sales, and taxes. In some cases there is a terminal net outlay to be considered. One approach is to work backward to the salvage value needed to reach zero NPV. For example:

```
Machine cost                    $10,000
10 year life SL $1,000.  Tax 40%
Saving $1,800.  Discount rate 10% net.  f6.145  f.386
Cash gain:   Saving          $ 1,800
             Depreciation -  1,000
                                800
             Tax          -    320
             Net income        480
             Depreciation + 1,000
             Cash            1,480
             f6.145 =      $ 9,095 PV
             Outlay         10,000
                        -      905 NPV
```

$905/f.386 = $2,345 after tax and $3,908 before tax, or 39% of cost.

The question now centers on how safe this terminal value appears to be. With no salvage value and negative NPV the yield is only 7.85% (10,000/1,480 = f6.757).

The project can be rewritten:

```
Cash gain    $1,480 f6.145 = $ 9,095 PV
Net salvage  $2,345 f.386  =     905 PV
                             $10,000 PV
                              10,000 outlay
                                   0 NPV
```

The project should be recorded and depreciated at cost without regard to salvage value. When the asset is disposed of a separate entry is made to an account for gain or loss on asset disposal for the net proceeds, which are subject to tax. The alternate practice of booking depreciation net of a future salvage gain is not desirable. With less annual book depreciation the tax credit is reduced and it is less conservative because of the highly speculative nature of the future disposal value. The effect of this net method is illustrated using $3,908 salvage deducted from

$10,000 cost for $6,092 net, or 609 SL per year. Note that after ten years the book value equals estimated disposal value so no tax is deductible from the $3,908 sales proceeds.

			Comparison:		
Saving	$1,800		Cash gain:		
Depreciation	- 609		Gross	$1,480	
	1,191		Net	1,324	
Tax	- 476			- 156	f6.145 = -959
	715				
Depreciation	+ 609		Salvage:		
Cash	1,324		Gross	2,345	
f6.145	$8,136 PV		Net	3,908	
$3908 at f.386	1,508 PV			+1,563	f.386 + 603
	9,644 PV		Net change		- 356
	10,000 outlay				
	- 356 NPV				

The net method thus shows negative NPV of $356 and the gross method with zero salvage has negative NPV of $905, a difference of $549.

Project NPV can actually decline with the recognition of salvage value--the depreciation reduction exceeds the salvage gain. For example:

Outlay $10,000---10 years---no salvage---SL $1,000
or salvage $4,000 = net outlay 6,000 - SL $600
Savings $3,000. Tax rate 50%.
Discount rate 15% net.

	No Salvage	With Salvage
Saving	$3,000	$3,000
Depreciation	-1,000	- 600
	2,000	2,400
Tax	-1,000	-1,200
Net income	1,000	1,200
Depreciation	+1,000	+ 600
Cash	2,000	1,800
PV f5.019	10,038	9,034
Outlay	10,000	10,000
NPV	+ 38	- 966
No salvage	0	
Salvage 4,000 f.247		988
NPV	+ 38	+ 22

The higher NPV with zero salvage is small but significant. Here again, the net calculation is misleading. The calculation of NPV $38 with no salvage value should be made first and then a separate estimate can be made for salvage of $4,000. With the asset fully depreciated on the books, the tax is $2,000. The $2,000 net proceeds at f.247 equals $494, which is then added to NPV $38 to total $532. The probability of NPV gain from salvage can be evaluated separately without the net calculations. Trials with a range of assumptions are constructive.

Shorter Life Valuation

For assets with long lives the calculation should be made for the full economic life. Use of a shorter period raises the difficult question of interim salvage value. For example:

Building cost $80,000--40-year life. No salvage.
Discount rate 10% net. Tax rate 50%.
Cash gain $9,000 f9.779 = $88,011 PV
                         80,000 outlay
                          8,011 NPV
Yield 80/9 = f8.889 = 11.1%.

If it is assumed that the building retains its cost value at the end of 40 years at $80,000, the gain is $40,000 after tax. The PV is $40,000 f.022 = $880. NPV is $8,011 + 880 = $8,891. If the salvage value is estimated to be 10% of cost, or $8,000, the net is $4,000, PV is $88, and NPV is $8,099.
For a ten-year calculation, salvage value can be worked backward from NPV zero:

	Recap	
Cash gain $9,000 f6.145 = $55,305	Cash gain	$55,305
Outlay 80,000	Salvage	24,695
NPV -24,695	PV	$80,000
$24,695/f.386 = $63,977 Salvage	Outlay	80,000
	NPV	0

If salvage value is estimated at $80,000 after 10 years the gain over book is $20,000 (80,000 - 60,000) and the $10,000 tax reduces the cash to $70,000.

Net salvage $70,000 f.386 = $27,020
Cash gain $9,000 f6.145   = 55,305
PV   82,325
Outlay   80,000
NPV   2,325

Project analysis should include net cash from salvage in the last year for correct measurements. An alternative method deducts salvage PV, based on the discount rate, from outlay to arrive at a net outlay. NPV is the same but both yield and payback are distorted. For example:

	Outlay	$6,000	5 years	
	Cash gain	$1,000	6% discount rate	
	Salvage	$3,000		
Correct Method:				
	Cash gain	$1,000	f4.212	$4,212
	Salvage	$3,000	f.747	2,241
				$6,453 PV
	Outlay			6,000
				$ 453 NPV

```
            Trial yield at 8%:
            Cash gain      1,000 f3.993          $3,993
            Salvage        3,000 f.681            2,043
                                                 $6,036 - yield about 8.1%
            Payback        $6,000/1,000 = 6 years
Alternate method:
            Outlay         $6,000
            Salvage PV     -2,241
            Net Outlay      3,759
            Cash gain       4,212
                              453 NPV - same
Yield 3759/1000 = f3.759 = 10.3% (cf 8.1%)
Payback 3759/1000 = 3.76 years (cf 6 years)
```

UNEVEN CASH FLOWS

The examples given above have used annuities for annual cash gains for the sake of brevity and clarity. In practice, equal periodic cash flows are rare. The analytic techniques are the same for uneven cash flows but some unique features call for explication.

Example

Uneven cash flows directly affect NPV. For example, with total cash gain of $12,000 in 3 years with three cash flow patterns:

Year	10% f	Cash Gain	PV	Cash Gain	PV	Cash Gain	PV
1	.909	$ 7,000	$ 6,363	$ 1,000	$ 909	$ 4,000	$3,636
2	.826	4,000	3,304	4,000	3,304	4,000	3,304
3	.751	1,000	751	7,000	5,257	4,000	3,004
Total PV		($12,000)	$10,418	($12,000)	$9,470	($12,000)	9,944
Outlay			9,944		9,944		9,944
NPV		+	474	-	474		0

A cash gain annuity is given first to compare with uneven cash gains by period:

```
            Outlay $80,000.  5-year life.  SL $16,000.
            Discount rate 10%.  Savings $32,000 a year.
            Tax rate 50%.  No salvage.
Savings        $32,000    Cash $24,000      f3.791   =   $90,984
Depreciation   -16,000    Outlay                          80,000
                16,000    NPV                             10,984
Tax            - 8,000    Yield $80,000/24,000 = f3.333 = 15.2%
Net income      8,000
Depreciation  +16,000
Cash           24,000
```

If the cash flows are uneven the effect on NPV may be up or down. For example, with total savings of $160,000 (32,000 for 5 years) restated by year:

	Year 1	Year 2	Year 3	Year 4	Year 5	Total
Savings	$10,000	$10,000	$30,000	$30,000	$80,000	$160,000
Depreciation	16,000	16,000	16,000	16,000	16,000	80,000
	- 6,000	- 6,000	14,000	14,000	64,000	80,000
Tax	+ 3,000	+ 3,000	- 7,000	- 7,000	-32,000	40,000
Net income	- 3,000	- 3,000	7,000	7,000	32,000	40,000
Depreciation	16,000	16,000	16,000	16,000	16,000	80,000
Cash gain	13,000	13,000	23,000	23,000	48,000	120,000
f	.909	.826	.751	.683	.621	-
PV	$11,817	$10,738	$17,273	$15,709	$29,808	$ 85,354
Outlay						80,000
NPV						5,345

NPV is reduced from $10,984 by over half to $5,345 because of lower cash flows in the earlier years.

Yield is found by trial and error.

Try 12%:

	Cash Gain	f	PV
Year 1	$13,000	.893	$11,609
Year 2	13,000	.797	10,361
Year 3	23,000	.712	16,376
Year 4	23,000	.636	14,628
Year 5	48,000	.567	27,216
	120,000	(3.605)	$80,190

Yield is a little over 12.0%, compared with 15.2% for the annuity. Cash payback is 4 1/6 years, compared with 3 1/3:

Year 1	$13,000
2	13,000
3	23,000
4	23,000
5	8,000 (8/48 = 1/6)
	$80,000

The accounting rate of return for the annuity is:

Year	Net Income	Asset Balance (opening)	ROA
1	$8,000	80,000	10.0%
2	8,000	64,000	12.5%
3	8,000	48,000	16.7%
4	8,000	32,000	25.0%
5	8,000	16,000	50.0%
	40,000	--	

Based on the uneven cash flows:

Year	Net Income	Asset Balance (opening)	ROA	Asset Balance (average)	ROA
1	-$3,000	$80,000	- 3.8%	$72,000	- 4.2%
2	- 3,000	64,000	- 4.7%	56,000	- 5.4%
3	+ 7,000	48,000	+ 14.6%	40,000	+17.5%
4	+ 7,000	32,000	+ 21.9%	24,000	+29.2%
5	+32,000	16,000	+200.0%	8,000	+400.0%
	$40,000	--			

Discrepancies between yield and NPV based on financial (cash) analysis and accounting rate of return (accrual) are wide but determinable as part of project evaluation. The distinction is lost in the accounting records and ROA is a weighted average of all projects on the books as measured to periodic cut-off dates.

Accelerated Depreciation

The effect on cash flows is more pronounced with the use of accelerated depreciation, rather than straight-line, allowed by tax law to encourage investments. The larger earlier deductions reduce taxes, with larger amounts payable later; the total is the same over project life. The early tax saving is in effect a tax-free loan. Many companies use accelerated depreciation for taxes but record straight-line depreciation on the books to avoid reporting the lower income occasioned by new projects. GAAP requires the reporting of tax provision on the taxable income difference as a deduction from income and a credit to deferred taxes payable; these amounts are expected to reverse over time.

The double-declining balance (DDB) method of depreciation applies a percent that is double the straight-line percent, to the opening balance each period. Switchover to SL is made when that amount exceeds the DDB amount so that a zero balance is reached. The SL rate for 5 years is 20%. The DDB rate is 40%.

Year	Asset	DDB at 40%	Switchover to SL
1	$80,000	$32,000	$32,000
2	48,000	19,200	19,200
3	28,800	11,520	11,520
4	17,280	6,912	8,640
5	10,368	4,747	8,640
Balance	6,221	73,779	80,000

Sum-of-the-years digits (SYD) is based on the arithmetic sum of the number of years. For five years, $1 + 2 + 3 + 4 + 5 = 15$. A short-cut is to add the first and last years = 6, divide the last year by 2 = 2 1/2, and then multiply--6 x 2-1/2 = 15. For the years 1 to 10 = 11 x 5 = 55. For the years 1 to 20 = 21 x 10 = 210.

Year	SYD on $80,000		Asset Balance
1	5/15	$26,667	$53,333
2	4/15	21,333	32,000
3	3/15	16,000	16,000
4	2/15	10,667	5,333
5	1/15	5,333	0

Many factors in the tax code relate to asset capitalization and depreciation methods, and there are specific allowances such as the investment tax credit. These provisions and their interpretation change frequently. Expert tax guidance is essential for both project analysis and tax liability calculations. The illustrations given are simplified to convey the approach and the method for handling uneven cash flows that are occasioned by operating as well as tax considerations.

SYD is applied to the example but the amounts are rounded:

	Year 1	Year 2	Year 3	Year 4	Year 5	Total
Savings	$10,000	$10,000	$30,000	$30,000	$80,000	$160,000
Depreciation	26,000	22,000	16,000	10,000	6,000	80,000
SYD						
	-16,000	-12,000	14,000	20,000	74,000	80,000
Tax	+ 8,000	+ 6,000	- 7,000	-10,000	-37,000	- 40,000
Net income	- 8,000	- 6,000	7,000	10,000	37,000	40,000
Depreciation	+26,000	22,000	16,000	10,000	6,000	80,000
Cash gain	18,000	16,000	23,000	20,000	43,000	120,000
f	.909	.826	.751	.683	.621	-
PV	$16,362	$13,216	$17,273	$13,660	$26,703	$ 87,214
Outlay						80,000
NPV						7,214

The NPV increases from $5,345 to $7,214 by using SYD in place of SL. Yield increases from 12% to 13%, by trial and error--not given. Cash payback becomes 4 3/43 years. The accounting rate of return is:

		Asset Balance		Compare
Year	Net Income	Opening	ROA	ROA-SL
1	-$8,000	$80,000	- 10.0%	- 3.8%
2	- 6,000	54,000	- 11.1%	- 4.7%
3	7,000	32,000	+ 21.9%	+ 14.6%
4	10,000	16,000	+ 62.5%	+ 21.9%
5	37,000	6,000	+616.7%	+200.0%
	40,000			

ROA is much more skewed by SYD as it is with all methods of accelerated depreciation.

The advantage for reduced taxes in earlier years with SYD is illustrated:

Year	SL Tax	SYD Tax	SYD Gain (Loss)	Cum
1 Credit	+$3,000	+$8,000	+$5,000	+$5,000
2 Credit	+ 3,000	+ 6,000	+ 3,000	+ 8,000
3 Expense	- 7,000	- 7,000	0	+ 8,000
4 Expense	- 7,000	-10,000	(3,000)	+ 5,000
5 Expense	-32,000	-37,000	(5,000)	0
	-40,000	-40,000	0	

The cum column shows the amount of the cash gain--an interest-free loan. It is assumed that the credits reduce total taxes payable.

Change of Signs

Some projects have cash flows that change signs from one period to the next in varying amounts and patterns. Use of the discount rate to determine NPV always provides the correct answer, and yield can then be found by trial and error. It is arithmetically possible for projects with sign reversals to have more than one yield, or none, but with NVP calculated first the correct yield is clear. An example of cash flow reversal shows the relationship between NVP and yield:

	Cash Flow				
Year	Plus	Minus	f10%	PV+	PV-
1	$10,000	$ 0	.909	$ 9,090	
2	0	2,000	.826		$1,652
3	10,000		.751	7,510	
4	0	11,000	.683		7,513
				16,600	9,165
				- 9,165	
PV				7,435	
Outlay				7,430	
NPV				5	

The yield appears to be slightly over 10% but is found to be 20%:

	Cash Flow				
Year	Plus	Minus	f20%	PV+	PV-
1	$10,000	$ 0	.833	$ 8,330	
2	0	2,000	.694		$1,388
3	10,000		.579	5,790	
4	0	11,000	.482		5,302
				14,120	6,690
				- 6,690	
PV				7,430	
Outlay				7,430	
NPV				0	

ASSET REPLACEMENT

It is a good practice to review all productive assets periodically for retention, disposal, or replacement. Replacements, often a major part of capital expenditures, are made to achieve some better combination of capacity, cost, and quality. Replacement projects have some distinctive features. For example:

New machine: cost $24,000---12-year life---
            SL $2,000 Salvage value $4,000 in 12 years
Old machine: book balance $6,000
            6 years remaining life---SL $1,000
            Sell for $7,000 (salvage value zero in 6 years)
Annual savings $3,250 Tax rate 40% Discount rate 10% f6.814 f.319

Outlay:

New machine			$24,000
Old machine			
Sell		$7,000	
Books		6,000	
Gain		1,000	
Tax		- 400	
Net cash (7,000-400)		6,600	- 6,600
Net outlay			$17,400

Cash gain:

Saving		$3,250	
Depreciation		- 2,000	
		$1,250	
Tax		- 500	
Net income		750	
Depreciation		+ 2,000	
Cash gain		2,750	
12 years 10%		f6.814	$18,738 PV

Salvage--new machine:

Sell		$4,000	
Tax		1,600	
Net		2,400	
		f.319	$ 766 PV
			$19,504

Tax lost on depreciation on old machine:

$1,000 at 40% = $400 6 years 10%		f4.355	$ 1,742
PV--net			$17,762
Net Outlay			17,400
NPV			$ 362

NPV is less than half the salvage PV of $766 for the new machine. Projecting a sales value of $4,000 on a $24,000 cost to be realized 12 years later is questionable. With a disposal value of $2,000, NPV becomes negative (2,000-800 = 1,200 at f.319 = 383 or half of 766, and NPV 362 - 383 = -21). Failure to recognize the tax lost on the depreciation of the old machine would inflate NPV by $1,742. If the old machine has projected salvage value in 6 years, not included in the example, that also is a sacrifice that is deductible for NPV. Replacement analyses require logical, complete, and accurate formats, and all amounts should be estimated within reasonable ranges. A most likely combination of data can be run to provide a point estimate for first evaluation. Replacement possibilities should be monitored closely to keep abreast of improvements. If a new machine offers positive NPV, it should be approved even though the old machine was only recently acquired. The fact that the old machine has become relatively unprofitable attaches to the decision to acquire it. Purchase of a new machine with a positive NVP should not be deferred because the delay might improve the NVP--the gain lost by the delay is not recoverable. Foresight as to possible improvements is visionary.

MUTUALLY EXCLUSIVE PROJECTS

Many projects require a choice among several feasible alternatives. Methods of analysis are illustrated using three examples of equalities.
First, equal outlays and yields:

Project	Outlay	Cash Gain	f	Years	Yield
A	$10,000	$1,490	6.710	10	8.0%
B	10,000	2,505	3.993	5	8.0%
		$1,015			

$\underline{A}$ locks in the 8% yield for an extra 5 years but $\underline{B}$ provides more liquidity with high cash gain.

Second, equal cash gain and yields:

Project	Outlay	Cash Gain	f	Years	Yield
C	$16,808	$2,505	6.710	10	8.0%
D	10,000	2,505	3.993	5	8.0%
	$ 6,808				

$\underline{C}$ requires higher outlay to provide 8% yield for an additional 5 years.

Third, equal lives and yields:

Project	Outlay	Cash Gain	f	Years	Yield
E	$16,808	$2,505	6.710	10	8.0%
F	10,000	1,490	6.710	10	8.0%
	$ 6,808	$1,015			

With equal years and yields, the question is liquidity. The extra outlay for $\underline{E}$ is recouped by higher cash gain in 6.7 years.
These examples are not apt to occur in practice but are presented to put a sharp focus on the nature of the analysis.
Two examples with equal lives and different yields follow:

1.	Project	Outlay	Cash Gain	f	Years	Yield
	G	$10,000	$1,993	5.019	10	15.0%
	H	18,000	3,186	5.650	10	12.0%
	(H-G)	$ 8,000	$1,193	6.710	10	8.0%

$\underline{G}$ offers higher yield in the same period with less outlay. $\underline{H}$ is, in effect, $\underline{G}$ plus $(\underline{H}-\underline{G})$. The incremental outlay offers a yield of 8%, thus lowering $\underline{H}$ to 12%. The choice depends on the discount rate. If it is lower than 8%, then $(\underline{H}-\underline{G})$ is desirable and $\underline{H}$ is chosen. If the discount rate is over 8%, then $(\underline{H}-\underline{G})$ is not acceptable and $\underline{G}$ is chosen. The decision is thus independent of the fact that the yield for $\underline{H}$ is lower at 12% than for $\underline{G}$ at 15%. As to liquidity, $\underline{H}$ requires a higher outlay with a slightly longer payback. Risk requires separate evaluation. Although mutually exclusive projects relate by definition to the same type of operation, and have equal lives in this case, possibly $\underline{H}$ at the higher cost is more dependable and thus less risky. Several scenarios are possible and could tip the scales.

Project	Outlay	Cash Gain	f	Years	Yield
I	$ 8,000	$1,193	6.710	10	8.0%
J	6,000	815	7.360	10	6.0%
(I-J)	$ 2,000	$ 378	5.291	10	13.6%

With a discount rate over 8% neither plan is acceptable. The incremental 13.6% raises J's 6% to 8% for I but (I-J) is not a separate investment. With a discount rate between 8% and 6%, I is acceptable. With a discount rate below 6%, J is acceptable but I is preferred because it is a combination of J and (I-J).

Two examples with unequal lives using the annuity method of analysis follow:

Projects	K	L	K to L
Life	10 years	5 years	
Cash gain	$3,000	$2,000	+$1,000
10% f	f6.145	f3.791	
PV	$18,435	$7,582	
Outlay	15,000	6,000	+ 9,000
NPV	3,435	1,582	+ 1,853
Divide	f6.145	f3.791	
Annuity	= $559	= $417	+ 142
Yield	$15,000/3,000 =	$6,000/2,000 =	
	f5.0 = 15.1%	f3.0 = 19.9%	

K has a higher NPV which is an annuity of $559 for 10 years compared with an annuity of $417 for 5 years for L. K is preferred although yield at 15.1% is lower than L's 19.9%. The project with the higher NPV may not always have a higher annuity.

Projects	M	N	M to N
Life	10 years	5 years	
Cash gain	$3,000	$2,000	+$1,000
10% f	f6.145	f3.791	
PV	$18,435	$7,582	
Outlay	15,000	5,000	+10,000
NPV	3,435	2,582	+ 853
Divide	f6.145	f3.791	
Annuity	= $559	= $681	- 122
Yield	$15,000/3,000 =	$5,000/2,000 =	
	f5.0 = 15.1%	f2.5 = 28.6%	

M is unchanged from K. N is changed from L only by lower outlay. M still has a higher NPV but the lower NPV of N provides an annuity of $681, or $122 more than M. The yield for N is also higher by a wider margin. Thus, the annuity method neatly and accurately adjusts NPVs for different periods to comparable annual equivalents.

An example of two projects analyzed on the basis of cost rather gain follows:

	O	P	P to O
Life	5 years	10 years	
Annual cost	$10,000	$12,000	+ $2,000
10% f	f3.791	f6.145	
PV	$37,910	$73,740	
Outlay	50,000	55,000	+ 5,000
Total cost	$87,910	$128,740	
Divide	f3.791	f6.145	
Annuity	=$23,189	=$20,950	- 2,239

P has a higher annual cost by $2,000 and costs $5,000 more to buy. But with a 10-year life the annual cost at $20,950 is substantially less than the 5-year annual cost for O at $23,189.

INTANGIBLE BENEFITS

Many projects are designed to provide benefits that cannot be quantified. Advertising budgets, often substantial, are developed as part of the overall marketing plan, but the amounts are necessarily judgmental and results are difficult to assess. Benefits are expected to persist into the future but for how long or to what extent is indeterminate. Research and development expenses are also large for many companies but the planned budgets cannot be guided by any estimate of gains. By definition, R&D is the pursuit of new knowledge. If gain can be estimated, the activity is not R&D. All advertising and all R&D expenditures are charged to expense as incurred; there is no basis for deferral because no gain is predictable. Other product-related efforts, such as product engineering or manufacturing and industrial engineering, may permit expense deferral to the extent considered chargeable to future revenue. The principle is matching expense and revenue to express income fairly. In practice, the decisions are pragmatic and often debatable. It is not unusual for such deferrals to be written off abruptly when plans go wrong. Large write-offs are often referred to as "taking a bath."

Projects for employee welfare or public relations are frequent but do not have quantifiable benefits. These projects can be defined as to amount of outlay and economic life, if only as estimates, and with a stated discount rate the gain can be expressed. For example, a project for a local community:

Outlay $80,000 Life 5 years 8% discount rate f3.993
Taxes 40%
Analysis: $\frac{\$80,000}{f3.993}$ = $20,036/.6 = $33,394 before tax

Evaluation can focus on the quantified benefit at $33,394, which is zero NPV, and on alternative projects. Variations of outlay and life can be explored. For example, with a 10-year life--$80,000/f6.710 = $11,940/.6 = $19,900. The required benefit for 10 years is 60% of that for 5 years. For reasons of profitability and liquidity, total budget limits may be set for such projects based on the consideration of overall profitability and liquidity prospects.

PROGRAM CONTROL

The capital expenditure program should be aided by a well-defined system, supported by procedures, forms, and timetables, and guided by trained and cooperative technical staff.

Project Definition

Each project must be fully identified, defined as to purpose, and be independent of all others. It must not require any undisclosed subsequent outlay or the approval of some other project. For mutually exclusive proposals, only the one selected should be included, but the others may be disclosed for reference. No project should include an activity better handled as a separate project.

Cash flows attributable to the project must be set out by amount and period. Cash amounts are those that occur with project approval; without approval there is no cash effect. Each cash item must be a specific element such as supplies, rent, taxes, insurance, wages, travel, cash collected from customers, cash outlays for fixed assets, or expenses by item. Excluded are depreciation, overhead, allocations, and fringe benefits. Interest is represented by the discount rate and is not a project expense. A financial lease option is a separate financing decision, and project approval rests solely on the analysis of cash flows without regard to the source of the funds.

Judgmental areas may be described separately and expressed as approximations if practical. A product proposal may affect the sale of other products. There may be competitive reactions. The proposed use of available space and existing facilities may hasten the time for their expansion. Such evaluations need to be guided by the effect of all related proposals and company plans.

Project Classification

For ease of administration, projects should be classified by some scheme that suits the situation. Classification schemes are arbitrary and pragmatic because of the variety of projects, and some overlap is unavoidable. A classification scheme is suggested:

Strategic--large sums; long lives; high risk; benefits not
  quantifiable; goals, strategies, policies involved; top-level
  approval
New and Improved Products--for old markets; for new markets
Existing Products--new markets
Increased Capacity--higher output; lower cost
Cost Reduction--same capacity
Replacements--technology changes
Current Assets--increase in net current assets not involving
  fixed assets
Expensed--outlays charged directly to expense, or deferred and
  amortized over short periods, such as plant rearrangement, product
  engineering, and consulting charges. Advertising is expensed as
  incurred but is usually included separately in the marketing plan.
  Research and development is also expensed as incurred but is usually
  a wholly separate proposal.

Communications--information systems, computers, telecommunications,
   fax
Mandated--required by law or contract
External Relations--public relations of all kinds
Internal Relations--employee benefit

The varied nature of proposals may call for some multiple listings and
cross-referencing.

Project Evaluation in Total

Proposals   approved   by   the   designated organizational units and
management levels are assembled and classified for top management review.
Only   then   is   it   possible to assess the overall   effect   on growth,
profitability, risk, and liquidity.   Some proposals may be   rejected
because of conflicts with goals, policies, strategies, or other
proposals. Some may appear to be too risky. Others may be deferred for
further analysis or to await pending developments. Management overload as
to time or skill may dictate holding up some projects.   Weight must be
given to the possible effect on both internal and external relations.
Profitability must be considered both in financial terms--NPV and yield--
and accounting results--ROA, ROE, net income, and EPS. Projects that are
deferred, rather than rejected, are eligible for resubmission.

Liquidity constraints may dictate project postponement when management
is not inclined to increase debt or to issue stock in light of conditions
in the financial markets. The profit foregone on the deferred projects is
the opportunity cost of reduced liquidity risk. Other factors bearing on
the evaluation are the dangers of corporate raiders, technological trends,
shifting   consumer   tastes,   competitive   developments,   tax   changes,
government programs, foreign exchange prospects, the economic climate, and
financial markets. These considerations are complex and subjective.   The
final decisions become the approved capital expenditure plan that enters
into the financial plans. The dropping or deferring of proposals for
liquidity reasons is often referred to as "capital rationing" but this
term is better avoided as being rather simplistic and possibly misleading.

The financial plans become approved budgets to guide and coordinate
performance throughout the organization.   However, capital expenditure
projects in the budget should be resubmitted for approval to start action
and commit funds. This may be done on a quarterly basis.   These
submissions may include more detail, changed analysis, and even new
projects.   Some projects included in the budget may be cancelled by the
proposers. Thus, the annual capital expenditure budget authorizes only
the submission of projects for review and approval at subsequent times
throughout the year.   The whole process should be guided by clear
procedures and specific designation of approval authority.

Project Control

After approval projects should be monitored for timely completion to
insure realization of anticipated benefits, and for compliance   with
budgeted outlays.   Some projects may have to be delayed or cancelled
because of adverse developments. A final report should summarize actual
results compared with the proposal as to dates, outlays, benefits, and

life. The time from approval to completion may range from a month to several years. This report completes the project control cycle and provides the basis for operation review.

Operation Review

At the time of project completion, a decision should be made as to whether a later review is advisable. For many projects it is neither necessary nor practical. For projects to be reviewed, a record should be made stating when, by whom, and for what factors. Data that will be needed should be clearly specified. If not now available from existing records, specific instructions and procedures must be instituted. Examples of information that may not be available currently include: machine operating time; reasons for downtime; setup times by machine and by process or product; machine maintenance; material usage; scrap or defective output; labor time and pay rates by operator; output rates; downtime by reason; inventory levels by machine and process; power consumption; and use of supplies.

At the time of review all the data should be evaluated and a report issued. The findings may be:

--Better performance than projected.
--Performance that should be improved.
--Poor performance that needs modification.
--Bad performance. Abandon or replace. Estimate net salvage
  value and authorize disposal.
--Reschedule review at a selected future date.

The evaluation should be based on the data found compared with the project as defined on completion. When applicable the data should be related to the risk ranges used for project review. When results are significantly better or worse than the point estimate they may still be within the risk range. The review should focus on encouraging constructive action, including prompt cessation of bad operations and search for acceptable alternatives.

The review program is often referred to as an audit but this is inaccurate and misleading. It is primarily an operational appraisal by technical staff as an integral part of the capital expenditure program. It can contribute to the preparation of better proposals and enlighten the search for opportunities. Bias in project factors may also become evident. The relation of performance to risk profiles may be illuminating. The success of some types of projects may increase efforts in that direction. Project preparers will be motivated to be clear and complete in their efforts.

4

Capital Expenditures: Special Applications

Several highly significant decision areas are unique except for a common link with capital expenditures.

. The learning curve (LC) requires close attention when projects involve new methods and the possibility of lower unit costs as experience is gained. The LC is also known as the experience curve.

. Purchase of a company--merger--requires evaluation as a capital expenditure but has distinctive features as to risk and liquidity.

. Investing in a new product calls for plans to achieve a designated market share, usually over a long period. The risk of substantial losses may be high.

. Refunding a bond issue is analyzed as a capital expenditure but it is a financing decision with unique features related to risk and accounting treatment.

. Financial leases are defined and illustrated as financing choices independent of the asset acquisition decision.

LEARNING CURVE

The learning curve--LC--refers to repetitive operations that can lead to higher output rates expressed as decreased average times per unit. The effect is measured primarily in terms of labor time, or labor and machine time. When other related activities respond with lower costs per unit, reference is made to the experience curve. The saving potential arises from new methods and technology, particularly those with substantial labor content. The effect can be significant in the evaluation of some capital expenditures. Failure to recognize LC can cause rejection of a project that should be accepted. Overestimatation of LC can cause a poor project to look attractive. (LC also applies to product costs and pricing, and to vendor quotations, both illustrated later in this section. The use of LC in measuring labor performance is presented in chapter 11. The accounting treatment of LC is explored in chapter 15.)

Estimating LC is difficult because many factors that are hard to predict and control are involved, including labor conditions, product revisions, method changes, and run sizes. LC calculations are usually based on linear assumptions--a simplification that is not always true in practice. For each doubling of quantity the time per unit is decreased by a constant percent.

Two illustrations are given at the extreme rates of 100% and 50% to demonstrate the method. 100% LC has no time saving:

Q Quantity Doubled	100% Avg. Time Per Unit	Total Time	Increment Time/Q	Per Unit
1	100	100	--	--
2	100	200	100/1	100
4	100	400	200/2	100
8	100	800	400/4	100

As $\underline{Q}$ doubles total time doubles and average time per unit is constant. 50% LC is not attainable:

Q	50% Avg. Time Per Unit	Total Time	Increment Time/Q	Per Unit
1	100	100	0	0
2	50	100	0/1	0
4	25	100	0/2	0
8	12.5	100	0/4	0

As $\underline{Q}$ doubles total time is constant and per unit time is zero.

The doubled quantites used for illustration may in practice be any amount relevant to the product and process: one aeroplane wing, ten control panels, sixty struts, one thousand clamps. The LC rate falls within a range generally between 65 and 90%, with a median of about 80%. The average time is expressed for convenience as 1.0 for Q1 and decreased progressively by the LC rate as shown. The total time is $\underline{Q}$ times LC average and it rises at a constant rate related to the LC rate. The increase in total time is divided by the increase in $\underline{Q}$ to arrive at the output time per unit for the bracket measured.

The procedure described is illustrated for 80% LC:

Q	80% LC	Total Time	Increment Time/Q	Per Unit (80%)
1	10,000	10,000	--	--
2	8,000	16,000	6,000/1	6,000
4	6,400	25,600	9,600/2	4,800
8	5,120	40,960	15,360/4	3,840
16	4,096	65,536	24,576/8	3,072

Time per unit decreases at 80% while the total increases at 60% for each doubling of Q.

Q3 and Q4 can be determined individually by use of a .calculator or found in a table:

```
                           Average
        Q3 is 506.312 or 506 - 480 = +26
        Q4 is 453.688 or 454 - 480 = -26
                 960.000     960 - 960 =   0
```

For Q5 + 6 + 7 + 8 the schedule is:

Time per Unit	Each	Average	Difference
Q5	418	384	+34
Q6	391	384	+ 7
Q7	372	384	-12
Q8	355	384	-29
	1,536	1,536	0

This level of detail is presented to clarify the workings of LC time calculations. The incremental effect on the weighted averages is derived as follows:

	Difference per Unit	Time Total	Divide by Q	LC 80% Average
Cum Q4	480	2,560	4	640.0*
add Q5	418	2,978	5	595.6
add Q6	391	3,369	6	561.5
add Q7	372	3,741	7	534.4
add Q8	355	4,096	8	512.0*

*These figures appear on the 80% LC table given above.

The level of detail given helps to illustrate LC applications. In purchase negotiations with vendors the time allowance for Q4 is 2,560 but the added time for Q5 is 418, lowering the Q4 average of 640.0 to a Q5 average of 595.6. The incremental time for Q8 is 355, and the average is 512. These time estimates would be transformed into dollars.

A similar process relates to product costing when the LC is applied to incremental amounts and price reductions lead to higher sales. Using an example for pricing with positive demand elasticity and incremental costing without LC:

	Q4		Q6		Q8	
Sales	@ $800	$3200	@ $700	$4200	@ $550	$4400
Cost	@ $640	2560	@ $610	$3660	@ $560	$4480
Margin	160	640	90	540	- 10	- 80

The schedule is rewritten with 80% LC using dollars in place of the time totals in the preceding table:

	Q4		Q6		Q8	
Sales	@ $800	$3,200	@ $700	$4,200	@ $550	$4,400
Cost LC 80%	@ $640	2,560	@ $561	3,366	@ $512	4,096
Margin	160	640	139	834	38	304
Increase	0	0	49	294	48	384

The 90% LC is illustrated:

Q	90% LC	Total Time	Increment Time/Q	Per Unit (90%)
1	10,000	10,000	--	--
2	9,000	18,000	8,000/1	8,000
4	8,100	32,400	14,400/2	7,200
8	7,290	58,320	25,920/4	6,480
16	6,561	104,978	46,656/8	5,832

The 70% LC is as follows:

Q	70% LC	Total Time	Increment Time/Q	Per Unit (70%)
1	10,000	10,000	--	--
2	7,000	14,000	4,000/1	4,000
4	4,900	19,600	5,600/2	2,800
8	3,430	27,440	7,840/4	1,960
16	2,401	38,416	10,976/8	1,372

Time per unit is summarized for several LCs:

	100%	90%	80%	70%	Ratio of 70% to 90%
Q2	10,000	8,000	6,000	4,000	50.0
Q4	10,000	7,200	4,800	2,800	38.9
Q8	10,000	6,480	3,840	1,960	30.2
Q16	10,000	5,832	3,072	1,372	23.5
Ratio of Q16 to Q2		72.9	51.2	34.3	

Use of the LC in the analysis of a capital expenditure project is given for both Q8 and Q16, each for LCs 90% and 80% and 70%:

Outlay $350,000 Life 10 years
Cash gain $25,000 No salvage
Discount rate 6% f7.36

No LC:

Cash gain $25,000 f7.360 = $184,000 PV
Outlay   350,000
                           -166,000 NPV

The cash gains in the following schedules are factored by LC averages given above.

90% LC: Apply to $25,000
                 Q8 .7290 = $34,294 f7.36 = $252,400
                 Outlay   350,000
                                             - 97,600 NPV
                 Q16 .6561 = $38,104 f7.36 = 280,445
                 Outlay   350,000
                                             - 69,555 NPV

80% LC: Apply to $25,000
                 Q8 .5120 = $48,828 f7.36 = $359,375 PV
                 Outlay   350,000
                                             +   9,375 NPV
                 Q16 .4096 = $61,035 f7.36 = 449,219 PV
                 Outlay   350,000
                                             +149,219 NPV

70% LC: Apply to $25,000
                 Q8 .3430 = $72,886 f7.36 = $536,441 PV
                 Outlay   350,000
                                              186,441 NPV
                 Q16 .2401 = $104,123 f7.36 = 766,345 PV
                 Outlay   350,000
                                              416,345 NPV

Summarizing NPV and computing yield:

	Q8		Q16	
	NPV	Yield %	NPV	Yield %
LC 90%	-$97,600	Loss	-$69,555	Loss
LC 80%	+ 9,375	6.6	+149,219	11.6
LC 70%	+186,441	16.2	+416,345	27.0

These wide ranges in NPV and yield underscore the importance of selecting an achievable LC percent and a realistic quantity limit. With no LC there is a large loss and at 90% LC losses continue. For 80% LC the yield range is 6.6% for Q8 to 11.6% for Q16, well above the 6% discount rate. 70% LC is probably not attainable.

Predictions of LC effectiveness for quantity are perilous because many circumstances can alter the situation affecting the learning rate. In practice, LCs do not regularly follow a fixed percent as shown in the tables, which are log linear. The longer the production period the greater the chance for the LC to be interrupted by extraneous developments that are not readily predicable.

Capital expenditure projects in operation should be reviewed for the LC effect for comparison with the estimates used in the proposals. Such evaluations can be critical in tempering overly optimistic estimates, and in other cases encouraging the use of less cautious assumptions. Projects rejected on the basis of LC analysis should be earmarked for later review.

THE PURCHASE OF A COMPANY

There are many reasons for a company to acquire another concern and a variety of ways for handling the transaction. A multitude of financial, tax, and accounting factors are involved. Motivation for merger springs from goals and strategies and the terms of deals depend largely on negotiating skills. The presentation here is limited to the purchase of a company to acquire productive assets in lieu of their separate purchase or construction--an extension of capital expenditure analysis. The prospective cash gains must be estimated and discounted to determine NPV and yield. Operating risk may be high. Liquidity may also be a critical factor if heavy borrowing is required. The combined effect of operating and financial risk has a major bearing on the price and terms. A long period of losses may be necessary before the acquisition becomes profitable. Capital expenditure analysis also includes disinvestment, or the spinning off a segment of the company because of poor profit prospects or a change in goals.

An example of a merger proposal is given for which estimated life is uncertain. The outlay is $75,000 and cash gain is $10,000. The perpetuity is $10,000 divided by 13.3%. For 7.5 years the total cash gain is $75,000 and the yield is zero. The following table illustrates a range of years with probabilities:

Life	Yield	Probability	Extension
8	1.5%	0%	0.00%
9	2.6	5	.13
10	5.6	5	.28
12	8.1	10	.81
15	10.2	10	1.02
20	11.9	20	2.38
25	12.7	30	3.81
30	13.0	20	2.60
	65.6%	100%	11.03%
Average	8.2%		

This wide range has an 8.2% average without weighting and 11% with the probabilities assumed. If the discount rate is 6%, the chance of loss is about 10%. With a 10% discount rate the negative odds are 30%. With a 12% discount rate, the odds are close to 50-50. Managers respond differently to risk exposure. Factors other than yield often have a major bearing on the evaluation.

Given a $75,000 outlay and 10-year life, cash gain estimates may vary:

Cash Gain	Yield	Probability	Extension
$ 8,000	1.5%	10%	.15%
10,000	5.6	20	.56
12,500	10.6	30	3.12
15,000	15.1	30	4.56
17,500	19.4	20	3.88
5	52.2%	100%	12.30%
Average	10.4%		

The odds are about 50-50 for $12,500 cash gain.

The cash outlay may also be variable, some deals call for future outlays conditional on specified developments. All variables need to be estimated in reasonable ranges and probable outcomes determined. The probabilities below the discount rate indicate the degree of downside risk, often the controlling factor.

Projected earnings growth is also a factor. Assuming a 6% annual growth rate, all earnings paid out in dividends and 1,000 shares of stock:

Year	Earnings	Yield on $75,000	EPS (1,000/sh)
1	$10,000	13.33%	$10.00
2	10,600	14.13	10.60
3	11,236	14.98	11.23
4	11,910	15,88	11.91
5	12,625	16.83	12.62
6	13,383	17.84	13.38

The increase rate is 6% for all three columns.

If all earnings are retained for reinvestment, yields drop but EPS continues to increase at 6% a year. Yield is based on the investment at the beginning of the year:

Year	Earnings	Investment	Yield	EPS
1	$10,000	$ 75,000	13.33%	$10.00
2	10,600	85,000	12.47%	10.60
3	11,236	95,600	11.75%	11.23
4	11,910	106,836	11.15%	11.91
5	12,625	118,746	10.63%	12.62
6	13,383	131,371	10.19%	13.38

The earnings increase the investment and constantly lower the weighted average yield. EPS is not affected--it reflects earnings without regard to the asset base and is thus not a good profit measure standing alone.

Retaining earnings to a yield of 6% is attractive only if the discount rate is below 6%. Projects in total should yield substantially more than the discount rate because many of them offer higher rates. For example, with a 5% discount rate a weighted average yield of 12% is statistically valid:

Yield Range	Yield Average	Project Totals		Extension %
5-10%	7%	$ 40	40%	2.8%
10-15	12	30	30	3.6
15-20	17	20	20	3.4
20+	22	10	10	2.2
		$100	100%	12.0

The project totals reflect the probability of relatively more investment opportunities at the lower rates and the relative scarcity of higher yield proposals.

Liquidity may also pose a problem, particularly with the expectation of variable earnings and higher interest expenses. The coverage ratio is earnings before interest divided by interest, both before tax. An example is given for a company before merger and after:

Before merger:

Earnings	$60	$72	$84	$96	$108
Interest	$12	$12	$12	$12	$ 12
Coverage ratio	5	6	7	8	9

The company considers 7 to be a safe ratio and 5 a minimum ratio.
After merger:

Earnings	$60	$80	$100	$120	$140
Interest	$20	$20	$ 20	$ 20	$ 20
Coverage ratio	3	4	5	6	7

Change:

Earnings increase	$ 0	$ 8	$ 16	$ 24	$ 32
Interest increase	$ 8	$ 8	$ 8	$ 8	$ 8
Gain (Loss)	$(8)	$ 0	$ 8	$ 16	$ 24
Ratio	--	1	2	3	4

The middle column shows a drop in the coverage ratio from 7 to 5 with
a change ratio of 2. The coverage ratio of 7 is kept after the merger
only at the highest earnings estimate. Evaluation would depend largely
upon the probabilities assigned to each of the outcomes.

The potent effect of leverage on ROE and liquidity is illustrated
with a merger example where capital increases 50% solely through debt at
a higher interest rate. After-tax figures are used. Earnings before
interest increase from $120 to $210.

Before merger:

Debt	$ 400			40% - interest 6% $24
Equity	$ 600			60% - D-E 4/6 = 67%
Capital	$1000			equals net assets
Earnings:	$120	Assets	$1000	12% ROA
Interest:	$ 24	Debt	$ 400	6% Debt Rate
Net	$ 96	Equity	$ 600	16% ROE

Merger accomplished with $500 new debt and no new equity:

Debt before merger	$ 400 at 6.0% = $24
New debt	500 at 9.6% 48
Debt after merger	900 at 8.0% 72

After merger:

Debt	$ 900	60%	interest 8% = $72
Equity	$ 600	40%	D-E 6/4 = 150%
Capital	$1500	100%	equals assets
Earnings:	$ 210	Assets $1500	14% ROA
Interest:	$ 72	Debt $ 900	8% Debt rate
Net:	$ 138	Equity $ 600	23% ROE

```
Incremental ROA:  90/500 = 18% (12% to 14%)
Incremental Debt: 48/500 = 9.6% (6% to 8%)
Incremental ROE:  42/0   =  -   (16% to 23%)
D-E rises from 67% to 150%.
```
The interest coverage ratio drops from 5.0 (120/24) to 2.9 (210/72).

The significant gain in profitability rests heavily in leverage with attendant financial risk. Evaluation would hinge to a large extent on the predictability of earnings. For example, if earnings increase only 40% from $120 to $168, ROE is unchanged at 16%:

```
Earnings    $168    Assets  $1500        11.2% ROA
Interest    $ 72    Debt    $ 900         8.0% Debt rate
Net         $ 96    Equity  $ 600        16.0% ROE
```

The interest coverage ratio drops to 2.3. ROA drops from 12.0% to 11.2%. Incremental ROA at 48/500 = 9.6% is equal to the interest rate and thus provides no leverage.

With no earnings increase, the added $48 interest reduces net from $96 to $48, and ROE is 8%. Leverage is negative.

INVESTING IN A NEW PRODUCT

Plans for new products are often based on achieving a target market share within a specified time frame. Outlays for the required capacity --staff and plant--must be made well in advance and be scheduled by period. Operating plans include sales quantities and prices, product costs based on planned capacity, expenses, taxes, and profits. Outlays and operating results must be annualized and expressed in both financial (cash) and accounting (accrual) terms. Measurements include financial NPV and yield, accounting rate of return, operating risk, and liquidity. For financial analysis losses in early years are counted as outlays.

Analysis is presented first in financial terms to express true profitability, and then in accounting terms to measure the impact by year on reported profits. Data is supplied as follows:

```
Annual sales goal to be reached in 4 years
1,000 units at $12 = $12,000
Variable costs--VC--50% of sales
Fixed production costs--$3,300
Fixed SGA costs--$1,200
Factory capacity 1,100 units
Sales goal       1,000 units
Extra capacity    100 units
Fixed factory cost per unit:  $3,300/1,100 = $3
Taxes at 40% of taxable income
Fixed asset cost $3,600  No salvage
15-year life = $240 SL depreciation
Net current assets--net CA--fully recovered
  Receivables--10% of sales
  Inventories--10% of sales
Project life--15 years
Discount rate 6%
```

Cash Outlays:	Year	0	1	2	3	4	15 Recovery
Fixed assets		$3,600	$0	$0	$0	$0	$0
Inventories		300	300	300	300	0	(1200)
Receivables		-	300	300	300	300	(1200)
Net CA		300	600	600	600	600	(2400)
Total		$3,900	$600	$600	$600	$300	$(2400)

Cash Gain:	Year	1	2	3	4	5-15 Each	Years 4-15 Percents
Sales units		250	500	750	1000	1000	
Sales at $12		$3000	$6000	$9000	$12000	$12000	100.0%
VC at 50%		1500	3000	4500	6000	6000	50.0%
VM at 50%		1500	3000	4500	6000	6000	50.0%
Factory fixed cost:							
at $3 per unit		750	1500	2250	3000	3000	25.0%
Volume variance		2550	1800	1050	300	300	2.5%
		3300	3300	3300	3300	3300	27.5%
SGA fixed cost		1200	1200	1200	1200	1200	10.0%
Total fixed cost		4500	4500	4500	4500	4500	37.5%
Profit (Loss)		(3000)	(1500)	0	1500	1500	12.5%
Tax at 40%		(1200)	(600)	0	600	600	5.0%
Net income (Loss)		(1800)	(900)	0	900	900	7.5%
SL depreciation		240	240	240	240	240	
Cash gain (loss)		$(1560)	$(660)	$240	$1140	$1140	

Cash Schedule:

Year	Outlay	Cash Gain (Loss)	Net In (Out)	6%f	PV	PV Cum
0	($3900)	$ 0	($3900)	1.000	$(3900)	
1	(600)	(1560)	(2160)	.943	(2037)	
2	(600)	(660)	(260)	.890	(1121)	
3	(600)	240	(360)	.840	(302)	$(7360)
4	(300)	1140	840	.792	665	
5-15 ea.	0	1140	1140	6.247*	7122	
15 Recov.	2400	0	2400	.417	1008	8795
						NPV +1435

NOTE: *11 years f
Year 15   9.712
Year 4   3.465
            6.247

The positive NPV of $1435 at 6% is a yield of 8% by trial and error.
The accounting rate of return is the ratio of net income to net CA plus net FA (fixed assets, net of depreciation) at the beginning of the year. Recovery of net CA at the end of year 15 is omitted.

Year	Net Income	Net CA	Net FA	Asset Total	ROA
1	$(1,800)	$ 300	$3,600	$3,900	(46.2%)
2	(900)	900	3,360	4,260	(21.1%)
3	0	1,500	3,120	4,620	0
4	900	2,100	2,880	4,980	18.1%
5	900	2,400	2,640	5,040	17.9%
15	900	2,400	240	2,640	34.1%

The principal concern is the negative effect in the early years on net income, and on ROA, ROE, and EPS. After year 5, ROA increases each year because net FA is reduced by depreciation, net CA is constant, and net income continues at $900. In financial terms the yield is 8% for the full 15-year period. Undue concern with performance in accounting terms for the early years can have an adverse influence when short-run results prevail over the long term, a policy question of the first order.

Cash payback is also important. Drawing from the cash schedule above:

Year	Net Cash	Cum
0	$(3900)	
1	(2160)	
2	(1260)	
3	(360)	$(7680)
4	840	(6840)
5+6+7+		
8+9+10		
= 6 x $1140	6840	0

It is 10 years before the outlays are fully recouped. The remaining five years provide 5 x $1140 = $5700 plus $2400 recovery of net CA. This cash drain enters into the cash plans, part of financial planning. In a period of tight liquidity this project might be deferred in favor of projects with better cash flows. Financial risk can be evaluated only in terms of overall operating, investing, and financing plans.

Some degree of operating risk, or probable range of outcomes, applies to all elements of the project. The effect of sales volume alone is illustrated for year 5 with 100 units over and under the plan:

Sales units	900	1,000	1,100
Sales at $12	$10,800	$12,000	$13,200
VC at 50%	5,400	6,000	6,600
VM at 50%	5,400	6,000	6,600
Fixed cost total	4,500	4,500	4,500
	900	1,500	2,100
Tax at 40%	360	600	840
Net income	540	900	1,260
Net CA	2,160	2,400	2,640
Net FA	2,640	2,640	2,640
Total assets	$4,800	$5,040	$5,280
ROA	11.3%	17.9%	23.9%

The range from 17.9% is about one-third each way. The gain in ROA from 900 to 1100 units is over two times--11.3% to 23.9%. At 1100 units the factory has reached planned output. If capacity is expanded to prepare for higher sales, fixed costs rise, assets increase, and ROA drops. Sales and profit projections must rest on the practical aspects of output capacity and asset requirements. For example, assuming an increase to 1200 units with higher fixed costs and more assets there may be no gain over the ROA for 1,000 units:

Sales units	1,200		
Sales at $12	$14,400		
VC at 50%	7,200		
VM at 50%	7,200		
FC $4500 + $900 =	5,400		
	1,800		
Tax at 40%	720		
Net income	1,080		
Net CA at 20% =	$ 2,880		
Net FA 2640 + 513 =	3,153	$6,033	ROA 17.9%

ROA returns to the 1,000-unit level. Failure to have capacity to meet demand entails the opportunity cost of lost sales and margins. Failure to generate enough sales results in the cost of unused capacity, both staff and plant. Principal factors to be weighed include the economies of plant size, the learning curve, reliability of sales forecasts, ability to shift product output quickly, and competitive reactions. Such considerations must enter into capital expenditure evaluation.

The handling of taxes is critical because of the large impact on profits. The tax code is complex and constantly changing, but some estimate for the future must be made. The current tax situation may be used for lack of any better basis for prediction. The cash gain schedule shows tax credits of $1,200 for year 1 and $600 for year 2, reducing the losses used to compute NPV. This treatment rests on the assumption that these losses can be absorbed by taxable income from other sources. If this is not true the change in NPV is:

	Tax Credit	6% f	PV
Year 1	$1200	f.943	$1132
Year 2	$ 600	f.890	$ 534
Reduction			-$1666
NPV as computed			+1435
Corrected NPV			- 231

Yield is below 6%. Losses may be carried back for application to reported taxable income and carried forward for possible future benefit under technical, and changing, tax regulations. However, an assumption that losses will be recouped is speculative at best. GAAP does not permit the anticipation of tax benefits.

Risk evaluation is a critical factor in the capital expenditure program but is almost intractable for strategic decisions such as for new products. An attempt can be made by setting out reasonable ranges and probabilities for each element of the proposal and computing the resulting outcomes as yields. (The process is explained in detail in the next chapter.) If twenty project elements are estimated for five outcomes each, there are 3,200,000 results. Simulation by computer may be useful but is complex and expensive. Risk evaluation is conducive to constructive communication and encourages closer attention to the validity of the details. If the exploration is limited to ten elements with three outcomes each there are 1,000 results--still too many to evaluate. A summary of the outcomes by yield ranges can be useful. Five yield ranges are enough and should be standard for all projects. The probabilities for each yield range would vary for each project. A project risk evaluation is illustrated:

Standard Yield Ranges	Project Probability	Cum
Loss	5%	5%
0-5	15%	20%
5-10	30%	50%
10-15	30%	80%
15 plus	20%	100%

With a discount rate of 5% there is a 20% chance of a negative result with a 5% chance of loss--the downside risk. The upside potential is strong. Few proposals have a more favorable prognosis but in most cases the risk analysis is not carried out. Individual reactions to a 20% downside risk vary greatly. To require no downside risk would be self defeating--very few investments would be made. Further detail within each yield range can be explored. For instance, the exact composition of the 5% loss probability could lead either to allaying concern or to heightening it. If the discount rate is 10% the odds are highly unfavorable: a 50% chance of a lower yield.

The final decision on strategic proposals such as for new products may be aided by risk appraisal, but the broader considerations are goals and policy tempered by the economic climate.

BOND REFUNDING

The question of refunding an outstanding callable bond issue is a financing decision rather than an investment decision. However, the method of analysis is the same as for capital expenditure proposals for NPV, yield, and cash payback. Evaluation of risk is unique for a bond refund, and the accounting treatment is different, as compared with investments in assets.

Bond refunding analysis compares a proposed new issue to pay off an old issue based on the principal amount and remaining years to maturity of the old issue. In practice, the new issue would usually be for a larger amount and for a longer period to extents based on financial planning. The cost of issuing a bond argues for a larger amount and longer maturity because the incremental expense is low.

The example used is simplified by using annual interest payments rather than the customary semiannual installments. Also, the usual overlapping interest expense between the call date and issue date is omitted.

Outstanding issue:
> $40,000 - 12% or $4,800 interest - due in 10 years
> call premium 5% - $2,000. Unamortized issue expense
> $2,000, or $200 a year.

New issue:
> $40,000 - 10% or $4,000 interest - due in 10 years
> no call premium. Issue expense $3,400, or $340 a year.
> Tax rate 40%.

Discount rate--interest on new issue--10% less tax = 6%.

The question of a call premium for the new issue is a financing decision not explored here. With no call provision the interest rate is slightly lower because buyers are not subject to a possible future call if interest rates drop. The company benefits with less interest cost but forfeits the right to call the bonds if rates fall.

```
Cash outlay:
        Call premium--5%                    $2,000
        New issue expense                    3,400
                                            $5,400
        Less tax credit:
          Call premium       $2,000
          Old issue expense   2,000
                             $4,000
          Credit at 40%                     $1,600
          Net outlay                        $3,800
Cash saving annually:
        Interest:
          Old issue--12%     $4,800
          New issue--10%      4,000
          Saving               800
          Less tax at 40%      320  $   480
        Expense write-off on books:
          Old issue             200
          New issue             340
          More expense          140
          Tax credit at 40%         $    56
          Net saving               $   536
```

The proposal calls for a net outlay of $3,800 cash to produce a cash annuity of $536 for 10 years, the analytic equivalent of a capital expenditure project.

```
Yield:  $3,800/536 = f7.090 - 10 years = 6.8%
NPV:  Gain $536 x f7.360 (6%, 10 years) = $3945 PV
      Outlay                                3800
                                           145 NPV
Cash payback:  $3,800/536 = 7.36 years
```

Liquidity is affected by the net outlay of $3,800 and the reduced interest of $536 net, which are elements of financial planning. Capital structure is unchanged for financial analysis, as explained.

Bond refunding is unique among all types of capital expenditures because of its riskless nature. All the factors in the analysis are known or closely determinable. If interest rates rise before the issue is made, eliminating NPV, it is deferred. If rates fall, a greater gain is realized. All other types of capital expenditure require separate evaluation of risk, but always based on NPV and yield computed with the same rate that is relevant for bond refunding, the current borrowing rate less tax.

The accounting treatment is also singular. The asset addition, a deferred charge, is for new issue expense $3400 less old issue expense $2000, or net $1400, amortized at $140 over 10 years. Capital structure is unchanged. There is no charge or credit to operating expenses. Interest expense is less by $800, offset by $140 more expense for amortization to $660 net before tax, or $396 after tax--an increase in annual net income. There is also a one-time extraordinary charge for the call premium ($2,000) and old issue expense ($2,000)--$4,000 or $2,400 after tax. EPS is calculated for income both before and after extraordinary charges. The effect on ROA and ROE is generally minor and without bearing on the decision. Management evaluation and market response are based both on the refunding per se and any concurrent additional financing deemed advisable.

FINANCIAL LEASES

Capital expenditure proposals are analyzed for profitability without regard to the source of financing. The amount and timing of proposed outlays and cash gains are part of overall financial planning. If concurrent analysis of a project is attempted for both the asset acquisition and its financing the result is spurious. If financial planning shows a need for borrowing, asset leasing is one source. A financial lease for an asset offered by the seller can be analyzed for the interest cost by comparison with other sources of funds, such as a bank loan. There are many other aspects to leasing not explored here-- tax, legal, insurance, maintenance, indenture provisions. Some leases are attractive even at higher cost for reasons such as convenience and cash flow--an opportunity cost.

The illustrations given provide a clear basis for analyzing the financial cost of leasing. For example, a project is analyzed as follows:

Asset cost $40,000. No salvage
4-year life - SL $10,000
Saving $14,000 a year Taxes 40%
Bank loan 15% less tax = 9% net
9% discount rate - 4 years - f3.240

	Books	Cash
Saving	$14,000	$14,000
SL	10,000	
	4,000	
Tax	1,600	1,600
Net	2,400	
SL	10,000	
Cash	$12,400	$12,400

```
                    f 3.240 =            $40,176 PV
                    Outlay =              40,000
                                            176 NPV
```

Yield: $40,000/12,400 = f3.226 = 9.2%

The project is acceptable for profitability.
The manufacturer as lessor offers a financial lease of 4 annual payments of $15,000 starting in one year in lieu of $40,000 now with ownership retained by the lessor. The lease payment is tax deductible but tax on depreciation is lost. The analysis is:

```
Lease payment                    $15,000
less tax at 40%                    6,000      $ 9,000
Lost tax on $10,000 SL                         4,000
Net cash at f3.24 =                           13,000
                        f3.240 =              42,120 PV
                        Outlay                40,000
                                            $ 2,120 NPV
```

The extra cost of the lease to the lessee over the bank rate is $2,120 in present dollars. The lease interest rate is $40,000/13,000 = f3.077 = 11.4%, compared with the bank rate of 9.0%.

Recap:	Bank	Lease
After tax	9.0%	11.4%
Before tax	15.0%	19.0%

The lessor retains ownership of the asset at the end of the lease. The lessee believes that the asset may have a substantial residual value and asks the lessor to assign ownership at the end of the lease. The lessor then raises the lease terms to $17,000 a year. The lessee then determines a probable residual value:

```
Lease payment                    $17,000
less tax at 40%                    6,800      $10,200
Lost tax on $10,000 SL                          4,000
Net cash                                      $14,200
                        f3.24 =               46,008 PV
                        Outlay                40,000
                                            $ 6,008 NPV
```

With no salvage the rate is 15.7% (40,000/14,200 = +2,817). The salvage value required to produce a 9% rate is as follows:

Special Applications   95

$6,0008 NPV/f.7084 (9% year 4) = $8,481 after tax or $14,135 before tax residual value, or 35% of the $40,000 asset cost. This determination of salvage value produces a 9% interest rate:

```
Cost                          $40,000
Salvage PV                      6,008
PV cost                       $46,008
$46,008/f3.24 =               $14,200 payment
```

These terms are attractive if the lessee is confident of a future residual value of $8,500 after tax. If the lessor waived ownership without changing terms the residual value would be: $2,120/f7.084 = $2,993/6 = $4,988. This change also lowers the net rate from 11.4% to 9.0%.

If the lease payment is quoted at an amount that computes to minus NPV it is a concealed price reduction. For example:

```
Payment                       $12,675
less tax at 40%                 5,070    $7,605
Lost tax on $10,000 SL                    4,000
                                         11,605
                              f3.24 = 37,600 PV
                              Outlay     40,000
                                     -    2,400 NPV
    -2400/.6 = 4,000 reduction on $40,000 cost.
```

The interest rate is 40,000/11,605 = f3.447 = 6.23%.
A break-even quotation at 9% with no salvage value can be computed as follows:

```
Cost                          $40,000
less tax saving--
$10,000 SL at 40% = 4,000 at 3.24    $12,960
Cost NPV                      $27,040
Payment--$27,040/f3.24 =        8,346
Lost tax on $10,000 SL          4,000
                              $12,346
                f3.24 =               $40,000
                Outlay                 40,000
                                           0 NPV
```

Interest: $40,000/12,346 = f3.24 = 9%
Lease payment: $8,346/.6 = $13,910 before tax

A bank loan for $40,000 at 15% for four years with annual payments of $14,010 is illustrated with rounded amounts. (The actual annual amount is $40,000/f2.855 = $14,010.058.)

Year	A Lease Payment	B Interest (at 15%)	Principal Reduction	Principal Balance
1	$14,010	$ 6,000	$ 8,010	$31,990
2	14,010	4,798	9,212	22,778
3	14,010	3,416	10,594	12,184
4	14,010	1,826	12,184	0
	$56,040	$16,040	$40,000	

Interest and depreciation are tax deductible.

Year	B Interest	Depreciation	Total	C Tax at 40%
1	$ 6,000	$10,000	$16,000	$ 6,400
2	4,798	10,000	14,798	5,919
3	3,416	10,000	13,416	5,366
4	1,826	10,000	11,826	4,731
	$16,040	$40,000	$56,040	$22,416

Cash schedule:

Year	A Lease Payment	C Less Tax	Net Cash	9%f	PV
1	$14,010	$ 6,400	$ 7,610	.917	$6,981
2	14,010	5,919	8,091	.842	6,813
3	14,010	5,366	8,644	.772	6,674
4	14,010	4,731	9,279	.708	6,572
	$56,040	$22,416	$33,624		27,040

Check: $27,040/f3.24 = $8,346/.6 = $13,910 lease payment before tax, as above.

This example demonstrates the interest cost equality of a bank loan and leasing at 9% net.

Leasing cost is often higher than bank borrowing but may be desirable for a variety of reasons such as uncertainty about equipment performance, useful life, salvage value, or less restrictive lease terms. Lessor terms may be attractive because the lessor has access to cheaper credit and to markets for used equipment. Lessors may be able to take full advantage of all tax credits.

Recap:

Lease Payment Before Tax	Interest Rate After Tax	PV Cost	Salvage Value Before Tax to Lessee for 9% Rate (f.7084)
$17,000	15.7%	$46,008	$14,135 (6008/f = 8481 = 14,135)
15,000	11.4%	42,120	4,988 (2120/f = 2993 = 4,998)
13,910	9.0%	40,000	0 (0/f = 0 = 0)

5

The Discount Rate and Risk: Keys to Profitable Growth

DETERMINING THE DISCOUNT RATE

A discount rate translates future cash flows into present dollars, referred to as discounted cash flow--DCF--or just present value--(PV). Outlays at the present time are subtracted to obtain net present value-- (NPV). The discount rate is a primary factor used in measuring both profitability and risk for investment decisions. Other terms used such as "hurdle rate," "cut-off rate," "investment rate," and "cost of capital" are ambiguous and misleading; they are better avoided in favor of "discount rate." The opposite of discounting is accumulation; interest is added to cash flows to a specified future time. An accumulated amount discounts back to NPV by application of the interest factor for the period. For example:

	Period	Cash Flow	With No Interest	Discount at 10% f	Cash	Accumulate at 10% f	Cash
Outlay	0	-$2,000	-$2,000	1.000	-$2,000	1.331	-$2,663
Cash Gain	1	+ 1,000	+ 1,000	.909	+ 909	1.210	+ 1,210
Cash Gain	2	+ 1,000	+ 1,000	.826	+ 826	1.100	+ 1,100
Cash Gain	3	+ 1,000	+ 1,000	.751	+ 751	1.000	+ 1,000
Net			+ 1,000		+ 486		+ 647

Future $647 f.751 = $486 NPV   Present $486 f1.331 = $647 future.

For investment decisions it is simpler and clearer to analyze in terms of NPV $486 relative to a current outlay of $2,000 now, designated as period zero. Subsequent periods are for years, as in this example, unless otherwise designated.

Most investment decisions are administered through the capital expenditure program; notable exceptions include mergers, bond refunding, leasing, research and development, advertising, management development, and public relations. Investment decisions rest on the concurrent evaluation of many factors--NPV, yield, risk, ROA, EPS, cash payback, and liquidity. Quantitative expression can guide decisions and may be indispensable in many cases, even though approximations are unavoidable. For some situations quantitative measures are not practicable. In all cases the decisions are basically subjective; the same data may elicit a range of responses. The overriding criteria are goals, strategies, and policies.

The discount rate used to determine NPV should be:
. the current <u>borrowing rate</u> for substantial sums for long periods, similar to a bond refunding rate and relevant to the capital expenditure program, less
. the current <u>effective tax rate</u> on a projected company basis to obtain
. the <u>net rate</u> for use throughout the company in discounting cash flows for all proposals for all purposes for all locations and for all segments or divisions, kept on a current basis by revision as necessary.

The borrowing rate allows for the cost of money. Projects earning more provide positive leverage--a favorable outcome for owners. In simple terms using one year and no taxes: Borrow $1,000 for a year at 10% and repay $1,100. Buy goods for $1,000 and sell for profit of $250. Gain to owners $250 less $100 equals $150 favorable leverage. If the profit is only $80, then the loss is $20 (80 minus 100)--negative leverage. If the owner does not elect to borrow but uses his own money to buy the goods there is an opportunity cost--the best alternative investment.
The effect of leverage on owners' equity is illustrated, again without taxes or discounting. The degree of leverage, with interest constant at 10%, depends on the ratio of debt to equity (D-E), as follows:

		Capital	Interest - Profit	Rate		
1	Debt	$ 0	$ 0	0%		
	Equity	1,000	200	20%	ROE	No debt
		1,000	200	20%	ROA	No leverage
2	Debt	333	33	10%		
	Equity	667	167	25%	ROE	
		1,000	200	20%	ROA	D-E 50%
3	Debt	500	50	10%		
	Equity	500	150	30%	ROE	
		1,000	200	20%	ROA	D-E 100%
4	Debt	600	60	10%		
	Equity	400	140	35%	ROE	
		1,000	200	20%	ROA	D-E 150%

The profit of $200 on capital of $1,000 is 20%, the return on assets --ROA--constant for all cases. Interest dollars increase with higher debt but the interest rate remains at 10%. The decreasing profits available to equity relate to a more rapidly declining equity, so the return on equity--ROE--increases. The change is dramatic--from 20% with no debt to 35% with D-E at 150%. Negative leverage occurs when ROA is less than interest. This is illustrated with the same cases but with 6% ROA in all cases:

	Capital	Interest - Profit	Rate		
1 Debt	$ 0	$ 0	0%		
Equity	1,000	60	6%	ROE	No debt
	1,000	60	6%	ROA	No leverage
2 Debt	333	33	10%		
Equity	667	27	4%	ROE	
	1,000	60	6%	ROA	D-E 50%
3 Debt	500	50	10%		
Equity	500	10	2%	ROE	
	1,000	60	6%	ROA	D-E 100%
4 Debt	600	60	10%		
Equity	400	0	0%	ROE	
	1,000	60	6%	ROA	D-E 150%

ROE declines from 6% to zero and interest claims all profit; there is no balance for owners. With even lower ROA the equity return becomes negative.

Taxes have a major impact on profits and the effect is highly uneven among projects. Those with the same yield before tax often have widely varying returns after tax. Conversely, projects with the same after-tax yields may have a wide range of results before tax, but this is not relevant to the investment decision. For example, no tax applies to the acquisition of land or current assets, the full tax applies at once to expensed items, and a future tax applies to depreciable assets over time. There are also numerous special tax credits. The tax code and its application vary constantly and unpredictably. Technical tax advice is mandatory. Because taxes are paid by a company as a taxable entity, the company tax situation is controlling. The guiding principle is to ascribe taxes to each project that reflect the net effect of that project on the total tax situation. If the project is not undertaken taxes are not affected. Of necessity investment decisions require forecasting cash flows and the effect of taxes by period. Uncertainty attaches to all cash flows and tax effects.

The discount rate should be kept current for changes in both interest rates and taxes. The discount rate should be reviewed periodically and adjusted for changes of one percentage point or more. If the rate used is too low, some projects with negative leverage would appear to be profitable. If the rate is too high, some projects with favorable leverage would appear to be unprofitable.

Arithmetic relationships are given to illustrate some selected ranges:

Interest Before Tax	8%	12%	16%	20%
Net rate after deducting				
tax rate of: 50%		4.0	6.0	8.0	10.0
40%		4.8	7.2	9.6	12.0
30%		5.6	8.4	11.2	14.0
20%		6.4	9.6	12.8	16.0

The full range is wide--4% to 16%. Higher interest rates may be accompanied by higher taxes, with little net effect: Interest 12% tax 20% = 9.6, and interest 16% tax 40% = 9.6. If interest rates rise and tax rates fall, the increase is cumulative. For instance, at 12% interest and 50% tax the net rate is 6%. With 20% interest and 20% tax the net rate is 16%. Investment is encouraged by lower net rates.

The discount rate should be clearly established for use throughout the organization. When the discount rate is changed, the cash flows must also be adjusted.

A company as a legal entity has only one set of owners, is obligated for all debts, and has one tax return with an effective tax rate on taxable income--the total tax payable for the year. A single discount rate should be used for all segments of the company to insure comparability and positive leverage. If a project has $100 NPV the effect is favorable regardless of its organizational or physical location, or its size, type, or life, or the composition of the outlays. In addition to NPV all projects are subject to evaluation relative to risk, liquidity, and accounting effect. It is a mistaken notion that different types of assets should provide different yields. Cash outlays and cash gains, regardless of purpose, are neutral and homogenous for financial analysis. It is appropriate to assess risk separately for different classes of assets but risk evaluation, as explained later, is a separate step that is only confused by the use of differential discount rates.

Projects with positive NPV have a wide range of NPVs and related yields. A weighted average can be derived from the total but decisions rest on incremental analysis. Lower yields apply to the bulk of the projects with relatively small amounts providing high yields. This condition simply reflects economics and competition. Exceptions exist for monopolistic positions such as provided by patents. A statistical pattern applies to a large number of projects, and it is reasonably predictable because of the law of large numbers.

If all projects are divided into four groups of equal yield ranges, the project amounts in each group will be skewed from the 25% arithmetic average. Using a 5% discount rate and 5 point yield ranges, the probable skew is illustrated as follows:

Yield Range %	Dollar Outlay %	Average Yield In Range
20-25%	10%	22%
15-20%	20%	17%
10-15%	30%	12%
5-10%	40%	7%

For the 5 to 10 yield range the outlays of 40% exceed the arithmetic average of 25 by 15 points. For the 10 to 15 yield range 30% exceeds the 25% average by 5 points. The higher yield ranges show the opposite effect. The validity of this distribution rests on a large number of projects, either in one year or longer, and can be tested in actual situations. The average yield in each range shows the same skew as that for the total dollars.

The schedule is rewritten with $100,000 total dollars:

Yield Range	Projects	Average Yield			Cum		
					Projects	Yield	%
20-25%	$10,000	22%	$2,200		$10,000	2,200	22
15-20%	20,000	17%	3,400		30,000	5,600	18 2/3
10-15%	30,000	12%	3,600		60,000	9,200	15 1/3
5-10%	40,000	7%	2,800		100,000	12,000	12
	100,000	(12%)	12,000				

The $100,000 outlay provides $12,000 for a weighted average yield of 12% using a 5% discount rate. An assumption that use of the 5% rate would result in a 5% average overlooks the vital distinction between increments and averages. With properly prepared projects the overall results should approximate the results given in the table; the over and under variations tend to net out for a large number of projects.

The 12% average, or ROA, is also 12% ROE with no leverage. With debt equal to equity, 19% ROE occurs, as follows:

Debt	$50,000	$2,500	5% debt rate
Equity	50,000	9,500	19% ROE
Capital	100,000	12,000	12% ROA

The cum columns in the schedule show the effect of higher discount rates. At 10%, project totals drop 40% from $100,000 to $60,000. At 15%, project totals drop to $30,000, or 50% from $60,000. At 20%, project totals drop 90% from $100,000, or 67% from $30,000, to $10,000. The cum yields rise from 12% to 22% as the investment base drops. The appeal of higher yield totals is meretricious; evaluation of the effect on growth and profits is needed.

The schedule is restated with cum amounts related to growth rates:

Yield Range	Yield Cum %	Cum Projects	Assumed Growth Rates
20-25%	22	$10,000	0 - replacements
15-20%	18 2/3	30,000	5% - selective
10-15%	15 1/3	60,000	12% - substantial
5-10%	12	100,000	22% - stretch goal

The growth rates are arbitrary but indicate the effect of larger investments. If industry growth is 16%, the 12% rate at the $60,000 project level trails to a dangerous extent. With $40,000 added investment the yield drops to 12% but the growth rate rises to 22%, exceeding the industry average by six points.

The growth goals of the company are reflected principally by the capital expenditure program, guided by considerations of risk and liquidity. As noted above, higher discount rates occur with higher borrowing costs and lower tax rates, and investment levels are necessarily restricted.

Sustained growth in profits and increasing sales and market share are primary factors in financial strength, reflected in rising stock prices and greater borrowing power. A lower discount rate qualifies higher investment levels, if suitable opportunities are developed. Growth also engenders employee morale and facilitates attracting and holding management and technical talent, essential to the generation of investment opportunities.

DEALING WITH RISK

The discount rate provides the primary measure of project profitability--NPV. This is enough to justify a proposal that has no risk. A bond refunding is virtually free of risk, but it is a financing, not an investing decision. Asset investments involve futurity and inescapable uncertainty. The elements of an investment proposal can be estimated as to a range of outcomes and related probabilities, and provide a useful guide to risk appraisal. Risk attitudes are personal, subjective, and ineluctable. Risk and profitability based on the discount rate are twin parts of the decision process.

Uncertainty is simply doubt and is not subject to rational prediction. Risk refers to possible outcomes with expressed probabilities. Individual risk attitudes can change over time, are affected by size, timing, and odds, and are not necessarily transitive. Aversion to loss--downside risk--usually outweighs possible gains--upside potential. The objective expression of these subjective feelings can be beneficial for individual evaluation, and it is essential for constructive communication in a group. Unexamined doubts can negate valid projects. Uncritical enthusiasm can promote reckless ventures.

Some examples illustrate the close relationship between the amounts at risk and the odds.

A certain $10 has been won but can be gambled to win $100 at odds of 1 to 10 (10%)--the arithmetic equivalent. The gambler takes nine chances in ten of losing out. The odds required to make this bet would vary among individuals, possibly from 1:20 for a high risk taker (5%), to 1:2 for a low risk taker (50%). These relationships are known as utility functions--a method for expressing dollar amounts in value terms based on individual risk attitudes. A person with a great need for $10 might not accept any chance of losing it. As the dollar amounts at risk increase their greater utility calls for safer odds:

Certain amount won	$ 100	$ 1,000	$ 10,000	$ 100,000
Possible win--1:10	1,000	10,000	100,000	1,000,000
Illustrative required odds	3:10	4:10	6:10	9:10

The odds given are illustrative. They would vary greatly among individuals and over time. A wealthy person might take odds of 1:10 on $100,000 because that amount is too small to worry about while a million-dollar win would be attractive. A very poor man might also bet the same way because he would like to be a millionaire and a loss would simply keep him in his accustomed state of poverty. As a rule most people are averse to risk most of the time and even more so for greater amounts.

Another dimension of risk is time--a series of payments or annuities. If a lottery pays $1,000 a week for 50 weeks the total is $50,000. If there is an election to be made each week either to get the sure $1,000 or take a 1:10 chance of getting $10,000 or nothing, the range of possibilities is wide:

                    50 weeks at $1,000 = $50,000
                    50 weeks at 1:10 =
                       all losses   0
                       all wins $500,000

The odds of all losses for 50 weeks at 1:10 or for all wins is statistically infinitesimal. If the chance is made each week, the result would move toward $50,000 statistically. With many players, there is a greater chance for the group result to average $50,000. Many would accept the $1,000 for a period of weeks and then elect to try to beat the odds. If the weekly payment is accepted for 25 weeks, the $25,000 sum could encourage a gamble for week 26. How many weeks of failed gambles before returning to the sure payment? How many weeks of successful gambles? Individual reactions would vary widely.

An example illustrates risk evaluation for an investment proposal:

        Outlay $100,000 Cash gain $20,000
        f 5.0 Life 12 years Yield 17%
        Discount rate 10% f6.814 NPV $36,280

The project appears to be acceptable but questions are raised about the outlay, the cash gains, and life. Possible outcomes and related probabilities are computed. The many possible results (say, 5 outlays, 6 lives, 10 gains) are summarized by yield ranges and probabilities:

Yield Range	Probability	Cum
Loss	10%	10%
0-10%	15%	25%
10-20%	35%	60%
20-30%	30%	90%
30% plus	10%	100%

A 10% chance of loss is acceptable in most circumstances, and usually exists even if not estimated. For very large sums the 10% chance of loss might be unacceptable. The worst case in the loss category can also be shown for large projects--in this case say 1:1000:

Outlay	$120,000	P.10
Cash gain	15,000	P.10
Life	6 years	P.10
Total cash gain	$ 90,000	
Outlay	120,000	
Cash shortfall	- 30,000	P.001

The chance of a yield between 0 and 10% is 15%. The probability of being below the 10% discount rate is cum 25% or 1 in 4. The 10 to 20% yield range has a 35% probability or 1 in 3 with a 60% cum. The 17% project yield splits the odds almost evenly so there is 1 chance in 2 of a lower yield. The odds of yields over 20% are promising, but potential gains seldom have as much weight, or utility, as downside risk. This relationship is at the heart of risk evaluation and the investment decision. NPV and yield are important measures but are not sufficient alone. This project with a 17% yield might be rejected because of risk while another project with a 12% yield might be accepted. For example:

Outlay $100,000   Cash gain $17,700
f5.65   Life 10 years   Yield 12%
Discount rate 10%   f6.145
$17,700 x f6.145 = $108,766 PV   NPV $8,766

Yield Range	P	Cum
Loss	5%	5%
0-10%	10%	15%
10-20%	50%	65%
20-30%	30%	95%
30% plus	5%	100%

The cum 15% chance of results below the discount rate is generally acceptable, and is well below the 25% cum above. The chance of falling below the 12% yield is about 25%. Thus profit and risk are twin parts of the decision process. Managers and companies are characterized by their investment decisions--principal factors in growth and profits. Necessarily like-minded individuals associate as managers and like-minded investors select similar stocks.

The risk evaluation should be kept for reference when the project is reviewed for performance. Below-par results may have a negative impact on project sponsors that can be mitigated by showing that the shortfall is within the risk limits set by management. Similarly, results better than the proposal may be within the probabilities, precluding unwarranted prescience.

Top management must set not only the discount rate for use throughout the organization but also specific limits on risk. The purpose is not just to weed out proposals beyond allowable amounts but more importantly to encourage project submissions for review. Lower management levels are more vulnerable to a negative impact from poor projects. Junior personnel may limit their submissions to the safest projects, thus preempting management selection. At the highest management level risk is borne more readily, and the greater the number of projects the more likely that high and low performance will average out. A recently employed junior engineer might hesitate to propose a large project that is risky, such as a new material handling system. However, as one of many projects the risk might be acceptable to management. For, say, 100 projects with a 17% yield the average is highly likely to be close to 17%; some will lose money, some will have higher yields. Management might well request submission of, say, proposals with a probability up to 10% for loss and up to 25% cum probability for yields below the company discount rate, and without specification at higher levels. These limits might also be· separate for different project types and sizes. Many of these projects would be acceptable and some would be subject to redetermination or deferral. This approach precludes the premature loss of good ideas and moves the onus of risk bearing up the line.

Project Risk Analysis

The elements of a project should be explored and reasonable outcome ranges set out with probabilities. Reasonably broad amounts are usually sufficient such as for a project with:

```
Life          8 years       4 to 10 years--in increments of 1 year
Outlay        $100,000      $85,000 to $130,000--in increments of $7500
Cash Gain     $20,000       $12,000 to $24,000--in increments of $2000
```
For this illustration total outcomes are:
life 7 x outlay 7 x cash gain 7 = 343

The probability per outcome could well be set at 10% with a minimum cum of .1%. This approach would encourage closer analysis of the project elements, promote better understanding among those involved, and lead to revision as necessary. Excessive detail and refinements should be avoided because the projections are necessarily speculative; the goal is to clarify the degree of risk in terms of specified risk ranges. The process can be time consuming but the potential benefits are great. Only the larger and more questionable projects require close analysis but it may be constructive to request a risk profile for each proposal. Proposers then submit the risk profile as a basis for performance evaluation and reviewers can more readily perceive the nature of the proposal.
Analysis of a proposal for risk is illustrated with point estimates:

```
Outlay $100,000
Cash gain $20,000   f5.0
Life 8 years   Yield 11.8%
Discount rate 10%   f5.335
$20,000   f5.335 = $106,700 PV - $100,000 = $6,700 NPV
```

Ranges of outcomes with probabilities expressed as decimals are next developed: first for life, then for outlay, and finally for cash gain, in each case holding constant the other elements (* denotes the point estimate):

Life	Years	f5.0 Yield %	Probability (P)	Cum
	10	15.1%	.1	.1
	9	13.7	.2	.3
*	8	*11.8	.3	.6
	7	9.2	.1	.7
	6	5.5	.1	.8
	5	-0-	.1	.9
	4	-8.4	.1	1.0

Project life may be subject to wide estimates in many cases. The table shows the effect on yield with no change in outlay or cash gain. Break-even is at 5 years. The 10% discount rate has about a .67 cum probability by interpolation; or a yield below 10% has a .33 probability. The 4 and 5 year lives are dropped after review and the estimates are revised as follows:

Life	Years	f5.0 Yield %	Probability (P)	Cum
	10	15.1%	.1	.1
	9	13.7	.3	.4
*	8	*11.8	.4	.8
	7	9.2	.1	.9
	6	5.5	.1	1.0

The odds for a yield below 10% are now about .22, down from .33.

Next, outlays range up from $85,000 in $7,500 steps with life held constant at 8 years and cash gain at $20,000:

Outlay	f	Yield	Probability (P)	Cum
$ 85,000	4.250	16.7%	.1	.1
92,500	4.625	14.1	.2	.3
*100,000	5.000	*11.8	.2	.5
107,500	5.375	9.8	.2	.7
115,000	5.750	8.0	.1	.8
122,500	6.125	6.3	.1	.9
130,000	6.500	4.9	.1	1.0

Outlays are generally more readily determinable because of nearby timing and more specific data. Exceptions include experimental projects, complex construction jobs, and situations involving future outlays. Residual value may also be a major factor. This risk table is generally favorable but after review the highest and lowest outlays are dropped:

Outlay	f	Yield	Probability (P)	Cum
92,500	4.625	14.1	.1	.1
*100,000	5.000	*11.8	.3	.4
107,500	5.375	9.8	.3	.7
115,000	5.750	8.0	.2	.9
122,500	6.125	6.3	.1	1.0

Next, cash gain increments of $2,000 are used with constant $100,000 outlay and life of 8 years, as follows:

Cash Gain	f	Yield	Probability (P)	Cum
$24,000	4.167	17.3%	.1	.1
22,000	4.545	14.6	.1	.2
*20,000	5.000	*11.8	.2	.4
18,000	5.546	8.9	.2	.6
16,000	6.250	5.8	.2	.8
14,000	7.143	2.6	.1	.9
12,000	8.333	- .9	.1	1.0

Cash gains are often difficult to estimate, particularly for longer periods. All anticipated gains and losses must be expressed incrementally and tax effects computed. All cash flows are after tax, as is the discount rate, to provide consonant calculations. Elements affecting cash flow should be expressed clearly with a separate estimate for each, including the effect of interrelationships. Simulation may be useful if expertly employed. The table shows the net effect of all cash gain explorations. The odds of 10% yield are about even. There is a 10% chance of loss. (Cash gain $12,000 x 8 years = 96,000 less $1000,000.) This table is recast by eliminating the first and last lines:

Cash Gain	f	Yield	Probability (P)	Cum
$22,000	4.545	14.6	.2	.2
*20,000	5.000	*11.8	.2	.4
18,000	5.556	8.9	.3	.7
16,000	6.250	5.8	.2	.9
14,000	7.143	2.6	.1	1.0

Project review depends on the outcome for all three tables of five items each, a total of 125 (5 x 5 x 5). The outcomes are then summarized by yield ranges to produce the risk profile. The details are not given here but some combinations are illustrated with yields and probabilities:

	Least Profitable	Most Profitable	Median
Life	6 (P.1)	10 (P.1)	8 (P.4)
Outlay	$122,500 (P.1)	$ 92,500 (P.1)	$107,500 (P.3)
Cash Gain	$ 14,000 (P.1)	$ 22,000 (P.2)	$ 18,000 (P.3)
f	f8.750	f4.205	f5.944
Yield	Loss 9.8% (P.001)	19.9% (P.002)	7.0% (P.036)

Total cash 6x	$14,000 = $84,000
Outlay	122,500
Cash loss	38,500

These results are an extra dimension for the point estimate of 11.8%. A summary of all 125 outcomes is not presented but would be used to develop the risk profile. If the combined results show more than a 10% chance of loss or over 25% for yields below the 10% discount rate, the project would be too risky for many despite the point estimate of 11.8%.

Risk Profiles

The many possible yield outcomes arising with risk estimates require summarization. Five categories are enough, with one for losses and an open-ended top range. The intervals should be even and based on the discount rate. Illustration is given for discount rates of 5, 8, and 10%.

Yield Ranges	5%	8%	10%
	LOSS	LOSS	LOSS
	0-5	0-8	0-10
	5-10	8-16	10-20
	10-15	16-24	20-30
	15+	24+	30+

Two ranges are below the discount rate and three are above. All outcomes are grouped by yield ranges and their probabilities are added. The five subtotals add to P 1.0.

Outcomes for six projects are illustrated with a 5% discount rate:

Yield Range:	A	B	C	D	E	F
LOSS	0	5	10	10	10	15
0-5	5	10	10	15	20	25
5-10	20	30	40	50	60	45
10-15	40	30	30	20	5	10
15+	35	25	10	5	5	5
	100	100	100	100	100	100

Projects A and B should be acceptable. Projects C and D are subject to close review. Projects E and F are highly risky. Actual evaluation would depend on the degree of risk aversion and other factors such as project size. In all cases further detail is available, such as probable loss amounts. In many cases borderline proposals will be reworked. The same yield ranges should be used throughout, and should be restated for each change in the discount rate.

As explained above, it is desirable to encourage proposals from all sources, and to avoid premature rejection at lower levels because of possible unfavorable results. Risk is better assumed at the highest levels and the degree of risk is significantly reduced by a large number of proposals. Acceptable risk ranges should be stated along with the discount rate and yield ranges. For example, with a 5% discount rate, the loss limit might be 10% and the cum limit 25% (including the loss):

Yield Range	Submit			Do Not Submit		
	1	2	3	4	5	6
LOSS	10	5	0	12	8	0
0-5	15	20	25	8	20	28
Cum	25	25	25	20	28	28

The first three projects are within both the 10% loss limit and the 25% cum limit. The range (0-5) is given but does not affect the result except as part of the cum. Project 4 exceeds the 10% loss limit. Projects 5 and 6 exceed the 25% cum limit. Separate risk limits could also be set by project classification or by size of outlay but complexity should be avoided. The objective is to relieve juniors of the onus of risk bearing and to encourage a maximum flow of submissions. Even if half of the added proposals are rejected there can be major gains in both investments and morale.

A simple comparison of planned and actual results is given for five projects to demonstrate the effect of combined risk. A one-year period is used to avoid discounting and outlay is a constant $1,000 for both plan and actual:

Project	PLAN			ACTUAL		
	Outlay	Gain	%	Outlay	Gain	%
1	$1,000	$ 50	5.0	$1,000	$-100	-10.0
2	1,000	80	8.0	1,000	0	0
3	1,000	110	11.0	1,000	+100	10.0
4	1,000	140	14.0	1,000	+240	24.0
5	1,000	170	17.0	1,000	+310	31.0
	$5,000	$550	11.0%	$5,000	$550	11.0%

The swings in cash gains even out to the planned total. The first three projects sum to zero gain, and the first four have a total yield of only 6 percent--$240 on $4,000.

The probability of a point yield estimate being realized within + 1 percentage point is very small. The probability of yield below the point estimate is often over 50 percent.

Examples of Project Risk

The following project is submitted for approval:

        Outlay $32,000
        Cash Gain $6,000
        Life 8 years   f5.333   Yield 10%
        Discount rate 5% f6.463 PV $38,778 - $32,000 = $6,778 NPV

For risk analysis the outlay is considered to be certain--P1.0. This could mean in practice that the probable variations in dollar amounts were too small to consider. Cash gains are estimated:

                $4,000 P.2
                $6,000 P.7
                $8,000 P.1
                        1.0

Life is estimated:

                7 years P.3
                8 years P.6
                9 years P.1
                        1.0

The nine possible outcomes are calculated:

Cash gain $4,000 (P.2) Outlay $32,000   f8.0:

Life Years	Yield	P
7 (P.3)	Loss $4,000	.06
8 (P.6)	0	.12
9 (P.1)	2.4%	.02
		.20

Cash gain $6,000 (P.7) Outlay $32,000   f5.333:

Life Years	Yield	P
7 (P.3)	7.3%	.21
8 (P.6)	10.0%	.42
9 (P.1)	12.0%	.07
		.70

Cash gain $8,000 (P.1) Outlay $32,000   f4,000:

Life Years	Yield	P.
7 (P.3)	16.4%	.03
8 (P.6)	18.6%	.06
9 (P.1)	20.2%	.01
		.10

The outcomes are listed in yield sequence with Ps:

Yield %	P
LOSS	.06
0	.12
2.4	.02
7.3	.21
10.0	.42
12.0	.07
16.4	.03
18.6	.06
20.2	.01

The outcomes are grouped into the designated yield ranges:

Yield Range	P	Cum
LOSS	.06	.06
0-5	.14	.20
5-10	.21	.41
10-15	.49	.90
15+	.10	1.00

The combined 20% risk of a yield below 5%, including a 6% chance of loss, would be acceptable in most circumstances. Very large or particularly innovative projects would get a closer look. Such projects may be reworked or deferred. Small changes in probable outcomes can alter the risk profile significantly. The risk profile used must be supplied by the proposers and be acceptable to management. The configuration of odds above the discount rate (5%) is of little relevance--the upside potential. The 59% (.49 + .10) chance for yields over 10% does not usually offset aversion to yields under the 5% discount rate despite the long odds; reactions vary widely according to utility functions. The point yield of 10% is often taken to be an average or median but this assumption rests on the false notion that risk is symmetrical--an unsupportable assumption.

If the discount rate is 10%, the yield is also 10% and NPV is zero. The risk profile does not change but evaluation does. There is now a 41% chance of yield below 10%, including the 6% chance of loss. The difference of 35% (.14 +.21) relates to the yield range (0-10%). This is probably unacceptable despite the 59% chance of better results.

For a second example 64 outcomes are used. Proposal:

```
Point Estimate:                        Outcome Ranges
     Outlay  $40,000      $32,000 - 40,000 - 48,000 - 56,000
     Cash gain $8,000     $ 6,000 -  8,000 - 10,000 - 12,000
     Life 10 years             6  -      8  -    10  - 12 years
     f5.000  Yield 15.1%
     Discount rate 10%  f6.145
     PV $49,160  NPV $9,160
```

The four estimates made for each of the three factors total 64 outcomes. Calculations for 12 results are given by three tables. Point estimates are designated by *.

Cash gain $8,000		Life 10 years	
Outlay	f	Yield	P
$56,000	7.0	7.1%	.1
48,000	6.0	10.6%	.3
*40,000	5.0	*15.1%	.5
32,000	4.0	21.4%	.1
			1.0

Outlay $40,000		Life 10 years	
Cash Gain	f	Yield	P
6,000	6.667	8.1%	.2
* 8,000	5.000	*15.1%	.3
10,000	4.000	21.4%	.3
12,000	3.333	27.3%	.2
			1.0

Cash Gain $8,000 Outlay $40,000 f5.0		
Years	Yield	P
6	5.5	.1
8	11.1	.3
*10	*15.1	.4
12	16.9	.2
		1.0

The point estimate yield of 15.1% has a P of .5 x .3 x .4 = P.06 or 6%. All 64 outcomes are not given so the chance of a yield below 15.1% is not evident. The full risk profile is needed for evaluation but several outcomes are given:

	Best		Point Estimate		Worst	
Outlay	$32,000	- P.1	$40,000	- P.5	$56,000	- P.1
Cash gain	$12,000	- P.2	$ 8,000	- P.3	$ 6,000	- P.2
Life	12	- P.2	10	- P.2	6	- P.1
f	f2.667		f5.0		f9.333	
Yield	36.6%	- P.004	15.1%	- P.03	-11.3%	- P.002

Discount rate	10.0%	10.0%	10.0%
	12 years f6.814	10 years f6.145	6 years f4.355
	PV $81,768	PV $49,160	PV $26,130
	-32,000	-40,000	-56,000
	NPV 49,768	NPV 9,160	NPV -29,870

The worst case loss is 6 years of gains at $6,000 = $36,000 and outlay of $56,000 or a shortfall of $20,000. The negative yield of 11.3% is not needed, nor is the negative NPV of $29,870, shown for comparison only. The $20,000 cash loss has a P of only .002 but the 64 outcomes would include other losses for smaller amounts.

Inflation

Cash flows are projected by period and by the individual elements of outlay and gain--a difficult and risky task. All of the factors must be expressed in cash and adjusted to cash after taxes at some assumed rate. Prices must be set for all elements, but prices are constantly changing in a random and unpredictable fashion. In addition to changes in specific prices, which move up and down at varying rates, inflation must also be considered. Rates of inflation are expressed by indices, and many are available. But predictions of inflation are highly variable for both the short and long term. Cash flows may omit adjustment for both price changes and inflation if they are considered too uncertain. There is an innate tendency to assume that prevailing conditions will continue. It may also be assumed that there will be some offsetting tendency for all price changes, with an unpredictable net gain or loss. In projecting revenues and costs it may be prudent to allow for costs to rise faster than revenues with declining margins, a condition occurring frequently in inflationary periods. For example, a project with $3,500 outlay, 5 year life, discount rate 10% f3.791:

Revenue	$2,000
Cost	1,000
Gain	1,000
f3.791	$3,791 PV
Outlay	-3,500
	$ 291 NPV Yield 13.2%

The proposal is reworked to reflect revenue increases of $100 a year and cost increases of $200 a year:

Year	Revenue	Cost	Gain	10% f	PV
1	$2,000	$1,000	$1,000	.909	$909
2	2,100	1,200	900	.827	744
3	2,200	1,400	800	.751	601
4	2,300	1,600	700	.683	478
5	2,400	1,800	600	.621	373
				(f3.791)	3,105 PV
					-3,500
	Yield about 5.3%				- 395 NPV

The NPV change is negative from +$291 to -$395, or $686 and yield drops from 13.2% to 5.3%. This outcome could be one of many trials in risk analysis.

The simplest course may be to disregard inflation but to allow for changes in specific cash flow elements. The situation changes by period and may be different for separate locations, industries, and types of projects. However developed, the point estimates used to measure NPV and yield should be subjected to risk analysis. The company should provide guidelines on methods for handling price changes and inflation, as well as for risk analysis, risk limits, the discount rate, and yield ranges for the risk profile.

The discount rate is based on the current borrowing rate, less taxes, and includes whatever risk premium attaches to the company--the company rate less the comparable Treasury rate. The balance of the rate is a combination of a basic or "real" rate and inflation as anticipated at that time. All interest rates respond quickly to changes in inflationary expectations. The underlying "real" rate changes more slowly. The risk premium is unique to each entity and changes infrequently as a rule. The resolution of rates between the basic or real rate--the price of money without risk or inflation--and the allowance for inflation is indeterminate. The distinction is debatable in economics but not relevant to the investment decision. Of necessity, the discount rate is used regardless of its composition. Possible future changes in rates are not relevant for current discounting; the decision must be made now.

The effect of inflation on interest rates is illustrated with an example of an 8% note purchased for $1,000 to pay $1,080 in one year. Taxes and discounting are omitted. The 8% interest rate, or nominal rate, is for a Treasury note, risk-free by definition. The determination of the inflationary content of the rate is moot but it can be measured by using a selected price index. The balance is the basic, or real rate, the reward for the sacrifice of liquidity according to one economic interpretation. For example, if 5% is the expected rate of inflation, the real rate is 2.9% (1.08/1.05 = 1.0286). If prices rise 8% in the year, the $1,080 proceeds have the same purchasing power as $1,000 a year earlier and the real rate is zero. With no change in the price level, the proceeds can buy 8% more--the real rate is 8%. A commonly used index to measure inflation is the consumer price index--(CPI). The relationship between any index of price movement and individual utility is loose.

THE "COST OF CAPITAL"

The term cost of capital is widely used but has no clear or agreed-upon meaning, either by definition or application. "Capital" refers to financial instruments of all kinds--principally debt and stock. "Cost" refers to yield, both the return to the owner and the cost to the issuer. The subject is defined in three categories to establish clarity and relevance:

Rate of Return. Yields to investors for securities, individually and in portfolio.

Cost of Funds. Weighted average cost of the funds comprising the capital structure. The calculations can be based on both book and market values, and on both actual and planned amounts.

Discount Rate. The rate used to discount future cash flows to determine NPV. Other terms used are cut-off rate, investment rate, hurdle rate, and cost of capital (the latter erroneously).

It would be constructive to eliminate entirely the term cost of capital and substitute the terms suggested. "Capital" can mean both financial and physical assets and is often used ambiguously. "Cost" refers to both income to one group and outgo to another.

Rate of Return

Yields, or rates of return to investors, are illustrated with a few simple examples for some common forms of bonds and stock. Taxes and transaction costs are omitted.

Bonds--Fixed Interest Payment Annually.

Contract rate 10%. Due in 10 years.

a) Market rate 10%	Contract	f	PV
Principal	$10,000	.3855	$3,855
Interest	1,000	6.1445	6,145
Current price			10,000
b) Market rate 12%	Contract	f	PV
Principal	$10,000	.3220	$3,220
Interest	1,000	5.6500	5,650
Current price			8,870
Discount			1,130 $10,000

Check: $1,130/f5.650 = $200 plus $1,000 = $1,200 = 12%

The cash interest payment of $1,000 is increased by the discount expressed as an annuity of $200 to provide 12%.

c) Market rate 8%	Contract	f	PV
Principal	$10,000	.4632	$4,632
Interest	1,000	6.7101	6,710
Current price			11,342
Premium			1,342 $10,000

Check: $1,342/f6.7101 = $200 deducted from $1,000 = $800 = 8%

The cash interest payment is reduced by the premium expressed as an annuity to yield 8%.

Bonds (Zero Coupon--Interest Paid at Maturity).

Principal $10,000   Price $5,000   f.500
a) Due in 9 years: = 8.0%
b) Due in 6 years: = 12.2%
c) Due in 12 years: = 5.9%

Preferred Stock. Most issues have stated dividends (nonparticipatory in profits) payable when declared by the board of directors. Most issues are also cumulative--passed dividends must be made up before any common dividend can be declared. Preferred stock face amounts and dividends are stated, like bonds, and prices vary with market conditions:

Face value	$1,000	Annual dividend $100:
Market price	$1,000	Yield $100/1,000 = 10%
Market price	$ 833	Yield $100/833 = 12%
Market price	$1,250	Yield $100/1,250 = 8%

   Common Stock. Yield is measured by dividends and changes in market price for a specified period. The illustrations are for one year for a share costing $100:

   a) Price $110
      Cost   100
      $$\overline{10} = 10\% + 5\% \text{ dividend} = 15\%$$
   b) Price $115
      Cost   100
      $$\overline{15} = 15\% + \text{no dividend} = 15\%$$
   c) Price $100
      Cost   100
      $$\overline{0} = 0 + 15\% \text{ dividend} = 15\%$$
   d) Price $ 90
      Cost   100
      $$-\overline{10} = -10\% + 10\% \text{ dividend} = 0\%$$
   e) Price $ 85
      Cost   100
      $$-\overline{15} = -15\% + 5\% \text{ dividend} = -10\%$$

   The method, sometimes called the dividend model, can be used for both the past and the future, and for any periods. An investor who projects a rate of return less than he requires for a stock refers to it as "overpriced"--at a lower price the return is higher. If the projected yield is higher than required, the stock is said to be "underpriced." These continuing evaluations by legions of investors move market prices quickly and efficiently based on news and expectations.
   A complementary valuation method is known as the "Capital Asset Pricing Model" (CAPM). This approach rests on yields and risk, excluding prices and dividends. The steps are:
   Determine the total yield for all stocks for a selected market such as the NYSE--say 15%.
   Select a risk-free debt rate such as Treasuries--say 9%.
   Compute the statistical relationship between the company stock yield and the total market yield for a number of periods. This is a measure of risk, known as the company characteristic line. The degree of risk is referred to as beta. Alpha is always zero theoretically, but otherwise the stock is said to be "mispriced."
   The risk of the market is 1.0 by definition. If the stock beta is 1.0, its changes in yields coincide with the market. At beta .5 stock yield changes are half the market; for beta 2.0 they are double the market rate.
   Equation:

1 Market Yield	2 Risk-Free Rate	3 (1-2) Difference	4 Beta	5 (3-4) Extend	6 (2+5) Yield	Difference From Market
15%	9%	6%	.5	3%	12%	-3%
15	9	6	1.0	6	15	0
15	9	6	1.5	9	18	+3
15	9	6	2.0	12	21	+6

Betas outside these ranges are rare. CAPM yields should agree in general with those obtained using the stock price and dividend model.

Investors hold portfolios designed to provide the preferred combination of yield and risk. Portfolio yields are weighted arithmetic averages of all holdings. Portfolio risk is a complex computation based on correlation. The security markets make any combination of return and risk available quickly and at low cost. The risk of a single stock can be reduced by selecting other stocks to modify the risk-return balance; risk can be reduced to a low level by holding a variety of securities. Thus, market prices are said not to include a premium for company risk (called "unsystematic" risk). The risk for the entire market-- "systematic" risk--remains. Investors pick stocks to meet their portfolio requirements.

Companies acquire physical assets at considerable cost and for use over long periods with some effect on operating risk. Debt is managed in line with financial risk to achieve goals for combined risk. Managers can only perform according to their own interests; stockholders as a group are unknown. In practice, investors choose companies. Managers work toward improved financial performance primarily to bolster their careers and estates. Stock prices reflect company prospects but also include expectations for the industry and the economy. These three elements combine in ever-changing relationships. In many cases the effect of the company on the price is smaller than the other elements. Stock prices quickly reflect all news (and rumors). The efficient market theory, well validated, states that past yields hold no information about the future, that all public information is rapidly and fully incorporated into the price, and that private (inside) information affects price to some unknown degree. Insider trading is kept under close surveillance but is not clearly definable.

Cost of Funds

Yields on securities to investors are costs to the issuers. Security offerings are designed to appeal to investors and to provide issuers with acceptable terms--a marketing approach similar to that used for products and services. Design features include issue amounts and denominations; rates and payment terms; fixed, participating, and variable rates; convertibility and callability; security; control; tax status; and market listing.

The weighted average cost of all securities, at book or market, and actual or planned, is referred to as the cost of funds, not "cost of capital."

Examples to illustrate the calculation method show varying proportions of debt (D) and equity (E). Varying net interest rates and yields on equity produce varying rates for the cost of funds:

1. D $ 0   5% $ 0
    E $10,000   20% $2,000
         $10,000 $2,000 = 20%

With no leverage the cost of funds equals equity yield.

2. D $ 2,000   5% $ 100
    E $ 8,000   18% $1,440
         $10,000 $1,540 = 15.4%

Use of a moderate amount of debt (D-E 25%) provides favorable leverage and lowers the cost of equity from 20% to 18% and the cost of funds to 15.4%. The stock is more attractive and the price rises.

3. D $ 4,000   5% $ 200
    E $ 6,000   16% $ 960
         $10,000 $1,160 = 11.6%

Higher D-E of 67% increases favorable leverage; the stock price rises and yield drops to 16%. Cost of funds shows another large decline--from 15.4 to 11.6%.

4. D $ 5,000   6% $ 300
    E $ 5,000   18% $ 900
         $10,000 $1,200 = 12.0%

With D-E at 100%, interest cost rises to 6% net and stock yield rises to 18% from 16% in response to higher liquidity risk. The cost of funds rises only slightly--from 11.6 to 12.0%.

5. D $ 6,000   7% $ 420
    E $ 4,000   20% $ 800
         $10,000 $1,220 = 12.2%

With D-E at 150%, the interest rate increases to 7% and yield is back to 20%, but the cost of funds rises only fractionally from 12.0%.

6. D $ 8,000   10% $ 800
    E $ 2,000   60% $1,200
         $10,000 $2,000 = 20.0%

This abnormal case brings the cost of funds back to the 20% rate found in the first example with no debt. With a jump to 10% net interest for a D-E of 400%, stock yield is 60%--three times that of example 5--representing a precipitous price drop. At this point, prices may reflect liquidating values. The six cases are recapped with stock prices added:

	D-E	Interest Rate	Avg. Cost of Funds	Stock Yield	Stock Price	Cum Change
1	0%	5%	20.0%	20%	$100.0	--
2	25%	5%	15.4%	18%	111.1	+11.1%
3	67%	5%	11.6%	16%	125.0	+25.0%
4	100%	6%	12.0%	18%	111.1	+11.1%
5	150%	7%	12.2%	20%	100.0	0
6	400%	10%	20.0%	60%	33.3	-66.7%

These examples demonstrate the "flat" curve for the cost of funds within a wide range of capital structures; examples 3, 4, and 5 have practically the same result. The extremes of no debt and excessive debt entail a high cost of funds because stock prices are depressed. The relevance of this form of analysis to specific decisions on capital structure is questionable and apparently has little recognition in practice. Use of the "cost of capital" (read "cost of funds") as the discount rate or hurdle rate to be used for investment decisions continues to be advocated by some academics, surprisingly, despite proof of its irrelevance by leading authorities. Its use in practice is not reported. Use of a discount rate higher than the net borrowing rate necessarily decreases total investment and growth.

Discount Rate

The discount rate--the net cost of borrowing--is a marginal rate used to compute the NPV for each investment proposal. The cost of funds is a weighted average for all securities. It is a result, not a causative agent relevant to investment. A high hurdle rate shuts off investment, slows growth, and depresses stock prices. Equally important, any rate higher than the net borrowing rate includes a risk factor that arbitrarily distorts present values, precluding rational risk appraisal. The damaging effect of using a "high" discount rate is dramatic: "Continuing reliance on the 20% ROI hurdle rate for capital projects has led many basic American industries to their demise" (Braxton Associates, Journal of Accounting [August 1987]: 42). The message is clear but unfortunately ROI is not defined either as to "investment" or "return," or whether it is before or after tax.

Internally generated funds have no explicit cost and provide the principal source for financing growth. The discount rate regulates the trade-off between investments and dividends. With good investment opportunities all earnings may be used to promote growth. With limited opportunities, available funds are paid out in dividends. An investor not receiving a dividend has an opportunity cost equal to the best alternative use of the funds, offset by possible future gain on the stock arising from investment of the retained funds by the company. To the company, a paid dividend has an opportunity cost related to investments not made. The correct company criterion is the discount rate, or net interest rate, that provides positive leverage and maximum growth for all qualified proposals of acceptable risk. In effect, the company is re-investing the unpaid dividends for the investor who stands to gain from future dividends and stock price increases.

A company may have qualified investment proposals that call for outlays in excess of available funds from retained earnings and borrowing capacity. It may be decided that added debt would impair liquidity and increase financial risk unduly. The NPV of the proposals not made is the opportunity cost of additional financing by stocks and debt. The incremental cost of funds can be developed as follows, assuming a need for $100,000, 100% D-E, 5% net interest, and 15% yield for a new stock issue, based on projected market acceptance:

```
New stock issue        $50,000 at 15% = $7,500
Added debt capacity     50,000 at  5% = $2,500
                       100,000          $10,000 = 10%
```

The incremental cost of 10% is relevant to evaluation of the investment projects, not the stock yield of 15%. The discount rate remains at 5% to enable rational risk analysis. Cumulative risk profiles are presented, based on the 5% rate, for three projects, deferred for lack of funds, and calling for $100,000 total outlay:

	Cumulative Risk Percents		
Yield Ranges:	A	B	C
0-5	10%	10%	10%
5-10	40	30	20
10-15	80	70	60
15-20	95	95	95
20+	100	100	100

Evaluation:

At 5% Debt Rate--   All projects are approved because yield below 5% is limited to an acceptable 10% risk. But the 5% rate is below the 10% incremental rate for funds.

At 15% Stock Rate--   Projects are unacceptable because the chance of a lower yield is over 50% in all three cases. But this rate is higher than the incremental funds rate of 10%.

At 10% Avg. Rate -   A is unacceptable because the 40% cum is too high. B, with a 30% cum, is marginal. C is acceptable with a 20% cum.

After evaluation of the risk-return relationship for all defined proposals using the risk profile based on 5% and the 10% incremental cost of funds, several outcomes can occur. All projects could be approved and full incremental financing planned; this entails careful time scheduling for investment outlays and financing proceeds. All projects could be deferred and the financing plan dropped. Most likely, some projects will be approved and others deferred. The balance sought is between yield for accepted projects and the incremental funds rate. In both cases the incremental rates are the criteria, not the new weighted averages for the cost of funds. A further problem is the relatively high cost of raising funds in small amounts and the constantly shifting costs of funds, coupled with the disparate nature of investment proposals.

This brief outline illustrates the central ongoing management decision of balancing investments (yield and operating risk) and financing (cost and financial risk) relative to goals and expectations.

QUESTIONABLE RISK INDICATORS

Standard Deviation

Standard deviation is an established measure of normal distribution and has many applications. Its validity rests on a large number of repetitive events taken from a large population of defined properties. There is little relevance to asset investment proposals because of their singular nature, the skew of probable outcomes, and individual risk attitudes--the utility function.

An example compares standard deviation with the risk profile for a proposal:

```
Outlay        $10,000
Cash gain     $ 3,000    5 years
              f3.333     Yield 15.2%
Discount rate 10%        5 years  f3.791
Cash gain     $ 3,000    f3.791 = $11,373 PV
                                  -10,000
                                  $ 1,373 NPV
```

Probable outcomes are estimated and summarized in the following risk profile:

Yield Range	Probability	Cum
Loss	6%	6%
0-10	12%	18%
10-20	54%	72%
20-30	22%	94%
30+	6%	100%

Standard deviation is calculated as follows:

1 Yield Range	2 Mid Point	3 P	4 (2x3)	5 (2-M)	6 (5 squared)	7 (3x6)
Loss	- 5	.06	-.30	-21	441	26.46
0-10	5	.12	.60	-11	121	14.52
10-20	15	.54	8.10	- 1	1	.54
20-30	25	.22	5.50	+ 9	81	17.82
30+	35	.06	2.10	+19	361	21.66
		Mean	16.00M		Variance	81.00

The square root of the variance is the standard deviation - 81 = 9 SD. The probabilities for outcomes within given standard deviations are provided by tables as stated below:

No. of SD	P	SD	M	M + SD = Yield Range	Compare Discount Rate	Point Yield
1	68.3%	9	16	+7 to 25	10	15.2
2	95.4%	18	16	-2 to 34	10	15.2
3	99.7%	27	16	-11 to 43	10	15.2

For one SD there is a 68.3% chance (2 in 3) of a yield between 7% and 25%--a spread of 18 points. Seven percent is three points below the discount rate and 25% is ten points over the point yield, and there is a one in three chance of being outside these limits. For 2 SD the range from -2 to 34% almost overlaps the yield range--the 95.4% assurance says little. At 3 SD--a near certainty--the range is too broad to be meaning-ful. This statistical procedure obliterates the skew and the critical element of downside risk. The significant indicators of risk are the 6%

chance of loss and the 18% cum for yield below 10%. The risk pattern over 10%-- upside potential--generally has little bearing on the decision.

For the comparison of projects of different size a coefficient of variation is computed -- SD divided by M, or 9/16 = .56. A higher coefficient denotes a higher degree of risk but there is no benchmark to indicate whether one or the other project should be accepted, or both, or neither.

Higher Discount Rate

The discount rate used should be risk-free in order to obtain unbiased present values of cash flows for determining NPV. Also, the evaluation of the risk profile is made against the same discount rate; a possible exception is the incremental funds rate as explained above. The technically applicable rate is that for treasury bonds, risk-free by definition. In practice, the company's current borrowing rate for substantial sums for long maturities, net of taxes, is acceptable. The difference is relatively small and avoids the danger of negative leverage. Differences between Treasury and company rates are unlikely to have practical significance. For example:

	Interest Rate	Tax at 40%	Net
Treasury	9.0%	3.6%	5.4%
Company A	10.0	4.0	6.0
B	11.0	4.4	6.6
C	12.0	4.8	7.2
D	13.0	4.2	7.8
E	14.0	5.6	8.4

Use of a higher rate to allow for risk is intuitively attractive but specious. For this approach, a risk schedule might be based on a net interest rate of 6%:

Discount Rate		Premium
6%	minimum risk	0
8%	moderate risk	+2
10%	average risk	+4
12%	high risk	+6

There is no logical foundation for such a scheme. Use of higher rates arbitrarily distorts present values. More distant cash flows are increasingly biased. The effect on PV is erratic because of varying amounts of cash flow and periods. With a risk-free rate there is no distortion and amounts can be logically evaluated for outcome ranges.

The following annuity table shows the PV for $1,000 for selected discount rates and periods to illustrate relationships:

			Rates			
Years	0%	4%	6%	8%	10%	12%
0	$ 1,000	$ 1,000	$ 1,000	$ 1,000	$ 1,000	$ 1,000
5	5,000	4,452	4,212	3,993	3,791	3,605
10	10,000	8,111	7,360	6,710	6,145	5,650
20	20,000	13,590	11,470	9,818	8,514	7,469
40	40,000	19,793	15,046	11,925	9,779	8,244

Note: Year zero means now--no discounting at any rate.
Rate zero means no interest--no discounting for any period.
The PV relationships are logarithmic, not linear.

Example:
	at 12%		at 4%	Change +8%
0	$1,000	0	$1,000	0
Year 40	$8,244	Year 10	$8,111	+ 30 years
	$+7,244		$+7,111	$+133

The PV is about the same for 12% for 40 years as for 4% for 10 years.

Example:
	at 10%		at 8%	Change +2%
0	$1,000	0	$1,000	0
Year 40	$9,779	Year 20	$9,818	+ 20 years
	$+8,779		$+8,818	-$39

Example:
	at 4%		at 10%	Change -6%
Year 5	$4,452	Year 5	$3,791	+$661
Year 20	13,590	Year 20	$8,514	0 years
	+9,138		+4,723	$+4,415

Example:
	at 4%		at 10%	Change -6%
Year 5	$4,452	Year 5	$3,791	+$661
Year 40	19,793	Year 40	$9,779	0 years
	$+15,341		+5,988	+$9,353

These examples demonstrate the nature of the time and rate relationships; they are not intuitive.

The following examples illustrate the effect of using rates arbitrarily inflated for risk.

Outlay gain $11,470 Cash gain $1,000 f11.47% 20 years
Yield 6%
Discount rate 6% $11,470 PV
                          11,470 Outlay
                               0 NPV

NPV for selected discount rates and 20 years:

Discount Rates	4%	6%	8%	10%	12%
f	f13.590	f11.470	f9.818	f8.514	f7.469
Cash gain (1000)	$13,590	$11,470	$9,818	$8,514	$7,469
Outlay	11,470	11,470	11,470	11,470	11,470
NPV	$+2,120	$ 0	$-1,652	$-2,956	$-4,001
Yield	6%	6%	6%	6%	6%
Discount rate above	4	6	8	10	12
Yield over (under)	2	0	(2)	(4)	(6)

If the discount rate used is 4%, instead of the correct 6%, NPV is overstated by +$2,120 and approval is encouraged for a marginal proposal.

Rates over 6% generate negative NPVs and discourage consideration of proposals that qualify with the 6% rate. The negative NPVs are meant to measure risk but are arbitrary and opaque; they are in no way related to a risk profile. When proposals show positive NPVs for rates over 6%, their acceptance is encouraged but without rational risk analysis. Such an approach would increase risk because high yield projects tend to be riskier.

If the correct discount rate is 8% and a project shows zero NPV at 8% for 20 years, spurious gains appear below 8%, and losses at higher rates:

Discount Rates	4%	6%	8%	10%	12%
f	f13.590	f11.470	f9.818	f8.514	f7.469
Cash gain	$13,590	$11,470	$9,818	$8,514	$7,469
Outlay	9,818	9,818	9,818	9,818	9,818
NPV	+ 3,772	+ 1,652	0	-1,304	-2,349

This table has the same pattern as that for the 6% table, but the focus shifts. The deceptive nature of the results is unchanged. Use of a rate below the correct discount rate shows spurious gains and encourages acceptance of marginal proposals; use of rates over the correct discount rate shows negative NPVs not correlated with risk. Proposals with positive NPVs for rates over 8% appear to be acceptable, but are apt to be riskier because of higher yields.

The following example compares a project evaluated with a risk profile compared with discount rates arbitrarily increased for risk:

```
Outlay      $6,710      Cash gain  $1,000  f6.710
10 years                Yield 8%
Discount rate 5%        f7.722  PV $7,722
                             Outlay  6,710
                             NPV     1,012
```

A risk profile is prepared for a range of cash gains but with outlay and years constant:

		10 year			
Cash Gain	Outlay $6,710	Yield	P	Cum	Yield Range %
(1) $ 671	f10.000	0%	.1	.1	0-5
(2) 869	f 7.722	5%	.2	.3	5-10
(3) 1,092	f 6.145	10%	.3	.6	10-15
(4) 1,337	f 5.019	15%	.2	.8	15-20
(5) 1,601	f 4.192	20%	.2	1.0	20+

(1) Based on the discount rate of 5%, risk is low at P.1. (2) If a 10%
rate is used for profit evaluation, the downside risk rises to P.3 cum
and is marginal.   (3) At a 15% rate for evaluation, the downside risk is
very high at P.6 cum. The risk profile is based on the company's net
borrowing rate and positive NPV is positive leverage. When applicable,
the risk profile adds a new dimension to the evaluation--some projects
with the same NPV are acceptable while others are too risky. The
arbitrary use of a higher rate for evaluation stacks the odds against
approval indiscriminately.   An exception is when the incremental funds
rate is used for projects requiring equity funding.

If the project is discounted at an arbitrary rate of 20%, a premium
of 15% over the discount rate of 5%, the result is a large decrease in
NPV:

```
As given:
        Outlay  $6,710          Cash gain $1,000   f6.710
        10 years                Yield 8%
        Discount rate 5%        f7.722      PV   $7,722
                                            Outlay  6,710
                                            NPV     1,012
        With discount rate 20%:  f4.192     PV   $4,192
                                            Outlay  6,710
                                            NPV    -2,518
        Yield remains at 8% but NPV drops by $3,530.
```

To obtain zero NPV at 20%, cash gain must be $6,710/f4.192 = $1,601
(5) compared with the $1,000 estimate: cash gain $1,601 f4.192 = 6,710 PV
and NPV 0. The risk profile shows that a cash gain of $1,601 has P.20 or
one chance in five. If a project shows positive NPV at 20%, it is highly
profitable, compared with the 5% minimum, but it is also probably very
risky.   But the odds are unknown. High yield projects tend to be
riskier--opportunities for high returns are scarce; the estimates may be
overly optimistic; the proposal may be innovative and uncertain. Without
a risk profile, approval is likely for long shots while some that are
acceptable are rejected.   The net effect is higher risk and less profit,
to some unknown extent. Like analysis applies to the other rates.

Payback Period

The cash payback period is the number of years required for cash
receipts to equal cash outlays. By definition the profit is zero--cash
out equals cash in. It is a measure of liquidity, a significant part of
cash planning.   It is not a measure of profit which can only arise when
cash gains exceed outlay. It is not a measure of risk because it simply
expresses a period without regard to the nature of the project. Shorter
periods suggest less risk but in fact relate only to uncertainty -- that
which cannot be estimated. A shorter period may well be riskier. Use of
a payback period as a profit criterion may be counterproductive; accepting projects with short paybacks that are riskier, rejecting projects
with larger paybacks that may be safer. Prior to the wide use of cash
discounting and risk analysis, the practice was to use a range of payback
periods relevant to asset life.

Project profitability (NPV, yield) is based on the discount rate with no added risk premium. Risk can then be portrayed by the risk profile. Evaluation rests on the risk-return relationship, particularly as to downside risk. All accepted proposals enter into the financial plans. In times of financial stringency it may be prudent to defer some projects. Outlays and cash flows could be factors in the selection of projects to meet short-term liquidity restraints, a process referred to as capital rationing.

The bond refunding decision is virtually risk-free, as described above. The discount rate used to determine NPV is the borrowing rate for the new bond issue less taxes, the rate that applies to all discounting. With a positive NPV the refunding is attractive and risk need not be considered. However, bond refunding is a financing, not an investing, decision. All investment decisions require some degree of risk evaluation, from informal hunch to elaborate modeling. Such analysis is independent of payback. Proposals with short paybacks that are highly risky include styles, customer tastes, CB radios, electric knives, novelties, and toys. Longer payback proposals may be relatively safe, such as production equipment with predictable performance, buildings, autos, and trucks. The following table illustrates four pair combinations with annual paybacks, and yields, using a 6% rate:

Cash Outlay	Cash Gain	Pay back	Life	Yield	Downside Risk	Decision
$10,000	$1,250	8	12	6.9%	LO	Accept
10,000	1,250	8	30	12.1	HI	Reject
10,000	2,000	5	6	5.5	LO	Reject
10,000	2,000	5	20	19.4	AVG	Accept
10,000	3,333	3	4	12.6	LO	Accept
10,000	3,333	3	6	24.3	HI	Reject
10,000	5,000	2	2	0	LO	Reject
10,000	5,000	2	5	41.0	AVG	Accept

Many combinations exist and the decisions indicated would rest on many considerations.

Portfolio Effect

Investing in a variety of assets spreads risk and averages the returns. A portfolio rate of return is a weighted average of the rates for all the securities held. The degree of risk is a more complex correlation calculation based on co-variances. Investors buy, hold, and sell securities according to the effect on their portfolios. A single security has a single rate of return and degree of risk. That risk can be measured by the relationship of the security's rate of return to the total market rate of return for a period, the characteristic line. It is expressed as beta; 1.0 means that the company and market rates move together. Beta .5 is a rate movement at one-half the market; beta 2.0 indicates a relationship of two to one. This method is known as CAPM--capital asset pricing model--which is described in chapter 5. Adding to the number of securities held reduces the portfolio risk, and it can approach zero. The moderation of company risk (or "unsystematic risk") is a choice for the investor. However, market risk ("systematic risk") remains. Thus investors can adjust for company risk quickly and cheaply, as circumstances change. A company that materially changes its risk posture may get a favorable, or unfavorable, market response. The effect on portfolios will also vary. Investors will buy, hold, or sell based on the effect on their portfolios.

Companies also hold a portfolio of assets and seek to regulate their risk posture. As compared with securities, asset management is more costly and riskier, and takes much more time. Risk moderation can be sought by investment in different industries and geographic locations, and by a range of markets and products. In theory, each decision should be made on the basis of the CAPM. In practice, the problem is too complex to be captured by CAPM or other mathematical approaches. Limitations include the need to simplify the facts to suit the formulation, the use of arbitrary assumptions, and sophisticated solutions lacking clarity and relevance. Portfolio risk analysis for productive assets is highly significant but necessarily judgmental. The dynamics of the economy dictate constant review and appraisal.

Research and experimentation continue in the use of CAPM for financial assets and for applicability to productive assets. Other mathematical models are available for use in special situations where there is good applicability with highly experienced people, and plenty of time and money, all guided by savvy managers.

RISK AND RETURN GUIDELINES

First, encourage and assist all people to submit investment proposals to foster growth. Provide technical guidance at all locations by designated staff to help define possibilities and expedite preparation in good form.

Second, specify the discount rate to be used for all calculations-- the current borrowing rate less the current tax rate. Keep the rate current by revision for net changes up or down of 1 percent or more. Use the same rate for all types of proposals, for all types of assets, for all locations, for all organizational units, and for all time periods. Use of a lower rate may cause negative leverage. Use of a higher rate lowers NPV, distorts results, and shuts off good projects.

Third, establish yield ranges for expressing the risk profile and the maximum acceptable downside risk limits. For example, with a 5% discount rate:

Yield Ranges	Risk Probability
Loss	10% maximum
0-5	25% cum
5-10	--
10-15	--
15+	Yield

The maximum allowable risk probability below 5% yield is 25% cum with a further 10% limit for the loss range. The other ranges--upside potential--do not require expression. Encourage preparation of risk profiles to aid review and to provide a basis for performance evaluation. Provide guidance on risk analysis methods such as practical limits or intervals for probabilities and for ranges of project elements such as outlays, cash gains, and life.

Fourth, provide clear and timely communication to proposers as to proposal status. If not accepted, explain the basis for rejection or deferral.

Fifth, insure the use of cash flows on an incremental basis, stated in detail for all elements. Compute the NPV, yield, accounting rate of return, and payback period. Express the risk profile and supply explanatory notes as needed. Designate mutually exclusive projects. Describe nonquantitative relative factors. Cash flow forecasts should take account of both changing prices and inflation, based on guidelines provided by the company. Probable ranges can be incorporated into the risk profile.

Sixth, monitor approved projects for timely completion so that operating plans are met. On completion restate projects for actual outlays and revise estimates for cash gains and life. This determination provides the basis for measuring the project as completed with the proposal as approved, and for performance review at a later date.

Seventh, review all approved projects in total for operating effects not determinable for each proposal alone, such as demands on limited facilities; opportunity costs; risk exposure relative to new products and markets; competitive reactions; and management capability. Risk must also be reviewed on a portfolio basis to evaluate the interrelatedness among the proposals and with existing operations. Also, the total cash flows must be entered into the cash plans for review of the impact on liquidity relative to financial planning. Review includes not only the capital expenditure program but also major outlays such as for research and development and advertising.

Eighth, review and approve projects first for planning and budgeting only. Actual authorization to commit funds should be made later on a separate submission, say quarterly, of each project. Projects may be restated. Base review on current conditions relative to operations, risk, and liquidity. Some proposals approved for the budget may not be resubmitted and others may be added. This approach provides needed flexibility for both proposers and management.

Ninth, explore the acquisition of other companies or their segments. Analyze assets for disposal or replacement. Evaluate callable bonds for refunding when NPV is positive to improve liquidity and ROE.

Finally, cultivate the financial markets to enhance reputation for the "quality of earnings" to achieve favorable borrowing terms and stock market strength. This should help lower the cost of funds. If the total of all approved projects requires outlay beyond the funds available from earnings as well as from additional debt, because of financial risk, the alternative is to issue stock or defer the proposals. The trade-off is between the cost of additional financing and the NPV of the deferred proposals. This is primarily a financing analysis but, briefly stated, the incremental costs of funds is used to evaluate the projects but the discount rate remains unchanged in order to provide logical risk analysis.

6

The Anatomy of Product Cost

PLAN AND PERFORMANCE

The specification of product cost is central to both cost control and profit measurement. A product profit plan, ideally, is developed by determining a market, designing a product, designating a market share, setting a price, estimating marketing expenses, costing the product, and specifying the assets required. Profit is then computed and the financing is planned. The product plan is expressed in both financial and accounting terms and evaluated relative to risk and liquidity over the period of expected life. Product plans are developed constantly and are accepted or dropped. Existing plans are expanded, contracted, or dropped. Decision factors include product costs, prices, volume, design, promotion, distribution, service expenses, and assets.

Planned product costs are the best basis for both charges to marketing for sales planning and for the control of manufacturing expenses. Marketing bases its product sales plans and profits on the planned product costs. Manufacturing plans are based on the sales plans --the process is reciprocal. The constant changes in products and output affect costs, and the actual output compared with the planned volume is a major factor.

Comparison of performance with plan is illustrated in terms of management responsibility expressed as three functions:

	Plan	Actual	Gain (Loss)
MARKETING:			
	500 units	550 units	50 units
Sales--at $2	$1000	$1100	$100
Standard cost	600	660	(60)
Margin	400	440	40
Expenses	100	125	(25)
Sales margin	300	315	15
MANUFACTURING:			
Product cost:			
Plan (standard)	600	660	
Actual	600	670	
Expense variance	0	10	(10)
Gross margin	300	305	5
ADMINISTRATION:			
Expenses	100	120	(20)
Profit margin	200	185	(15)
Volume variance	50	25	25
Profit	$150	$160	$10
Percent to sales	15.0%	14.5%	10.0%
Assets	$500	$500	
Turnover rate	2.0	2.2	
ROA	30.0%	32.0%	

Note: Volume variance: Capacity 600 units   Fixed overhead $300:
       Per unit $300/600 = $.50
       Plan   500 units - 100 short at .50 = $50
       Actual   550 units - 50 short at .50 = $25
       Gain   50 units   at .50 = $25

This format shows marketing performance with a gain in sales and margin of 10 percent and higher expenses (25 percent) for a sales margin increase of $15 on $300, or 5 percent. The planned sales margin is 30 percent and the incremental sales margin is 15 percent; the actual sales margin is reduced to 28.6 percent. Manufacturing expenses exceed plan by $10. Administration expenses are $20 over plan. The profit margin is $15 less. The expected charge for unused capacity of $50 is reduced by $25 because of higher sales and output, with inventories unchanged. Volume variance is set out as a separate factor because responsibility for it is diffused. It is part of the capital expenditure program and hence long term, but is also affected by sales volume and factory output. Sales exceeded plan by 50 units, thus reducing the variance charge by $25. The sales margin gain of $15 plus the directly related volume gain of $25 is a combined gain of $40 on the added sales of $100. The manufacturing and administration expense variances of $30 (10 + 20) reduce the $40 gain to $10 profit. The added volume was handled with no increase in assets so turnover increased and ROA rose from 30 to 32%. Incremental ROA is the profit gain of $10 divided by zero asset gain.

This illustration is based on management accountability, called "responsibility accounting," on planned product costs called "standard costs," and on planned expenses, called "budgets."

The illustration is restated in more conventional terms to contrast the two formats:

		Plan	Actual	Gain (Loss)
Sales		$1,000	$1,100	$100
Cost of sales:				
at standard		600	660	(60)
variances	(1)	50	35	15
		650	695	(45)
Gross profit		350	405	55
Expenses	(2)	200	245	(45)
Profit		$ 150	$ 160	$ 10

(1) Variances include both expense and volume: Plan $0 + 50 = 50 and actual $10 + 25 = 35. (2) Expenses include both marketing and administration. Gross profit is 35 percent plan and 55 percent incremental; actual gross profit is 36.8 percent (405/1,100).

PRODUCT COST STANDARDS

Costs and Expenses

The costs of production are expressed as "product costs" and carried in inventory until sold (or otherwise disposed of). Inventory sold is charged to "cost of sales" which is an expense. "Costs" are outlays for the acquisition of assets. "Expenses" are charges against income in the current period. Costs not expensed remain as assets. In practice the distinctions in terminology are often ignored.

Product costs include "all costs necessary for production"--material, labor, and factory overhead. Costs not "necessary" are variances and expensed as incurred because they were avoidable. Costs not for "production" are "period expenses" charged to income as incurred. Material and labor are "direct costs" that can be charged directly to product, known as "prime costs" and fully variable with output. Factory overhead includes all other expenses of production, separated into fixed and variable components for use in expense control. Factory overhead and labor combined are called "conversion costs." Departmental expense budgets are variable--"flexible budgets"--when part of the allowed expense is based on a selected activity basis. Factory overhead is applied to product costs with "costing" rates based on a defined basis of activity for each production department and its budgeted overhead, including the allocated expenses of service departments. Factory overhead is an "indirect cost" assigned to products by some causal relationship. All company expenses other than direct costs (labor and material) are "overhead." Factory overhead is applied to product cost. Other overhead is period expense and is not measured to products. It is designated "selling, general, and administrative expenses" (SGA). The distinction between product cost and period expense is important but not always carefully defined in practice.

Some theorists believe that all overhead should be handled as a product cost. Others advocate charging only direct costs to products (material and labor). In practice, and by the requirements of GAAP (and the IRS), overhead is divided between the two categories. How this is done, and to what effect, is not clearly defined, remains debatable, and has no established and consistent practice.

Variances from standard are expensed as incurred to individual accounts in cost of sales--period expenses. Variances are not given product identity because they define departures from plans as inefficiencies. They are not related to individual product standards or to sales plans. Variances are defined by management responsibility to aid both expense control and profit planning.

Standard Cost Elements

Direct Material. A "bill of materials" for each product states kind of material used, required quantity, price, and dollar totals. Purchased amounts allow for necessary loss in processing, expressed as a separate standard. Purchasing is responsible for prices, and differences between standard and actual are "price variances." Manufacturing is responsible for the quantity used, and differences from standard are "usage variances." Any price variance relating to usage variance remains a purchasing responsibility, debit or credit. Price and usage variances are charged (credited) to costs of sales as incurred.

Direct material is often the largest single cost element. Changes in price or usage should be incorporated into the standards promptly. Delay causes erroneous reporting of variances. The adjustments needed should be reviewed annually, at the least, with debit to inventory and credit to a separate cost of sales account (or vice versa). Lower material costs should be sought through product design, substitution, and vendor sourcing. Changes in material prices and usage should be anticipated for pricing and sales planning. Sales planners should be aware of all current changes and new developments, and maintain close communication with purchasing, engineering, and manufacturing. For custom-made products with special material components, vendor price quotations serve as standards.

Price variance example: Purchase 1,000 units at $8.50--standard $8.20 = variance $.30 = $300, or $8,500--$8,200. Usage variance example: Use 200 units--standard 185 units = 15 units at $8.20 = $123 or $1,640--$1,517.

Some direct materials are treated as indirect material and charged to a separate overhead account for practical reasons of measurement or small amount. Such items may need separate attention when product plans are reviewed.

Direct Labor. Each direct labor operation is stated:
1. By department, cost center, type of operation
2. For time required per unit of output
3. Labor rate per hour, and total
Example:
1. Machining--Lathes
2. 6 minutes per unit, or .10 hour
3. $12.60 per hour (department average) = $9.00 pay rate plus $3.60 fringe.
Operations are totaled to arrive at the product total.
Rate variance can arise as follows:

Total earnings	300 hours at $13.20	=	$3,960
Total standard	300 hours at $12.60	=	$3,780
Variance	300 hours at .60	=	$ 180 DR

This example assumes 100 percent time efficiency. Rate variance is charged to cost of sales as incurred and is the responsibility of manufacturing and personnel. It may reflect a lag in updating standards or a shift in the average.

Time, or efficiency, variance can arise as follows:

```
Actual output   3150 units in 300 hours        at $12.60 = $3,780
Standard        3150 units at .10 = 315 hours   at $12.60 = $3,969
Variance = 15 hours                             at $12.60 = $189 CR
```

Efficiency rate: 300/315 = 95.24% or 315/300 = 105.00%

Time efficiency measurement depends on accurate time and quantity records. The analysis is recast in table form:

	Actual	Standard		Variance
Time	300	315	= 15 at $12.60 =	$189 CR
Rate	$13.20	$12.60	= $.60 at 300 =	180 DR
Total	$ 3960	$ 3969		
		3960		
		9 CR		9 CR

The distinction between rate and time variance is important. Workers are classified as direct or indirect. All indirect labor is overhead. Direct time is divided between productive time and downtime, which is part of overhead. Direct labor productive time is actual physical units produced times standard time per unit.

Factory Overhead. All production costs not defined as direct material or direct labor are classified as overhead, including material and labor not directly measurable to products for reasons of expediency. All company expenses not classified as factory overhead are period expenses, often referred to as SGA--selling, general, and administrative. The dividing line between SGA and factory overhead is loosely defined and actual practice varies widely, even in companies with several plants. The classification does not affect expense control because all departments are budgeted. It does affect the level of inventory cost on the balance sheet but the effect on cost of sales is limited to the periodic net change and is small. Product cost standards are lower, to a minor degree, by the exclusion of staff functions such as purchasing, accounting, and production control, which could be included only by arbitrary allocation.

All factory overhead is classified first by department-- responsibility accounting--and then by expense accounts designed to aid budgeting and expense control. Some examples:

Downtime for direct labor--time paid for but not charged to production. Segregated by cause. Production labor variance is a separate cost element.

Indirect labor--supervision, clerical, technical, inspection, cleaning, maintenance, rework, material handling. Number of accounts based on number of departments and need for detail.

Overtime premiums--for all labor.

Fringe benefits--one account for each type or a jumbo account. May be included in pay rates and thus not separately reported, but readily available in the records.

Indirect materials--closely related to products--glue, sandpaper, padding, casters.

Supplies--lubricants, maintenance, cleaning, laboratory, office, medical.

Utilities--electricity, steam, gas, water.
Telephone, telegraph, fax.
Scrap, waste, spoilage.
Travel, fees, postage, licenses.
Insurance, taxes, licenses.
Depreciation, amortization.

Department overhead totals are reported and summarized by responsibility. Expense accounts can be cross-totaled for all departments as a matter of general information but not for control.

All departments can be classified as office or service or production.

Office. Classification for a plant could be as follows: plant manager - product engineering - manufacturing engineering - industrial engineering - plant engineering - purchasing - production control - quality control - cost accounting - time keeping - personnel. These activities are conducted largely by salaried people working in offices and without any direct or continuing relationship to particular products or factory operations. Budgets are fixed and expense control is discretionary. These departments are often excluded from factory overhead, obviating the need for arbitrary allocation to product costs. When relevant to a decision, such as "make or buy," the effect on the alternative can be determined by incremental analysis.

Service. Departments directly support factory operations and contain both salaried people and hourly workers. Examples are: maintenance, stores, tool room, utilities, material handling, receiving, shipping, floor inspection. Flexible budgets are based on selected activities within a relevant range based on planned output levels. Expense control is exercised in advance for major changes in plans, such as hiring beyond the budget or overtime schedules. Monthly reports compare the expense accounts for actual and budget amounts. Service departments are allocated to production departments to determine overhead costing rates, not expense control. The allocation method is based on derived relationships of service departments to each other and to the production departments.

Production. Departments work directly on the product and have both direct and indirect labor. Direct labor time spent on production is measured by standards and the balance, downtime, is charged to overhead. The number and types of departments depend on the nature of the operations, size, and technology. Examples are: machining, wood-working, finishing, assembly, plating, crating, mixing. Budgets are based on production plans for the relevant range of activity. The rate of change in expense related to the rate of change in output, based on a selected causal factor, is a guide to budget flexibility to determine actual expense allowances for comparison with actual expenses. Monthly reports compare actual and budget by expense account. The budget allowance for each account may be fixed, fully variable relative to the activity base, or partly variable. Activity bases include direct labor time and direct labor earnings for productive time, machine time, material handled or processed, or some combination. Wholly automated processes have no direct labor; all labor is part of overhead. The monthly accounting reports provide formal summaries but actual expense control can be exercised only in real time during operations.

Variable and Fixed Expenses

Departmental expense budgets are prepared on the basis of planned activity levels for the coming year, known as the relevant range. Budgets are prepared for each account for each month, or other period, according to the planned output level and the degree of expense flexibility. These budgets serve as advance approval for expenses and for comparison with actual results. The budgets also provide the basis for calculating overhead rates to be applied to product costs, based on an estimate of production capacity known as practical capacity--an approximation of what output can be achieved relative to current technology and efficiency.

The relationship of expense to activity is not always clear. Relatively little overhead is fully variable or fully fixed; the major portion is mixed. In practice, budgets are arrived at by evaluation of plans and reasonable performance levels as determined by production and engineering personnel and subject to review by management. Past records are a source of information but a fallible guide to the future. Expense elements have widely varying characteristics. For example, some expenses:

    increase with activity in steps--supervision
    decrease with activity--clean-up, maintenance
    increase and decrease with usage levels--electricity rate schedules
    increase gradually and become fixed--rentals
    increase slowly--general supplies
    vary with purchases, not usage--expensed items
    An illustration is given for activity levels in units:

	Units	60	80	100	120
Expense Totals in Groups:					
Variable		$ 90	$120	$150	$180
Fixed		250	250	250	250
Mixed		440	510	600	650
Total		780	880	1,000	1,080
Per Unit:					
Variable		$1.50	$1.50	$1.50	$1.50
Fixed		4.17	3.13	2.50	2.08
Mixed		7.33	6.37	6.00	5.42
		$13.00	$11.00	$10.00	$9.00
Percents:					
Variable		11.5%	13.6%	15.0%	16.7%
Fixed		32.1	28.4	25.0	23.1
Mixed		56.4	58.0	60.0	60.2
		100.0	100.0	100.0	100.0

If 100 units is the base chosen for practical capacity, the total expense budget is $1,000 and the rate is $10 per unit. If output is actually 100 units, inventory is charged at the $10 rate with $1,000. If actual expense is $1,000 there is no variance. For output under or over 100 units it is necessary to separate variable and fixed expenses in the budget to determine both volume variance and expense variance. Volume variance is the difference between actual and planned units, times the budgeted fixed overhead rate. Expense variance is the difference between actual and budgeted expense--the actual output times the variable rate

plus the budgeted fixed expense. Thus, it is necessary to separate the $10 costing rate for 100 units into total variable and total fixed rates, which requires separation of the mixed overhead into the two categories. For 100 units, the rates are $1.50 variable, $2.50 fixed, and $6.00 mixed. The individual accounts in the mixed category have erratic patterns, as described above. There are several methods for separating the $600 into its two parts but only the simplest one is illustrated. The dollar difference divided by the unit differences yield the variable (V) rate, and the fixed (F) expense is then calculated:
Several combinations are calculated:

	Output Units	Total Mixed Dollars	V x Output = Variable Expense	Total - V = Fixed Expense
1.	120	$650	$300	$350
	100	600	250	350
	20	50		
	V rate $50/20 = $2.50			
2.	100	600	450	150
	80	510	360	150
	20	90		
	V rate $90/20 = $4.50			
3.	100	600	400	200
	60	440	240	200
	40	160		
	V rate $160/40 = $4.00			

The total budget for 100 units is computed for each trial:

		1	2	3
V	a)	$1.50	$1.50	$1.50
F	b)	2.50	2.50	2.50
Mixed		6.00	6.00	6.00
		10.00	10.00	10.00
Mixed V	a)	2.50	4.50	4.00
Mixed F	b)	3.50	1.50	2.00
Combined V	a)	4.00	6.00	5.50
Combined F	b)	6.00	4.00	4.50
		10.00	10.00	10.00

The budget formula for example 3 is: total overhead allowed = (V) actual output times $5.50 plus (F) $450 (250 + 200). The allowable budgets for each output level are compared with the original budgets:

Units	60	80	100	120
V at $5.50	$330	$440	$550	$660
F at $450	450	450	450	450
Allowable	780	890	1000	1110
Original	780	880	1000	1080
Difference	0	10	0	30

This arbitrary analysis is necessary to adjust allowed expenses for volume to aid expense control, reported at the account level. It is also necessary to measure volume variance. Both topics are explored in depth in subsequent chapters.

OVERHEAD RATES

Volume of Production

The formula established for the flexible budget was: V $5.50 times actual units plus F $450. The results of using this formula for given output levels are:

Units		60	80	100	120
	V	$330	$440	$550	$660
	F	450	450	450	450
		780	890	1000	1110
Rates					
	V	$5.50	$5.50	$5.50	$5.50
	F	7.50	5.62	4.50	3.75
		12.00	11.12	10.00	9.25

The question is what rate to use for product costing. For 60 units, the rate is $12.00 and for 120 units it is $9.25, or $3.75 less. The fixed overhead rate alone drops from $7.50 to $3.75. The overhead rate is used to determine volume variance, separate from expense variance, to signal the cost of available but unused capacity, a vital factor in planning and control.

The effect of several output levels is presented first to provide a basis for evaluation. Each output level in units is multiplied by the fixed overhead rate for that level to arrive at the total amount of fixed overhead absorbed--charged to inventory and credited to overhead. This amount is compared with the fixed budget to determine the difference-- underabsorbed is a debit (DR) to cost of sales and overabsorbed is a credit (CR).

These amounts exclude expense variance which is always computed separately.

80 Units: Fixed Rate $5.62

Actual Output	Absorbed	Budget	Volume Variance
120	$675	$450	$225 CR
100	562	450	112 CR
80	450	450	0
60	337	450	113 DR

100 Units: Fixed Rate $4.50

Actual Output	Absorbed	Budget	Volume Variance
120	$540	$450	$ 90 CR
100	450	450	0
80	360	450	90 DR
60	270	450	180 DR

120 Units: Fixed Rate $3.75

Actual Output	Absorbed	Budget	Volume Variance
120	$450	$450	$ 0
100	375	450	75 DR
80	300	450	150 DR
60	225	450	225 DR

Current sales are 60 units, and 80 units are budgeted for next year. 100 units could be produced with achievable labor efficiency based on planned volume, mix, and seasonality, and on available facilities and technology. Output at 120 units represents a theoretical maximum that does not allow for any practical limitations.

Use of 80 units--the sales plan--would result in zero variance if 80 units are made and sold. Lower output creates a debit, charged to cost of sales. Production over 80 units creates credits to cost of sales and inventory is overvalued. It must be written down to avoid a "bookkeeping" profit. Product cost includes the $5.62 charge for fixed overhead which enters into sales planning. The plant capacity of 100 units is not separately stated.

Use of 100 units--practical capacity--reduces the fixed costing rate from $5.62 to $4.50 and thus both inventory costs and product costs are lower. For output at 80 units, the sales plan, volume variance of $90 is shown, the cost of capacity provided but not used. This amount is charged to cost of sales. Inventory costs include the $4.50 rate, which represents "all the costs necessary for production." The use of the 100-unit capacity basis, rather than the 80-unit sales basis, represents investment in plant and people according to plans. There is often a significant lead time that results in the establishment of capabilities before their use because of the installation delays and uncertain sales demand. For instance, sales at 80 units are 80% of capacity at 100 units. As sales plans call for higher amounts, the supporting facilities must be put in place in a timely manner. To illustrate the process with two extreme points:

Units	Capacity	Sales	Percent
Norm	100	80	80%
Add 20%	--	16	
	100	96	96%
Add 50%	50	0	
	150	96	64%
Add 25%	--	24	
Average	150	120	80%

At 96% production capacity becomes strained at bottleneck points. Added capacity brings the utilization rate down to 64%. Thus, there is a 16-point range over and under 80%. The size and timing of these increments is basic to strategic planning. Overcapacity has costs measurable by volume variance. Inadequate capacity has costs associated with lost sales, overtime, subcontracting, work pressures, and performance inefficiencies.

The difference between practical capacity and planned production is volume variance, an important element in the budget. It represents the degree by which capacity is in place to handle rising volume. It is compared with actual volume variance to measure gains and losses against plan. Reasons for differences are as various as all the factors entering into the planning and budgeting. Because the responsibility for volume variance is diffused over several functional areas, it is reported as a separate item. The degree of investigation rests on the size of the variance and the possible benefit of analysis. Setting the practical capacity is a pragmatic problem resting on many factors, including shifting bottlenecks. The purpose is to have sound costing that is most constructive for measuring product profit margins and volume variance. With 100 units as the base, there is small likelihood of higher output and a credit variance. Short-term credit variances are not uncommon and require no correction if the year-end amount is not expected to be a credit.

Use of 120 Units represents a theoretical maximum. Debits arise for any output below 120 units. At 80 units the debit is $150 while the debit with the 100-unit base is $90. The $60 excess is meant, by purists, to prod management toward an impractical goal. Overstating the volume variance obscures the practical amount subject to useful analysis. The costing rate is understated, thus raising product profit margins and inflating volume variance. However, it is often difficult to set practical capacity closer than plus or minus 10%--a range from 90 to 110 units.

When capacity is available according to plans there is an opportunity to pick up additional business by pricing based on variable costs and ignoring the fixed costs (sunk) that exist in any event. Such decisions are the subject of incremental analysis, explored in the next chapter. A separate possibility exists in a decision to decrease volume variance, and increase profits, by production over planned needs. The profit gain must be related to the extra inventory holding cost, requiring a time estimate for sales, plus the question of shifting the volume variance to a future period. An example is offered for a representative product:

Unit standard cost:

Direct material	$10
Direct labor	5
Variable overhead	5
Variable costs	$20
Fixed overhead	5
Total costs	$25

Production of 20 units over needs:

Debit finished goods (20 x $25)	$500 Total
Credit inventory and payables (20 x $20)	400 Variable
Credit absorbed overhead (20 x $5)	100 Fixed

By increasing output from 80 to 100 units, the debit variance of $100 (20 units at $5) is eliminated and profit increased. The cost of carrying $500 in inventory at a marginal rate of 24% is $120 a year, or $10 a month. The break-even point is: $100 profit gain divided by $10 monthly carrying cost, or 10 months, based on accrual accounting. The decision to reduce current volume variance by production for stock over schedule can increase accounting profit for the period substantially but with conjectural effect for the future.

Departmental Overhead Rates

A single plant overhead rate for costing is sufficient when all production departments have the same rate, and if expense control is effective at that level. That is also the case if all products have relatively the same time in all departments even with differing costing rates. Plant overhead should be subdivided into departments, for both expense control and product costing, to the degree required for effective results. All expenses are assigned to departments according to established responsibilities. Budgets for service departments are allocated to production departments to determine costing rates, not for expense control. The resulting total overhead by production department is divided by an activity factor relevant to the expenses incurred, such as productive labor or machine time, to determine the costing rate. The departments may be subdivided into "cost centers" for more accurate product costing and better expense control. Actual overhead expenses are charged to a clearing account that is credited with absorbed (or applied) overhead charged to inventory--actual output, based on the activity factor, times the costing rate. The difference is some combination of expense variance, based on flexible budgets, and volume variance, based on planned output. Variances are charged to cost of sales as incurred and are not analyzed by product. Product margins are based on standard costs only. Variances relate to operating efficiency only.

The following example is for a plant with three cost centers. Overhead is based on units for convenience, rather than the more customary basis of labor or machine time. The cost center (CC) overhead totals include allocations from service departments. CC rates applied to units are comapred with the plant rate as follows:

	Plant	CC1	CC2	CC3
Overhead	$6,000	$2,640	$2,280	$1,080
Units	2,000	440	760	800
Rate per unit	$ 3.00	$ 6.00	$ 3.00	$ 1.35
Overhead at $3	$6,000	$1,320	$2,280	$2,400
CC over (under) plant rate	0	+1,320	0	-1,320

The effect of using CC rates rather than the plant rate for product costing is zero for CC2 but large for CC1 and CC3. The effect on product cost depends on the time in each CC. The following combination of CC outputs produces an average $3 rate:

	Units	Percent	CC Rate	Extension
CC1	440	22%	$6.00	$1.32
CC2	760	38%	3.00	1.14
CC3	800	40%	1.35	.54
Plant	2,000	100%		$3.00

If a product has equal time in all three CCs:

	Rate	One-third
CC1	$6.00	$2.00
CC2	3.00	1.00
CC3	1.35	.45
		$3.45 (Plant $3.00)

Product overhead cost is higher with the CC rates by $.45.

Many combinations are possible with product costs using CC rates differing from costs with the plant rate in varying degrees. Some combinations are given for 100 units to demonstrate the range of possible results.

Method of calculation--Product E is used for illustration--is as follows:

        CC1   60 units at $6.00 =$360
        CC2   20 units at $3.00 = 60
        CC3   20 units at $1.35 = 27
               100 units   447
        Plant 100 units at $3   300 + 147/300 = 49%

Products	CC1 - $6.00	CC2 - $3.00	CC3 - $1.35	CC Total	Over Plant	Percent on $300
A	100/600	--	--	600	+ 300	100%
B	--	100/300	--	300	+ 0	0
C	--	--	100/135	135	- 165	-55%
D	80/480	--	20/27	507	+ 207	69%
E	60/360	20/60	20/27	447	+ 147	49%
F	40/240	40/120	20/27	387	+ 87	29%
G	30/180	50/150	20/27	357	+ 57	19%
H	20/120	60/180	20/27	327	+ 27	9%
I	10/60	50/150	40/54	264	- 36	-12%
J	20/120	--	80/108	228	- 72	-24%
K	--	40/120	60/81	201	- 99	-33%
L	--	20/60	80/108	168	- 132	-44%

Use of a plant rate rather than CC rates can have a significant effect on profits, both in terms of expense control and product margins. With a plant budget, the individual expense accounts are budgeted in total and are stated in variable and fixed components based on the range of planned output--the relevant range. Actual expenses are charged to a single overhead control account which is credited with absorbed overhead--actual units made times the plant costing rate. The expense variance, a charge (credit) to cost of sales, is a measure of expense control. Work in CC1 has a budget based on $6 but credit is allowed only at $3, the plant rate, causing a built-in variance. This is not known because CCs are not established. The difference is illustrated for 1,000 units in CC1:

	Plant	CC1
Actual expense	$6,000	$6,000
Allowance at $3	3,000	
Allowance at $6		6,000
Expense variance	3,000	0

The plant basis indicates 100% expense variance but any attempt to reduce expenses would be counterproductive. The lower plant rate also causes a lower product cost with likely underpricing and misdirection of product profit planning. The lower pricing encourages more sales, and this exacerbates the expense control problem--a vicious circle.

CC2 has the same rate as the plant so there is equality by coincidence. CC3 has a $1.35 rate distorting both expense control and product costing in the opposite direction from CC1. For example, for 1,000 units:

	Plant	CC3
Actual expense	1,350	1,350
Allowance at $3	3,000	
Allowance at $1.35		1,350
Expense variance	1,650 CR	0

The reported expense saving is illusory and expense variances are disguised. Product costs are overstated, leading to overpricing and lower sales, with impaired profits.

The net effect on expense control using the plant rate rather than CC rates depends on the ratio of time in each CC. An equality, shown above, occurs for the following time ratios:

	Output	CC rate	
CC1	22%	$6.00	$1.32
CC2	38%	3.00	1.14
CC3	40%	1.35	.54
Plant	100%		3.00

Distortion exists to the extent that actual output time ratios depart from this equality, but this is an unknown, variable, and unpredictable factor. The upshot is misdirection of expense control and profit measurement--confusing and frustrating with a potentially serious loss of profits.

The effect of costing rates on product costs and prices is complex. Prices affect the quantity demanded relative to demand elasticity. Forecasting price-volume relationships is neat in microeconomics but messy in practice. Volume affects cost depending on the relationship of variable and fixed costs, expressed for a relevant range and limited period--an arbitrary analysis as explained above. An optimum (theoretical) profit is derived from some combination of price-volume-cost, but it must be measured against assets to determine ROA, the basic measure of operating profit. Asset requirements are variable with sales, particularly for receivables and inventories.

The effect of CC rates on product profits is illustrated with products $\underline{X}$, $\underline{Y}$ and $\underline{Z}$. The first profit plan is based on the plant costing

rate of $3. The second schedule develops product costing rates based on the CCs. The third schedule shows the profit plan restated for CC costing rates. Prime cost is direct material and direct labor: per unit - X $3 - Y $2 - Z $6. SGA is 30% of sales. Tax is 50% of profit.
Profit plan with plant costing rate of $3:

Products	X		Y		Z	Total	
Units	1,200		600		200	2,000	
Overhead	(3) $3,600	(3)	$1,800	(3)	$600	$6,000	
Prime cost	(3) 3,600	(2)	1,200	(6)	1,200	6,000	
Cost	(6) 7,200	(5)	3,000	(9)	1,800	12,000	
Margin	(6) 7,200	(5)	3,000	(9)	1,800	12,000	
Sales	(12) 14,400	(10)	6,000	(18)	3,600	24,000	100%
Margin	7,200		3,000		1,800	12,000	50%
SGA	4,320		1,800		1,080	7,200	30%
Profit	2,880		1,200		720	4,800	20%
Tax	1,440		600		360	2,400	10%
Net	1,440		$ 600		$ 360	$2,400	10%
Assets (turnover 2)						$12,000	
ROA							20%

Product costing rates based on CC rates:

The percentage of time for each product in each CC is multiplied by the CC rate and cross-totaled to arrive at a product rate:

Product	CC1 $6.00	CC2 $3.00	CC3 $1.35	CC Total	Plant Total
X	20%/1.20	80%/2.40	0	$3.60	$3.00
Y	4%/.24	16%/.48	80%/1.08	1.80	3.00
Z	11%/.66	69%/2.07	20%/.27	3.00	3.00

Profit plan restated with CC rates and cross-reference to (1):

Product Rate		X $3.60	Y $1.80	Z $3.00	Total
Units	(1)	1,200	600	200	2,000
Overhead		$4,320	$1,080	$ 600	$6,000
Prime cost	(1)	3,600	1,200	1,200	6,000
Cost		7,920	2,280	1,800	12,000
Sales	(1)	14,400	6,000	3,600	24,000
CC margin		6,480 45%	3,720 62%	1,800 50%	12,000 50%
Plant margin	(1)	7,200 50%	3,000 50%	1,800 50%	12,000 50%
		- 720 -5%	+ 720 +12%	0	0

The increase in overhead cost for product X from $3,600 to $4,320 drops the product margin by $720, or from 50 to 45% of sales. The decrease in overhead cost for product Y from $1,800 to $1,080 raises the product margin from $3,000 to $3,720, or from 50 to 62% of sales. Product Z is not affected, nor is the total margin. Product X appears to be underpriced with a 45% CC margin relative to the present 50% margin. The effect of a higher price on volume and costs should be explored relative to any possible improvement in ROA. Product Y appears to be overpriced with a 62% CC margin and should also be studied for the effect of a lower price.

A proposed plan for product X increases the price by 10% to $13.20 and number of units from 1,200 to 1,160. The overhead is variable (V) at $1.50 per unit and fixed cost (F) is $1,800. The proposal is compared with the present plan:

	Present Plan 1200 units			Proposed Plan 1160 units			Increments	%
Sales	$12.00	$14,400	100.0%	$13.20	$15,312	100.0%	$+912	6.3%
Prime cost	3.00	3,600		3.00	3,480			
V Overhead	1.50	1,800		1.50	1,740			
V Cost	4.50	5,400		4.50	5,220		- 180	
V Margin	7.50	9,000	62.5	8.70	10,092	65.9	+1092	12.1%
F Overhead		1,800			1,800			
Margin		7,200	50.0		8,292	54.2		
SGA fixed		4,320			4,320			
Profit		2,880	20.0		3,972	26.0	+1092	37.9%
Tax		1,440			1,986			
Net		1,440	10.0		1,986	13.0	+ 546	37.9%
Assets (turnover 2)		7,200	(turnover 2.08)		7,355		+ 155	2.2%
ROA		20%			27%		+ 352%	

Relatively small changes in sales and costs cause a very large jump in profit--37.9%--and in ROA, even with increased assets. The many variables in the proposal call for estimates of probable ranges and risk analysis. The unit sales decrease from 1,200 to 1,160 is small relative to the 10% price increase to $13.20. The $912 sales increase shows positive elasticity. One form of risk analysis is a break-even calculation to find the number of units at $13.20 that produce a variable margin of $9,000 thus eliminating the $1,092 gain. Calculation: $1,092 divided by V margin $8.70 = 125.5 units; 1,160 units minus 125.5 = 1,034.5 units; 1,034.5 units times $8.70 = $9,000; sales of 1,034.5 units times $13.20 = $13,655, a drop of $745 from $14,400; demand is inelastic. The safety margin for profit break-even is the reduction in units from 1,200 to 1,034.5, or 165.5 = 13.8%.

The proposal for product Y drops the price from $10.00 to $7.60 with a unit increase from 600 to 1000 units. The large sales jump from $6,000 to $7,600 indicates high elasticity. Overhead is V $1.00 and $1,200 F.

	Present Plan 600 units			Proposed Plan 1,000 units			Increments	%
Sales	$10.00	$6,000	100%	$7.60	$7,600	100%	+$1600	26.7%
Prime cost	2.00	1,200		2.00	2,000			
V Overhead	1.00	600		1.00	1,000			
V Cost	3.00	1,800		3.00	3,000		+ 1200	
V Margin	7.00	4,200	70	4.60	4,600	60.5	+ 400	9.5%
F Overhead		1,200			1,200			
Margin		3,000	50		3,400	44.7		
SGA-fixed		1,800			1,800			
Profit		1,200	20		1,600	21.0	+ 400	
Tax		600			800	10.5		
Net		$ 600	10		$ 800	10.5	+ 200	33.3%
Assets (turnover 2)		$3,000	(turnover 2.4)		$3,200		+ 200	6.7%
ROA		20%			25%		+ 100%	

   This increase in ROA of 5 points almost matches that for product X of
7 points, but arises from a price decrease. The test for a drop in units
to equal the present variable margin of $4,200 is computed as follows:
$400 divided by V margin $4.60 = 87 units; 1,000 - 87 = 913 units; 913
times $4.60 = $4,200. The unit increase from 600 to 913 provides no
profit gain. The gain in units from 600 to 1,000 provides $400 gain.
This is a narrow limit.
   In practice there are frequent opportunities to vary the combination
of factors to improve ROA, often substantially. This can be done
independently of other actions such as product cost reduction, expense
control, and asset management. Product margin and ROA analysis may lead
to dropping some products and retaining others scheduled for
elimination. The incremental approach to profit analysis is described in
the next chapter.

Overhead Rates for Material

   The analysis to this point has related all factory overhead to
products using CC rates applied to units, with emphasis on product cost
differentials. In some cases it is constructive to develop separate
costing rates for material, in addition to the CC rates, to refine
product cost measurement and expense control. The procedure is to study
all factory operations and separate out, by department and expense
account, the amounts applicable to materials such as buying, inspecting,
receiving, storing, handling, and waste. These amounts are then related
to types of material on a selected basis such as material cost, weight,
size, physical characteristics, or a factored base. The material
overhead application rates are applied to purchases by debit to inventory
and credit to applied material overhead. The inventory amounts are
carried at the combined amount of purchase cost and material overhead.
The balance of factory overhead is expressed as CC rates, applied to
production and credited to applied production overhead. The net effect
is to revise the amounts of overhead charged to products and credited to
department expense. The rates developed are necessarily arbitrary but
can be enlightening.
   An illustration first presents three products with all overhead
applied by CC without recognition of material overhead. The product
overhead rates are given without break-out by CC and are applied to units:

Products	A	B	C	Total
Units	400	600	800	1800
CC Rate	$7	$5	$4	(5)
Overhead--Total	$2800	$3000	$3200	$9000
Material	4200	3000	4800	12000
Labor	400	1000	1600	3000
Cost	7400	7000	9600	24000
Margin	7400	7000	9600	24000
Sales	$14,800	$14,000	$19,200	$48,000

   A study of overhead is made to break out material overhead and revise
the CC rates to determine the effect on product costs and sales.

Products	A	B	C	Total
Units	400	600	800	1800
CC Rate--revised	$5	$4	$3.50	
Process Overhead	$2000	$2400	$2800	$7200
Material Overhead new	1290	110	400	1800
Total Overhead revised	3290	2510	3200	9000
Material	4200	3000	4800	12000
Labor	400	1000	1600	3000
Cost	7890	6510	9600	24000
Sales (50% margin)	15780	13020	19200	48000
Present Sales	14800	14000	19200	48000
Change	+$980	-$980	-	-
Percent	+6.62%	-7.00%		

Total overhead of $9,000 consists of material $1,800 and process $7,200. The CC rates are lower in unequal proportions. The material rates are shown for the total of all materials used in each product:

	A	B	C	Total
Material overhead	$1,290	$ 110	$ 400	1,800
Material	4,200	3,000	4,800	12,000
Rate	30.71%	3.67%	8.33%	15.0%

In practice a separate rate would be established for each material. The new product cost is doubled to determine the revised sales amounts with a 50% margin. Product A appears to be underpriced while product B is overpriced. The effect of price changes on ROA must be explored as described above. The ranges illustrated are wide but do occur in practice.

In the example all the products sold are manufactured by the company. For sales of products purchased and resold without processing it is particularly important to segregate all factory overhead between production and material. To illustrate, all processed products are presented in total and all purchased products, sold without processing, are also given in total:

	Process	Purchase	Total
Sales	$8,000	$2,000	$10,000
Cost:			
Material	1,600	800	2,400
Labor	1,200	0	1,200
Overhead	2,400	0	2,400
Total	5,200	800	6,000
Margin	$2,800	$1,200	$4,000
Percent	35.0%	60.0%	40.0%

It appears that process costs are too high. Analysis of overhead finds that total overhead of $2,400 includes $400 for material and $2,000 for processing. The schedule is recast:

	Process	Purchase	Total
Sales	$8,000	$2,000	$10,000
Cost:			
Material	1,600	800	2,400
Labor	1,200	0	1,200
Overhead	2,000	400	2,400
Total	4,800	1,200	6,000
Margin	$3,200	$ 800	$4,000
Percent	40.0%	40.0%	40.0%

The relatively small change in overhead allocation drastically alters the margin percents.

The exploration of overhead relative to material illustrates the necessity for careful analysis of operations and determination of cause-and-effect relationships. The process is unavoidably arbitrary in both expense segregation and product application. However, approximations can provide useful guidelines to product cost differentials. Sharper pricing and better expense control can contribute significantly to ROA.

STANDARD PRODUCT COST DETAIL

Standard product costs have a central role in profit measurement, expense control, and inventory valuation. The details should be carefully organized to serve the needs of different users. They should be kept on a current basis for major changes and brought up to date periodically, at least annually. A product history of standard unit costs, prices, and sales volume is a valuable reference.

Standard product costs are particularly consequential to profit planning. They are the equivalent of a quoted price by manufacturing to marketing. If product pricing based on the competitive situation shows a low margin the product may be dropped, while large margins encourage extra sales effort. The combined effect on product mix and volume affects costs in turn. Changes in costs require reconsideration of profit margins. The process is circular. Sales planning needs both current costs and ranges of cost expectations. Actual sales and costs differ from plans and call for close evaluation.

Standard product cost details are described as follows:

Product Cost Schedule

Direct Materials:
Source - Type - Quantity - Price - Totals.
Price is weighted average of vendor prices, plus equalization for freight and discount, plus overhead applied by material type.

Direct Labor:
Department - CC - Operation - Time - Rate - Totals.
Time is standard productive time. The rate is a weighted average. A factor may be added for fringe benefits, otherwise included in overhead.

Overhead:
Material: Type - Purchase Cost - OH rate (V+F) - Totals.
Process: Department - CC - OH rate (V+F) - Totals.
Application basis: standard labor time or dollars, machine time, units

Product Total:
    Additional items may be needed such as:
    Packed for export
    Extra parts supplied
    Factory test runs for customers
    Special finishing
    Installation

A separate schedule for overhead detail is presented for three service departments supporting three production departments using budgets based on the planned volume of material purchases and production. The service department allocations are sequential and the bases used are omitted. (Bases used in practice include number of people, square feet, wages, number of requisitions, machine hours, all selected to achieve logical costing rates.) The total budget is first allocated to material in total but the amounts of material and application rates are not given. The budgeted overhead allocated to production is presented in detail with rates based on planned standard labor.

	Service			Production			
	A	B	C	1	2	3	Total
Total Budget:							
V	$1000	$500	$ 0	$2000	$4000	$4500	$12000
F	1500	2000	1500	600	5000	2000	18000
T	2500	2500	1500	8000	9000	6500	30000
Allocated to Material:							
V	600	300	0	600	350	150	2000
F	500	500	500	400	550	550	3000
Total Material	1100	800	500	1000	900	700	5000

Material overhead applied to individual materials with dollar rates.

Allocated to Production:	A	B	C	1	2	3	Total
V	$400	$200	$ 0	$1400	$3650	$4350	$10000
F	1000	1500	1000	5600	4450	1450	15000
Process	1400	1700	1000	7000	8100	5800	25000
Close A:							
V	-400	100	0	100	100	100	
F	-1000	200	100	200	300	200	
	-1400	300	100	300	400	300	
	0	2000	1100	7300	8500	6100	25000
Close B:							
V		-300	100	100	50	50	
F		-1700	400	500	400	400	
		-2000	500	600	450	450	
		0	1600	7900	8950	6550	25000
Close C:							
V			-100	50	50	0	
F			-1500	0	1000	500	
			-1600	50	1050	500	
Total Process			0	7950	10000	7050	25000
Recap:							
V				1650	3850	4500	10000
F				6300	6150	2550	15000
Applied by CC				$7950	$10000	$7050	$25000
Planned standard labor				$1000	$2500	$3000	$6500

Process rates:

V	1.65	1.54	1.50
F	6.30	2.46	.85
T	$7.95	$4.00	$2.35

This degree of detail seems formidable but is necessary for clarity and communication, and to avoid the "black box" reaction. It supports the summary listings for overhead on the product cost schedule, namely, OH rate for each CC, both V and F. The schedule provides clear answers to any questions on overhead. The budgets are given for every department with V and F amounts given separately. All allocations are shown, so that direct and indirect charges are separated. The distinction between material and production overhead is clear. The wide range of CC rates from the average emphasizes the need for close analysis. The total overhead related to material is $5,000 but application rates by type of material are omitted. A summary of CC overhead by both V and F is given above. A separate schedule is given to break out direct and indirect amounts and rates:

		1	Rate	2	Rate	3	Rate	Total	Memo- Rate Avg.
Standard labor		$1,000	Rate	$2500	Rate	$3000	Rate	$6.50	Avg.
Production overhead:									
Direct	V	$1400	$1.40	$3650	$1.46	$4350	$1.45	$9400	$1.45
	F	5600	5.60	4450	1.78	1450	.48	11500	1.77
		7000	7.00	8100	3.24	5800	1.93	20900	3.22
Service	V	250	.25	200	.08	150	.05	600	.09
	F	700	.70	1700	.68	1100	.37	3500	.54
		950	.95	1900	.76	1250	.42	4100	.63
Combine	V	1650	1.65	3850	1.54	4500	1.50	10000	1.54
	F	6300	6.30	6150	2.46	2550	.85	15000	2.31
		7950	7.95	10000	4.00	7050	2.35	25000	3.85

This schedule summarizes the service overhead allocations. Distinctions between direct and indirect overhead and between V and F expenses are often useful. The product cost summary emphasizes unit product cost, not the underlying rates.

The details given can ·be arranged editorially to suit user needs. Sales planners can readily adapt to cost changes such as material substitutions, vendor prices, labor rates, and overhead revisions. Questions on the legitimacy of any cost element can be readily handled.

Another schedule is a useful reference--a list of all SGA departments and budgets. These expenses are not allocated to products but are covered by mark-up on cost for profit planning.

PRICE-COST RELATIONSHIPS

Margin Measurement

The product costing detail described above is related to prices for several products in the following schedule:

VC is variable cost--direct material, direct labor, and variable overhead, both direct and indirect (allocated). VM is variable margin. F. OH direct is incurred in the CC, and F. OH indirect is allocated. SGA is selling, general, and administrative expense--fixed and not allocated.

Product	1	2	3	4	5	Total	Percent
Sales	$1000	$2000	$3000	$4000	$5000	$15,000	100%
VC	1000	1000	1000	1000	1250	5,250	
VM	0	1000	2000	3000	3750	9,750	65%
F. OH direct	500	1000	1000	1000	1000	4,500	
Gross	(500)	0	1000	2000	2750	5,250	35%
F. OH indirect	500	500	1000	500	500	3,000	
Margin	($1000)	($500)	$ 0	$1500	$2250	2,250	15%
SGA						1,500	10%
Profit						750	5%
Tax						300	2%
Net						$ 450	3%
					Assets	5,000	
					ROA	9%	

Product 1. VC is the equivalent of a cash outlay; by definition this amount is spent in direct proportion to sales. When price equals VC, it is said to be "trading dollars." F. OH direct is incurred in the CC and does not vary with volume.   F. OH indirect is incurred in service departments and allocated to CCs on the basis of service to be rendered. The resolution of overhead into V and F components depends on time and volume assumptions.   The CC overhead costing rate is based on a selected CC activity factor. The loss of $1,000 is failure to recover any F. OH.
Product 2. The VM covers F. OH direct but F. OH indirect is not recovered.
Product 3. The VM covers all F. OH and the margin is zero.
Product 4.   The VM covers all F. OH and provides a margin of $1,500. At this point the cum results for the four products are:

Sales	$10,000
VC	4,000
VM	6,000
F. OH Direct	3,500
Gross	2,500
F. OH Indirect	2,500
Margin	0

Product 5. Sales of $5,000 provide $2,250 margin, also the margin of total sales of $15,000. Net income of $450 on total assets of $5,000 is 9% ROA, all earned on product 5.
The schedule demonstrates the necessity for the breakout of product groups into product lines and separate products. A guideline is a separate margin analysis in all cases where standard product costs differ, regardless of prices, and where prices differ, regardless of costs.   There are cases where product distinctions call for different prices, but there is only one product cost. There are also cases where product costs differ but there is only one sales price. Such detail is essential for disclosing the internal dynamics of profit results, as illustrated for the five products above.

Study of alternatives to improve ROA is based on incremental analysis, fully described in the next chapter. The bookkeeping system underlying the reports states the results in terms of conventional accounting. Analysis of change must consider factors that cannot be kept in the records as a matter of practicality.

Product pricing is a critical and continuing challenge to management. It is a matter of both broad policy and pragmatic response to recurring pressures. Macroeconomics has no theory of pricing. Microeconomics offers definitive models of price relative to demand (elasticity), cost relative to volume (incremental), and marginal relationships, among other topics. These data are difficult to apply in practice but provide guiding principles. Managerial economics attempts to bridge the gap by providing practical guidance on decision making. Managerial accounting is cost accounting with emphasis on the future-- the use of accounting for profitability analysis. Ideally, pricing is directed toward obtaining the "optimum" ROA; price-volume-cost-assets. In practice, optimum is a concept that is indeterminate, but improvement can be planned and measured. Pricing is only one factor in the marketing program that includes other factors: design, quality, suitability, service, delivery, terms, promotion, warranty, and salesmanship.

ROA Combinations

One approach to pricing is based on the improvement of ROA by combinations of price, volume, cost, and assets. The following illustration shows five pricing alternatives for a product with price-volume amounts (elasticity) and volume-cost based on VC at $4 for all cases and F. OH at $400.

The cost total is adjusted for changes in net current assets but not for output capacity.

	1	2	3	4	5
Quantity-Price	100-$10	95 -$12	90 - $15	80 - $20	50 - $25
Sales	$1,000	$1,140	$1,350	$1,600	$1,250
VC at $4	400	380	360	320	200
VM	600	760	990	1,280	1,050
F. OH	400	400	400	400	400
Margin	200	360	590	880	650
Assets	$2,000	$2,140	$2,270	$2,430	$2,240
ROA	10.0%	16.8%	26.0%	36.2%	29.0%

As price increases, the sales quantity falls. Sales are elastic to 4 but drop off at 5. With VC constant at the $4 rate, VM rises to 4 and dips for 5. With constant F. OH margins are lower but differences are unchanged. Assets are adjusted for changed receivables and inventories. ROA increases sharply to 4 but falls off at 5, but 5 at 29% is higher than 3 at 26%. The example is simplified and magnified for exposition.

ROA is a valid measure of profit, both actual and planned, but one year is a very short time frame. Strategy may stress growth and a target market share over short-term performance. This goal may best be served by the low $10 price, high volume sales at 100 units, and low 10% ROA. The objective is to enjoy the profitability that can be realized only by dominant market position and economies of scale. The lower profit

accepted in this growth period is a form of opportunity cost. It is the
equivalent of a capital expenditure plan--below par profit over time
recouped by above par profit in the future.

Pricing by Cost Markup

Custom-made products are priced on the basis of costs estimated to
meet customer specifications. The required materials, labor, and
overhead are calculated from tables of data for cost elements, and new
estimates are prepared as necessary. These amounts are, in effect,
standards for each order and can be used for expense control as well as
profit performance when the order is completed. Variances from the
estimates are carried in inventory for each job and expensed when
billing is made. The following example omits many special cost factors
such as freight, special packaging, royalties, and agent fees.

<table>
<tr><td colspan="2">Cost Estimate Summary</td></tr>
<tr><td>Direct material</td><td>$100</td></tr>
<tr><td>Direct labor</td><td>60</td></tr>
<tr><td>V. OH</td><td>80</td></tr>
<tr><td></td><td>240</td></tr>
<tr><td>F. OH</td><td>60</td></tr>
<tr><td>Cost</td><td>300</td></tr>
<tr><td>Expense mark-up 50%</td><td>150</td></tr>
<tr><td></td><td>450</td></tr>
<tr><td>Profit--10% on price</td><td>50</td></tr>
<tr><td>Formula price</td><td>500</td></tr>
<tr><td>High price</td><td>550</td></tr>
</table>

A quotation at $500 would be routine in most cases. Reasons for
quoting a higher price could include disposing of a solicitation not
considered to be serious; avoiding an undesirable customer; delaying
action because of plant overload; belief that the higher price will be
accepted or a counteroffer received. Reasons for quoting a lower price
include need for the order to utilize available capacity and avoid
layoffs; pressure to please a customer with an unusual request;
competitive bidding for a new customer; low pricing to introduce a new
product or to meet a charitable request.

It is useful to maintain a schedule of the shop workload, by CC and
by period for orders accepted, plus orders quoted that are expected to be
obtained. The schedule should be updated promptly as a guide to bidding
to utilize available capacity and to avoid overbooking that would cause
serious shipping delays or extra costs.

It is also helpful to maintain an order log for all orders accepted
to use for production scheduling and another log for all quotations still
open as a basis for planning. A third log should be made for all orders
lost as a guide to pricing and the competitive situation.

Date	Bid #	Customer	Lost Order Log Formula Price	Price Quoted	Reason Lost
			$ 600	$ 660	price shopper
			820	820	competition
			900	800	?
			500	480	price too high
			750	700	delivery date not met
			860	920	counteroffer 800
			675	625	business closed
			880	820	make own product
			900	875	pending too long
			480	480	dissatisfied w/quality
			770	770	relocating
			690	690	using single supplier
			810	810	change in plans

Reasons are not always available or clear, but customer reactions are worth tracking as well as competitive practices.

7

Evaluation of Alternatives

BREAK-EVEN (B-E) ANALYSIS

The relationships among sales price, quantity, variable cost, and fixed cost determine profit. When profit is zero it is called the break-even point, or B-E. For analysis the elements are varied to learn the effect on profits. When profit is positive the decline in sales to reach B-E can be measured and expressed as the safety margin (SM). Combinations of elements and profits can be compared to help select the most desirable plan among the feasible alternatives. The accounting classifications and relevant output ranges are not directly usable for B-E analyses. Variable and fixed costs include both product and period expenses, and both direct and traceable expenses. Taxes are omitted because they do not affect the evaluation. Assets are omitted when they are not directly related, or traceable, to the analysis to a significant degree. Risk analysis is also omitted but the safety margin (SM) is a measure of risk for comparative purposes. After B-E evaluation, choices can be further analyzed for ROA and risk. Taxes are introduced when their recognition is appropriate. B-E is a useful tool for quick appraisals at the detail level for the short term, but subject to the limitations of linear relationships, timing and volume assumptions, and cost patterns. Relationships between price and quantity, or market elasticity, are particularly important. It is assumed that sales and production units are equal, that is, no change in inventory.

The B-E Model

A basic example is used to illustrate the technique:

	Units	at	Total	Percent
S Sales	125	$10	$1250	100%
VC Variable Cost	125	6	750	60
VM Variable Margin	125	4	500	40
FC Fixed Cost			400	32
PR Profit			$100	8

The sales price of $10 produces sales of 125 units. The variable cost of $6 includes all costs that vary fully with units, both direct and indirect but traceable. VM is then S less VC. Fixed cost remains unchanged by definition, both as to time and output, and includes both direct and traceable indirect costs. Both VC and FC contain allocations. The format does not correspond with customary profit statements; it is an abbreviated method.

The calculation of B-E is as follows:

```
     FC     $400
     VM     $  4   = 100 units.  At $10 = $1,000 sales
OR   FC     $400
     VM %    40%  = $1,000 sales     $1,000/$10 = 100 units
```

The percentage method must be used when unit amounts are not relevant because sales include items with different prices.

By working backward from zero profit:

Steps		Units	at	Total	Percent
5		100	$10	$1,000	100%
4		100			
3	VM	100	4	400	40%
2	FC			400	
1	PR			0	

Use of a model helps to derive answers from the known elements.

The safety margin (SM) measures the drop in sales that causes zero profit:

	Units	Dollars
S	125	$1,250
B-E	100	1,000
Decrease	25	$ 250
SM	20%	20%

This single expression is an indicator of risk that may be of some value in comparing alternatives.

The model is restated with S $1,250 (1), VM $500 (2), and PR $100 (3) but with different units and price:

	Units	at	Total	Percent
S	100	$12.50	$1,250 (1)	100%
VC	100	7.50	750	60
VM	100	5.00	500 (2)	40
FC			400	32
PR			$100 (3)	8

```
B-E:  FC $400
      VM $  5  = 80 units.  At $12.50 = S $1,000.

      FC $400
      VM  40%  = S $1,000.  Divided by $12.50 = 80 units.
      SM:  $1,250 - $1,000 = $250 = 20%
```

Elasticity is unitary:

125 units at $10 = $1,250
100 units at $12.50 = $1,250

Profit, B-E, and SM are unchanged. VC increases from $6 to $7.50 per unit, with VM rising from $4 to $5. FC is not changed. Thus, the price increase of 25% results in a unit decrease of 20% with sales and profit unchanged. This requires that unit VC increase from $6 to $7.50 which is contrary to the basic assumption that VC per unit is constant. This could happen in practice if variable costs for labor, material, and other elements increase because of inflation or other causes. It would then be necessary to increase the price to maintain the profit. The critical factor is the elasticity effect of the price increase. With a derived number of 100 units, judgment can be exercised as to its feasibility. At 80 units profit is zero. Several examples illustrate the flexibility of B-E in probing alternatives.

Examples of Price-Unit Changes

Increase price 20% To $12. Decrease units 20 to 100:   VC $6 and FC $400 unchanged.

	Units	at	Total	Percent	Model	Change
S	100	$12	$1200	100%	$1250	- $50
VC	100	6	600	50	750	- 150
VM	100	6	600	50	500	+ 100
FC			400		400	0
PR			200	16.7%	100	+ 100

Profit doubles with a small sales decrease (inelastic).

B-E: $\dfrac{\$400}{\$6}$ = 66 2/3 units. At $12 = S $800.

SM: $1,200 - $800 = $400 = 33-1/3%. Up from 20%.

Increase price 30% to $13. Decrease units 28% to 90. VC $6 and FC $400 unchanged.

	Units	at	Total	Percent	Model	Change
S	90	$13	$1170	100%	$1250	- $80
VC	90	6	540		750	- 210
VM	90	7	630	53.8%	500	+ 130
FC			400		400	0
PR			230	19.7%	100	+ 130

B-E: $\dfrac{\$400}{\$7}$ = 57+ units. At $13 = S $743.

SM: $1,170 - 743 = 427 = 36.5%. Up from 20%.

Sales elasticity is negative but profit exceeds the model by $130, and the first example by $30.
Decrease price 20% to $8. Increase units 20% to 150. VC $6 and FC $400 unchanged.

	Units	at	Total	Percent	Model	Change
S	150	$ 8	$1200	100%	$1250	- $50
VC	150	6	900		750	- 150
VM	150	2	300	25%	500	- 200
FC			400		400	0
PR			- 100	- 8.3%	100	- 200

B-E: $400
      $ 2 = 200 units. At $8 = S $1600.
SM: 1200 - 1600 = -400 Negative.

Sales must increase by 50 units (200-150) to reach B-E.
   Increase price 10% to $11. Profit goal $100. How many units?

Steps		Units	at	Total	Model	Change
5	S	100	$11	$1100	$1250	-$ 150
4	VC		6	600	750	- 150
3	VM	100	5	500	500	0
2	FC			400	400	0
1	PR			100	100	0

B-E: $400
      $ 5 = 800 units. At $11 = S $880.
SM: $1,100 - 880 = 220 = 20%.

In this example the model is used by inserting the data given and deriving the unknowns.

$$\text{PR} \qquad \$100$$
$$\text{FC} \qquad \underline{\quad 400 \quad} \qquad 500$$
$$\text{divided by VM } \$5 = 100 \text{ units at } \$11 - \$1,100.$$

The higher $11 price decreases units and S drops by $150, but profit is unchanged. The model has a lower price and more units for higher sales, and could be the preferred choice.

   Sell 160 units, 28% more than 125 units. Profit goal $80. What price?

Steps		Units	at	Total	Model	Change
5	S	160	$9	$1440	$1250	+ $190
4	VC	160	6	960	750	+ 210
3	VM	160	3	480	500	- 20
2	FC			400	400	0
1	PR			80	100	- 20

B-E: $400
      $ 3 = 133 1/3 units. At $9 = $1,200.
SM: $1,440 - 1200 = 240 = 16.7%.

The 28% gain in units requires a $9 price--10% less than $10. Sales increase by 15.2%--$190/1,250--a high degree of elasticity, and SM is low at 16.7%. This example could illustrate the objective of higher market share at lower profit.
  Price drops from $10 to $9. Profit goal $200. How many units?

Steps		Units	at	Total	Model	Change
5	S	200	$9	$1800	$1250	+$ 550
4	VC	200	6	1200	750	+ 450
3	VM	200	3	600	500	+ 100
2	FC			400	400	0
1	PR			200	100	+ 100

B-E: $400
      $ 3 = 133 1/3 units. At $9 = $1,200.
SM: S $1,800 - 1200 = 600 = 33-1/3%.

Units at 200 are 60% higher than 125, an unlikely degree of elasticity.
  Profit goal $225. Units remain at 125. What price?

Steps		Units	at	Total	Model	Change
5	S	125	$11	$1375	$1250	+$ 125
4	VC	125	6	750	750	0
3	VM	125	5	625	500	+ 125
2	FC			400	400	0
1	PR			225	100	+ 125

B-E: $400
      $ 5 = 800 units. At $11 = 880.
SM: S $1,375 - 880 = 495 = 36%.

This large gain in profit poses the problem of selling the same number of units at a higher price--$11 compared with $10, an unlikely prospect.
  The alternative solution method is:

```
PR              $225
FC               400      $625
Units - divide            125    =    VM  $5
                                      VC   6
                                   Price  11
```

  This example illustrates the percentage method used when unit price and unit cost are not known. PR Goal 8%. VM 40%. FC $400.

Step 1 - Data Given			Step 2 - Complete Percents	
S		100%		100%
VC				60%
VM		40%		40%
FC	$400		$400	32%
PR		8%		8%

Then: $400/32% = $1,250 sales, and 60% = $750, and 40% = $500.

```
S                   $1250      100%
VC                    750        60
VM                    500        40
FC                    400        32
PR                    100         8
```

B-E: $400
      ---- = $1,000
       40%
SM: 1,250 - 1,000 = 250 = 20%.

This result is the original model but units are not specified.
    When the analysis relates to a group of products with different units
and unit amounts, the total units may be given for reference but the unit
amounts are weighted averages.
    To illustrate the mix effect, three products are assumed to comprise
the model.

	Desks	Tables	Chairs	Total
Units	5	10	35	50
Price	$100	$ 40	$ 10	$(25)
Sales	$500	$400	$350	$1250

The weighted average price of $25 is not useful. Total units may be
shown for reference. (Product line analysis is presented later in this
section.)
    These examples have been limited for clarity to the effect of
elasticity, holding unit VC and total FC unchanged.

Examples of Changes in VC and FC

Costs may change because of external causes--material prices, labor
rates, utility charges, taxes--or for internal reasons--product design,
technological changes, output efficiency, research, advertising, or
employment levels. VC may change because agents who are paid fees for
sales may replace salaried salespeople, or vice versa. FC may increase
because of higher advertising expenditures. VC may decrease because of
higher efficiency achieved through higher FC. FC may increase for more
research or greater output capacity to achieve longer-range goals. Thus,
there is a mix of time horizons and trade-offs between unit VC and total
FC. These relationships can be explored with B-E.

Sales--125 units at $10. VC is reduced from $6 to $5 per unit. FC
is increased from $400 to $525. How much profit?

	Units	at	Total	Model	Change
S	125	$10	$1250	$1250	$ 0
VC	125	5	625	750	- 125
VM	125	5	625	500	+ 125
FC			525	400	+ 125
PR			100	100	0

B-E: $525
$\overline{\$\ 5}$ = 105 units. At $10 = $1,050.
SM: S $1,250 - 1,050 = 200 = 16%.

The added investment in FC lowers VC but PR is unchanged and SM drops from 20 to 16%.

Profit goal $225. FC $525. Price $10. 125 units. What VC per unit?

Steps		Units	at	Total	Model	Change
5	S	125	$10	$1250	$1250	0
4	VC	125	4	500	750	- 250
3	VM	125	6	750	500	+ 250
2	FC			525	400	+ 125
1	PR			225	100	+ 125

B-E: $525
$\overline{\$\ 6}$ = 87.5 units. At $10 = S $875.
SM: S $1,250 - 875 = 375 = 30%.

The higher FC must reduce VC to $4 per unit from $5.

Profit goal $250. VC $8 per unit. Price $10. Units 125. How much FC?

	Units	at	Total	Model	Change
S	125	$10	$1250	$1250	$ 0
VC	125	8	1000	750	+ 250
VM	125	2	250	500	- 250
FC			0	400	- 400
PR			250	100	+ 150

B-E: $0
$\overline{\$2}$ = 0

FC at zero is not possible. If FC remains at $400 the loss is $150. If FC is reduced to $250 the profit is zero, or B-E. To reach PR $250 with $400 FC or $650/2 = 325 units, not a practical prospect. Or, with FC $400 and PR $250: $650/125 units = VM $5.20, plus VC $8 = price $13.20:

	Units	at			
S	125	at $13.20	=		$1650
VC	125	at $ 8.00	=		1000
VM	125	at $ 5.20	=		650

This example shows the nature and extent of the problems of dealing with a big jump in VC and finding a feasible combination of price and units relative to FC.

Profit goal $200. FC increase from $400 to $600 for sales promotion. Price $10. How many units?

	Units	at	Total	Model	Change
S	200	$10	$2000	$1250	+$750
VC	200	6	1200	750	+ 450
VM	200	4	800	500	+ 300
FC			600	400	+ 200
PR			200	100	+ 100

B-E: $\dfrac{$600}{$4}$ = 150 units. At $10 = $1,500.

SM: S $2,000 - 1,500 = 500 = 25%.

Units must increase by 60% or 125 to 200--with the sales promotion. Profit doubles from $100 to $200. With 175 units, profit remains at $100:

$$\begin{array}{l} 175 \text{ at } \$4 = \$700 \text{ VM} \\ \underline{\hspace{1.2cm} 600} \text{ FC} \\ \hspace{1cm} 100 \text{ PR} \end{array}$$

A combination example: Price drops from $10 to $9. Units increase from 125 to 150. VC drops from $5 to $4 per unit. FC increases from $400 to $650. How much profit?

	Units	at	Total	Model	Change
S	150	$ 9	$1350	$1250	+$100
VC	150	4	600	750	- 150
VM	150	5	750	500	+ 250
FC			650	400	+ 250
PR			100	100	0

B-E: $\dfrac{$650}{$5}$ = 130 units. At $9 = $1,170.

SM: S $1,350 - 1170 = 180 = 13.3%.

The gain in VM is offset by higher FC.

Product Line Analysis

B-E analysis for a product line is the weighted average of the individual products but with FC not allocated:

	A	B	C	Total
Sales				
Units	10	30	100	(140)
Price	$20	$10	$ 5	($7.14)
Total	$200	$300	$500	$1000
VC	100	180	350	630
VM	$100	$120	$150	$ 370
Percent	50%	40%	30%	37%
FC				$ 222
PR				$ 148

B-E: $\underline{\$222}$
 37% = $600 sales
SM: $1,000 - 600 = 400 = 40%

   B-E and SM are relevant to the total only, as a weighted average. Total units of 140 and the average price of $7.14 are not part of the analysis. VC for A, B, and C is both direct and traceable and includes both product and period expenses. FC for the total is also direct and traceable to the product line and includes both product and period expenses. Further allocation to the products would be arbitrary and misleading. These classifications do not follow the customary reporting format; they are directed toward relevance for analysis.
   Changes in the product prices and units, with VM percents and FC unchanged, illustrate the effect on B-E:

	A	B	C	Total
Sales				
Units	50	30	20	(100)
Price	$10	$10	$10	($10)
Total	$500	$300	$200	$1000
VC	250	180	140	570
VM	$250	$120	$ 60	$ 430
Percent	50%	40%	30%	43%
FC				$ 222
PR				208

B-E: $\underline{\$222}$
 43% = $516 sales
SM: $1,000 - 516 = 484 = 48.4%

   The profit change arises from the effect of the VM percents on the change in sales:

A   S + 300 at 50% = $150
B   S +   0 at 40% =   0
C   S - 300 at 30% = - 90
 Change   + 60
 First plan   +148
 Second plan   208

INCREMENTAL ANALYSIS

   Alternatives can be evaluated by analyzing the changes, or increments, in both profit and assets to determine the incremental ROA. These ROAs can be compared with each other and the discount rate. All the elements changed by the alternative are determined by analysis and set out as increments for increases, or decrements for decreases. Costs that do not change can be omitted because they are not relevant. They are called "sunk" costs or "unavoidable" costs for that particular analysis. Increments may be shown net or with the present and proposed amounts expressed, called "differential" analysis. The changes in revenue, costs, and assets attributable to an alternative can be arrived at only by close study. The components of product cost used for the records, based on factors of direct-indirect and fixed-variable are not applicable but may be useful for reference. The alternatives chosen become part of the budget when taxes are applied. Risk and liquidity are separately evaluated.

The following examples illustrate a variety of applications in breif form.

Increase Receivables and Inventories

The purpose is to increase sales by extended terms from 36 to 72 days as a form of price reduction and by doubled inventories to expedite delivery:

	Present	Alternative	Increment
Sales	$80,000	$100,000	$ 20,000
Cost--80%	64,000	80,000	16,000
Margin--20%	16,000	20,000	4,000
Expenses			2,800
Gain			1,200

Receivables:

       $ 80,000 - 36d (1/10) $ 8,000
       $100,000 - 72d (1/5) $20,000   + $12,000

Inventories (net of payables):

       $ 64,000 - 45d (1/8) $ 8,000
       $ 80,000 - 90d (1/4) $20,000   + $12,000
Net assets   total - $16,000 to $40,000 $24,000

ROA: 1,200/24,000 = 5% before tax. This low rate is not attractive. The $20,000 ambitious sales increase requires a net asset increase of $24,000. The schedule given is limited to increments. Restated with all expense:

	Present	Alternative	Increment
Margin--above	$16,000	$20,000	$ 4,000
Expenses--all	13,600	16,400	2,800
Gain	$ 2,400	$ 3,600	$ 1,200
Net Assets	$16,000	$40,000	$24,000
ROA	15%	9%	5%

In practice, this degree of analysis is not practical because expenses and assets are not known at the detail level explored, and allocations are not meaningful. The expense increment of $2,800 is the net amount of change in all activities affected by the alternative.

The ROA erosion indicated by the analysis can also occur without plan if inventories and receivables are allowed to get out of control. This may occur because of lax collection, delayed billing, forward billing, liberal return policy, consignments not billed until sold by customer, holding inventory for future delivery, and poor inventory control.

Sell to a New Market with High Risk

	Increment
Sales	$40,000
Cost	24,000
Margin--40%	16,000
Expenses	6,000
	10,000
Bad debts--20%	8,000
Gain--5%	$ 2,000
Receivables--45d (1/8 on sales)	$ 5,000
less bad debts--20% on receivables	1,000
Net	4,000
Inventory 60d (1/6 on cost)	4,000
Net assets	$ 8,000

ROA: $2,000/$8,000 = 25% before tax

On a cost basis:	
Receivables--net	$ 4,000
less margin 40%	1,600
	2,400
Inventory	4,000
Net assets at cost	$ 6,400

ROA: $2000/$6400 = 31% before tax

The book basis, 25% ROA, is ordinarily used but the alternative 31% ROA is the basis used for financial, rather than accounting, analysis. The ROA is attractive but risk may be high.

Sell to a Market through an Agent

	Present	Agent Alternative	Increment
Sales	$60,000	$ 50,000	-$10,000
Cost	30,000	25,000	- 5,000
Margin	30,000	25,000	- 5,000
Expenses	20,000	15,000	- 5,000
	10,000	10,000	0
Freight	1,000	0	- 1,000
	9,000	10,000	+ 1,000
Bad debts (1/15)	4,000	0	- 4,000
Gain	$ 5,000	$ 10,000	+ 5,000
Receivables:			
72d (1/5)	12,000	10,000	
Bad debts (1/15)	- 800	0	
	11,200	10,000	- 1,200
Inventories	8,800	10,000	+ 1,200
Net assets	$20,000	$ 20,000	0
ROA:	25%	50%	0

The agent assumes freight and bad debts for a commission of 30% ($15,000 on $50,000 sales). Sales drop $10,000 but the variable margin remains 50%, with a $5,000 drop equal to the expense saving. The total $5,000 reduction in freight and bad debts is a net gain. Receivables deop with lower sales, offset by a higher inventory requirement. ROA doubles with no asset increase to achieve 50% ROA with the present operation, expenses of $20,000 would have to be reduced to $15,000.

Open a New Market with an Agent

	Increment
Sales	$20,000
Cost	10,000
Margin	10,000
Agent fee	3,000
	7,000
Expenses	5,000
Gain	$ 2,000
Receivables--90d (1/4)	$ 5,000
Inventory	5,000
Net assets	10,000
ROA	20%

This alternative is attractive, particularly if the market can be reached only through an agent.

Enter the Private Label Market

	Increment
Sales	$50,000
Cost	45,000
Margin	5,000
Expenses	2,000
Gain	$ 3,000
Receivables--18d (1/20)	$ 2,500
Inventory	5,000
Net assets	7,500
ROA	40%

Private label business is priced closely with the low margin of 10%, but there is little marketing expense. Payment is prompt, averaging 18 days. Inventories are low because shipments are made on completion of production runs. There is some risk in the loss of business on short notice. There may also be demands for output beyond capacity levels. Consideration of the time factor (fixed-variable) and the volume factor (capacity) enter into the cost and pricing analysis. Entering private label, and private brand, markets is a policy decision affecting both marketing and capital expenditure planning.

Accept a One-time Export Order

A product profit plan per unit is:

Price		$50	100%
VC		20	
VM		30	60%
FC:	$18,000		
	1,000 units	18	
PR		$12	24%

An order is received for 1000 units at $40, including export packing. The per unit profit is:

Price	$40	100%
VC	20	
VM	20	50%
FC	18	
Balance	2	5%
Packing	2	
PR	0	

The current sales plan for 900 units is compared with the sales plan including the export order for 100 units:

		Sales Plan		Add Export Order	Combined
	at	900 Units	at	100 Units	1000 Units
Sales	$50	$45,000	$40	$4,000	$49,000
VC	20	18,000	20	2,000	20,000
VM	30	27,000	20	2,000	29,000
FC	18	16,200	0	0	18,000
	12	10,800	20	2,000	11,000
Volume variance		1,800		0	0
		9,000		2,000	11,000
Packing		0	2	200	200
PR		$ 9,000		$1,800	$10,800
Percent to sales		20%		45%	22%

The added profit of $1,800 for the export order equals the volume variance without the order. If FC at $18 per unit is applied to the export order, PR drops to zero. This example illustrates the practice of omitting FC for the use of available capacity. ROA is omitted because the effect on receivables and inventories is negligible. Evaluation should be guided by several considerations:

Is $1,800 PR enough to justify handling a special one-time order? Will there be cost overruns? Can the available capacity be used to better advantage? Will this order complicate relations with other customers? Will the production timing jibe with present schedules by department so that shipment can be made on time? Does this order push ahead planned capacity expenditures?

Close a Profit Center

A profit center has low earnings and poor prospects. Its assets can be sold at market. The increments are negative:

	Decrements
Sales	$80,000
Cost	56,000
Margin	24,000
Expenses	16,000
Gain lost	$ 8,000

The drop in sales is $80,000 and the $8,000 gain is lost. The ROA is:

Receivables	$25,000	
Inventory	15,000	
Other Assets	85,000	
	$125,000	$8,000/125,000 = 6.4% ROA

This return is far below the target 25% ROA. Asset realization is scheduled:

	Book	Cash	Net
Receivables	$25,000	$22,000	- $3,000
Inventory	15,000	10,000	- 5,000
Other Assets	85,000	128,000	43,000
	125,000	160,000	35,000

Market ROA: $ 8,000/160,000 = 5.0%

The gain for other assets reflects current market compared with historical book cost. The land and buildings were acquired 12 years ago:

Other Assets:	Book	Market	Net	12-Year Gain at Annual Rate
Land	$15,000	$47,000	+32,000	10%
Buildings--net	40,000	80,000	+40,000	6%
Machinery--net	30,000	1,000	-29,000	--
	85,000	128,000	+43,000	

Land and buildings have substantial market appreciation. Machinery is fully depreciated and sold in bulk for scrap. The total cash proceeds of $160,000, less tax, become available for other purposes.

Capital expenditure analysis is based on the market rate of 5%, not the 6.4% book ROA. The book realization gain of $35,000 for all assets is credited to gain from discontinued operations, net of tax, shown on the income statement after net income from continuing operations. The distinction is significant for financial analysis and profit projections.

Discontinue a Product Line

A company has three product lines--A, B, C--and C has poor results and prospects. Its elimination requires consideration of the effect on customers and the sales force. Other product lines may be affected. The

study must consider all costs with and without C to determine how much is
"escapable" (can be eliminated). A and B costs must be redetermined and
capacity utilization evaluated. The relationships of variable and fixed,
and of direct and indirect expenses must be redetermined.   The effect on
assets   must be analyzed to calculate ROAs.   The analysis must be
localized to the specifics of the choice; book data are a source of
information only.

The present profit plan:

	A	B	C	Total
Sales	$3,000	$2,000	$1,000	$6,000
VC	900	800	500	2,200
VM	2,100	1,200	500	3,800
FC--direct	900	600	300	1,800
Product profit	1,200	600	200	2,000
Allocation	600	400	200	1,200
PR	600	200	0	800
Assets--direct	$2,000	$ 800	$ 400	$3,200
ROA	30%	25%	0	25%

The ROA goal is 30% total, with a 15% minimum for each product.   With
product line C dropped, the effect is:

	From	to	Change	
Sales A	$3,000	$3,900	+$ 900	30% up
B	2,000	1,600	- 400	20% down
C	1,000	0	- 1,000	100% down
	6,000	5,500	- 500	8% down

VM remains at the same percents to sales:

		From	To	
A	70%	$2,100	$2,730	+$630
B	60%	1,200	960	- 240
C	50%	500	0	- 500
		3,800	3,690	- 110

FC direct:

	From	To	
A	900	980	+ 80
B	600	520	- 80
C	300	0	- 300
	1800	1500	- 300

The revised schedule for product profit:

	A	B	C	Total	Change
Sales	$3900	$1600	$ 0	$5500	- $500
VM	2730	960	0	3690	- 110
FC direct	980	520	0	1500	- 300
Product profit--new	1750	440	0	2190	+ 190
present	1200	600	200	2000	
Gain (Loss)	550	(160)	(200)	190	

The FC saving of $300 is offset by the $110 loss of VM to net $190 for all three lines.

Total costs of $1,200 are allocated to the product lines in the ratio to sales--20%--because there is no causal relation. The elimination of C does not reduce the total. The new ratio is 3900/5500 times 1200 = $850 for A and $350 for B. The allocations are:

	From	to	Change
A	$600	$850	+ 250
B	400	350	- 50
C	200	0	- 200
	1200	1200	0

Allocations are made primarily to provide comparability of company ROA with product line ROAs.

Asset requirements traceable to product lines are recomputed:

	From	to	Change
A	$2000	$2500	+ 500
B	800	692	- 108
C	400	0	- 400
	3200	3192	- 8

The $400 assets of C are disposed of at book value.
The profit schedule is completed:

	A	B	Total	Change
Product profit	$1750	$440	$2190	+$190
Allocation	850	350	1200	0
PR	900	90	990	+ 190
Assets	2500	692	3192	- 8
ROA	36%	13%	31%	

Total ROA at 31% is 1% over the 30% target but B at 13% is 2% below the 15% target.

For A: PR increase $300 = (600 to 900)
         Asset increase $500 = (2000 to 2500)
         ROA   60% incremental
         ROA rises from 30% to 36%
For B: PR decrease $-110 = (200 to 90)
         Asset decrease $-108 = (800 to 692)
         ROA   -102% decremental
         ROA drops from 25% to 13%
For Total PR $190 = (800 to 990)
         Asset   - 8 - (3200 to 3192)
         ROA rises from 25% to 31%

If B is dropped the product profit of $440 is lost. The $350 allocation to B is applied to A and reduces profit from $900 to $550. On assets of $2,500 the ROA is 22%; total ROA is now 22%, not 31%. The elimination of B would require a new study.

Studies of this type are difficult and require approximations of sales elasticity and cost functions. But valuable insights can be gained and new direction given to sales plans and capacity commitments, with salutary effect.

Make-or-Buy

How much a company buys or makes is a long-term policy question relating to investment costs, quality, and delivery. Companies vary widely in this respect. Decisions to buy more, or less, involve productive capacity and long-term planning.

Short-run decisions arise more frequently and often with little advance notice. The relevant factors include available capacity, short-run costs, and vendor quotations. For example, a warehouse fire destroys 5,000 parts which must be replaced promptly to maintain schedules. One alternative is to run overtime because production is at capacity; the other is to purchase from a vendor. The unit cost for making the part is:

VC	$8		
FC	4	12	
Overtime		3	$15

A vendor quotes 5,000 parts at $12, or $60,000. The company cost is the VC $8 plus overtime at $3, or $11 a unit, a total of $55,000. The $4 FC is excluded because it is the same either way--a "sunk" cost; it is not "avoidable." The question is whether the $5,000 saving by not purchasing is worth the extra production effort and disruption. The longer-term question is why full company cost at $12 equals the vendor price.

A related problem concerns two products whose requirements exceed available capacity in the short run. The question is which product to buy outside and how much to minimize total cost. An example is based on costs per machine hour (MH). Fixed costs are excluded. A machine failure reduces total available MH from 15,600 to 9,600:

	Part A	Part B	Total
Total units	1,800	4,000	
at MH each	2	3	
Total MH	3,600	12,000	15,600
Available MH			9,600
Shortage MH			6,000
Per unit:			
Output VC	$ 10	$ 7	
Purchase price	16	10	
Extra cost	6	3	
MH	2	3	
Per MH	$ 3	$ 1	

Part A is more expensive to buy so it is scheduled for production first with any remaining time assigned to B.

Alternatives for Growth and Profit

	MH		Cost to	
			Make	Buy
Total Available	9,600			
Part A--1,800 at 2 MH	3,600	at $10	$18,000	
Balance MH	6,000			
Part B:				
Make 2000 at 3 MH	6,000	at $7	$14,000	
Buy 2000 at $10				$20,000
			$32,000	20,000

Total cost $32,000 plus $20,000 = $52,000
Extra cost   2,000 B at $3   =   6,000
Cost to make:
  A 1800 at $10 $18,000
  B 4000 at $ 7   28,000 $46,000

If B is scheduled first in error:

				Extra Cost
Total Available	9,600 MH			
Part B 3,200 at 3 MH 9,600 MH	3,200 at $7	$22,400		
Buy 800 at	800 at $10	8,000	$3	$2,400
4,000		$30,400		
Buy Part A 1,800	1,800 at $16	$28,800	$6	10,800
Total Cost		$59,200		
Cost to make		$46,000		
Extra cost--run B first		13,200		13,200
Extra cost--run A first		6,000		

This type of situation is usually complex but can be solved handily with linear programming.

PROFIT MEASUREMENTS

ROA

ROA is an average that responds to the alternatives selected by evaluations such as those described above. The following schedule illustrates the effect of all choices made from the evaluation of alternatives in the sales plan:

	Present	Drop	Total	Add	Total	Net Change
Sales	$80,000	-$10,000	$70,000	$30,000	$100,000	$+20,000
Profit	3,200	- 200	3,000	5,000	8,000	+ 4,800
Assets	40,000	- 10,000	30,000	20,000	50,000	+10,000
ROA	8.0%	- 2.0%	10.0%	25.0%	16.0%	48.0%
% to Sales	4.0%	- 2.0%	4.3%	16.7%	8.0%	24.0%
Turnover	2.0	- 1.0	2.3	1.5	2.0	2.0

The drop decisions raise ROA from 8% to 10%, further boosted to 16% by the add choices. Incremental ROA for the net change is 48%. The percent to sales shows a big jump from 4 to 8% or 24% change. Asset turnover is unchanged at 2. The doubling of ROA from 8 to 16% is the weighted average

result of the incremental ROA of 48%. This example demonstrates the
potential for selective analysis. Even greater gains occur in practice and
justify continuing intensive studies.

The Discount Rate

The discount rate is a marginal rate used to guide investment
decisions. ROA is a weighted average. An investment gain justified by the
discount rate may move the ROA average up or down. It is necessary to
provide both measures for clarity. Four examples with 15% ROA and a 10%
discount rate illustrate possible combinations:

		Now	Add	Total	
1	Profit	$150	$ 60	$ 210	
	Assets	1000	400	1400	
	ROA	15%	15%	15%	No change
	at 10%	$100	$ 40	$ 140	
	Net gain	$ 50	$ 20	$ 70	
	Percent	5%	5%	5%	No change
2	Profit	$150	$ 50	$ 200	
	Assets	1000	250	1250	
	ROA	15%	20%	16%	Up 1%
	at 10%	$100	$ 25	$ 125	
	Net gain	$ 50	$ 25	$ 75	
	Percent	5%	10%	6%	Up 1%
3	Profit	$150	$ 60	$ 210	
	Assets	1000	500	1500	
	ROA	15%	12%	14%	Down 1%
	at 10%	$100	$ 50	$ 150	
	Net gain	$ 50	$ 10	$ 60	
	Percent	5%	2%	4%	Down 1%
4	Profit	$150	$ 45	$ 195	
	Assets	1000	500	1500	
	ROA	15%	9%	13%	Down 2%
	at 10%	$100	$ 50	$ 150	
	Net gain	$ 50	- 5	+ 45	
	Percent	5%	- 1%	3%	Down 2%

The company benefits from investments with yields over the discount rate
even though ROA drops. Examples 1, 2, and 3 show net gains over the
discount rate so all are acceptable. Example 3 provides a net gain of $10
even though ROA is lowered from 15 to 14%. Example 4 shows an investment
with a negative net which is not acceptable. Failure to recognize the
distinction between ROA alone and the discount rate can be confusing and
misleading, as is any display based on averages. The net gain is also known
as residual profit. If the project yield equals the discount rate, net gain
is zero. The illustrations bring out the distinction between margins and
averages and help to bridge the gap between conventional accrual accounting
and financial analysis for investments.

The comparison of actual results with plan is illustrated in similar
fashion:

1

	Plan	Actual	Change
Profit	$480	$ 576	+$96
Assets	3000	3200	+200
ROA	16%	18%	48% UP
at 10%	300	320	+ 20
Net Gain	180	256	+ 76
Percent	6%	8%	38% UP

The ROA increase is achieved by the incremental net gain of $76 and incremental ROA of 48%.

2

	Plan	Actual	Change
Profit	$480	$ 420	-$60
Assets	3000	2800	-200
ROA	16%	15%	-30%
at 10%	300	280	- 20
Net Gain	180	140	- 40
Percent	6%	5%	-20%

The ROA change is from 16 to 15% but the incremental ROA is 30% negative. Net gain is short by $40.

3

	Plan	Actual	Change
Profit	$480	$ 324	-156
Assets	3000	3600	+600
ROA	16%	9%	x
at 10%	300	360	+ 60
Net Gain	180	- 36	-216
Percent	6%	- 1%	x

The large drop in ROA occurs with lower profits and higher assets. Actual ROA at 9% is below the 10% discount rate. The profit drop of $156 increases to $216 because of the requirement for $60 on the added assets.

Operating and Financial Leverage

Operating leverage is the effect on profit for changes in sales based on the ratio of fixed cost to variable margin. The rate of change is the VM divided by PR, known as the DOL--degree of operating leverage.

Sales	$833	$1000	$1250	$1667	$2500	$10,000
VM 60%	500	600	750	1000	1500	6,000
FC	500	500	500	500	500	500
PR	$ 0	$ 100	$ 250	$ 500	$1000	$ 5,500
VM/PR = DOL	0	6	3	2	1.5	1.09

The DOL is based on assumed time and volume parameters. It gradually approaches but does not reach zero: S $100,000 = VM 60,000 - FC 500 = PR 59,500 = DOL 1.0084. If FC is zero (unrealistic) VM = PR.

The DOL can be used to project an increase in PR for a given increase in sales by ratio. A new DOL is needed for each change in sales, VM, and FC. The method is illustrated:

1. Sales $1,000 to 1,250 = 25%
    PR $ 100 to   250 = 150%, OR
    Sales $1,000 DOL 6 x 25% = 150%
2. Sales $1,250 to 2,500 = 100%
    PR $ 250 to 1,000 = 300%, OR
    Sales $1,250 DOL 3 x 100% = 300%
3. Sales $2,500 to 10,000 = 300%
    PR $1,000 to 5,500 = 450%, OR
    Sales $2,500 DOL 1.5 x 300% = 450%

This short-cut approach is prone to error; it is preferable to write out all the amounts. For instance, if sales increase from $1,250 to $2,000, what is the profit? The first column is a direct calculation without use of the DOL formula, followed by the DOL details.

```
Sales $2,000          $1,250 + 750 = 60%
VM 60% 1,200               750
FC      500                500
PR   $  700           $    250
DOL                        3 x 60% = 180%
                      $   250 x 180% = 450 = $700
```

The DOL formula is longer and more complex.
Financial leverage is the effect on profit of fixed financing expenses such as interest. The degree of financial leverage--DFL--is illustrated by continuing the DOL schedule with $200 interest deducted:

Sales	$1,000	$1,250	$1,667	$2,500	$10,000
PR	100	250	500	1,000	5,500
Interest	200	200	200	200	200
Net	- 100	50	300	800	5,300
PR/Net = DFL	x	5.00	1.67	1.25	1.04

DOL may exist without DFL. When both exist DOL times DFL = DCL, the degree of combined leverage. The two schedules are combined:

Sales	$1,000	$1,250	$1,667	$2,500	$10,000
VM	600	750	1,000	1,500	6,000
PR	100	250	500	1,000	5,500
DOL	6	3.00	2.00	1.50	1.090
Net	- 100	50	300	800	5,300
DFL	x	5.00	1.67	1.25	1.040
VM/Net or DOL x DFL = DCL	x	15.00	3.33	1.875	1.132

Example: Sales $1,250 to $2,500 = 100%
          Net $ 50 to   800 = 1,500% OR
          Sales $1,250 DCL 15 x 100% = 1,500%

DOL can be used without regard to DFL, which relates to financial planning and capital structure. High fixed costs, both operating and financing, increase leverage but also increase risk to the extent that sales and margins are variable.

Product Profit Risk Evaluation

Product profit margins are included in sales plans to meet profit goals. Each product plan includes single amounts for sales, cost, and margin--a point estimate. The degree of risk can be explored by estimating ranges and probabilities for each element. The degree of detail is a pragmatic decision. The study can set reasonable boundaries for each variable and isolate the more sensitive elements to help achieve consensus. A simple illustration is used to minimize detail and clarify the method.
A point estimate is:

Sales	10 units at $10 =	$100
Cost	10 units at 6 =	60
Margin	10 units at 4 =	40 = 40%

Ranges of outcomes and their probabilities in decimals are given in three tables with exaggerated amounts to highlight outcomes.

A Constant sales--variable cost:

Sales	$100	$100	$100	$100
Cost	80	60	50	40
Margin	20	40	50	60
%	20%	40%	50%	60%
P	.3	.4	.2	.1

B Variable sales--constant cost:

Sales	$ 60	$ 75	$100	$150
Cost	60	60	60	60
Margin	0	15	40	90
%	0	20%	40%	60%
P	.1	.2	.5	.2

C Variable sales--variable cost

Sales	$ 80	$100	$120	$140
Cost	72	75	72	70
Margin	8	25	48	70
%	10%	25%	40%	50%
P	.2	.4	.3	.1

The tables are collected by margin percents and P:

Margin %	A	B	C	Total	Divide by 3	Restate As %
0	--	.1	--	.1	.033	3.3
10	--	--	.2	.2	.067	6.7
20	.3	.2	--	.5	.167	16.7
25	--	--	.4	.4	.133	13.3
40	.4	.5	.3	1.2	.400	40.0
50	.2	--	.1	.3	.100	10.0
60	.1	.2	--	.3	.100	10.0
	1.0	1.0	1.0	3.0	1.000	100.0%

Recap:

Margin %	P Percent	Cum
0	3.3	3.3
10	6.7	10.0
20	16.7	26.7
25	13.3	40.0
40	40.0	80.0
50	10.0	90.0
60	10.0	100.0

Summary:

Margin % Range	P Percent	Cum
0 - 10	10.0	10.0
10 - 40	30.0	40.0
at 40	40.0	80.0
over 40	20.0	100.0

The point estimate of 40% margin has a 40% probability matched by a 40% probability of a lower return, with a 20% chance of a higher percent. There is a 10% chance of a margin below 10%. The worst case is zero margin at P 3.3%. The best case is 60% margin at P 10%. Evaluation of these odds is necessarily subjective. Risk aversion usually weighs lower returns more heavily, according to the individual's utility function. The odds expressed are well within actual experience. The probabilities for returns below the 40% target must be recognized. A reasonable limit could be set at no more than a 20% chance of margins below 20%; this would defeat the proposal because the odds are P 26.7%. This method of risk analysis can be revealing, and the tables may be reworked in many ways to help achieve agreement.

8

Formulating Marketing Plans

Forecasting sales by markets and products is basic to all planning. The sales plans express all revenues, costs, and expenses for comparison with goals. After review and approval the plans become budgets for comparison with actual performance.

An example:

	Goal	%	Plan	%	Short
Sales (S)	$110,000	100	$100,000	100	$10,000
Cost	66,000		61,000		
Gross Margin (GM)	44,000	40	39,000	39	5,000
Sales Expenses	22,000		23,000		
Sales Margin (SM)	22,000	20	16,000	16	6,000
Assets	$ 88,000		$ 87,000		
Sales ROA	25.0%		18.4%		

The balance of the financial plan is:

Sales Margin (SM)	$ 22,000	$ 16,000
General Expenses	4,400	4,400
Profit	17,600	11,600
Tax	4,400	2,900
Net	$ 13,200	$ 8,700
Percent to S	12.0%	8.7%
Assets	$ 88,000	$ 87,000
ROA	15.0%	10.0%

The composition of the sales plan is presented in terms of markets, branches, and products for review and analysis aimed at better results.

SALES PLANS

Markets

	Total	Branches	Government	Export	Private Label
Sales	$100,000	$60,000	$15,000	$15,000	$10,000
Cost	61,000	39,000	7,500	9,000	5,500
GM	$ 39,000	$21,000	$ 7,500	$ 6,000	$ 4,500
Percent to S	39.0%	35.0%	50.0%	40.0%	45.0%
Expenses (*23,000):					
Direct	* 13,000	6,000	3,000	2,400	1,600
Direct SM	26,000	15,000	4,500	3,600	2,900
Percent to S	26.0%	25.0%	30.0%	24.0%	29.0%
Indirect	* 10,000				
SM	$ 16,000				
Percent to S	16.0%				

Total expenses of $23,000 are $13,000 direct to the four markets as shown. Each market has its own salespeople. The central staff departments with a $10,000 total serve two or more markets and can be allocated on some traceable or arbitrary basis. For example:

	Total	Branches	Government	Export	Private Label
General Mgmt.	$ 2,500	$ 1,500	$ 450	$ 300	$ 250
Order Handling	800	550	50	150	50
Advertising	3,500	2,500	--	1,000	--
Warehouse	900	500	100	200	100
Market Research	600	450	--	150	--
Training	800	675	125	--	--
Credit	900	625	75	200	--
Total	$10,000	$ 6,800	$ 800	$2,000	$ 400
Percent	100%	68%	8%	20%	4%
Percent to S	10.0%	11.3%	5.3%	13.3%	4.0%

The plan after expense allocation is:

	Total	Branches	Government	Export	Private Label
Sales	$100,000	$60,000	$15,000	$15,000	$10,000
Direct SM	26,000	15,000	4,500	3,600	2,900
Allocation	10,000	6,800	800	2,000	400
SM	$ 16,000	$ 8,200	$ 3,700	$ 1,600	$ 2,500
Percent to S	16.0%	13.7%	24.7%	10.7%	25.0%

The SM relationships are materially altered but some insight is provided for analysis of both staff departments and the four markets.

The sales totals are summaries of all products, with supporting detail by product group, product line, and individual products stated in quantities and prices. Cost is standard product cost; it is fully direct and fully variable to sales with quantities sold by debit from inventory. The gross margin reflects both product pricing and product mix. The company sells five products through the branches. The government sells two products that are differently labeled and packaged.

Export sells three products with print in foreign languages and separately packaged for each country. Private label includes two products labelled with the name of the customer.

The only assets directly related to markets are receivables, planned as follows:

	Sales	Terms	Receivables
Branches	$60,000	120 days (1/3)	$20,000
Government	15,000	36 days (1/10)	1,500
Export	15,000	36 days (1/10)	1,500
Private Label	10,000	18 days (1/20)	500
	$100,000		$23,500

ROA can be developed only by arbitrary allocation of all assets other than receivables: $87,000 minus $23,500 = $63,500. One method is to allocate on the basis of total product costs:

	Cost	Percent	Assets Other	Assets Receivables		Total
Branches	$39,000	63.9%	$40,576	$20,000	$60,576	
Government	7,500	12.3%	7,811	1,500	9,311	
Export	9,000	14.8%	9,398	1,500	10,898	
Private Label	5,500	9.0%	5,715	500	6,215	
	$61,000	100.0%	$63,500	$23,500	$87,000	

	SM	Assets	ROA	Goal ROA SM	Goal ROA Assets	Goal ROA Percent
Branches	$ 8,200	$60,576	13.5%	$13,200	$60,000	22.0%
Government	3,700	9,311	39.7%	4,000	10,000	40.0%
Export	1,600	10,898	14.7%	2,400	12,000	20.0%
Private Label	2,500	6,215	40.2%	2,400	6,000	40.0%
	$16,000	$87,000	18.4%	$22,000	$88,000	25.0%

Branches and export are short on SM and with high assets the result is low ROAs. Government and private label are close to target, but have limited potential for the short term. Export has growth prospects but the SM at 10.7% is too low. The branches, with 60 percent of total sales, handle all products and offer the best opportunity for growth. The SM at $8,200 is $5,000 short of the $13,200 goal and is most of the total SM shortage of $6,000 (22,000 - 16,000). Close analysis is dictated. The sales plan for the five branches is presented next.

Branches

The sales plan for each branch is:

	Total	1	2	3	4	5
Sales	$60,000	$18,000	$10,000	$12,000	$14,000	$16,000
Cost	39,000	4,000	5,400	7,800	9,800	12,000
GM	21,000	4,000	4,600	4,200	4,200	4,000
Percent to S	35.0%	50.0%	46.0%	35.0%	30.0%	25.0%

```
Expenses *($6,000):
Direct--branches    *4,500      740      800    1,020      960      980
Indirect--allocated *1,500      300      300      300      300      300
                     6,000    1,040    1,100    1,320    1,260    1,280
SM                 $15,000  $ 2,960  $ 3,500  $ 2,880  $ 2,940  $ 2,720
Percent to S         25.0%    37.0%    35.0%    24.0%    21.0%    17.0%
Allocated total    $ 6,800
SM                 $ 8,200
Percent to S         13.7%
```

The expenses incurred directly in the branches total $4,500. Home office branch expenses of $1,500 are charged equally to all branches at $300 each. The SM of 25% for all branches has wide variations among the branches. The $6,800 expense allocation for all branches is not further allocated to each branch. Assets also are not allocated. Analysis is directed to product pricing and product mix to explain variation in GM: branches 4 and 5 are well below average. Branch expenses also need to be reviewed. For all branches the expenses are 10 percent of sales: the direct portion is 7.5 percent--$4,500/$60,000. The next step is to study the sales plan for the five products.

Products

Sales plans are prepared by individual products with quantities and prices, then summarized by product lines and product groups. The following illustration is not related to the sales plans:

	Quantity	Price	Sales	Cost	GM	Percent
Product 1	10,000 at	$ .50	$ 5,000	$ 3,000	$ 2,000	40%
2	5,000 at	$2.00	10,000	7,500	2,500	25%
3	5,000 at	$3.00	15,000	7,500	7,500	50%
Product Line A	20,000	[1.50]	$30,000	$18,000	$12,000	40%
Product Line B		(detail)				
Product Line C		(detail)				
Product Group I						
Product Group II						
Product Group III						
Total			$450,000	$315,000	$135,000	30%

The summary for product line A may, or may not, show the combined quantity of 20,000 depending on whether it is considered useful. It is not usually shown beyond that point because of the mix disparity. The weighted averaged price of $1.50 for product line A is not usually of any value. The GM percent is shown for all levels.

The sales plan for the five products sold through the branches is next given; product sales plans for the other markets are omitted.

		Products				
	Total	A	B	C	D	E
Sales	$60,000	$18,000	$15,000	$12,000	$ 9,000	$ 6,000
Cost	39,000	10,800	7,500	9,000	6,300	5,400
GM	21,000	7,200	7,500	3,000	2,700	600
Percent to S	35.0%	40.0%	50.0%	25.0%	30.0%	10.0%

Expenses *($12,800):						
Direct	* 3,000	1,800	900	120	180	0
Direct SM	$18,000	$ 5,400	$ 6,600	$ 2,880	$ 2,520	$ 600
Percent to S	30.0%	30.0%	44.0%	24.0%	28.0%	10.0%
Indirect	* 9,800					
SM	$ 8,200					
Percent to S	13.7%					

Branch direct expenses are $4,500 of which $3,000 is direct to products as shown. The balance of $1,500 is indirect and is added to the $1,500 allocated to the total branch allocated expenses of $6,800; the $9,800 total is not allocated. No branch expenses are direct to product. Worksheets are required to relate expenses to classification such as markets, branches, and products, or other classes such as customers or salesmen.

Product A direct expenses of $1,800 are 10 percent of sales compared with the 5 percent average--$3,000/$60,000. The plan is to build market share. B has a high 44% direct SM with 6 percent direct expenses. C has a low 24% direct SM and 1 percent direct expenses. D is also low at 28% direct SM with only 2 percent direct expenses. E sales are only 10 percent of total sales and have a 10% direct SM. There is no direct expense.

Analysis at the level of quantities and prices is discussed in chapter 10.

The product sales plan for each branch is also reviewed as illustrated for branch 3 which sells only products A, B, and C.

Branch 3	Total	Product		
		A	B	C
Sales	$12,000	$3,000	$3,000	$6,000
Cost	7,800	1,800	1,500	4,500
SM	$ 4,200	$1,200	$1,500	$1,500
Percent to S	35.0%	40.0%	50.0%	25.0%

Future sales are planned for products D and E. No branch expense is direct to product and expense allocations are not made. The product SM percents for the branch agree with those for the product totals, reflecting both fixed prices and consistent product mix. Further analysis can be made at the quantity-price level for possible deviations.

The plan may also be expressed by salesman:

Branch 3		Product		
Salesman Z:	Total	A	B	C
Sales	$ 2,000	$ 900	$ 900	$ 200
SM	860	360	450	50
Percent	43%	40%	50%	25%
Salesman Y:				
Sales	$ 3,000	$ 2,000	$ 0	$ 1,000
SM	1,050	800	0	250
Percent	35%	40%	0	25%

The sales plan may also be shown by salesman and by customer and product, and by customer totals by product as needed.

The product totals are also summarized by branch:

Product A:	Sales	SM	Percent
Branch 1	$3,000	$1,200	40%
Branch 2			
Total	$18,000	$7,200	40%
Product B:			
Branch 1			
Total	$15,000	$7,500	50%
Products Total	$60,000	$21,000	35%

The plans illustrated are designed to meet individual responsibilities and the degree of detail needed at each management level.

SALES EXPENSES

Expense Control

The product costs quoted by manufacturing to marketing are used for sales planning--quantities, prices, and margins. The product costs are based on standards for material, labor, and factory overhead. Variances from standard are expensed as incurred and are the responsibility of manufacturing. The product standard costs are charged to inventory and shipments are charged to cost of sales.

All expenses other than factory overhead are charged to expense as incurred. These expenses are budgeted by department and by account according to organizational responsibility and degree of delegation. The amounts are planned to meet operational requirements and are fixed; variations in activity within the planned range have little or no effect on the expense level. Possible exceptions are commissions, royalties, and freight-out, but such accounts are excluded from departments and shown separately. Variations from departmental expense budgets are generally small or approved in advance to reflect a change in plans. If sales are down some expenses may be increased. Sales above plan do not generally require extra expense dollars. A large amount of expense is discretionary such as product development, market research, advertising, and training. Such expenditures are designed to benefit the future to some unknown extent. Some expenses are susceptible to improved methods and procedures such as order handling, warehousing, credit, and collections.

Expense control is secondary to accomplishment. The relationship of expenses to markets and products is direct only to a limited extent. Allocation of indirect expense is arbitrary and not necessary for either expense control or profitability analysis.

Number of Sales Orders

The cost of handling customer orders may be analyzed to determine possible benefits from setting a minimum order size, or imposing a surcharge. A method of analysis is illustrated. All orders for a month are sorted into five sales ranges, arbitrarily selected for the first trial analysis:

	Sales Range	No. of Orders	Total Sales	Sales Per Order
1	Under $200	200	$16,000	$ 80
2	$200 -- $400	100	24,000	240
3	$400 -- $600	80	40,000	500
4	$600 -- $1,000	70	56,000	800
5	$1,000 up	50	114,000	2280
		500	$250,000	$(500)

The sales plan is stated as follows:

Sales	$250,000	100%
Direct material and labor	60,000	24%
	$190,000	76%
All company overhead	$140,000	56%
Profit	$ 50,000	20%

The analysis requires definition of the relation of the activities and expenses of all departments to the handling of sales orders, and the incremental costs for a change in the number of orders. Many departments are not involved and can be omitted. The other departments require individual attention to arrive at an approximate incremental cost based on an assumed decrease in total orders handled. The process is pragmatic. Manufacturing overhead may be reduced if fewer production orders are needed --fewer setups, longer runs--depending on the production process. Sales effort may be more effective and less expensive with larger orders. Office expenses could also be lower. For this example departments not affected have total expense of $40,000. The balance of $100,000 is expected to drop by 20 percent, or $20,000, with a 40 percent decrease in the number of orders from five hundred to three hundred. The $20,000 increment is $40 per order for five hundred orders:

	Sales Range	No. of Orders	Incremental Cost at $40
1	Under $200	200	$ 8,000
2	$200 -- $400	100	4,000
3	$400 -- $600	80	3,200
4	$600 -- $1,000	70	2,800
5	$1,000 up	50	2,000
		500	$20,000

The sales plan is restated with the incremental order cost deducted:

Sales		$250,000	100%
Direct material and labor		60,000	24%
		$190,000	76%
Total overhead	$140,000		
Less increment	20,000	$120,000	48%
Margin		$ 70,000	28%

Sales are restated with the 28% margin and incremental order costs:

	Sales Range	Sales	Margin at 28%	Order Cost	Incremental Profit	% to S
1	Under $200	$ 16,000	$ 4,480	$ 8,000	-$ 3,520	-22.00%
2	$200 -- $400	24,000	6,720	4,000	2,720	11.25%
3	$400 -- $600	40,000	11,200	3,200	8,000	20.00%
4	$600 -- $1000	56,000	15,680	2,800	12,880	23.00%
5	$1000 up	114,000	31,920	2,000	29,920	26.25%
		250,000	$70,000	$20,000	$50,000	20.00%

If the first sales range is eliminated the balance becomes by difference:

	Sales	Margin	Order Cost	Profit	% to S
Total	$250,000	$70,000	$20,000	$50,000	20.00%
#1 Range	- 16,000	- 4,480	- 8,000	+ 3,520	-22.00%
Balance	$234,000	$65,520	$12,000	$53,520	22.87%

-- Sales decrease by $16,000 from $250,000 to $234,000, or 6.40%.
-- Profit increases by $3,520 from $50,000 to $53,520, or 7.04%.
-- The profit percent to sales rises from 20.00% to 22.87%.
-- Order costs drop from $20,000 to $12,000, or 40%, and the number of orders also drops 40% from 500 to 300.

For this example all overhead is variable, true for long terms. Short-term fixed overhead such as used for annual expense control, would remain after eliminating the #1 range. The margin lost is decreased because fixed cost remains. With fixed cost of $3,520 there is no profit gain by eliminating the #1 range.

A further major consideration is the effect of a large reduction in the number of sales orders on plant capacity. The degree of change depends on the production process but the increase in capacity could be large, with significant impact on the capital expenditure program as to timing and amounts.

The analysis illustrated should be made with different sales ranges and incremental costs to establish a reasonable range of outcomes. The first sales range to $200 might divide at, say, $120, with a loss for sales up to $120, and profit above $120. The use of a surcharge should also be evaluated, possibly based on a target price to provide a 20% profit. For example:

Order amount $100	$250	$400	$500	
Cost at 72% 72	180	288	360	
Margin at 28%	28	70	112	140
Order cost 40	40	40	40	
Net profit - 12	30	72	100	
Add surcharge	32	20	8	0
Profit at 20%	$ 20	$ 50	$ 80	$100

For an order for $100, the surcharge is 32 percent of sales, for $250 it is 8 percent of sales, and for $500 it is zero. A combination rule might be to accept no orders below $100, and a surcharge per order for orders from $100 to $400 to provide a 20 percent profit.

After analysis and evaluation, actual trials may be taken to test the reaction of customers, the effect on sales expenses, and the change in production costs and output capacity.

Storage Charges

When prices are based on shipment at completion of production, storage beyond that point involves extra cost. Such expenses are not separated in the records and constitute an "invisible" cost that may be significant. When a quantity discount is offered for large orders, customers are encouraged to buy and may delay delivery to meet their needs. If storage charges are quoted separately, customers may forego the quantity discount, or order the larger quantity and take full delivery. If the election is to take deferred shipments, storage charges should be billed monthly. It is assumed in all cases that the sales amount is billed on order completion regardless of shipping dates.

An example illustrates the use of storage charges:

	100 Units				600 Units 10% off	
Price at $10	$1,000	100%	Price at $9		$5,400	100%
Cost at $6	600	60%	Cost at $6		3,600	67%
Margin at $4	400	40%	Margin at $3		1,800	33%
Expenses at $2.40	240	24%	Expenses at $2.10	1,260		23%
Profit	$160	16%	Profit		$ 540	10%

The order quantity increase does not affect the $6 unit production cost. Total expenses at 24% of sales or $2.40 per order, are reduced to $2.10 per order, or 23% of sales. ($1,260 is 21% of sales at $6,000.) Profit is increased from $160 to $540, but the percent to sales drops from 16 to 10%.

By incremental analysis:			Increment
Sales	$1,000 to	$5,400	$4,400
Margin	400 to	1,800	1,400
Profit	160 to	540	380
Percent	16%	10%	8.6%

Assume the following delivery schedule in units:

Total Order		600
at once	100	500
Month 1	100	400
2	100	300
3	100	200
4	100	100
5	100	0

If incremental storage costs are 36 percent a year or 3 percent a month, based on cost, the charge for one month is $18--3% of $600 (100 units at $6). The monthly charge schedule for the delivery schedule is:

In Storage	Unit Balance	Inventory Cost	Storage at 3%
Month 1	500	$3000	$90
2	400	2400	72
3	300	1800	54
4	200	1200	36
5	100	600	18
6	0	--	--
		$9000	$270

The profit in the order for 600 units is $540 as shown above. If storage is not charged the total cost of $270 cuts the profit in half. The customer has saved $600 with the quantity discount. If the storage charges are billed, the net saving to the customer is $330 ($600 - $270).

The company bills $5,400 for the total order on completion and storage charges each following month, as shown by the schedule, for a total of $270. In summary:

Sales	$5400	100.0%
Cost	3600	
Margin	1800	33.3%
Expenses	1260	23.3%
Profit	540	10.0%
Storage billed	270	5.0%
Total	810	15.0%

This result can be compared with six separate orders at $1,000 ($6,000) with a profit at $160 ($960) or 16% as shown above.

If the quantity order is held for six months, storage charges are:

Cost $3,600 at 15% (5 months at 3%) 540, double the amount for monthly shipments. The order profit becomes zero if storage is not charged. Billings for storage are debited to receivables and credited to expense recovery--a credit account in the warehouse department. The credit would be to revenue if the warehouse is run as a profit center.

Goods Returned by Customers

Customers may be given credit for shipments for a variety of reasons, all of which warrant investigation: poor quality, late delivery, not ordered, wrong quantity, overstock, wrong specification, going out of business. Allowance may be made to receivables by credit memo without return of the goods. If goods are returned various classifications may apply: no value, sell as scrap, resell as is, resell after reconditioning. Goods may be delivered to a retailer in consignment, with returns unrestricted. Larger amounts in display encourage higher sales but may entail higher returns at some cost. An example is the retail paint market. Another is the bakery business where product freshness is primary but returns can be resold within a limited time at a sharp discount. If a retail outlet sells all goods delivered there are no returns but the likelihood of missed sales is high. If returns are high the proceeds of resale at a discount and disposal expenses must be considered. There is a limit to how much a retailer will accept based on customer demand and shelf space. There is a limit on how much returned goods can be sold. The problem is one of relative demand at retail and at a discount, and the margins for each.

Marketing Plans   189

An example for a retail outlet is given at retail prices:

Delivered	$600	$700	$800	$900	$1000
Sales	600	650	700	750	800
Returned	$ 0	$ 50	$100	$150	$ 200
Percent to sales	0	7.7%	14.3%	20.0%	25.0%

The delivery increases of $100 are split evenly between sales and returns for analysis, with $1,000 as the maximum the store will accept.
The sales plan is:

Sales	$600	$650	$700	$750	$ 800
Cost	300	325	350	375	400
GM 50%	300	325	350	375	400
Expenses--fixed	210	210	210	210	210
SM	$ 90	$115	$140	$165	$190
% to sales	15.0%	17.7%	20.0%	22.0%	23.7%

Fully variable cost is 50 percent of sales. Total fixed expenses are $210; they are not affected by the quantities sold or returned. The sales value of returns at cost are:

Returns (above)	$ 0	$ 50	$100	$150	$ 200
Cost at 50%	0	25	50	75	100

If the returns had no value the effect would be:

SM	90	115	140	165	190
Less return	0	25	50	75	100
Net	90	90	90	90	90

The net is unchanged with higher sales. If the returns are disposed of to realize cost, the SM is not affected and rises from $90 to $190 as shown.
If the returns can be resold at 10 percent over cost with $5 resale expense the sales plan is:

Returns at cost	$ 0	$25.0	$50.0	$75.0	$100.0
Gain 10%	0	2.5	5.0	7.5	10.0
Resale expense	5.0	5.0	5.0	5.0	5.0
Net gain	-5.0	-2.5	0	+2.5	+ 5.0
Retail SM above	90.0	115.0	140.0	165.0	190.0
Total SM	85.0	112.5	140.0	167.5	195.0
Percent to retail sales	14.2%	17.3%	20.0%	22.3%	24.4%

Break-even for returns is reached with delivery of $800, sales at $700, and return of $100, or $50 cost. The outlet handles returns from all retailers but is illustrated with simplified amounts for the retailer. If total returns exceed $200, or $100 cost, the mark-up drops to zero on the excess because of limited demand, and the net gain remains at $5.
Retailers are served by bakery delivery routes, each with its own characteristics. A route is illustrated for one week:

Retail:

Deliver	$1250	125%
Return	250	25%
Sell	1000	100%
Cost	500	
GM	500	50%
Expenses	350	
SM	150	15%

Resales:

Return	$ 250.0	
at cost	125.0	
Mark-up 10%	12.5	
Expenses	2.5	
SM	10.0	
Total SM	160.0	16%

Each route should be separately planned and monitored for each retailer. Margins could run from a loss to over 30 percent with variable conditions. Returns from all routes are sold through one or more resale outlets, and excess amounts may be donated and taken as a tax deduction.

MANAGEMENT DECENTRALIZATION

As a business grows in size and complexity the top managers become less able to make timely and informed operating decisions and need more time for planning and control. One remedy is to redefine the company into separate entities, such as divisions and profit centers, each with its own mission and defined markets, products, facilities, and assets--a quasi-company. Evaluating this approach may be difficult.

. New organization plan, new positions, personnel reassignments by job and location, hiring new people, training, implementation schedule
. Relations with customers, vendors, stockholders, the financial community
. More formal controls, revised information systems, more written reports
. Extra costs and probable benefits over time
. Probable need for recurring changes to meet changing conditions

The aim is to increase profits through more localized and specialized management, but staff costs increase and top management control is less direct. The separation of performance responsibility provides the basis for clearer measurement with ROA for each unit but two basic challenges arise: (1) allocation of company staff expenses for the separate operating units; and (2) transactions between the units, or intracompany billings.

These two topics are often subsumed under the single phrase transfer pricing but each topic is unique and requires separate attention.

The degree of complexity can be considerable. A company may own other companies--wholly or partially, domestic and foreign. Reports may be:

. Consolidated for all companies
. Consolidated for all except for some specific exclusions, such as a finance company or a nonoperating subsidiary. Such companies are carried in the consolidation at cost plus undistributed earnings, and a separate report is made for each.
. Parent company only, with a separate report for each subsidiary, shown by the parent at cost plus undistributed earnings--known as "the equity method."
. Combined reports for selected groups of companies such as those in a separate country, or in a geographic area such as Europe or the Far East.

Tax returns are prepared for each company in each country according to local regulations; they may or may not be consolidated. Allocation of taxes may be difficult or necessarily arbitrary, if done at all. A division set up by management as an independent operation may include more than one company in more than one country and consist of several profit centers. Each unit can have revenues--sales, rentals, service--with outside customers, within its own division, and with other divisions. Entries by company must be classified as to:

```
          Inter Division - Inter Country
              Div A      - PC 1    USA
              Div B      - PC 4    Mexico
          Inter Division - Intra Country
              Div A      - PC 2    USA
              Div B      - PC 3    USA
          Intra Division - Inter Country
              Div A      - PC 3    Canada
              Div A      - PC 2    USA
          Intra Division - Intra Country
              Div B      - PC 2    Mexico
              Div B      - PC 4    Mexico
```

Transactions within a profit center are simply transfers of production to sales at standard cost. Sales may include both manufactured and purchased products, including purchases from other divisions. Production may be for sales both to customers and to other divisions.

Expense Allocation

The following table shows a sales plan for a company with three divisions in one country; the example applies equally to a division with three profit centers.

Division	Total	I	II	III
Sales	$10,000	$5,000	$3,000	$2,000
Cost	5,500	2,700	1,800	1,000
GM	4,500	2,300	1,200	1,000
Expenses	3,300	1,650	990	660
Profit	1,200	650	210	340
Assets	$ 5,500	$2,500	$1,000	$2,000
ROA	22%	26%	21%	17%

```
Company
Div. Profit  $ 1,200
Co. Expenses      320
Co. Profit        880
Div. Assets  $ 5,500
ROA              16%
```

This example excludes, for simplicity, company assets, income taxes, interest, and other items of income and expense. When income taxes apply, the best practice is to use a planned uniform rate for all units, leaving unit and company ROAs in the same ratio. It is simpler to recognize income taxes at the company level only. Interest expense applies to debt, solely a company responsibility relative to capital structure and financial leverage. ROE and EPS relate only to the company--there is only one shareholder group.

The example is continued to tie together the division ROAs with the company ROA and ROE to present a complete plan. The capital structure is:

```
Total assets                          $6,000
   Debt (6 2/3% = $200 interest)       3,000
   Equity                              3,000
Financial Plan:
   Co. profit--above                  $  880
   Other income                          220
Profit before tax                     $1,100
   Income tax (40%)                      440
   Profit after tax                      660
   Total assets                       $6,000        ROA 11%
   Profit after tax                   $  660
   Interest              $ 200
   Less tax              $  80           120
   Net income                            540
   Equity                             $3,000        ROE 18%
```

Recap:

```
Assets     $6,000        Net $660        ROA 11%
Debt        3,000        Net  120        Debt 4%
Equity      3,000        Net  540        ROE 18%
```

The divisions have a combined ROA of 22% but after company expenses of $320 it is 16%. Allocation of the expenses to the divisions puts all ROAs on an equal footing. The allocations represent expenses the divisions would have as separate legal entities and avoids an overblown view of division performance. Allocations are largely arbitrary and should not stifle or blur accountability. The following method is advised:

. Budget all home office departments and expenses and select allocation bases.
. Notify the divisions of the allocations for inclusion in the profit plans.
. Enter allocations in the books at planned amounts only. Variances are not allocated.

The sales plans after allocation of company expenses are as follows:

	Total	I	II	III
Sales	$10,000	$5,000	$3,000	$2,000
Div. Profit	1,200	650	210	340
Allocation	320	150	90	80
Co. Profit	880	500	120	260
Div. Assets	$ 5,500	$2,500	$1,000	$2,000
New ROA	16%	20%	12%	13%
Prior ROA--above	22%	26%	21%	17%
Change	- 6	- 6	- 9	- 4

The ROA relationships are considerably different:

	New	Prior
I to II:	8 points higher	5 points higher
I to III:	7 points higher	9 points higher
II to III:	1 point lower	4 points higher

Division plans can be compared with actual results both before and after allocation as illustrated for Division I:

		Actual	Plan	Actual Over Plan
	Sales	$5,400	$5,000	$400
1	Div. Profit	810	650	160
	Allocation	150	150	0
2	Co. Profit	660	500	160
	Assets	$3,000	$2,500	$500

ROA

		Actual	Plan	Increment
1	Div.	$810/3,000 = 27%	$650/2,500 = 26%	$160/500 = 32%
2	Co.	$660/3,000 = 22%	$500/2,500 = 20%	$160/500 = 32%

The division operating ROA increases from 26% plan to 27% actual with an incremental ROA of 32%, which is the same at the company level. At the company level the gain in financial ROA is from 20% plan to 22% actual. Expense allocation thus does not distort division ROA, and company interpretation is improved. Allocation of actual expenses would be unproductive, as would the recording of income taxes; the divisions are not responsible in either case.

A variety of allocation methods are available for use as applicable; they are described briefly:

1. Ratio of planned revenues for all general expenses without determinable relationships to divisions, such as top management, legal, financial, planning, and public relations. The expense total of $120 is allocated:

Div.	Sales	Allocation
I	$ 5,000	$ 60
II	3,000	36
III	2,000	24
	$10,000	$120

2. Ratio of planned employment for all activities related to number of employees such as, compensation, benefits, recruiting, and retirement. The expense total of $40 is allocated:

Div.	People	Allocation
I	300	$15
II	200	10
III	300	15
	800	$40

3. Ratio of estimated time required for services related to divisions based on experience and projections such as auditing, communication, and systems analysis. The expense total of $64 is allocated:

Div.	Percent	Allocation
I	50	$32
II	25	16
III	25	16
	100	$64

4. Ratio based on division missions relative to company goals such as for research and development, for a total of $32:

Div.	Percent	Allocation
I	50	$16
II	50	16
III	0	0
	100	$32

5. Ratio of planned usage for central services such as market research, data processing, and printing. The department expense budgets are commitments to provide service at an estimated level for both the company and the divisions, based on cost-benefit analysis. Fixed costs should be allocated on the basis of planned usage. Actual usage should be charged at variable rates by debit to users and credit to the supplying departments. Service departments are measured both by comparison of actual expense with budget and by comparison of actual and planned usage. Variance remains with the service departments and is not allocated. This procedure encourages usage and precludes uneconomic outside purchases. The total fixed expense budgets are allocated:

Div.	Allocation
I	$27
II	12
III	25
	$64

The allocations are summarized by division:

Method	I	II	III	Total
1	$60	$36	$24	$20
2	15	10	15	40
3	32	16	16	64
4	16	16	0	32
5	27	12	25	64

Total	$150	$90	$80	$320
Percent	47%	28%	25%	100%
Sales	$5,000	$3,000	$2,000	$1,000
Percent	50%	30%	20%	100%
Ratio of Expense to Sales	3%	3%	4%	3.2%

Division expenses are allocated to profit centers in the same way, including allocation from the home office. The purpose is the same--to express PC ROAs that are consonant with the division ROA and to avoid the impression of inflated PC results. A common simplification is to base all allocations in the ratio of planned sales, particularly when there is little effect on ROA. For this example, the ratio of 3.2% would be used for all divisions.

Intra-Company Billings

Reports should designate separately transactions with customers, with other divisions, and with other profit centers. This is illustrated for Division I with sales through its three PCs to customers, to other divisions, and to other PCs within the division:

	Sales	Cost	GM	Percent
PC 1:				
Customers	$100	$ 60	$ 40	40%
Div. II	20	15	5	25%
PC 2	30	27	3	10%
	$150	$102	$ 48	32%
PC 2:				
Customers	$150	$105	$ 45	30%
Div. III	50	45	5	10%
	$200	$150	$ 50	25%
PC 3:				
Customers	$250	$140	$110	44%
PC 2	50	50	0	0
	$300	$190	$110	37%
Memo: Combined	$650	$442	$208	32%
Consolidated:				
Customers	$500	$305	$195	39%
Div. II, III	70	60	10	14%
	$570	$365	$205	36%
PC elimination	80	77	3	4%

PC 2 purchases from PC 1--$30 with $3 GM--and from PC 3--$50 with no GM, make for a combined total of $80 with $3 GM. The PC 2 cost total of $150 contains the $80 received, assuming no amount in inventory. This information is kept on the PC 2 records but is not separately reported. It applies to both customer and Division III sales. Sales by the PCs to the other divisions are at higher percents but well below customer margins. If transfers at a profit remain in inventory at closing, the gross margin is charged to cost and credited to inventory on the division work sheet; this entry is reversed the next period.

The division reports are consolidated by the company as follows:

	Sales	Cost	GM	Percent
Div. I:				
Customers	$500	$305	$195	39%
Div. II & III	70	60	10	14%
	$570	$365	$205	36%
Div. II:				
Customers	$300	$150	$150	50%
Div. I	100	90	10	10%
	$400	$240	$160	40%
Div. III:				
Customers	$400	$220	$180	45%
MEMO: Combined	1370	825	545	40%
Consolidated:				
Customers	1200	675	525	44%
Div. Elim.	170	150	20	12%

Each manager with a profit responsibility measurable by ROA must be free to buy and sell without direction or interference from division or company management. Decisions to buy or sell within the company must be made by the manager on the same basis that applies to transactions with vendors and customers outside the company. The purpose of decentralization is profit improvement stemming from autonomous local management, acting within approved plans and policies. Decisions imposed by higher authority vitiate this objective. If deemed necessary the decentralization plan should be restructured to reflect realities.

For example, PC 1 may have a vendor quotation of $10 per unit and a quote of $11 per unit from PC 2. PC 1 can choose either one but would be expected to buy from the vendor at $10 with freedom of choice. PC 2 would lose the order. The PC 2 price reflects its target pricing method for all customers:

Variable cost	$ 6
Fixed cost:	
$40,000/20,000 units	2
	$ 8
Mark-up	3
Target price	$11

For the company, PC 1 pays $10 to a vendor but only the $6 variable cost is saved by PC 2, a putative loss of $4. From this viewpoint the decision has been called "suboptimal," an academic concept that is not relevant. PC 2 is free to quote $9, or $1 below the vendor price, if it so chooses for its own purposes, based on both short- and long-term factors. The price reduction equals FC $2. The two quotes can be compared:

	Full	Discount $2 Full Cost	VC
Price	$11	$9	$9
VC	6	6	6
	5	3	3
FC	2	2	--
Mark-up	$ 3	$1	$3
Percent to price	27.3%	11.1%	33.3%

Even the $11 sales price may be unattractive to PC 2 if the order would require overtime or the loss of long-term customer business. If the order utilizes available capacity, the outlay cost is only $6 and the margin is $3, or 33.3 percent of $9. PC 2 would have to guard against the $9 quote being a precedent and PC 1 would have to be concerned about a profit plan based on this low price. If PC 1 asks for a long-term price commitment, PC 2 must necessarily recognize long-term costs--all fixed costs are variable in the long run. The PC managers must deal at arm's length to preserve the integrity of separate ROA accountability.

Sales within the company may entail less expense and thus justify lower pricing. Such expenses may include advertising, selling, warranty, market research, training, and installation. Internal price may be established by discounting target prices or on an ad hoc basis. The purpose would be the same--improved profit.

Special situations can arise for major customer contracts when a substantial amount may be procured either from a vendor or from within the company. It may be highly desirable to keep all the work in the company for reasons of quality control, scheduling, handling contract changes, and administration.

For example, Division I makes a competitive bid on a contract at $10,000, with $8,000 total cost and a $2,000 margin. The $8,000 cost is $4,000 internal with $4,000 to be subcontracted. Division II is invited to bid. Several possibilities arise:

	1	2	3	4
Quote to customer	$10,000	$10,000	$10,000	$10,000
Div. I cost	4,000	4,000	4,000	4,000
Balance	$ 6,000	$ 6,000	$ 6,000	$ 6,000
Div. II quote	$ 6,000	$ 4,000	$ 5,000	$ 4,600
Div. I margin (1)	0	2,000	1,000	1,400
Div. II quote	$ 6,000	$ 4,000	$ 5,000	$ 4,600
Div. II cost	4,000	4,000	4,000	4,000
Div. II margin (2)	2,000	0	1,000	600
Company margin (3)	$ 2,000	$ 2,000	$ 2,000	$ 2,000

Alternative:

1	Div. II gets full margin
2	Div. I gets full margin
3	Equal dollar margins to each
4	Div. I margin $1,400 = 14% on sales of $10,000
	Div. II margin $600 = 13% on transfer price of $4,600.

This alternative recognizes Div. I's lead position.

If a vendor quotes $5,000, the Division I margin is $1,000 (alternative 3) but Division II loses its margin of $1,000, as does the company. Division II might be "requested" to lower its bid to $4,600 to shut out the vendor. The problem would move into the political arena and career angles would come into play. One technique is to notate Division II reports with the $400 price concession, a memo not affecting ROA. An alternative is to allow Division II to bill $5,000, with $4,600 charged to Division I and $400 debited to the company. The inflated division profits are deflated by company consolidation. This is a debatable choice. The basic answer is to let the divisions decide independently. Each situation must be evaluated on its merits at the time it arises. Top management can keep informed of developments for major contracts and provide the degree of guidance it considers appropriate; good division managers are good company men.

The nature and degree of intracompany relationships must be carefully evaluated in the decentralization analysis. The delegation of responsibility must be matched by requisite authority to establish validity for ROA accountability. A decision that may impair short-run profits presumably increases long-term performance; in any event the decision has been delegated to the local manager. Decentralized organization plans require constant reappraisal to adapt to changing markets, products, and technology. The fundamentals remain--prices, volume, costs, expenses, and assets, managed over time.

ECONOMIC EVALUATION AND MANAGEMENT PERFORMANCE

The evaluation of managers' performance rests on their assigned organizational responsibilities, comparing actual results with plans. Plans are made according to forecasts and expectations, guiding both organizational structure and asset investment. Economic evaluations may require redefining data separate from organizational units. For instance, evaluation may be made of a foreign country in which several divisions operate independently, or for a class of customers served by more than one company entity. Also, emerging technologies and new products may occasion economic study. Such analysis is basic to strategic planning, a continuing top management challenge. Information provided by reports based on organizational units may have to be adapted to a defined economic area. This is a difficult subject to illustrate but an example is given in simplified form to demonstrate the process.

A company sells custom-made products throughout three regions, each of which is directed by a manager with sales and production responsibilities. Each sales office sells to customers located in its region but orders may call for delivery to any location in the country. Each plant produces for a territory limited by freight cost. Thus, each plant can produce for all sales offices and each sales office can sell for all plants. Each manager is responsible for sales to customers in his region regardless of shipping plant, and for plant costs for all production. Sales quotations are based on customer specifications and cost estimates prepared by the producing plant. The business is highly competitive and delivery time is a factor. Each sales office is responsible for pricing, sales, and expenses. Each plant is responsible for timely production at the quoted costs based on its own standards.

The sales plan shows sales by sales office and by producing plant for each region:

	Sales by Region			
Production by:	A	B	C	Total
A	$1,600	$ 400	$ 600	$2,600
B	0	1,800	0	1,800
C	0	200	1,400	1,600
	$1,600	$2,400	$2,000	$6,000

Region A: Sales for A only--$1,600. Production for A-B-C--$2,600.
Region B: Sales for all three plants--$2,400. Production for B only--$1,800.
Region C: Sales for A and C--$2,000. Production for B and C-- $1,600.

The schedule can also be written:

	Production by			
Sales by:	A	B	C	Total
A	$1,600	$ 0	$ 0	$1,600
B	400	1,800	200	2,400
C	600	0	1,400	2,000
	$2,600	$1,800	$1,600	$6,000

The next schedule shows sales (S), costs (C), gross margin (GM), and percent to sales for each sales office by producing plant. S and C are totaled, region expenses (EXP) are deducted in total; sales margin (SM) is given, with percent to sales (rounded):

		Sales by			
Production by:		A	B	C	Total
A	S	$1,600	$ 400	$ 600	$2,600
	C	800	196	330	1,326
	GM	800	204	270	1,274
		50%	51%	45%	49%
B	S	0	$1,800	0	$1,800
	C		900		900
	GM		900		900
			50%		50%
C	S	0	$ 200	$1,400	$1,600
	C		132	700	832
	GM		68	700	768
			34%	50%	48%
Total	S	$1,600	$2,400	$2,000	$6,000
	C	800	1,228	1,030	3,058
	GM	800	1,172	970	2,942
		50%	49%	48%	49%
	EXP	$ 544	$ 656	$ 600	$1,800
	SM	$ 256	$ 516	$ 370	$1,142
		16%	22%	18%	19%

   Production is debited to inventory at standard, based on the order estimate, and charged to cost on shipment. Variances are not budgeted but are the responsibility of the producing plant. (Planned volume variance is omitted here but will be considered later.) The region office expenses are budgeted.

   Region A. A sales and A costs have a 50% GM. Expenses of $544 are 34% leaving a 16% SM. The plant also produces for B sales--51% GM--and for C sales--45% GM. Each sales office is responsible for its sales and pricing. Competition relates to the shipping (production) area rather than to the location of the sales offices. B sales at 51% GM are higher, and C sales at 45% GM are lower, than A's 50% GM. The weighted average is a 49% GM for plant A for all three sales offices.

   Region B. The sales office has a 50% GM for the B plant, with 51% GM for plant A (above) and 34% GM for plant C. The plant produces only for B. The sales office has a 49% GM, and a 22% SM. Expenses are 27% of sales.

   Region C. The sales office GM is 50% for plant C compared with 45% for plant A (above), an average of 48% GM and 18% SM. Expenses are 30% of sales. The plant GM is 48% for sales by B and C.

   Totals. The GM is 49% and the SM is 19%, with expenses at 30%.

   Each region is responsible for the planned performance as shown. ROA measurement by regional manager for all sales is not practical because the bulk of the assets--inventories and fixed assets--are related to the producing plant for sales of all offices. Arbitrary allocation would not be useful. ROA evaluation can be made by plant without need for allocation. This is an economic evaluation of a plant area and its performance and potential for all sales regions.

Planned assets are:
   Receivables--36 days (1/10 of sales)
   Inventory--60 days (1/6 of cost)
   Plant--at cost before depreciation

| | Plant | | | |
	A	B	C	Total
Receivables:				
Sales	$2600	$1800	$1600	$6000
at 1/10	260	180	160	600
Inventory:				
Cost	1326	900	832	3058
at 1/6	221	150	139	510
Plant:	1144	1470	1155	3769
Asset Totals	1625	1800	1454	4879

The sales plan is restated by plant:

	A	B	C	Total	Percent
S	$2600	$1800	$1600	$6000	100%
C	1326	900	832	3058	51%
GM	$1274	$ 900	$ 768	$2942	49%
Expenses	832	488	480	1800	30%
SM	$ 442	$ 412	$ 288	$1142	19%
	17%	23%	18%	19%	

This schedule is taken from the sales plan by sales office, above, for S-C-GM. The expenses incurred by each region do not relate to producing plants. The allocated expenses for this schedule were derived by using the expense ratio to sales for each region and the sales for each plant--detail omitted.

	A	B	C	Total
ROA:	$442/1625	$412/1800	$288/1454	$1142/4879
	= 27.2%	= 22.9%	= 19.8%	= 23.4%

Volume variance is now examined. The plant cost standards include fixed expenses at practical capacity. The planned sales for each plant are translated into capacity. Differences from plant capacity and planned sales are volume variance--the quantity times the fixed overhead rate. These calculations are not given but the results are presented as follows:

	A	B	C	Total
Sales	$2600	$1800	$1600	$6000
SM	442	412	288	1142
Volume Variance	42	124	0	166
Margin	400	288	288	976
Assets	$1625	$1800	$1454	$4879
New ROA	24.6%	16.0%	19.8%	20.0%
Prior ROA	27.2%	22.9%	19.8%	23.4%

The planned ROA drops to 20% after total volume variance of $166. Volume variance can be related to cost in the sales plan:

	A	B	C	Total
Cost	$1326	$ 900	$ 832	$3058
Volume Variance	42	124	0	166
Ratio	3.2	13.8	0	5.4

Plant A. The high ROA and low volume variance suggest study of plant expansion, depending on the sales potential for the three sales offices. The expense rate could be lowered with higher sales, calculated above at 32%-- $832 divided by $2,600. Expanded capacity could lower unit costs but volume variance would be higher while sales catch up.

Plant B. The high volume variance reduces ROA to a low 16% from 22.9%. This plant serves only the B sales area. Sales potential needs to be explored with the possibility of reduced plant capacity or relocation. The 23% SM is much higher than A at 17% and C at 18%.

Plant C. Production is planned at capacity. GM is 50% for C sales but only 34% for B sales. The SM is 18%, after 30% for expenses. ROA at 19.8% is low compared with 22.9% for B and 27.2% for A. The question of increasing capacity needs immediate attention, as well as the low 34% GM for B sales. Perhaps the B sales office is cutting prices to gain customers but the impact is to lower ROA for plant C.

This example shows the need for economic evaluation and financial analysis separate from manager responsibilities.

PART 2

CONTROLLING CURRENT PERFORMANCE: WHO NEEDS TO KNOW WHAT, AND WHEN?

Introduction: Management Reports and Effective Control of Operations

Periodic financial statements provide final results of operations, with comparison of plans and past periods. The published statements conform with GAAP, but internal reports can be adapted to meet management needs and can include relevant data from any source. All financial reports are summaries of past transactions, both completed and in progress, and require time to prepare--some ten to fifteen days. The books must be closed at a specified time--the cut-off date: transactions must be recorded, estimates and adjustments made, and statements written. The closing time interval can be shortened at the expense of accuracy and added cost but this is not a matter of primary concern. An effective system of control and communication provides continuous and timely information to all those concerned; it endeavors to serve the injunction "NO SURPRISES." Periodic formal reports provide a full record that is essential for overall review and evaluation, and they should substantially bear out expectations. Any consequential deviation should be reviewed for cause and correction.

Periodic statements should be fully articulated with all published and internal reports to assure clear communication. They should correspond with established responsibilities, budgets, and plans to aid evaluation of individual performance. They should be recast as needed to permit economic evaluations independent of organization structure. They must serve the purposes of technical requirements, such as taxes, insurance, associations, loan terms and indentures, government units, and public releases. Consolidated, consolidating, and combining statements may be required.

Meeting the formidable demands for published and internal reports is the job of the management control system. The direct responsibility of management was legally established in 1977 by act of Congress--the Foreign Corrupt Practices Act--FCPA. This act specifies that records be kept in reasonable detail and accuracy, and with an effective system of internal control. The purpose is both the prevention and the detection of errors. The system should assure management that nothing significant has been omitted or wrongly represented, economize management time in reviewing reports, and direct attention toward constructive analysis. Anything unusual or unexpected should be readily identified and resolved.

Management reports should be interdependent with the current operating controls, the means by which corrective action is taken on a continuing basis as transactions occur. Timing is geared to events. For example, reports may include: constant clocking of labor and machine time; downtime by shift; daily scrap; weekly use of supplies; weekly logs of purchase orders; daily record of sales orders; weekly record of sales calls; periodic summary of media commitments for advertising; and monthly reports on capital expenditure projects. The timing need not be consonant with accounting periods but the two should be reconcilable. Cut-off points for physical processing must be specified to meet control needs in addition to those used for accounting.

The system should be designed to avoid the problem of information overload but all essential data must be available. Accuracy is relative and timely approximations are often sufficient. No system can provide all information at all times. Individual needs vary over time and are not readily predictable. Operating data is usually voluminous and complex. The system design should be based on "building blocks" of information that can be arranged to meet shifting reporting needs and to facilitate analysis. The control system also includes oral communication, personal observation, walking around, and outside contacts (such as with customers, vendors, financial analysts, stockholders, business associates, and auditors).

The cost of the information system should be acceptable, the responsibility of both management and systems analysts, based on cost-benefit analysis. Essentially it is a matter of not keeping unnecessary records or providing unneeded reports. The primary mission of the system is to provide timely, relevant information to aid managers in exercising effective control. The system is supported by procedures, forms, manuals, charts, office layout, data processing equipment, methods, training, supervision, and audit. Systems analysts are charged with the design, and auditors for the review, of all systems, as directed by top management. Frequent change is to be expected to meet new conditions and to utilize more efficient technologies. The costs of systems design and its operation are small relative to the potential for improved management control and decision making. It is not always readily apparent that managers who do not receive satisfactory reports develop their own sources of information to meet their perceived needs, either supplanting, or co-existing with, the system in operation. With such an idiosyncratic situation, inaccurate and incomplete information can cause flawed decisions, unnecessary expense, and garbled communications. These deviant procedures need to be eliminated by good systems design. All systems deteriorate over time and with inadequate attention. When improved systems help to control a problem so that it becomes minor there is a tendency to eliminate or reduce the control method. The control system may become progressively enervated to the point of requiring a major overhaul. This pendulum effect is expensive. The problem also develops from short-term and short-sighted economy drives.

Plans and budgets are essential to guide operations but there is a sharp limit to prescience. Changing conditions constantly alter the operating environment. The ability to respond rapidly and with assurance is a valuable asset provided by the control system. This requires constant feedback, distinction between internal and external factors, anticipation of the effect of a change internally, and evaluation of possible external reactions. Performance evaluation is an ongoing process and includes review, and possible revision, of the budgets, plans, programs, objectives, strategies, and policies. As a practical matter there is a limit to how much data can be assimilated quickly, but at the same time there are relatively few factors that are critical to results. Attention to these key elements in the operation on a current basis should provide effective control. Management of these key variables should lead to the best results obtainable in the circumstances. The "bottom line" is simply an end result.

Part 2 presents specific descriptions of the major information needs for the organization levels ranging from sales supervisor and foreman to the board of directors. The coverage runs from real time efficiency to planned utilization of capacity, from sales orders booked to changes in market share, from profits by products and markets to net income. Illustrative reports and analytic methods are provided in detail. Both plans and the control system should try to anticipate contingencies and avoid the fire-fighting reaction to unforseen developments.

Robert S. Kaplan, professor of accounting at the Harvard Business School, notes:

> Internal accounting practices should be driven by corporate strategy, not by FASB and SEC requirements for external accounting...Companies... must devise cost accounting systems that reflect their investment decisions and cost structures... Today's global competition requires that non-financial measures--on quality, inventory levels, productivity, deliverability and employees...also be used. ("Yesterday's Accounting and Today's Economy," Harvard Business Review [July-August 1984])

9

Management Reports

COMPANY FINANCIAL STATEMENTS

Published statements are based on GAAP, industry practices, management
judgments, and the advice of independent accountants. There is a wide
latitude in both statement content and presentation format, with a tilt
toward public relations and minimum disclosure. These reports serve the
public purpose, not management needs. In this chapter internal reports
are presented and examined for use in planning and control. External and
internal reports are complementary.
   The statements are:

   --Income statement (profit and loss statement)
   --Balance sheet (statement of financial position)
   --Funds statement (statement of changes in financial position)

These statements include a comparison of the actual results with the
plans given in chapter 1 with additional detail.

Income Statement

	Plan	%	Actual	%	Increase	%	% Change
Sales	$4,000	100.0%	$4,600	100.0%	$600	100.0%	15.0%
Standard Cost	2,200		2,438		238		10.8
Standard GM	1,800	45.0	2,162	47.0	362	60.3	20.1
Variances	200	5.0	230	5.0	30	5.0	15.0
Gross Profit	1,600	40.0	1,932	42.0	332	55.3	20.8
Expenses:							
Sales	600		660		60		10.0
Admin.	500		520		20		4.0
R&D	100		112		12		12.0
	1,200	30.0	1,292	28.1	92	15.3	7.7
Operating Profit	400	10.0	640	13.9	240	40.0	60.0
Interest	80	2.0	80	1.7	0	0	0
	320	8.0	560	12.2	240	40.0	75.0
Tax (37.5%)	120	3.0	210	4.6	90		
Net Income	200	5.0%	350	7.6%	150	25.0%	75.0%
Dividend	0		50		50		
Retained	$ 200		$ 300		$100		

This format discloses the effect of increments on averages. Gross profit rises from 40% plan to 42% actual, but the incremental rate on the $600 sales increase is 55.3%. The sales gain of 15.0% over plan provides a 20.8% gain for gross profit, a 60.0% gain for operating profit, and a 75.0% gain for net income. The incremental net income at 25.0% raises the 5.0% plan to 7.6% actual, a significant boost.

Standard GM reflects the summation of several major factors: sales prices, standard product costs, sales mix, and volume of production. Standard product costs are used for profit planning and inventory valuation. Variances from standard are expensed as incurred and remain at 5% of sales. The major components are:

	Plan	Actual	Change	Percent
Material purchase prices	$80	$ 64	-$16	-20%
Operating expenses--usage, efficiency, spending	20	26	+ 6	+30%
Volume of production	100	140	+ 40	+40%
Variances	200	230	+ 30	+15%
Standard cost	$2,200	$2,438		

The planned variances are provided for fiscal prudence; standards are set on a tight but achievable basis. The purchase price and operating expense variances reflect a wide range of transactions. (These results are purely fiscal in this summary report. The actual control of operations is described in subsequent chapters.) Volume variance is the budgeted fixed factory overhead expense not absorbed by production based on practical capacity. The $100 plan is based on production planning and the capital expenditure program. Actual volume variance of $140 exceeded plan by $40 for a variety of reasons: order volume, product mix, seasonality, breakdowns, strikes, delay in project installation, and inefficiencies. Effective management of volume is a key variable in profitability, explored in depth in later chapters. To illustrate, if volume variance had decreased by $40 rather than increase by $40 the $80 change would have increased net income by $50 from $350 to $400 (increase $80 less $30 tax).

Inventory on the balance sheet is valued at product cost standards that are revised periodically and updated near the end of the year to currently attainable performance. Adjustments to inventory are made to the variance expense accounts. Standard cost of sales includes only charges that are credited to inventory at the current standard product cost. Variances are the total, or net, of both the continuing operating variances and the periodic inventory adjustments for changes in standards. The total variances, as shown, are a direct deduction from profit. The use of higher (looser) standards to reduce variance is not constructive: the measure of operating performance is slack; product cost is too high thus inhibiting sales planning; inventory is overvalued by credit variances; profit measurement is distorted. Another undesirable alternative is to defer on the balance sheet some variances to be expensed with usage such as purchase price variances. This practice also serves no purpose. The costing principle is that inventory should include all costs necessary for production, thus excluding any unnecessary or avoidable costs, and all expenditures not for production, that is, selling, general, and administrative, which are period expenses.

All departments are budgeted to aid expense control. Factory departments are included in standard product costs by overhead application rates. Period expenses--SGA--are budgeted by department and grouped as shown in the income statement. Sales expenses rose 10% while sales increased 15%. All expenses increased $92, or by 7.7%, with the ratio to sales dropping from 30 to 28.1% actual. With no change in interest expense and taxes at 37.5%, net income rose by 75% from $200 to $350. The $150 increase was 25% of the $600 sales gain. Dividends are deducted to show the amount of net revenue retained, shown on the balance sheet as retained earnings.

Balance Sheet

	Ending Balances		Increase
Net Assets:	Plan	Actual	(Decrease)
Net current assets:			
Cash	$ 200	$ 290	$ 90
Receivables	300	460	160
Inventories	500	600	100
	$1,000	$1,350	$350
Payables	250	300	50
Taxes	50	150	100
Dividend	0	50	50
	$ 300	$ 500	$200
Net current assets	$ 700	$ 850	$150
Net fixed asset:			
Land	$ 100	$ 80	(20)
Buildings	600	690	90
Machinery	900	1,050	150
Projects	200	280	80
	1,800	2,100	300
Accum. Depr.	900	1,000	100
Net fixed assets	900	1,100	200
Deferred charges	100	100	0
Deferred taxes	(200)	(250)	(50)
Net assets	$1,500	$1,800	$300
Capital:			
Debt: Bank loan (15%)	$ 100	$ 200	$100
Bonds (13%)	400	300	(100)
Current portion	100	100	0
Debt	600	600	0
Equity: Capital stock			
(100 shs)	300	300	0
Retained earnings	600	900	300
Equity	900	1,200	300
Capital	$1,500	$1,800	$300

The cash balance fluctuates constantly with the changing amounts and timing of receipts and disbursements. It reflects liquidity and is managed daily by the cash control system. High cash balances and strong liquidity represent a trade-off with profitability, reflecting the economic climate and management predilection. Receivables increase substantially relative to the sales increase, raising a question of longer terms or account delinquency. Inventories also exceed plan by a major amount, suggesting questions about the efficiency of the inventory control system. Payables and taxes arise in the regular course of business and have no explicit cost--"spontaneous credit." The declared dividend is a liability charged to retained earnings. The totals are deducted to arrive at net current assets, the amount used in operations and financed by the capital structure. The portion of bonds currently payable--$100--is included in debt in order to measure profits logically on both assets and equity. Published statements include debt currently payable (within one year) in current liabilities because of an outmoded convention based on an archaic notion of liquidity. Fixed asset increases are net of any retirements at book value. A piece of land was sold. There were net increases in buildings and machinery. Projects show the balance spent on capital expenditures still in process. On completion, the amounts are charged to fixed asset accounts. Accumulated depreciation increased by $100 for a net increase in fixed assets of $200. Deferred charges, unchanged at $100, represent expenditures deemed beneficial to future periods by management.

A deferred tax liability arises because the tax provision at 37.5% on accrued income contains both the tax actually payable (according to the tax regulations and the tax return) and credited to taxes payable, and a tax provision for accounting income required by GAAP but not currently payable. The $50 difference for the year increases the deferred total to $250, another liability without explicit cost. Net assets are thus reduced to the amount supported by the capital structure of debt and equity. This tax treatment is known as interperiod tax allocation. In future years the amounts are expected to reverse, or turn around, with debits made to the deferred tax liability. The account can have a debit balance. The election to pay less taxes currently and more later provides a loan without interest and so is utilized extensively. The question of how to report deferred taxes is highly controversial. It is speculative what the future will bring in both tax regulations and company earnings. The expectation that the deferred tax account will reach zero is visionary. The balance is an accumulation, usually from several years. One suggestion is to revise the balance to current tax regulations, and another is to use projected amounts. Others would use present values or abolish deferred taxes entirely. Taxes are a complex area with other problems: intratax allocation to transactions within the period; assigning taxes for consolidated returns to the constituent companies; foreign subsidiary remittances; equity changes in foreign investments; providing for tax assessments. The principal concern of management lies in tax planning for both profitability and liquidity, and in the logical application of taxes to operating decisions and investment analysis.

The $300 increase in net assets used in operations is supported by an equal increase in capital, a financing decision relative to debt and equity. Total debt is unchanged--the bank loan increase of $100 equals payment on the bonds. The debt section of the balance sheet includes all obligations that must be repaid at a specified time with interest. Capital stock is unchanged at $300, the total paid in by the original stockholders. Retained earnings increase by $300--net income $350 less $50 dividend declared, as shown on the income statement.

Changes in the balance sheet are accounted for in the funds statement which deals with differences in accruals, including cash. The term funds must be strictly understood in this context--changes in all accrual balances. Cash is only one account and a cash report deals solely with cash (currency) received and disbursed.

Funds Statement

Financing
Net income:

Plan	$200		
Increase	150		
Actual		$350	
Less dividend:			
Plan	0		
Actual	50	50	
Retained income			$300
Add: Depreciation		$100	
Deferred taxes		50	150
Equity funds available			450
Debt:			
Bank loan		$100	
Bonds		(100)	0
Available for investment			$450

Investing

Net current assets	Plan	Actual	Net
Current assets	$1,000	$1,350	$350
Current liabilities	300	500	200
Net	$ 700	$ 850	$150
Fixed assets:			
Land	$ 100	$ 80	$(20)
Bldgs. & machinery	1,500	1,740	240
Projects	200	280	80
	$1,800	$2,100	300
Total invested			$450

Net income of $350 less dividends of $50 provides retained income of $300. Depreciation of $100 deducted from income is added back because it is simply an allocation taken into expense. The purpose is to match the use of the depreciable asset over its life with revenue by periods to express periodic net income, a principal purpose of accrual accounting. This practice is known as the "matching principle," a part of GAAP. Both interpretation and application are relatively loose but fall within general guidelines. The expenditure for fixed assets is taken as incurred, and the recorded depreciation is added back to income. Depreciation is not a source of funds. For financial analysis of investments, the period is the asset life so the question of allocation does not arise. The $50 increase in deferred taxes is also added back to income because it is only a book entry for a possible future liability and does not require current funds. An alternative format adds both the $100 and $50 to net income of $350 to arrive at $500, called "funds available from operations." The $50 dividend declaration is then deducted, leaving $450 available for investment. Debt is unchanged so a total of $450 is left for investment in assets. The asset increases are summarized on the statement.

As a technical note, depreciation is often a major item in the total funds available from operations, a principal source of financing. Other items not currently requiring funds frequently add to, or decrease, the funds available from operations, excluded here but disclosed in published statements. It is also worth noting that most depreciation expense is actually charged on the books to factory overhead and applied to product cost. The cost stays in inventory until the product is sold; cost of goods sold is an expense account. There is no attempt to determine the amount of depreciation included in cost of goods sold. The problem is finessed by analysis of the credits to the accumulated depreciation accounts. The actual depreciation taken to period expense is known. The amount of depreciation shown on the funds statement is not apt to be of consequence.

The funds statement is not a cash report. The change in cash of $90 is one of all the accounts shown which necessarily balance--because balance sheets "balance." Accordingly the presentation format could follow any desired sequence and grouping. One alternative is to list everything but cash which is then the balancing item. Use of the title cash statement is wrong. Cash reports consist solely of actual receipts and disbursements; the historical record is of little or no interest. Projected cash is essential to cash management and preservation of liquidity. The funds statement is basic to measuring the relationship of changes in financing and investing. It is also basic to establishing the cash plans that express the expected timing of cash flows.

Financial Analysis

Profitability. The profit earned on assets is the single most important performance measurement--return on assets (ROA). The profit earned on equity--return on equity (ROE)--is the same as ROA with no debt. With debt, the debt rate is measured separately; if it is less than ROA then ROE is higher--positive leverage. Leverage can also be negative--the return to stockholders is less than the debt rate. All calculations are after tax to provide consistency and comparability. The calculations required do not appear separately on the statements as usually prepared. They are easily derived by the separate application of net tax to tax on operating profit and on interest:

	Plan		Actual	
Operating profit	$400		$640	
Less tax	150*	$250*	240*	$400*
Interest	80		80	
Less tax	30*	50*	30*	50*
Income	320		560	
Less tax	120	200	210	350

The * designates amounts not shown separately on the income statement.

The balance sheet amounts are:

	Plan	Actual
Net assets	$1500	$1800
Debt	600	600
Equity	900	1200
Capital	1500	1800

The following calculations are based on ending balances. In practice, calculations are made periodically and moving averages are generally required.

	Plan		Actual	
ROA--net assets	$250/$1500	16.67%	$400/$1800	22.22%
Debt	50/ 600	8.33%	50/ 600	8.33%
ROE--equity	200/ 900	22.22%	350/ 1200	29.17%

Incremental ROA:	Plan	Actual	Increment
Profit	$250	$400	$150
Net assets	1500	1800	300
ROA	16.67%	22.22%	50.00%

ROA Equation:

	Plan	Actual
Asset turnover: Sales	$4000	$4600
Net Assets	1500	1800
Times	2.67	2.55
Profit percent: Profit	$ 250	$ 400
Sales	4000	4600
Percent	6.25%	8.70%
ROA: $250/1500 = 16.67%		$400/1800 = 22.22%
2.67 x 6.25% = 16.67%		2.55 x 8.70% = 22.22%

The ROA gain derives from the higher profit percent to sales, reduced by a slightly lower turnover rate. Note that the profit percent to sales does not appear in the income statement.

Leverage.

	Plan	Actual
ROE	22.22%	29.17%
ROA	16.67%	22.22%
Ratio	1.333	1.313

ROE is higher than ROA because the debt rate is lower than ROA-- interest claims a relatively smaller part of the whole. The leverage ratio is little changed. The ratio of debt to equity or D-E drops:

Plan $600/ 900 = 66.7%
Actual $600/1200 = 50.0%

The $300 increase in net assets is financed entirely from equity (net income less dividends), thus reducing the degree of leverage. Capital structure is strengthened by less debt but at the expense of reduced leverage and ROE. ROA is unaffected.

Liquidity. The ratio of interest expense to operating profit before interest is a common measure of ability to meet payments on time. The amounts are before tax. It is called "times interest earned":

	Plan	Actual
Profit	$400	$640
Interest	80	80
Times interest earned	5	8

Coverage has increased substantially with no increase in interest--both debt and the interest rate are unchanged. These amounts are shown on the income statement and so are accruals rather than the cash needed to make payment. Payment ability is actually managed as part of the cash control plan but this information is not available to outsiders. In practice the ratio is widely used and frequently includes other fixed financial payments similar to interest.

The D-E ratio and the interest rate must be considered together relative to profit before interest to determine liquidity and leverage, a major area in finance.

The widely publicized ratios of current assets to current liabilities (current ratio and acid test ratio) are used by outsiders as measures of liquidity because better information is not available. These ratios are of little use to management because they are too broad for either decision making or control. They can be derived from the balance sheet but are not given here.

Assets. All assets enter into the ROA turnover ratio. The challenge is to keep the ratio high--relatively more sales to assets--along with the profit rate on sales which require asset support. The common published data is not useful to management. (The planning and control of assets is examined in detail in part 1 and only briefly reviewed here.)

Cash is managed as part of liquidity. Higher cash balances improve liquidity but lower ROA. Receivables are analyzed as investments to improve ROA by relating sales to profits based on receivables--incremental analysis.

Inventories are managed by the entire production control system, part of which is based on analysis of EOQ and safety stocks.

Current liabilities arise principally in the regular course of business, a source of capital without explicit cost.

Fixed assets, acquisition and disposal, are managed through the capital expenditure program. Analysis uses NPV, yield, risk, and the accounting rate of return.

Stock Market Measures. The one hundred shares of stock outstanding have a current market value of $21 a share.
. The price to earnings ratio, or P-E, is the market price divided by earnings per share. EPS = net income $350/100 sh. = $3.50. Price per share $21. P-E = $21/$3.50 = 6. P-E is referred to as the "multiple"--price is six times earnings.
. The reciprocal is the earnings to price ratio: E-P = $3.50/21.00 = 16.67%.

. Book value per share is $1,200/100 sh. = $12. Ratio of market to
  book is $21/$12 = 1.75. ROE per share $3.50/$12 = 29.17%.
. Dividend yield--dividend per share $50/100 sh. = $.50 and $.50/$21
  = 2.38%. Book rate $.50/$12 = 4.17%.
. Dividend payout ratio--$50/$350 net income = 14.29% Per share
  $.50/$3.50 = 14.29%.

PROFIT CENTER REPORTS

The company totals are supported by three profit centers (PC) and a
home office (HO):

Summary Report

Plan	A	B	C	Total	HO	Company
Sales (S)	$1800	$1200	$1000	$4000	$ 0	$4000
Net assets	600	500	300	1400	100	1500
Profit	108	66	86	260	$(10)	250
Profit % to S	6.00%	5.50%	8.60%	6.50%		6.25%
Turnover	3.00	2.40	3.33	2.86		2.67
ROA	18.00%	13.20%	28.67%	18.57%		16.67%
Actual						
Sales (S)	$1600	$1800	$1200	$4600	$ 0	$4600
Net assets	640	560	500	1700	100	1800
Profit	96	120	194	410	$(10)	400
Profit % to S	6.00%	6.67%	16.17%	8.91%		8.70%
Turnover	2.50	3.21	2.40	2.71		2.55
ROA	15.00%	21.43%	38.80%	24.12%		22.22%

The analysis of company profitability can now be made for each PC.
The effect of HO expense of $10 and assets of $100, both plan and actual,
increases the ROA plan from 16.67% to 18.57% for the PCs and the ROA
actual from 22.22 to 24.12% for the PCs. ROE is not calculated at the PC
level because debt is solely the province of the HO. Incremental summary
for plan to actual:

	A	B	C	Total	Company
Profit change	-$12	+$54	+$108	+$150	+$150
Net asset change	+ 40	+ 60	+ 200	+ 300	+ 300
Incremental ROA	- 30%	90%	54%	50%	50%

PC A.   Sales drop from $1,800 to $1,600 but the profit percent holds
at 6%. Profit dollars drop from $108 to $96 while net assets rise from
$600 to $640. Turnover slows and ROA is down to 15% from the 18% plan.
The incremental ROA is negative 30%, far below the other two profit
centers.
PC B.   Sales are up sharply and the profit percent also rises, with a
profit gain from $66 to $120. Assets rise modestly and turnover is more
rapid. The combined effect is to increase the ROA plan from 13.20% to
21.43%; the incremental gain is 90%.

PC C. Sales increase 20 percent from $1,000 to $1,200 while the profit percent rises sharply from 8.60% to 16.17%. The profit increase of $108--$86 to $194--is double that for PC B at $54. The asset increase from $300 to $500 lowers turnover from 3.33 to 2.40 but ROA rises from 28.67% to 38.80%. Incremental ROA is 54% compared with 50 percent for total ROA.

Comparison of actual with the past period, as well as with plan, is useful to gauge actual changes and to review the plan's validity in view of developments. The analysis is given for PC A only, as follows:

	Last Year	Actual	Plan
Sales	$1200	$1600	$1800
Net assets	500	640	600
Profit	60	96	108
Profit % to S	5.0%	6.0%	6.0%
Turnover	2.4	2.5	3.0
ROA	12.0%	15.0%	18.0%

Sales increased $400, short of plan by $200, but the profit percent was raised from 5 to 6% as planned. Net assets increased more than plan with a slight gain in turnover to 2.5 but well under the 3.0 plan. ROA at 15% was three points over the past year and three points short of plan. This comparison enlightens interpretation of both results and plans.

Income Statements

Plan	A	B	C	Total	HO	Company
Sales	$1800	$1200	$1000	$4000	$ 0	$4000
Standard cost	980	660	560	2200		2200
Standard GM	820	540	440	1800		1800
Variances	150	60	(10)	200		200
Gross profit	670	480	450	1600		1600
Expenses	400	330	270	1000		1000
PC profit	270	150	180	600		600
HO expenses	0	0	0	0	200	200
Allocation	97	45	42	184	(184)	0
Profit	173	105	138	416	(16)	400
Tax (37.5%)	65	39	52	156	(6)	150
Net profit	$ 108	$ 66	$ 86	$ 260	(10)	$ 250
Percent to S	6.0%	5.5%	8.6%	6.5%		6.25%
Actual (details omitted)						
Sales	$1600	$1800	$1200	$4600	$ 0	$4600
Net profit	96	120	194	410	(10)	400
Percent to S	6.00%	6.67%	16.17%	8.91%		8.70%

HO expenses are allocated on bases not given but described above, with $16 left in the HO as corporate expenses not relevant to PC operations. The planned HO expense allocations are booked as planned and variances are left in the HO. Tax provision of 37.5% applies to both plan and actual.

Balance Sheets

Plan	A	B	C	Total	HO	Company
Net current assets:						
Cash	$ 10	$ 10	$ 10	$ 30	$170	$ 200
Receivables	140	100	60	300	0	300
Inventory	220	160	120	500	0	500
	370	270	190	830	170	1000
Liabilities	100	90	60	250	50	300
Net CA	270	180	130	580	120	700
Net fixed assets	330	320	170	820	80	900
Deferred charges					100	100
Deferred taxes					(200)	(200)
Net assets	$600	$500	$300	$1400	$100	$1500
Actual (details omitted)						
Net assets	$640	$560	$500	$1700	$100	$1800
Change	+$40	+$60	+$200	+$ 300	-0-	+$ 300

Funds Statements

Sources	A	B	C	Total	HO	Company
Company net						$350
Deferred taxes						50
PC net	$ 96	$120	$194	$410	$(10)	400
Depreciation	50	30	10	90	10	100
	146	150	204	500	0	500
Dividend					50	50
Funds available	146	150	204	500	(50)	450
Uses						
Net CA	20	50	70	140	10	150
Fixed assets	30	100	150	280	20	300
Invested	50	150	220	420	30	450
Net change	+96	-0-	-16	+80	-80	-0-

The PCs provided net funds of $80. The HO used $30 for asset additions and $50 for dividends. The PC funds statements provide the basis for cash planning and cash management.

SUMMARY OPERATING REPORTS

Management needs condensed and selective operating reports that highlight significant current developments in a clear format. For decentralized companies, each profit center should design appropriate reports for division management, and each division should design appropriate reports for the company managers. Separate reports are also needed for the board of directors.

Factors entering into report design include:

    Plan - actual - last period - projection
    Week - month - cumulative - future
    Dollars - quantitative data - other items - from within
      the company or outside
    Estimates - approximations - ranges of outcome - probabilities
    Articulation covering all reports
    Written analysis as needed after oral reviews
    Redesign to adapt to current needs

When progress gets off course, or adverse events occur or threaten, it is necessary to revise plans and actions based on the available alternatives and probable results. It is not practical or even desirable to prepare a full set of new plans and budgets for the balance of the year. Revision can be limited to selected items and new estimates made of overall outcomes. Management has a need, and a right, to know promptly of any major developments--negative or positive. The watchword is NO SURPRISES! The continuing flow of communications--meetings, visits, memos, telephone calls--is the operation control link, aided by the system of written reports.

Profit Center A to Division X

I.   Income Summary--PC A

Six months to date:	Actual		Plan		Last Year	
Sales	$800		$900		$750	
Standard GM	360	45.0%	410	45.6%	340	45.3%
Operating profit	125	15.6%	144	16.0%	112	14.9%
Net income	48	6.0%	54	6.0%	42	5.6%
Net assets	600		600		600	
Turnover (annualized)		2.67		3.0		2.5
ROA (annualized)	16.0%		18.0%		14.0%	

Fiscal year:	Original Plan		Projection		Change	
Sales	$1800		$1600		-$200	
Net income	108	6.00%	90	5.62%	- 18	
Net assets	600	3.00%	600	2.67%	- 0	
ROA	18.0%		15.0%			

Six-month ROA is (16%) behind plan (18%) by two points and ahead of last year (14%) by two points. The current projection for the year shows ROA slipping to 15.0%, with net income at $90--off by $18 from the original plan. Such estimates are significant for directing attention to operating decisions that may remedy the situation, for financial planning relative to liquidity, and to good internal and external communications. Financial analysts thrive on forecasts.

II.   Balance Sheet Items--PC A--at Six Months:

		Actual	Plan
A.	Receivables	$158	$175
	No. of days	40 days	34 days
	Past due	$ 14	$ 5
B.	Inventories	$132	$127
	Turnover to cost of sales	6.6	7.3
C.	Capital expenditures:		
	Completed projects	$ 65	$ 80
	In progress	85	70
	Authorized balance	180	195
	Cost overrun	12	0

III.   Funds Changes--PC A--Six Months
        Operating profit $144
        Depreciation   26
        Funds provided $170
        Net current assets   35
        Fixed assets   150
        Funds used   185
        Net funds used   -15
        Plan--net funds provided   +$25
IV.   Operating Data--PC A--Six Months (as selected)
        Sales returns   Lost orders
        Sales allowances   Late shipments
        Quality complaints   New customers
        Orders received   Lost customers
        Orders cancelled   Order backlog--actual and plan
        Capacity utilization   No. of employees--actual and plan
V.   Income Statement--PC A--Six Months

	Actual		Plan		Last Year	
Sales	$800		$900		$750	
Standard GM	360	45.0%	410	45.6%	340	45.3%
Marketing:						
Sales deductions	16		17		18	
Commissions	40		45		45	
Advertising	19		28		16	
Department expenses	70		70		60	
	145	18.1%	160	17.8%	139	18.5%
Sales margin	215	26.9%	250	27.8%	201	26.8%
Manufacturing:						
Expense variance	5		10		8	
Volume variance	10		10		6	
	15		20		14	
Gross profit	200	25.0%	230	25.6%	187	24.9%
Administrative	75		86		75	
Operating profit	125	15.6%	144	16.0%	112	14.9%
Allocations	77		90		70	
Net income	$ 48	6.0%	$ 54	6.0%	$ 42	5.6%

VI.   Product Margins--PC A--Six Months

			Products	
Plan	Total	#1	#2	#3
Sales	$900	$400	$300	$200
Standard GM	410	200	120	90
	45.6%	50.0%	40.0%	45.0%
Direct expenses	$104	$ 60	$ 30	$ 14
Product margin	$306	$140	$ 90	$ 76
	34.0%	35.0%	30.0%	38.0%
Indirect expense	56			
Sales margin	$250			
	27.8%			

Total marketing expenses of $160 are $104 direct to products and $56
indirect.

Actual

Sales	$800	$360	$220	$220
Standard GM	360	162	88	110
	45.0%	45.0%	40.0%	50.0%
Direct expenses	$ 96	$ 54	$ 11	$ 31
Product margin	$264	$108	$ 77	$ 79
	33.0%	30.0%	35.0%	36.0%
Indirect expense	49			
Sales margin	$215			
	26.9%			

Total marketing expense of $145 are $96 direct to products and $49 indirect.

VII. Market Margins--PC A--Six Months

Plan	Total	Wholesale	Gov't.	Export	Private Label
Sales	$900	$400	$220	$180	$100
Standard GM	410	192	99	90	29
	45.6%	48.0%	45.0%	50.0%	29.0%
Direct expenses	86	20	44	18	4
Market margin	$324	$172	$ 55	$ 72	$ 25
	36.0%	43.0%	25.0%	40.0%	25.0%
Actual (detail omitted)					
Sales	$800	$360	$200	$140	$100
Market margin	272	144	54	49	25
	34.0%	40.0%	27.0%	35.0%	25.0%

VIII. Units Sold - Industry Analysis

When good data are available on industry unit sales for defined products, markets, and periods, comparable with company data, comparative analysis can be made of the relationship of company unit sales to both market share and industry totals. The following examples demonstrate the process. The amounts are unrelated to the information given above which does not include units.

Example 1	Prior	Current	Change
Company	1200	1320	+120 e
Industry	4800	4400 b	-400 d
Market share	25% c	30%	+ 5% a

Market share: +5% a times 4400 b = +220
Industry volume: 25% c times -400 d = -100
                                        +120 e

By increasing its market share by 5% the gain is 220 units on the industry total of 4,400. The drop of 400 units for the industry is a loss of 100 units for the company at the 25% market share. The company is working against a falling market. If industry sales had increased equally with company sales:

Company	1200	1320	+120 e
Industry	4800	5280 b	+480 d
Market share	25% c	25%	-0- a

Market share: 0 a times 5280 b =   0
Industry volume: 25% c times 480 d = 120
                                       120 e

With no increase in market share the gain comes entirely from industry volume. With no increase in industry units, the gain arises solely from company sales:

```
Company              1200      1320      +120 e
Industry             4800      4800 b     -0- d
Market share          25% c    27.5%     +2.5% a
```

```
Market share:    2.5% a times 4800 b = 120
Industry volume:  25% c times    0 d =   0
                                        ───
                                        120
```

Example 2	Prior	Current	Change
Company	2000	1500	- 500 e
Industry	10000	12500 b	+2500 d
	20% c	12%	- 8% a

```
Market share:   - 8% a times 12,500 b  = -1,000
Industry volume:  20% c times 2500 d   = +  500
                                        ────────
                                        -  500 e
```

The loss of market share has caused a loss of 1000 units, with 500 regained from industry volume. The company is lagging a growing market.

Example 3	Prior	Current	Change
Company	800	1,100	+ 300 e
Industry	8,000	10,000 b	+2,000 d
	10% c	11%	+ 1% a

```
Market share:    + 1% a times 10,000 b = +  100
Industry volume   10% c times  2,000 d = +  200
                                         ───────
                                         +  300 e
```

The company is gaining in a rising market.

Example 4	Prior	Current	Change
Company	400	400	0 e
Industry	1,600	2,000 b	+ 400 d
	25% c	20%	- 5% a

```
Market share     -  5% a times   2,000 b   -  100
Industry volume    25% c times + 400 d     +  100
                                            ──────
                                               0 e
```

The industry gain is offset by the loss of market share. The company is losing ground.

Example 5	Prior	Current	Change
Company	400	400	0 e
Industry	1,600	1,000 b	- 600 d
	25% c	40%	+ 15% a

```
Market share:    + 15% a times  1,000 b   +  150
Industry volume:   25% c times - 600 d    -  150
                                           ──────
                                              0 e
```

The company has offset the loss in industry volume by gain in market share.

Example 6	Prior	Current	Change
Company	400	360	- 40 e
Industry	2,000	2,400 b	+ 400 d
	20% c	15%	- 5% a
Market share:	- 5% a times	2,400 b	- 120
Industry volume:	20% c times	400 d	+ 80
			- 40 e

The company has a 10 percent loss in units while the industry has jumped 20 percent. The 120 units lost to market share are largely recovered by industry volume.

Division to Company

Division management and profit center managers work together on the communication and reporting system for each PC. The divisions in turn develop systems with the company to meet their mutual requirements. Principal factors include personal relationships, management style, and economic developments. The keys are relevance, significance, timing, clarity, and flexibility. The reports to the company for the division are illustrated for PC A. Other PC reports would generally be similar, and there would also be some summary reports and other division data; these are not illustrated.

I. Income Summary: PC A--Div. X

Six months	Actual		Plan		Last Year	
Sales	$800		$900		$750	
Gross profit	200	25.0%	230	25.6%	187	24.9%
Operating profit	125	15.6%	144	16.0%	112	14.9%
Net income	$ 48	6.0%	$ 54	6.0%	$ 42	5.6%
Net assets	$600		$600		$600	
Turnover--annualized		2.67		3.0		2.5
ROA--annualized		16.0%		18.0%		14.0%

Fiscal Year	Original Plan		Projection		Change	
Sales	$1800		$1600		- $200	
Net income	108	6.00%	90	5.62%	- 18	
Net assets	600		600		- 0	
ROA		18.0%		15.0%		

II. Balance Sheet Items: PC A--Div. X at Six Months

	Actual	Plan
Receivables	$158	$175
No. of days	40 days	34 days
Inventories	$132	$127
Turnover	6.6	7.3
Capital expenditures		
Authorized balance	$180	$195

III. Funds Changes: PC A--Div. X--Six Months

Funds provided	$170
Funds used	185
Net funds used	- 15
Plan--net funds provided	+ 25

   IV.   Operating Data: PC A--Div. X--Six Months--Selective:
          Order backlog--actual and plan
          Sales allowances
          Quality complaints
          Expense variances
          Volume variances
          Changes in unit sales by market share and industry volume
    V.   Product Margins: PC A--Div. X--Six Months
          Plan--sales, margins, %s
          Actual--sales, margins, %s
   VI.   Market Margins: PC A--Div. X--Six Months
          Plan--sales, margins, %s
          Actual--sales, margins, %s

The actual design, content, detail, and analysis would be selective in all cases; the examples given can only be generally illustrative.

Company to Board of Directors

The board should receive some operating reports for each PC and for each division in addition to the regular financial statements. The responsibility of the board obligates company management to supply all information that is consequential to financial performance and to observe the admonishment no surprises. The board must be able to evaluate performance by individual managers and the economic prospects for financial entities not directly related to organizational structure. The information flow is both written and oral, both periodic and intermittent, and adapted to both the current situation and the individuals concerned.

Operations Summary: PC A--Div. X

Six Months	Actual	Plan	Last Year
Sales	$800	$900	$750
Net income	48	54	42
Net assets	600	600	600
ROA (annualized)	16%	18%	14%

Fiscal Year	Original Plan		Projection
Sales	$1,800		$1,600
Net income	108		90
Net assets	600		600
ROA (annualized)	18.0%		15.0%

Capital Expenditures	Actual	Plan
Authorized balance	$180	$195
Funds changes	Used $15	Provided $25
Order backlog	--	--
Volume variance	--	--

Product margins--selective
Market margins--selective
Changes in market share and industry volume--actual, plan, projections.

Each corporation will face a number of issues--I call them
"vital issues"--which ... largely determine its success or
failure ... the critical areas and policy questions which a
board   ...   must monitor....The directors can be adequately
briefed ... without drowning in an incomprehensible flood of
reports....The   standard   of   "no   surprises"--favorable   or
unfavorable--should apply....Frequent tendency to have a short-
term bottom-line oriented focus--a myopia which could have a
severely negative impact...(Harold M. Williams, excerpts from an
address given to the Financial Executives Research Foundation/
Society of Corporate Secretaries, Philadelphia, Pa., September
16, 1980).

PROFIT MEASUREMENT FOR FOREIGN SUBSIDIARY

Investment in a foreign country has many dimensions, including the
uncertainty of currency exchange rates. Exchange rates may fluctuate
widely and unpredictably in direction and amount, and currency movement
may be subject to government regulations. When money moves across
borders the transactions are recorded at the actual exchange rates;
exchange rate gains and losses are booked as incurred. When a company
prepares consolidated statements including a foreign subsidiary the
foreign currency amounts must be restated in dollars at selected
translation rates. Differences that arise in the process are
translation, as distinguished from transaction, gains, and losses.
Current practice, per GAAP, is to carry the net translation amount
directly to a separate account in the equity section of the consolidated
balance sheet, bypassing the income statement. This account is
identified as a cumulative currency translation adjustment, debit or
credit. It is an anomaly but is generally preferable to the prior
practice of taking the adjustment through income, with erratic effect on
profit measurement. The records and reports of the subsidiary, kept in
local currency, are not affected.
U.S. companies must consolidate all subsidiaries, domestic and
foreign, with minor exceptions, for published reports. Practice in other
countries varies widely. The parent company carries investments in all
subsidiaries at cost. Periodically the net income of a subsidiary is
added to the investment account and credited to income from subsidiary.
Dividends received are debited to cash and credited to the investment
account. This practice is known as the "equity method" and is also
referred to as "one-line consolidation."
The translation process is illustrated with an investment in a
foreign country as follows:

Invest $1,000 or 4,000K in local currency
Exchange rate $1 = 4K or 1K = $.25
Borrow 4000K locally at 15%, or 600K interest
Target: 20% ROE
At the end of one year the local statements are:

Income Statement			Balance Sheet		
Sales		10,000K	Open:		
Profit	(a)	1,800K	Debt	(b)	4,000K
Interest	(b)	600K	Equity	(c)	4,000K
	(c)	1,200K	Total	(a)	8,000K
Tax		400K	End:		
Net		800K	Debt		4,000K
Equity		4,000K	Equity		4,800K
Balance		4,800K	Total		8,800K

Based on the opening balance sheet:

ROA	Profit	(a) 1800K - tax 600K = 1200K/8000K = 15.0%
Debt	Interest	(b) 600K - tax 200K = 400K/4000K = 10.0%
ROE	Profit	(c) 1200K - tax 400K = 800K/4000K = 20.0%

Performance is on target. The statements are submitted and evaluated in K. The translation of K into dollars is illustrated with three assumptions about exchange rates.

Case A   No change in exchange rate from $1 = 4K
          Invest 4,000K at 4K = $1,000
          Net   800K at 4K =   200
          Total   4,800K at 4K = $1,200
          ROE: K 800/4,000 = 20.0% $200/1,000 = 20.0%.

This is a parity situation. No tax adjustment is made on the assumption that the foreign tax obligation provides for U.S. tax liability. This tax area is technical and not fully resolved; in some cases the translation of net income after tax must be adjusted.

Case B   Exchange rate increases to $1 = 6K
          Year average 4 + 6 = 10/2 = 5K
          Invest 4,000K at 4K = $1,000
          Net   800K at 5K =   160
                                  1,160
          Total 4,800K at 6K =   800
          Translation Loss $ 360
          Net: Invest 4,000K = $1,000
          Total 4,800K   800
              (160 - 360)   - 200
          ROE: K 800/4,000 = 20.0% $160/1,000 = 16.0%.

ROE in dollars at 16% is below target. The $360 translation loss is carried to the "accumulated translation adjustment" in the equity section of the balance sheet. The alternative would be to carry the $200 net decrease to income, with ROE -200/1,000 = -20%, hardly a useful expression. In summary:

Investment	4,000K at 4K =	$1,000
Total balance	4,800K at 6K =	800
	+ 800K	- 200
Net income	800K at 5K =	+ 160
Translation Loss		$ 360

Case C   Exchange rate decrease to $1 = 2.4K
         Year average 4.0 + 2.4 = 6.4/2 = 3.2K
         Invest   4,000K   at   4K = $1,000
         Net   800K   at 3.2K   250
                                          1,250
         Total balance 4,800K at 2.4K =   2,000
         Translation gain $ 750
         Net: Invest 4,000K   = $1,000
               Total 4,800K   =   2,000
               (250 + 750)   +1,000
         ROE: K 800/4,000 = 20.0% $250/1,000 = 25.0%

ROE in dollars at 25% is above target. The $750 translation gain is
credited to equity, as described. The alternative would be to carry the
$1,000 net gain to income, with ROE $1,000/$1,000 = 100%--again, hardly a
useful ratio. In summary:

         Investment   4,000K at 4K = $1,000
         Total   4,800K at 2.4K = 2,000
                    + 800K   +1,000
         Net income   800K at 3.2K =   250
         Translation gain $ 750

These examples are based on current practice: ending balances at
current exchange rates and transactions at average (or specific) rates
for the period. The subject is controversial. Several methods have been
used in the past.   The present procedure continues to evoke criticism.
Many alternatives are proposed.   An attractive proposal is to present
foreign operations in foreign currency only without translation. The
parent would carry the investment at cost and record dividends as income
when received.   This would relieve the consolidated statements of almost
meaningless translated dollars and put the onus of financial interpretation   on   statement   users.   As a passing note, extensive research
establishes that financial markets "see through" accounting conventions
in establishing value. The principal concern to management is the proper
interpretation of foreign operations. There is surprising variety in the
techniques of translation manipulation--neither desirable nor necessary.
A foreign company operates locally exactly as a U.S. company does in the
United States.   Performance evaluation should be done in the local
currency only.   Economic evaluation rests on overall evaluation of
prospects in each country, paralleling the original investment decision.

10

Operating Controls for Marketing Performance

DEFINING PERFORMANCE RESPONSIBILITY

Good plans help to get good results. Equally important, good performance controls are needed to adapt to changing circumstances and unforeseen developments. Good information supports good decisions, capitalizing on opportunities, minimizing setbacks, and avoiding dangers.

The information system should provide timely, relevant data on all activities of significance to those responsible. Control can be exercised only for the future--after the event the record is history; accepting an order, changing credit terms, fixing a sales price, introducing a new product, entering a new market, contracting for advertising.

Performance records compared with plans and past periods are instructive but decisions must be made in the light of current information and expectations. The information system encompasses all written data and oral communication, both within the company and from outside. It includes, but is not limited to, the accounting system which is charged with the formal recording of all financial transactions, both completed and in progress, to meet all internal and external requirements based on GAAP. Statements to the effect that accounting is "inadequate" or "out-of-date" or "fails to meet current requirements" are misguided. Each manager must take the responsibility for performance in his or her area of accountability, and that must include responsibility for obtaining the information needed for planning and control. The needs of all managers must be served by an integrated company system including all accounting requirements. Design assistance is provided by systems analysts; review is provided by company auditors; operation is provided by clerks, bookkeepers, and data processors; but appraisal is the province of all managers, including accounting managers. The process is ongoing, evolutionary, and subject to cost-benefit analysis. It does not provide answers to questions, or make forecasts, or evaluate choices, but it helps people to do so.

The formal accounting reports include all recorded transactions for stated periods expressed in financial terms. Net income--the "bottom line"--receives too much attention, along with EPS. Profit must always be related to a base amount--net assets for ROA and equity for ROE. "But net income ... is not an adequate measure of company strength in the view of most economists. A far better measure is return on assets ....(New York Times, November 30, 1987 p. A1).

The well-informed manager can make timely decisions on the significant variables as events unfold and be assured that the results will be the best attainable under the circumstances. He will also know the degree and direction of change from plan within reasonable limits. He can anticipate the effect on the formal reports and keep superiors informed to an appropriate extent to avoid surprises. The process is analagous to a sports coach--he trains players, plans the game, develops plays, assigns players to positions, defines their jobs, calls the plays, assesses performance, evaluates the competition, adjusts to developments, and uses written, oral, and visual information. The final score is for the books.

The clear definition of responsibility among marketing, manufacturing, and administration is central to both planning and performance accountability. A pivotal role is played by the planned cost of a product, or standard cost per unit. It is in effect a price quoted by manufacturing to marketing--the equivalent of a vendor price. It is basic to sales planning. The sales margin is sales less standard product costs less marketing expenses. The plan specifies the quantity and price of each product to be sold by period, and excludes the products not to be sold because of poor promise.

Manufacturing plans production for the products to be sold, by quantity and period, including changed inventory levels. Production costs are based on the standards used for both inventory valuation and comparison with actual costs. Variances from standard are chargeable to manufacturing; they are not carried to inventory or transferred to marketing. Variances are also not identified with products because they are inefficiencies of operation by definition. Accountability is established by responsibility: purchase prices, material usage, wage rates, labor time efficiency, overhead spending and efficiency, and volume variance. Close coordination between manufacturing and marketing is essential for both timely production and cost control. Administrative expenses are based on the sales and production plans, plus other management considerations. The combined plans are coordinated and translated into departmental budgets and the company profit plan.

The product cost standards thus measure standard gross margin for sales and expense variances for manufacturing.

A product cost standard is outlined in brief form with illustrative amounts:

               CC = cost center
               V = variable expense
               F = fixed expense

Direct Material (V)

CC	TYPE	Qty.	Price	Amount	
				$115	46%

Direct Labor (V)

CC	Operation	Time	Rate		
				$ 45	18%

Factory Overhead
    Direct:

	Absorption	Rate:		
CC	Basis	V-F		
			V $30	12%

Direct--Variable Subtotal			V 190	76%
Direct--Fixed--OH			F 25	10%
Total Direct			215	86%

    Indirect:

		Allocation				
Dept.		Basis	%			
Total Indirect				V $20 + F $15 = 35	14%
Total Product Cost				V $210 + F $40 = $250	100%
				84% 16%	

Factory Overhead Recap

Direct	V $30 + F $25 = $55	61%
Indirect	V $20 + F $15 = $35	39%
	V $50 + F $40 = $90	100%
	V 55.6% F 44.4%	

A detailed format with subtotals helps all users to grasp the nature of the cost structure and focus attention clearly, facilitating communication and analysis. It also aids marketing in updating costs currently as factors change.

Reporting by responsibility using standard costs is illustrated:

	Plan	Actual	Gain (Loss)	% to Plan
Marketing				
Sales	$1,000	$1,100	$100	10%
Standard cost	400	464	(64)	16%
Standard GM	600	636	36	6%
Expenses	200	220	(20)	10%
Sales margin	400	416	16	4%
	40%	38%	16%	
Manufacturing				
Actual	420	481	(61)	
Standard	400	464	(64)	
Variances	20	17	(3)	
Operating margin	380	399	19	5%
Administration				
Expenses	220	215	5	
Profit before tax	$ 160	$ 184	$ 24	15%
Percent to sales	16%	16.7%	24%	
Assets	$1,000	$1,024	$ 24	
ROA before tax	16%	18%	100%	

The 10% sales increase provides a 4% sales margin increase, with both standard costs and expenses higher than plan. The incremental gain of 16% in the sales margin lowers the weighted average from 40 to 38%. The balance of this chapter examines the details underlying this marketing summary in terms of operating controls, profitability analysis, and accounting reports.

Planned manufacturing variances of $20 are only $17 less by $3. The resulting operating margin of $399 is a gain of $19 on $380, or 5%. This is not a gross profit, shown on conventional reports, because sales expenses are deducted. The standard costs in marketing equal the standards in manufacturing, indicating no change in total inventory at standard. Manufacturing operations are examined in detail in the next two chapters. Administration includes all other departments; expenses are $5 under plan. The profit before tax thus increases by 15% from plan, with a small increase in percent to sales--16 to 16.7%. Assets increase by $24 on the sales increase of $100. The plan ROA of 16% jumps to 18%, with incremental ROA of 100%. Nonoperating income and expense, interest, and taxes are not relevant to operations and are omitted.

The statement is recast in conventional terms:

	Plan	Actual	Gain (Loss)	% to Plan
Sales	$1,000	$1,100	$100	10.0%
Costs	420	481	(61)	14.5%
Gross profit	580	619	39	6.7%
SGA	420	435	15	3.6%
Profit before tax	$ 160	$ 184	$ 24	15.0%

This format is useful only for general financial purposes.

MARKETING

The marketing organization is responsible, with varying degrees of delegation, for functions such as selection of markets and products; prices and terms; quantities sold; warehousing and freight; warranty; commissions; sales discounts; returns and allowances; credit, collection, and bad debts; advertising and promotion; market research; sales forecasts for production scheduling; finished goods inventory levels, and all department expenses. It is responsible for the cost of products sold, at standards set by manufacturing and at purchase cost from vendors for resale products. Marketing depends on manufacturing for efficient production, embodied in the cost standards, for quality output and for timely shipment.

Product sales and costs, and their mix, produce the standard gross margins in all categories. The costs are by debit from inventory on billing.

Sales categories include:
Products--lines, classes, items (units and prices)
Source--production or purchase
Markets--wholesale, retail, original equipment, government, export,
         private label, private brand, catalog, factors
Geography--country, state, region, territory, city, zip code
Sales Channel--branches, salesmen, brokers, agents, direct sales
Customers--individual, industry, by location and size

Sales expenses are classified as variable and fixed, based on time and volume factors, to the extent useful for expense control. The expenses are direct or indirect relative to each specific sales category, and may be traceable to varying degrees. Allocations are arbitrary and not needed for either expense control or profit analysis. Other distinctions used in analysis as appropriate include book costs without expenditure (depreciation), out-of-pocket (disbursement required), avoidable or unavoidable (sunk costs), opportunity cost (best alternative), and implicit cost (interest assumed).

Sales

Sales are recorded on the books when shipped and billed. A sales report for four products is illustrated:

	Total	1	2	3	4
Sales	$10,000	$4,000	$3,000	$2,000	$1,000
Standard cost	4,000	1,800	1,200	700	300
Standard GM	6,000	2,200	1,800	1,300	700
	60%	55%	60%	65%	70%

The time intervals from order acceptance to shipment may be both long and variable. The sales effort is complete with order acceptance; some commissions are paid on that basis. The sales report for shipments made reflects orders accepted earlier, perhaps dating back from a week to a year, with varying time combinations for each product. Operating control requires a current record, or log, of all orders accepted, cancellations, shipments, and backlog, kept daily on a cumulative basis by day, week, and month. The log can also show future shipping dates and standard gross margins. The classifications should be made according to need-- product, market, channel, location, and customer. The focus should be selective to provide timely data on the most relevant activities, the vital factors, sometimes referred to as key variables. The order log facilitates timely decisions to deal with emerging changes. The results in the formal reports can thus be largely anticipated to avoid surprises in the historical reports. The distinction is between effect operating control and financial history.

An example of a weekly order report drawn from an order log is given for four products:

Date	Total	1	2	3	4
Backlog	$43,000	$18,000	$15,000	$ 7,000	$ 3,000
Accepted	12,000	6,000	4,000	1,000	1,000
Cancelled	- 1,000	0	- 1,000	0	0
Shipped (report)	-10,000	- 4,000	- 3,000	- 2,000	- 1,000
Backlog	44,000	20,000	15,000	6,000	3,000
To be shipped:					
Month 1	$12,000	$ 8,000	$ 3,000	$ 1,000	0
2	8,000	2,000	2,000	2,000	2,000
3	10,000	1,000	6,000	2,000	1,000
4	14,000	9,000	4,000	1,000	0

Standard GM:
  Month 1

Ship	$12,000	$ 8,000	$ 3,000	$ 1,000	0
Std. GM %		55%	60%	65%	70%
Std. GM	$ 6,850	$ 4,400	$ 1,800	$ 650	0
	57%				

The shipped line corresponds with the sales report given above. The timing of order acceptance for these shipments is not given and is not relevant, but it is determinable if needed. The backlog by product changes by varying degrees. The amounts to be shipped by month are shown for the backlog. With this report prepared weekly, the amount to be shipped next month would usually be reliable, even with long lead times between acceptance and shipment. At the other end of the time spectrum, if all orders are shipped on receipt, there is no need for this report; a daily record of shipments suffices. Projection for shipments beyond the next month are less certain but management is alerted to changes in patterns relative to plans and past performance. The standard gross margins for shipments in the first month are shown at the rates used in the sales report, but this would usually not be the case because of changes in prices, costs, and mix. The shift in total from 60% in the sales report to 57% in the order log arises from the product weighted average only. Shifts in backlog and shipping dates may affect inventories and production schedules. The records must be kept carefully and audited regularly but approximate accuracy is acceptable.

Sales Deductions

Sales are subject to deduction for customer returns and allowances, freight-out, and sales discounts. Each deduction must be carefully defined and closely controlled to avoid possible profit impairment. Reporting must be explicit for each item; netting against sales obscures essential information.

Returns and allowances. Customers should be required to obtain advance written approval for returns, with the reason stated. Returned goods are credited to receivables at the billed amount and debited to an account for sales returns. The goods are inspected and valued at current standard cost less any expenses needed to restore full inventory value. This net amount, ranging from zero to full standard cost, is debited to inventory and credited to the sales return account. If the return is valued at full standard cost without any repair needed, the sales return account has a debit for the standard gross margin--sales debit less standard cost. The debit is higher to the extent of estimated repair costs. These expenses are debited to inventory at standard with a credit to the actual expenses incurred. Control is exercised through work orders. In some cases it is preferable to grant an allowance without return of goods; such credits should explain the reason and carry management approval. Allowances may be given for a variety of reasons: late delivery, poor quality, wrong quantity, price error, freight adjustment, unauthorized shipment, delivery to wrong location, repairable damage. The allowed amount is credited to receivables and charged to sales allowances rather than returns. In some cases a return is replaced with a new shipment with memo paperwork. Any extra freight is charged to sales allowances. All returns and allowances should be closely monitored and a daily log maintained with appropriate sales categories (products, markets, customers). Weekly and monthly summaries should be provided for management review. There may be a tendency for these deductions to become excessive because of a desire to please customers, such as the return of obsolete, unsaleable goods. The daily log and periodic recaps are not illustrated but should be similar to the order log illustrated above.

The handling of returns and allowances (R&A) in the management reports is illustrated for the four products.

	Total	1	2	3	4
Sales	$10,000	$4,000	$3,000	$2,000	$1,000
Standard GM	6,000	2,200	1,800	1,300	700
	60%	55%	60%	65%	70%
R&A	1,000	200	600	200	0
Net	$ 5,000	$2,000	$1,200	$1,100	$ 700
	50%	50%	40%	55%	70%

Returns and allowances are usually combined for financial reports. Operating control is exercised through the logs described in which entries are made as approvals are granted. The booking in the records comes at a later date similar to the timing difference for order acceptance and shipment. In the financial report sales are for shipments billed in the period and for returns and allowances approved in the period but which relate to earlier shipments for various time intervals.

The financial report on a net basis with R&A deducted from sales:

	Total	1	2	3	4
Net Sales	$ 9,000	$3,800	$2,400	$1,800	$1,000
Standard GM	5,000	2,000	1,200	1,100	700
	55.5%	52.6%	50.0%	61.1%	70.0%

This net basis, regularly used for published reports, has no value to management and may be misleading; in some cases net sales are negative.

Freight-Out. The cost of delivery to a customer by any means is designated freight-out. There are four situations:

	Freight-Out Expense	Customer Receivables	Freight-Out Payable
Price includes delivery:			
Ship prepaid	DR		CR
Ship collect	DR	CR	
Price excludes delivery:			
Ship prepaid	0	DR	CR
Ship collect	0		

The last category is most common; the customer pays the freight.

Pricing with or without delivery cost is a company decision, usually following industry practice. Shipping prepaid or collect may be at the customer's option. If the price includes delivery the cost is charged to an account for freight-out, a deduction from sales because the cost has been included in the price. Price quotations may be made with freight-out as a separate item, with shipment to be made either collect or prepaid.

Some industries include a fixed amount for freight-out in the price for all sales. Sales to shipping zones with higher freight costs thus have lower margins. For example, for five freight zones:

	Total	1	2	3	4	5
Sales	$10,000	$2,000	$2,000	$2,000	$2,000	$2,000
Standard GM	5,000	1,000	1,000	1,000	1,000	1,000
Freight-out	2,300	0	200	400	800	900
Net	2,700	1,000	800	600	200	100
	27%	50%	40%	30%	10%	5%

If the plan requires 25% net, zones 4 and 5 are seriously short. The 27% net is a weighted average. If zones 4 and 5 are dropped, the totals become: sales $6,000 - standard GM - $3,000 - freight-out $600 - net $2,400, or 40%. Plants are located according to potential sales volume and freight costs for specified zones, with a planned weighted average for all zones. A sales quotation for shipment beyond the plant area would require separate analysis (incremental).

If the sales schedule given is rewritten on a net basis the result is misleading, as follows:

	Total	1	2	3	4	5
Net sales	$7,700	$2,000	$1,800	$1,600	$1,200	$1,100
Net	2,700	1,000	800	600	200	100
	35.1%	50.0%	44.4%	37.5%	16.7%	9.1%

These results are skewed to the degree of freight cost, the total increase from 27 to 35.1%. Zone 1 is unchanged at 50% and zone 5 jumps from 5 to 9.1% .

When some sales are priced with freight included and other sales exclude freight cost, a careful distinction must be made in the reports for consistent measurement. For example:

	Sales Include Freight		Sales Net of Freight
Sales	$4,000		$3,600
Standard cost	1,440		1,440
Standard GM	2,560	64%	
Freight-out	400	10%	
Net	$2,160	54%	$2,160 60%

If the sales price includes delivery, the report totals must be shown net for consistency. The net amount is the equivalent of sales with prices excluding delivery. If needed, a supporting schedule can show the gross method. Freight-out can be a significant cost and actual amounts should be carefully analyzed relative to the amounts used in pricing.

Sales Discounts. A variety of discounts may be granted as part of pricing policy such as cash discounts, trade discounts, early order discounts, order size discounts, and discounts for total purchases in a period.

Cash discounts are a common practice: for example, 2% discount allowed for payment within 10 days with the full balance due in 30 days: 2/10 net 30. The computation for a $100 invoice is: Pay $98 in 10 days or $100 in 30 days. The extra $2 to hold $98 for 20 days is 2/98 times 360/20 on an annual basis or 2/98 = 2.04% x 18 = 36.72% effective annual rate. When payment is received cash discount is credited to receivables and charged to a separate account for cash discounts allowed. This account is a sales deduction and should not be netted against sales. An alternative view holds that cash discount is a financing expense, the cost of obtaining cash sooner, classified in reports as nonoperating expense. If interest is charged on past due balances, the credit is made to interest income and reported as nonoperating income.

Discounts allowed that are larger than cash discounts are trade discounts, charged to separate accounts as sales deductions. There is no specific cut off point. For example, 6/15 net 30 = 6/94 or 6.38% times 360/15 or 24 = 153%. Trade discounts follow industry practice and are a convenient method for adjusting prices to particular situations.

Discounts for orders placed early in the season permit better production scheduling. Discounts for larger orders are based on lower handling costs. Discounts for total purchases encourage customers to buy more each season. The estimated total discounts for a year may be accrued and charged to expense periodically. When the discount is earned by a customer for total purchases for the period, the actual amount is credited to receivables and charged to the accrual account.

The effect of sales discounts is illustrated for five customer sales classes (returns and allowances and freight-out are omitted):

	Total	1	2	3	4	5
Sales	$15,000	$5,000	$4,000	$3,000	$2,000	$1,000
Standard GM	6,000	1,500	1,200	1,500	1,200	600
	40%	30%	30%	50%	60%	60%
Discounts:						
Cash	180	100	60	20	0	0
Trade	540	400	140	0	0	0
Early orders	300	200	0	100	0	0
Order size	140	40	0	60	40	0
Total purchases	40	10	0	30	0	0
	1,200	750	200	210	40	0
Net	$ 4,800	$ 750	$1,000	$1,290	$1,160	$ 600
Net to sales	32%	15%	25%	43%	58%	60%
Discounts to sales	8%	15%	5%	7%	2%	0

The net sales percents as planned should be used in projecting standard gross margin from the order log illustrated above. Because the sales deductions are necessarily expense provisions based on plans, there is no need for current operating control. If deemed useful, each account could be reviewed quarterly to see whether the provisions are still in line with expected results. The effect of sales discounts on sales and profitability should be subject to incremental analysis carried out at selected intervals.

Sales Expenses

All expenses to be incurred by marketing should be budgeted by departments according to organizational responsibilities and by individual expense. The primary purpose is accomplishment rather than expense control in the narrow sense of efficiency. If the need for substantially higher expenses arises, advance approval should be obtained to avoid any surprise in the financial reports. The departmental budgets should also be subject to interpretation as to direct and traceable expenses relative to sales classes as needed for profit reporting and profitability analysis. An illustrative list of departments is given:

General marketing:

    Sales management
    Market research
    Advertising
    Credit and collection
    Operations control and analysis

Customer sales: Distribution:

    Branch sales management   Order handling
    Product line managers   Scheduling
    Sales training   Warehouses
    Customer service   Shipping
    Promotion   Traffic
    Government sales
    Export sales
    Private label sales

Individual expense accounts are provided to help with budgeting, reporting, and analysis of salaries, fringe, overtime, temporaries, fees, travel, entertainment, professional services, supplies, printing, telephone, postage, insurance, taxes, depreciation, and utilities. Control is by department but the accounts can be cross-totalled for reference if desired for analysis. Some accounts may be additionally coded by sales class to aid analysis.

Monthly reports comparing actual with budget and past periods are sufficient for expense control. Major changes should be approved in advance to preclude surprises. The department expenses are fixed as planned to meet objectives and seldom vary with volume alone. A large increase in orders could require some higher handling expenses. A change in policy could lead to more, or less, market research, or other discretionary function. If sales drop materially, some expenses may be increased in an effort to restore volume. A change in plans could add or drop a market or product. Major departures from plan may require a new forecast for the balance of the year. The constant concern is how actual performance will compare with plans and what actions are being taken to remedy problems.

Some marketing expenses are better handled separately for control and reporting such as sales commissions, bad debts, warranty, and advertising.

Sales commissions and agent fees are based on sales, and they are often fully variable with volume and direct to products. They may be payable after shipment or with order acceptance, particularly when shipment is in the future. Sales commission expenses over budget are favorable because the sales budget has been exceeded. Commissions are usually at a constant percent but may vary by product or sales totals or other factors. Changes in commissions should be analyzed incrementally.

Bad debts are provided for by charge to bad debt expense and credit to allowance for bad debts, usually based on a percent to sales. The percent may vary by customer class according to risk and projected losses. The balance in the allowance may have to be adjusted periodically as experience indicates or as credit conditions change. The allowance balance is deducted from receivables in the balance sheet. Uncollectible accounts are credited to receivables and charged to the allowance account on approval of a credit officer. Credit policy is subject to incremental analysis; a customer class with potential large write-offs may still be profitable. The actual and planned bad debts should be monitored. A policy of minimum bad debt expense can well be counterproductive by precluding profitable sales.

Warranty expense is provided for by charge to expense and credit to a liability account, as determined by the warranty terms and expectations. Actual expenses are charged to the accrual as incurred. The entries need to be revised periodically and the potential liability re-estimated-- often a broad approximation. Warranties are part of the sales plan and often reflect competitive pressure. Warranty expenses should be monitored for proper approval and for indication of preventable quality failure.

Direct advertising expenses are better controlled with separate accounts outside of the departmental budget. These expenses are often large, of concern to several management levels, and unique in nature as to planning and control. All advertising is expenses as incurred because its future value is indeterminate. Its current value is also not readily determinable. Advertising plans and programs are made on the basis of past practice, policy, marketing goals, competition, and hunch. Advertising expenditures are a form of capital expenditure; quantitative analysis is elusive but models have been developed by the "quants."

If payment is made ahead of time it is charged to a deferred (asset) account and written off when the advertising runs (goes on the air or is published in print). If payment follows the run date, the expense is accrued in a liability account. Sales for a period are matched with the advertising run in the period, with no deferral for possible future value.

The operational control of advertising is significantly different and rests on detailed planning for the year and beyond. The advertising control plan includes details on media, run dates, commitment dates, penalties for late cancellation, and payment dates. The commitment dates are the key factor for authorizing runs or for cancelling programs without penalty. An advertising log should be kept to show all the relevant data, with a summary drawn off periodically. The data should tie in with accounting records for prepaid and accrued balances and expenses. The log should contain both plans and actual data. Budget control rests on comparing the amounts committed with budgets. Commitments are made ahead of the run dates, with a wide range of time intervals. Programs can be fully committed early in the year and be on target for expenses. Differences between commitments and budgets are known and reported at once. Any later difference between actual and committed expense is reported at the time. Amounts in the accounting records are supported and articulated with the entire program. The means for avoiding surprises in the accounting reports is, again, provided by a log that facilitates operational control with timely and relevant data. The total amount of advertising expense reported in the current period is of little relevance by itself.

Sales Reports

The subjects explored are set out in an illustrative report:

	Plan		Actual		Gain (Loss)
Sales (shipped)	$100,000		$110,000		$10,000
Standard cost	42,000		44,000		(2,000)
Standard GM	58,000	58%	66,000	60%	8,000
Deductions:					
R&A	800		600		
Freight-out	1,000		1,200		
Sales discounts (all)	4,200		4,800		
	6,000	6%	6,600	6%	(600)
	52,000	52%	59,400	54%	7,400
Expense accounts:					
Commissions	2,300		2,800		
Bad debts	1,100		400		
Warranty	800		1,200		
Advertising	7,800		8,800		
	12,000	12%	13,200	12%	(1,200)
	40,000	40%	46,200	42%	6,200
Departments:					
General	5,000		5,200		
Sales	7,000		7,400		
Distribution	4,000		3,900		
	16,000	16%	16,500	15%	(500)
Sales margin	$24,000	24%	$29,700	27%	$5,700

This accounting report displays the actual results in comparative form on a responsibility basis in historical terms. But it becomes available only ten to fifteen days after the closing date. It should contain no surprises if the operating control system is functioning properly. Otherwise, postmortems misdirect attention from constructive decisions. Defensive managers are tempted to manipulate results and engage in "constructive" accounting--the opportunities abound. The income statement shown is a summary for a given period of all sales classes and all levels of management; supporting statements are supplied as needed. The accounting reports thus are formal summaries of results but are not oriented toward control or analysis.

The operating control system presented above deals with "who needs to know what, and when?" The logs and data described are summarized:

Order log--orders accepted, cancelled, shipped, backlog, with
         projection of shipping periods and standard GMs
Standard cost--product cost standard for each item, updated
         currently; record of price and cost for all items
Returns and allowances--approval log
Advertising--log of commitments, run dates, budgets, expenses

Other expenses are ordinarily reported only periodically, supplemented by timely advance notice of impending changes and major developments: freight-out, sales discounts, commissions, bad debts, warranty, and department expenses.

CONTROLS BY PRODUCT

Marketing deals primarily with products and markets, and each may have many classifications. Revenue includes sales, leasing, service, and other income. Only sales to customers are considered here; inter- and intracompany transfers are excluded. Sales details are extensive but can be applied selectively within company units and among management echelons. All analysis must rest on the relevant details and decisions should focus on the key variables.

Product Profits

Products are analyzed at the successive levels of product lines, product classes, and individual products--the primary basis for analysis.
Product Line Report

	Total	1	2	3
Sales	$100,000	$50,000	$30,000	$20,000
Standard cost	40,000	22,000	12,000	6,000
Standard GM	60,000	28,000	18,000	14,000
	60%	56%	60%	70%
Direct expenses:				
Deductions				
(Total 6,000)	5,000 a	1,000	2,000	2,000
Expenses				
(Total 10,000)	7,000 b	4,000	2,000	1,000
Departments				
(Total 14,000)	8,000 c	3,000	3,200	1,800
Total direct	20,000	8,000	7,200	4,800
Product line margin	$40,000	$20,000	$10,800	$ 9,200
	40%	40%	36%	46%

	Total
Indirect expenses:	
Deductions	1,000a
Expenses	3,000b
Departments	6,000c
Total indirect	10,000
Sales margin 30%	$30,000

All sales are classified by products together with the related product cost standards, which are credited to inventory for each shipment. Standard gross margin is a weighted average. Deductions, expense accounts, and department expenses are shown in total. The $6,000 deductions total is found to be direct, or traceable, to product line 1 for $1,000, to product line 2 for $2,000, and to product line 3 for $2,000--a total of $5,000. The balance of $1,000 is indirect, relative to products, and is given in the list of indirect expenses. These determinations can be made by account subcoding, memo records, analysis, or estimate. The method should be established as part of the information system, with degree of accuracy guided by benefit and cost. In the same manner, total expense accounts are found to be direct for a $7,000 total, with $3,000 indirect. The departments total of $14,000 is $8,000 direct and $6,000 indirect. The product margin is the basis for study and varies considerably from the standard gross margins. Product line 1 compared with product line 2 has a lower standard gross margin by four points but a higher direct margin by four points. Compared with product line 3, product line 1 has a fourteen point lower standard GM but only a six point lower direct margin. Direct expenses total $20,000 compared with the indirect expenses of $10,000 that are not allocated. The direct-indirect expense classification varies with each sales class such as markets, considered below.

Product lines are composed of product classes. Product line 1 is illustrated for its three product classes as follows:

Product Line 1 Report--Product Classes

	Total	A	B	C
Sales	$50,000	$26,000	$14,000	$10,000
Standard cost	22,000	10,400	7,000	4,600
Standard GM	28,000	15,600	7,000	5,400
	56%	60%	50%	54%
Direct expenses--all				
(Total 8,000)	6,000a	4,420	980	600
Product class margin	22,000	11,180	6,020	4,800
	44%	43%	43%	48%
Indirect expenses	2,000a			
Product line margin 40%	$20,000			

Expenses are shown in total only for deductions, expenses, and departments, both direct and indirect. The $8,000 direct to product line 1 is only $6,000 direct to the product classes. The direct margin percents vary considerably from the standard GM percents.

Product classes are composed of the individual products, as sold to customers, and each has a specific price and cost standard. Averages are meaningful at this level, such as average sales price, not relevant at higher levels. Product class A is illustrated for its three individual products as follows:

Product Line 1 Report--Product Class A--Individual Products

	Total	Ax	Ay	Az
Sales	$26,000	$10,000	$10,000	$6,000
Standard cost	10,400	5,000	3,000	2,400
Standard GM	15,600	5,000	7,000	3,600
	60%	50%	70%	60%

Direct expenses--all				
(Total 4,420)	3,900 a	1,000	2,000	900
Product margin	11,700	4,000	5,000	2,700
	45%	40%	50%	45%
Indirect expense	520 a			
Product class margin 43% $11,180				

The direct expense of $4,420 to the product class is direct to the individual products for only $3,900 in total. The direct margins again vary widely. At this level study can be made for product mix, price-cost-volume relationships, incremental analysis, and comparison with competitors.

This product level may include cases where a single price is used for a narrow range of costs, such as for sizes or colors. For example:

	1	Break-out 2	3	4	Total	Avg.
Single price	$200	$200	$200	$200	$800	$200
Cost range	94	98	100	108	400	100
Margin	106	102	100	92	400	100
	53%	51%	50%	46%	50%	50%

There is usually predictable stability in these detail relationships so that the average can be used safely. Also a single cost standard may apply to a product sold at different prices, for a variety of reasons, but each price should be handled as a separate product. A case of this kind is presented below.

It can be useful to maintain a historical record of each product-- description, prices and costs by elements by date, quantities sold by period, markets--thus tracking price-cost margins, and costs relative to efficiency and inflation.

Margin Analysis

The Product Class A report is restated with quantities and unit amounts:

This Period		Ax		Ay		Az	Total
Quantity		2,000		5,000		1,000	X
Sales	$5.00	$10,000	$2.00	$10,000	$6.00	$6,000	$26,000
Cost	2.50	5,000	.60	3.000	2.40	2,400	10,400
Margin	2.50	5,000	1.40	7,000	3.60	3,600	15,600
		50%		70%		60%	60%

No quantity totals or averages appear in the total column. The schedule for the last period is:

Last Period		Ax		Ay		Az	Total
Quantity		2,000		4,500		1,000	X
Sales	$4.50	$9,000	$2.00	$9,000	$6.00	$6,000	$24,000
Cost	2.50	5,000	.60	2,700	2.62	2,620	10,320
Margin	2.00	4,000	1.40	6,300	3.38	3,380	13,680
		44.4%		70.0%		56.3%	57.0%
Margin increase		$1,000		$ 700		$ 220	$ 1,920
Sales increase		$1,000		$1,000		0	2,000

The change in margin is analyzed for each product for the separate effect of price, cost, and volume. The differences are this period less last period:

Quantity This Period		Ax 2,000		Ay 5,000		Az 1,000	Total X
Price	$5.00		200		600		
	-4.50	+ .50	- 200	0	-600	0	
		$1,000		0		0	$1,000
Cost	$2.50		.60		2.40		
	-2.50	0	-.60	0	-2.62	+.22	
		0		0		$ 220	220
Volume	2,000		5,000		1,000		
	-2,000	0	-4,500	500	-1,000	0	
Margin last period		$2.00		$1.40		$3.38	
		0		$ 700		0	700
Total		$1,000		$ 700		$ 220	$1,920

The price increase of .50 for Ax on 2,000 units sold this period provides a gain of $1,000. Products Ay and Az had no price change. Only Az had a cost change--down $.22 on 1,000 units for $220 gain. Only Ay had a volume change--up 500 units for a $700 gain at the margin for last period of $1.40. Each type of change has been limited to one product for clarity of explanation. Thus the product totals and cross-totals agree. For Ax the price increase does not affect volume. For Ay volume increases at the same price. For Az, cost was lower with no change in price or volume.

Another example shows the relationships for a product when all three factors change--the common situation in practice.

		Last Year		This Year	Gain (Loss)
Quantity		100		112	+12
Sales	$10	$1000	$9	$1008	$ + 8
Cost	6	600	5	560	+40
Margin	4	400	4	448	+48
		40%		44.4%	

The margin percent is up and the dollar gain is $48.
Price: $10 to 9--down $1 on 112 units = -$112 loss
Cost: $ 6 to 5--down $1 on 112 units = +$112 gain
Net effect   0
Volume: 100 to 112--up 12 units on $4 margin = $48 gain.

The margin gain of $48 arises solely from higher volume achieved with a lower price. The lower unit cost offsets the effect of the lower price. The additional units provide $48 at last year's margin of $4. The gain (loss) column in the schedule is misleading.
Reconcilement:

	Gain (Loss)	Analysis	Difference	
Sales	+ 8	-112	+120	= 12 units at $10
Cost	+40	+112	- 72	= 12 units at 6
Margin	+48	0	+ 48	= 12 units at 4

Similar analysis can be made for comparing actual with plan:

Plan		Ax		Ay		Az	Total
Quantity		2000		5500		800	X
Sales	$5.500	$11000	$2.00	$11000	$5.00	$4000	$26,000
Cost	2.595	5190	.62	3410	2.25	1800	10,400
Margin	2.905	5810	1.38	7590	2.75	2200	15,600
		52.8%		69.0%		55.0%	60.0%
This Period (above)							
Margin		$5,000		$7,000		$3,600	$15,600
		50%		70%		60%	60%
Margin Increase							
(Decrease)		$ (810)		$ (590)		$1,400	0

The changes in individual products are large but cancel out. The analysis for each product:

Ax	Price:	$-.50	x 2000 =	$1000 Loss			
	Cost:	-.095	x 2000 =	190 Gain			
	Volume:	0		0		$810 Loss	
Ay	Price:	0		0			
	Cost:	-.02	x 5000	100 Gain			
	Volume:	- 500	x $1.38	690 Loss		590 Loss	
Az	Price:	+1.00	x 1000	$1000 Gain			
	Cost:	+ .15	x 1000	150 Loss			
	Volume:	+ 200	x 2.75	$ 550 Gain		1400 Gain	

Summary:

	Ax	Ay	Az	Total
Price	1000 Loss	0	1000 Gain	0
Cost	190 Gain	100 Gain	150 Loss	140 Gain
Volume	0	690 Loss	550 Gain	140 Loss
	810 Loss	590 Loss	1400 Gain	0

The cross-totals show no net change for price, with the cost gain and volume loss offsetting. These are statistical amounts not relevant for analysis. Ax had a lower price with no volume gain and a small reduction in cost. Ay had a loss of volume with no price change, and a small cost gain. Az had large gains in both price and volume, with a small cost increase. The examination of actual performance with both the past period and the plan should be constructive.

An additional step in analysis can be taken when the performance of products is interrelated. Comparison is made of the weighted average for both plan and actual to isolate the effect of mix variance from volume variance. This process splits volume variance into two parts, relevant only when the products are not independent. A new example is used for illustration:

Plan		a		b		c	Total
Quantity		10		20		30	
Sales	$10	$100	$8	$160	$6	$180	$440
Cost	5	50	3	60	4	120	230
Margin	5	50	5	100	2	60	210

Actual							
Quantity		10		20		42	
Sales	$11	$110	$8	$160	$6	$252	$522
Cost	5	30	4	80	4	168	298
Margin	6	60	4	80	2	84	224
Gain (Loss)		10		(20)		24	14

a--Price: $11 - 10 = $1 at 10 = $10 gain
   Cost and volume--no change
b--Cost: $4 - 3 = $1 at 20 = $20 Loss
   Price and volume--no change
c--Volume: 42 - 30 = 12 x $2 = $24 Gain
   Price and cost--no change

The analysis thus far parallels that given above. The separation of mix from volume based on quanitity ratios can be made as follows:

	Plan	Ratio	Actual	At Plan Ratio	Actual to Plan	Plan Margin	Mix
a	10	1/6	10	12	- 2	$ +5	$-10
b	20	2/6	20	24	- 4	$ +5	$-20
c	30	3/6	42	36	+ 6	$ +2	$+12
	60		72	72	0		$-18

	Total Volume Variance	Mix Variance	Net Volume Variance
a	$ 0	- $10	+ $10
b	0	- 20	+ 20
c	+ 24	+ 12	+ 12
	+ 24	- 18	+ 42

The mix variance for a and b is negative becuase actual sales were a smaller percent of total than planned. For a, the plan ration of 1/6 applied to the actual total of 72 is 12 units, but only 10 were sold--a shortage of 2 units. At the plan margin of $5, the loss is $10 due to mix. By the same method, b is short 4 units for a mix loss of $20. C gains 6 units for a mix gain of $12. With mix variance a loss of $18 and a total volume variance of $24 gain, the resulting net volume variance is $42. Thus, for a and b mix variance and net volume variance are offsetting. For c the total of $24 splits $12 and $12. These relationships are useful to the extent that a and b sales fall when c sales rise.
Summary:

	a	b	c	Total
Price	+$10	$0	$0	+$10
Cost	0	-20	0	-20
Mix	-10	-20	+12	-18
Net volume	+10	+20	+12	+42
	+10	-20	+24	+14

In most situations the mix variances can be omitted.
Industry volume can be analyzed to advantage if reliable quantities are available that relate directly to company products. Changes in

company sales quantities can be separated into the components attributable to market share and industry volume. This topic was introduced in the previous chapter and is now reviewed with several examples. All amounts are in units and percents. (Co. is company; Ind. is industry; mkt. sh. is market share.)

	Prior	Current	Change
Co.	100	150	+ 50
Ind.	1000	1250 B	+250 at 10% A = 25
Mkt. Sh.	10% A	12%	+ 2% at 1250 B = 25
			50

With a 10% mkt. sh., the industry increase of 250 provides 25 units. The 2% increase in mkt. sh. times the current industry total of 1,250 yields 25 units. Thus the gain of 50 units is from each source--a growing share of a growing industry provides a 50% gain--from 100 to 150 units.

	Prior	Current	Change
Co.	100	150	+ 50
Ind.	1000	1000 B	0 at 10% A = 0
Mkt. Sh.	10% A	15%	+ 5% at 1000 B = 50
			50

With no industry increase, the co. gain of 50 units comes solely from mkt. sh. Thus, with a stagnant industry, mkt. sh. had to rise by 5% rather than 2% to achieve the 50 percent increase.

	Prior	Current	Change
Co.	100	150	+ 50
Ind.	1000	750 B	-250 at 10% A = - 25
Mkt. Sh.	10% A	20%	+ 10% at 750 B = + 75
			50

With a declining industry, mkt. sh. had to increase to 20% to gain 50 units.

	Prior	Current	Change
Co.	100	150	+ 50
Ind.	1000	1500 B	+500 at 10% A = + 50
Mkt. Sh.	10% A	10%	0 at 1000 B = 0
			50

Industry volume provides the 50-unit gain, with mkt. sh. unchanged.

	Prior	Current	Change
Co.	100	150	+ 50
Ind.	1000	2000 B	+1000 at 10% A = +100
Mkt. Sh.	10% A	7.5%	-2.5% at 2000 B = - 50
			50

The gain in industry volume more than offsets the loss of mkt. sh.
It is clear that a company gain of 50 units can arise from a variety of
combinations and that such information can be significant. For these
examples the co. gain of 50 units and the prior market share of 10% were
held constant to help clarify the relationships.
Further examples are based on the products analyzed above.

Product Ax	Prior	Current	Change
Co.	2,000	2,000	0
Ind.	10,000	12,500 B	2,500 at 20% A = +500
Mkt. Sh.	20% A	16%	- 4% at 12,500 B = -500
			0

The large industry gain is lost by drop in mkt. sh.

Product Ay	Prior	Current	Change
Co.	4,500	5,000	+ 500
Ind.	18,000	20,000 B	+2000 at 25% A = +500
Mkt. Sh.	25% A	25%	0 at 20,000 B = 0
			500

The company gain comes entirely from industry volume.

Product Az	Prior	Current	Change
Co.	1,000	1,000	0
Ind.	10,000	8,000 B	-2000 at 10% A = -200
Mkt. Sh.	10% A	12.5%	+ 2.5% at 8,000 B = +200
			0

The loss of industry volume offsets the increase in mkt. sh.

Dropping a Product

The elimination of the sales of a product must be related to the
decrease in expenses for that product, based on the analysis of
traceability and assumptions of time and volume. Intangible
considerations are also important. Estimates must be made of the effect
on other products, customers, sales staff, and competitors. The change
in profit must also be related to changes in assets to determine
incremental ROA.
A brief example illustrates the procedure:

	Total	Escapable	Not Escapable
Sales	$10,000	$10,000	$ 0
Product cost: Variable	4,000	4,000	0
Fixed	2,000	1,500	500
Sales deductions	1,000	900	100
Expense accounts	2,000	1,800	200
Department expenses	3,000	800	2,200
	12,000	9,000	3,000
Gain (Loss)	(2,000)	1,000	(3,000)

Escapable, or avoidable, costs of $9,000 can be eliminated but $3,000 is not escapable based on the traceability of costs. This is a form of incremental analysis. If the product is dropped profit is lower by $1,000; the sales loss of $10,000 avoids only $9,000 expense. This would not be evident in the records. The product should be analyzed for possible profit improvement. The nonescapable costs become escapable over time by reduction, or by use for other purposes. The decision often hinges on intangibles but some quantification can help even though approximations are necessary. Costs may be expressed in ranges for the degree of escapability, depending on degrees of traceability and the time horizon. If nonescapable costs drop to $2,000, escapable costs are $10,000 and the difference is zero, rather than a $1,000 gain. If the cost split goes to $10,500 and $1,500, profit increases $500 if the product is dropped. Costs can be reduced by $10,500 against sales of $10,000.

A more complex example is based on three products:

	1	2	3	Total
Sales	$6,000	$5,000	$4,000	$15,000
Cost	2,600	2,000	2,600	7,200
Margin	3,400	3,000	1,400	7,800
SGA	1,740	3,080	2,580	7,400
Gain (Loss)	$1,660	$(80)	$(1,180)	$ 400

This accounting summary is restated in management form and with SGA separated as to direct product expenses:

	1	2	3	Total
Sales	$6,000	$5,000	$4,000	$15,000
Cost	2,600	2,000	2,600	7,200
Margin	3,400	3,000	1,400	7,800
SGA--Direct	640	780	880	2,300
Direct margin	2,760	2,220	1,520	5,500
SGA--Traceable	1,100	2,300	1,700	5,100
Gain (Loss)	$1,660	$ (80)	$(1,180)	$ 400

Analysis for escapability is made as follows--Yes = Escapable and No = Not-Escapable:

	1	2	3	Total
Cost: Yes	$2,200	$1,700	$2,550	$6,450a
No	400	300	50	750
	2,600	2,000	2,600	7,200
SGA--Direct:				
Yes	640	780	880	2,300b
SGA--Traceable:				
Yes	300	500	800	1,600c
No	800	1,800	900	3,500
	1,100	2,300	1,700	5,100
Expense totals	4,340	5,080	5,180	14,600
Recap: Yes	3,140	2,980	4,230	10,350
No	1,200	2,100	950	4,250d
	4,340	5,080	5,180	14,600

A revised product margin report is prepared:

	1	2	3	Total
Sales	$6,000	$5,000	$4,000	$15,000
Escapable--Direct				
Cost	2,200	1,700	2,550	6,450a
SGA--Direct	640	780	880	2,300b
	2,840	2,480	3,430	8,750
Direct margin	3,160	2,520	570	6,250
Escapable				
SGA--Traceable	300	500	800	1,600c
Indirect margin	2,860	2,020	(230)	4,650
Not escapable	1,200	2,100	950	4,250d
Gain (Loss)	$1,660	$ (80)	(1,180)	$ 400

Product 1 provides a $2,860 indirect margin to cover $1,200 not escapable costs and leaves $1,660 gain. Product 2 contributes $2,020 indirect margin; if it is dropped $2,100 expense continues. Product 3 has a direct margin of $570 but escapable costs of $800 turn the margin into a loss of $230--sales $4,000 and escapable costs $4,230. The report is recast:

	1	2	New Total	Drop 3	Old Total
Sales	$6,000	$5,000	$11,000	$4,000	$15,000
Escapable	3,140	2,980	6,120	4,230	10,350
Indirect margin	2,860	2,020	4,880	(230)	4,650
Not escapable total			4,250	0	4,250
Gain (Loss)			$ 630	$ (230)	$ 400

With lower sales, receivables and inventories should be less. ROA is based on total assets with receivables and inventories for product 3 reduced to relative to sales.

	Old Total	Drop	New Total
Gain (Loss)	$ 400	$(230)	$ 630
Assets	$4,000	$ 850	$3,150
ROA	10%		20%

If the schedule is read in reverse, it indicates that an investment of $850 would cause a loss of $230. Even with no reduction in assets the new ROA is $630/4,000 = 15.75%. Elimination of losing products, or other sales categories, can have a dramatic impact on results but all intangibles must be carefully evaluated.

CONTROLS BY MARKET

Reports and analysis are needed for each market, and for the products in each market. The preceding discussion of products was based on a single market. Presentation is made first for four markets in total, and then for markets and products by market.

Market Profits

	Total	Branches	Government	Export	Private Label
Sales	$100,000	$ 50,000	$ 20,000	$ 20,000	$ 10,000
Standard cost	42,000	22,000	6,000	8,000	6,000
Standard GM	58,000	28,000	14,000	12,000	4,000
	58%	56%	70%	60%	40%
Deductions--all direct:					
R&A	800	800	0	0	0
Freight-out	1,000	0	1,000	0	0
Discounts	2,200	2,200	0	0	0
	4,000	3,000	1,000	0	0
Expense accounts--all direct:					
Commissions	2,800	2,000	0	800	0
Bad debts	1,300	1,300	0	0	0
Warranty	600	0	600	0	0
Advertising	7,800	6,200	0	1,600	0
	12,500	9,500	600	2,400	0
Departments (Total 13,500):					
Direct	8,500a	3,000	3,600	1,400	500
Direct total	25,000	15,500	5,200	3,800	500
Direct margin	33,000	12,500	8,800	8,200	3,500
	33%	25%	44%	41%	35%
Departments--indirect:	5,000a				
Sales margin 28%	$28,000				

Deductions and expense accounts are fully direct to the four markets. The departments have $8,500 direct and traceable to markets and $5,000 indirect, which is not allocated. The traceability of expenses is separate for each expense and for each purpose. An expense may be traceable to both markets and products or to neither, or to one and not the other. The identification process must be carried out for all sales classes at all levels. The transactions are coded for accounting records but subcoding may be used to aid classification by sales class. Memo records, analysis, and estimates may be used to achieve the degree of accuracy desired. Approximations are acceptable; traceability is judgmental to some extent.

The exploration of the four markets is undertaken in this sequence: private label, export, government, branches.

Private label often has a low gross margin and a high direct margin because expenses are low. ROA may be high when shipments are made as lots are completed and payment is prompt, keeping current assets at a low level. Each product has a separate product cost even though the only change from the company product is to replace identification with that of the customer. The reports may be broken out by customer as follows:

Private Label Report by Customer

	Total	J	K	L	M	N
Sales	$10,000	$3,000	$2,500	$2,000	$1,500	$1,000
Standard cost	6,000	1,740	1,400	1,240	960	660
Standard GM	4,000	1,260	1,100	760	540	340
Customer margin	40%	42%	44%	38%	36%	34%
Department	500					
Direct margin 35%	$ 3,500					

No part of the department expense is traceable to customers, and no allocation is made. Further analysis of customer by product, or contract, may be made. Long-term contracts should be disclosed, particularly with fixed prices. Private brands are products specified by the customer but are otherwise similar to private labels.

Export sales are illustrated for three regions of a foreign country:

	Total	North Bay	West Way	South Key
Sales	$20,000	$10,000	$ 6,000	$ 4,000
Standard cost	8,000	4,200	2,400	1,400
Standard GM	12,000	5,800	3,600	2,600
	60%	58%	60%	65%
Direct expenses	2,400	1,100	300	1,000
Region margin	$ 9,600	$ 4,700	$ 3,300	$ 1,600
	48%	47%	55%	40%
Department	1,400			
Direct margin 41%	8,200			

Further break-out by product, or customer, may be needed.

Government sales are classified by contract; it is assumed that all business is with a single government agency.

	Total	J4	K7	L5	M6
Sales	$20,000	$8,000	$6,000	$4,000	$2,000
Standard cost	6,000	2,800	600	600	2,000
Standard GM	14,000	5,200	5,400	3,400	0
	70%	65%	90%	85%	0
Direct	1,600	0	1,200	0	400
Contract margin	12,400	5,200	4,200	3,400	(400)
	62%	65%	70%	85%	(20%)
Department	3,600				
Direct margin 44%	$ 8,800				

Profits by contract can be highly variable. Margins may be high but cost overruns are not unusual. Tight time and cost control must be exercised. Network techniques such as critical path or program evaluation review (PERT) may be needed. Contracts may be reported for accounting either as completed or by the percentage of completion based on estimates of work yet to be done relative to the job budget. Substantial adjustments may be necessary when the job is completed. The status of all contracts should be reported regularly; time delays and cost overruns call for prompt attention. Close control of collections and inventories is also essential to achieve ROA goals.

Branch Reports

Branch sales are illustrated with reports by territory, branch, and product.

Sales Report by Territories

	Total	I	II	III	IV
Sales	$50,000	$20,000	$15,000	$10,000	$5,000
Standard cost	22,000	9,200	6,600	4,200	2,000
Standard GM	28,000	10,800	8,400	5,800	3,000
	56%	54%	56%	58%	60%
Direct expenses:					
R&A	800	800	0	0	0
Discounts	2,200	0	0	1,600	600
Commissions	2,000	1,200	600	0	200
Bad debts	1,300	300	200	500	300
Advertising (Total 6200)	1,700a	500	400	300	500
	8,000	2,800	1,200	2,400	1,600
Direct:					
Departments (Total 3000)	2,500b	600	750	500	650
Total direct	10,500	3,400	1,950	2,900	2,250
Territory margin	$17,500	$7,400	$6,450	$2,900	$ 750
	35%	37%	43%	29%	15%
Indirect:					
Advertising	4,500a				
Departments	500b				
	5,000				
Direct margin 25%	$12,500				

Territory I has ten branches. Branches 1 and 2 are illustrated, with the other eight branches given in total.

Sales Report for Territory I by Branches

	Total	Branch 1	Branch 2	All Other Branches
Sales	$20,000	$2,000	$2,000	$16,000
Standard cost	9,200	1,040	800	7,360
Standard GM	10,800	960	1,200	8,640
	54%	48%	60%	54%
Direct:				
R&A	800	160	0	640
Commissions	1,200	120	120	960
Department	600	60	60	480
	2,600	340	180	2,080
Branch margin	8,200	620	1,020	6,560
	41%	31%	51%	41%
Indirect:				
Bad debts	300			
Advertising	500			
	800			
Territory margin 37%	7,400			

Sales Report for Territory I--Branch 1, by Products

	Total	D	E	F	G
Sales	$2,000	$800	$600	$400	$200
Standard cost	1,040	440	300	208	92
Standard GM	960	360	300	192	108
	48%	45%	50%	48%	54%
Direct expenses (Total 340):					
R&A	160	120	0	20	20
Commissions	120	40	36	24	20
	280	160	36	44	40
Product margin	680	200	264	148	68
	34%	25%	44%	37%	34%
Department	60				
Branch margin 31%	620				

Sales Report for Territory I--Branch 2, by Products

	Total	D	E	F	G
Sales	$2,000	$600	$400	$200	$800
Standard cost	800	270	160	90	280
Standard GM	1,200	330	240	110	520
	60%	55%	60%	55%	65%
Direct expenses:					
Commissions	120	18	12	10	80
Product margin	1,080	312	228	100	440
	54%	52%	57%	50%	55%
Department	60				
Branch margin 51%	1,020				

Further analysis can be made for relevant sales classes such as customers, salesmen, and order size. Expense traceability must be made separately in each case.

All the reports given come from the accounting records, supplemented by expense analysis, to establish formal accountability for financial performance. Control of operations is based on order logs and other relevant current records of significant transactions. Fast and appropriate response is needed as events occur and decisions must be guided by current data. Also the situation can be described along with the actions to be taken, with the estimated effect on results as compared with plans. With a good control system the accounting reports are largely a formality--the results agree with expectations or the control system is faulty.

Product Line Reports

The reports described follow organizational lines of authority-- responsibility accounting. Staff people with functional duties may need separate reports. For example, a product line manager may be needed for each product line in a large marketing operation with a variety of products. The product line manager is responsible for guiding performance of products in terms of all factors: price, terms, quality, advertising, design, packaging, discounts, warranty, credit, costs, expenses, safety

stocks, warehousing, and freight. These are the responsibilities of a
sales manager when there is only one product. Actual performance is the
direct responsibility of other managers with line authority. The product
line manager is an adviser, coordinator, and advocate, and thus needs
reports designed for his or her needs. Sales managers for government,
export, and private label do not need a separate line manager. Branch
sales require a separate line manager for each product.

Product line managers use all the information and reports provided to
line managers, each concentrating on his or her assigned product. The
product line managers keep files of standard product costs, constantly
updated for changes, anticipating the less frequent formal cost
revisions. Close communications are maintained within the company to
learn of developments and forecasts of changes.

A summary report for both line and staff is illustrated in brief form:

	Sales	Standard GM	%	Returns
Territory I				
Branch 1	$2,000	$ 960	48%	$200
Branch 2	2,000	1,200	60%	0
(all other branches)				
Total	20,000	$10,800	54%	$800
Territory II				
(Branches)				
Total	15,000	$ 8,400	56%	0
(all other territories)				
TOTAL	50,000	$28,000	56%	$800

A report by product line is developed from the branch reports--

Product Line D	Sales	Standard GM	%	Returns
Territory I				
Branch 1	$ 800	$ 360	45%	$120
Branch 2	600	330	55%	0
(all other branches)				
Total	6,000	3,000	50%	$150
Territory II	2,500	1,000	40%	20
Total	12,500	6,000	48%	$200
Product Line E				
Territory I				
Branch 1	$ 600	$ 300	50%	0
Branch 2	400	240	60%	0
Total	50,000	28,000	56%	$800

Other detail includes recaps by product class by customers and by
salesmen in selected formats. The logs described above to provide current
operating control can also include recaps for product line managers. The
reporting system must be designed to serve the needs of management, be
kept relevant and current, concentrate on the key variables, and be
adapted constantly to changing circumstances. This is the job of the
information system, designed by system analysts who understand the
management process and directed by managers who understand the dynamics of
effective control.

11

Operating Controls for Manufacturing Performance

MEASURES OF PERFORMANCE

Manufacturing costs are stated as operating standards for material, labor, and overhead as an aid to cost control. These standards are also translated into product cost standards for inventory valuation. They are quoted by manufacturing to marketing for use in pricing and sales planning.

Manufacturing costs are the function of many factors such as product specifications, quality level, prices of inputs, technology, automation, total output, rate of output, plant size and location, and management. The scheduling of production must be balanced to reflect customer delivery dates, inventory levels, product mix, run sizes, and costs. Lack of coordination with sales can lead to shortages in products in greater demand and over-supplies for products in lesser demand. Underscheduling involves lost capacity costs (volume variance) and possibly low inventory balances. Overscheduling involves bottleneck costs and possibly high inventories. Rapid shifts in schedules can upset orderly work flow. Capital expenditures provide for output capacity and cost reduction but with relatively long lead times.

Scheduled product sales and inventory levels are the basis for the production plans, translated into budgets and standards based on planned cost factors. Operating reports provide current measures of performance for each cost element, comparing actual with standard, by organizational responsibility. Accounting reports provide periodic historical financial statements based on accrual accounting as part of the formal financial accounting system. These reports should contain no surprises. The information system should provide the current operating data needed for exercising effective control as events occur, and for projecting the probable dollar effect in the financial reports well ahead of their issuance.

The following table specifies the relationships between operating standards and product cost standards for five products to be produced in quantities of 100 each:

Direct Material	Standards	Total	A	B	C	D	E
No. A	100 pcs. at $ 10	$1000	$ 600	$ 200	$ 0	$ 0	$ 200
No. B	40 lbs. at $ 60	2400	0	1200	600	400	200
No. C	200 yds. at $ 20	4000	1000	0	1000	1000	1000
No. D	80 doz. at $ 30	2400	0	600	800	400	600
No. E	1000 ft. at $ 2	2000	200	400	800	300	300
		11800	1800	2400	3200	2100	2300

Direct Labor	Hours	Rate						
Dept. 1	60	$18	$1080	$480	$300	$200	$100	$ 0
Dept. 2	40	$17	680	80	100	200	200	100
Dept. 3	50	$16	800	200	600	0	0	0
Dept. 4	40	$19	760	120	90	100	150	300
Dept. 5	$34	$20	680	130	100	300	50	100
			4000	1010	1190	800	500	500
Prime Cost			15800	2810	3590	4000	2600	2800

Overhead

a) Department expense budgets at practical capacity:

Production	Variable	Fixed	Total
Dept. 1	$800	$400	$1200
Dept. 2	600	400	1000
Dept. 3	400	400	800
Dept. 4	300	300	600
Dept. 5	100	300	400
	2200	1800	4000
Service			
Dept. 6	800	600	1400
Dept. 7	600	600	1200
Dept. 8	400	600	1000
Dept. 9	300	500	800
Dept. 10	200	400	600
	2300	2700	5000
Total overhead	4500	4500	$9000

b) Costing rate--plant:
   Total budget above $9,000
   Practical capacity:
     Direct labor
     250 hours at $18 $4,500
   Rate: $9,000/4500 = $2.00

c) Applied overhead:

		A	B	C	D	E
Direct labor above	$ 4000	$1010	$1190	$ 800	$ 500	$ 500
at $2 rate	8000	2020	2380	1600	1000	1000
Total cost (15,800 + 8,000)	$23800	$4830	$5970	$5600	$3600	$3800
per unit		$48.30	$59.70	$56.00	$36.00	$38.00

This production plan calls for total direct labor of $4,000 with plant capacity rated at $4,500 direct labor. The total fixed expense is budgeted at $4,500. Planned capacity utilization is $4,000 direct labor divided by $4,500 capacity, or 8/9. Unused capacity is 1/9 times budgeted fixed expense of $4,500, equals $500. This is the volume variance, part of the operating and financial plans. The calculation can be made as follows:

Budgeted fixed overhead	$4,500
Plant capacity in direct labor dollars	$4,500
Fixed overhead rate	$1.00
Output in direct labor dollars:	
--Capacity	$4,500
--Scheduled	4,000
--Underutilization	$ 500
Volume variance	$ 500

The variable overhead is also budgeted at $4,500 and the overhead application rate is also $1, based on $4,500 direct labor. The expense budget total is:

Variable--direct labor $4,000 at $1 =	$4,000
Fixed	4,500
	$8,500

The overhead costing rate can be expressed:

	Capacity $4,500 direct labor	
	Expense	Rate
Variable	$4,500	$1
Fixed	4,500	1
	$9,000	$2

With $4,000 direct labor at the $2 rate the charge to inventory is $8,000, the debit to volume variance is $500, and $8,500 is credited to absorbed overhead. If the actual overhead is higher, the difference is a debit to expense variance. Actual overhead expenses--variable and fixed--are compared with budgets to guide expense control. Differences in actual volume (direct labor) from planned volume generate volume variances which may be more or less than plan. Both expense and volume variances are expensed as incurred. Variances are subject to operating control by responsibility; they are not allocated to inventory and they are not analyzed by product. Standards must be kept current to provide best results.

Expense variances are differences between actual and standard for each cost element:

> Material--prices and usage
> Direct labor--time efficiency and rates
> Overhead--expense (spending and time efficiency)

Volume variance is a measure of capacity utilization at budgeted fixed expense. Standards apply to expense control and product costs. Expense variances are booked as incurred. For financial planning only, some expense variance may be provided as a matter of prudence. With tight budgets a degree of expense variance is common. Accountability is based on departments, according to the extent of authority, and by type and cause to the degree practical. Accountability for volume variance is separate because responsibility is more diffuse, involves longer time spans, and relates to the capital expenditure program.

The control of material and labor is explained in the balance of this chapter and overhead in the next chapter.

CONTROLS FOR MATERIAL

Material cost is a major cost element, dependent on vendor prices and product specification (design, performance requirements, types of material). Several vendors may be used to encourage competition and provide more safety in delivery. Or a single vendor may be developed as a participant in the production process relative to design, quality, cost, and delivery. The question of whether a part should be purchased or produced (make-or-buy) requires incremental analysis for the short term and capital expenditure evaluation for the longer term. The cost of materials should be reviewed regularly for possible reductions by design changes, by material substitutions, by revised processing methods, or by lower purchase prices.

Materials are measured directly to products when feasible and when significant in amount. Standards are set for each product for each material, by quantity required for production and by estimated vendor prices. Other materials not directly measurable but related to products are indirect materials, charged to a separate overhead account. The amounts are budgeted and enter into the overhead rate applied to all products. Greater product cost accuracy is obtained by classifying material as direct but there are practical limits to useful measurement. Examples of materials that may be classified as indirect include glue, nails, ink, paste, sandpaper, rivets, paper, padding, washers, and bindings. These items are usually charged to inventory when purchased and debited to indirect materials expense by department when requisitioned for production. Actual expenses are compared with budget to the level of budget detail needed, including the use of price and quantity standards. Reclassification between direct material, a separate cost element, and indirect material, part of overhead, should be reviewed on occasion. All supplies, as distinct from indirect material, should be separately expensed in appropriate accounts. Some common items may require separation between supplies and indirect material when issued.

Price Variance

Standard purchase prices are set by the purchasing department for all direct materials, and possibly some indirect materials, for each vendor based on quantity requirements. The standards are a basis for both product costing and actual price comparisons. Timely revisions are needed to maintain the validity of the measurements; inventory values are adjusted and product costs are revised. The offsetting debit (credit) is made to a separate account for inventory adjustments for purchase price revisions, separate from the purchase price variance account. These companion accounts are a measure of purchase price performance. They are recognized in income as booked. The financial plan may include some allowance for these accounts as a matter of prudence in profit planning.

Vendor quotations must be put on a comparable basis relative to unit price, freight, and discounts. An example is given for four vendors.

	A	B	C	D
Price	9.50	10.00	11.00	11.50
Freight	+1.50	+1.50	0	0
Discount	0	- .50	0	- .50
Standard	11.00	11.00	11.00	11.00

With a vendor price range from $9.50 to $11.50, all four equalize at
$11.00 per unit. Invoices are booked net of discount. If a discount is
lost it is charged to a separate account, usually classified in the
nonoperating section of the income statement. When freight is not
included in the price--A and B--the $1.50 per unit inventory debit for a
collect shipment is credited to a freight clearing account, to be charged
with the freight bill. For a prepaid shipment, the $1.50 would be added
to the invoice with the total credited to payables to reimburse the
vendor. With freight prepaid for C and D, inventory is debited and
vendor payables credited. If freight is collect, it is credited to
freight clearing and debited to payables. Freight clearing is planned to
reach zero; in practice the entries are complex and small differences are
expensed. The procedures described keep the price standard at $11 in all
cases. Freight-out in product pricing is recorded in a similar manner,
as described in chapter 10.

When several vendors are used for a single material it is necessary
to have a single weighted average price for product costing. For example:

Vendor	Purchase Ratio	Unit Price Standard	Extension
A	60%	$10.00	$6.00
B	30	9.50	2.85
C	10	11.50	1.15
Standard	100		10.00

The unit price standard for each vendor is used to measure price
variance. The weighted average is used for the product cost standard.
The price for A at $10 happens to equal the average in this example.
Shifts in purchase ratios affect the average. For example:

Vendor	Ratio	Price	Extension
A	30%	$10.00	$3.00
B	10	9.50	.95
C	60	11.50	6.90
	100		10.85

Such differences are part of price variance, a balance remaining
after purchase price variance is determined separately for each vendor.

Purchase price variances are booked after delivery and acceptance of
the order, and completion of paperwork for vendor invoice, receiving
record, and purchase order. Inventory is debited at standard and
payables credited at actual, with the difference charged (credited) to
purchase price variance. The entries are made in a purchase (voucher)
journal and totals for the period are carried into the financial
statements. Timing thus relates to financial rather than operating
considerations. The total price variance as booked is deducted from

revenue for the period. It is not part of overhead. It is not allocated to inventory or product cost. The timing differences between accrual accounting and purchase commitments can be substantial. The purchases booked relate to vendor commitments made over a long period. Effective control requires the recording and reporting of variances as they occur, separate from the accounting procedures.

Purchasing should keep a log of all purchase orders issued on a daily basis showing actual, standard, and variance amounts. Classifications could include buyer, vendor, order number, type and quantity of material, standard and actual price, and delivery date. A purchase log is illustrated in outline:

Buyer A	Purchase Log Quantity	Unit Price	Date _____ Actual Amount	Standard	Variance	
Vendor I:						
Order No.						
Material 1	100 units	$ 8	$ 800	$ 800	$ 0	
Material 2	60 lbs.	12	720	700	20	
Material 3	80 pcs.	6	480	490	(10)	
Vendor II:						
Order No.						
Material 4	600 lbs.	2	1,200	1,160	40	
(Detail omitted)						
Buyer A Total			$28,119	$27,300	819	3.0%
Buyer B Total (detail omitted)			$79,200	$80,000	(800)	(1.0%)
All Buyers			$586,500	$575,000	$11,500	2.0%

The log can be summarized daily, weekly, and monthly for management review, and classified as to buyers, vendors, and materials. If needed for planning, the scheduled delivery dates can be used to project the timing of transaction entries and the amounts of variances and payables for the impact on cash flow and profit. The accounting reports include booked purchases, and variances can be traced back to origin dates but this need would be unlikely. Marketing can follow material price trends in the purchase log for use in product cost planning to anticipate changes in standards.

Reports from the log should be limited to the more significant items by setting variance limits in dollars and percents. A $100 variance limit is illustrated with decreasing percents to standard:

Actual	Standard	Variance	Percent
$ 2,600	$ 2,500	$100	4.0%
4,100	4,000	100	2.5
5,100	5,000	100	2.0
10,100	10,000	100	1.0
20,100	20,000	100	.5
50,100	50,000	100	.2
100,100	100,000	100	.1

A 2% limit is illustrated with decreasing variance dollars:

Actual	Standard	Variance	Percent
$ 20,400	$ 20,000	$400	2.0%
10,200	10,000	200	2.0
5,100	5,000	100	2.0
2,550	2,500	50	2.0
1,275	1,250	25	2.0

These schedules suggest possible report limits for individual
listings, perhaps at a combination of $100 and 2%. Applying this rule to
the two schedules only the first three items would appear separately.
The remaining items would be grouped into a single total. Debits and
credits should be kept separate in subtotals and totals to avoid
misleading net amounts.

A weekly report drawn from the purchase log is illustrated for type
of material only, with buyers and vendors omitted, using the limits of
$100 and 2% for individual items, both debit and credit:

Material Purchases	Actual	Standard	Variance	Percent
Debit Variances:				
A	$ 1,100	$ 1,000	$100	10.0%
B	5,100	5,000	100	2.0
C	10,200	10,000	200	2.0
D	4,200	4,000	200	5.0
	20,600	20,000	600	3.0
Credit Variances:				
E	7,350	7,500	(150)	(2.0)
F	4,800	5,000	(200)	(4.0)
	12,150	12,500	(350)	(2.8)
Subtotal	32,750	32,500	250	
Other debits	40,320	40,000	320	.8
Other credits	9,800	10,000	(200)	(.2)
Subtotal	50,120	50,000	120	
Total	82,870	82,500	370	
Recap:				
All debits	60,920	60,000	920	1.5
All credits	21,950	22,500	(550)	(2.4)
	82,870	82,500	370	

Reports for higher management levels could be further condensed.
Formats should be responsive to changing conditions and management
preferences. Significant deals relative to purchase totals and variances
would be cleared in advance of commitment and so noted in the purchase
log.

Usage Variance

Standard purchase quantities are based on product specifications for
each material, with allowance for necessary shrinkage and waste in
processing. Production schedules by product are broken down into the
individual material requirements in amounts and timing. Purchases are

charged to inventory at standard prices. Withdrawals from inventory are
at standard cost and in the amounts authorized by production orders. For
example, 100 finished units require 105 units of material at $20, or
$2,100 direct material cost. With no usage variance:

    Issue 105 units at $20 CR RM - DR WIP $2100
    Complete 100 units at $21 DR FG - CR WIP   2100

With usage variance:

    Issue 105 units at $20: CR RM - DR WIP $2100
    Complete 96 units at $21 DR FG - CR WIP   2016
                                    CR WIP   84
    Charge to usage variance   DR   84

Usage variance may be a credit. If 101 units are completed the usage
credit variance is $21. If extra material is issued because of excess
usage, the charge is directly to usage variance. After the first
production countpoint labor and overhead are added. Spoilage and scrap,
illustrated later, are booked at the total cumulative cost to the
countpoint.

Material processing must be correctly recorded at all steps of
production to assure valid reporting. Manipulation can occur by
switching material from one job to another, by requisitioning material
for one job and using it for another, by delayed counts, and by wrong
quantities. Floor operators are motivated to minimize the disclosure of
variances. Periodic floor counts by job at each work station, close
control of material quantities issued to production, and correct count of
pieces put into finished goods are requisite. Close control is also
needed for indirect materials and operating supplies that tend to be
hoarded on the floor for convenience.

Usage variance is expensed as incurred, as a separate cost element.
It is not part of overhead and is not identified by product. The
financial statements contain usage variance based on the timing of
accounting procedures and the period reported. This meets accounting
requirements but is inadequate for operating control. All usage variance
is at standard price and is the responsibility of manufacturing. All
price variance is a purchasing responsibility.

Material usage can be effectively controlled only during the
production process. A log for recording material usage as it occurs is
needed on the factory floor. If recording is made only at the time
materials are issued from stock and when production is completed, the
work done to date and not completed can be substantial. It is known as
"float." It is necessary to establish countpoints at selected process
intervals to determine work done to that point and any material waste or
scrap. These points are specified on the product processing sheets that
are also used to determine standard product costs. Countpoints may be
weigh stations, inspection posts, or count locations, in addition to the
completed pieces put into finished goods. The work done between
countpoints, or float, should be kept to a practical minimum. Piece
counts are the basis for debiting work-in-process inventory at standard

and crediting absorbed cost. Difference between actual and standard are variances, debit or credit. At the countpoint following the introduction of direct material the good pieces are recorded and material usage can be measured. At later countpoints the additional labor and overhead must be added to record scrap expense, a separate overhead account. The material usage log for waste and shrinkage, without labor and overhead, is the basis for floor control, illustrated as follows:

Material Usage Log   Department _____   Date _____
Countpoint: Quantity

		Actual	Standard	Variance	at	Amount	Cause
Job:							
Material	A	1000	920	80	$11	$880	Poor material
	B	600	660	(60)	3	(180)	High standard
	C	1620	1500	120	8	960	Wrong spec's.
	D	128	112	16	5	80	Floor damage

The log can be summarized in daily and weekly reports, with limits on dollars and percents for individual items. For example:

Material Usage Report   Department _____   Week _____
                               Quantity

		Actual	Standard	Variance	at	Amount	Quantity Percent
Material:	A	1100	1000	100	$11	$1100	10%
	B	5610	5500	110	3	330	2%
	C	1236	1200	36	8	288	3%
	D	285	300	(15)	5	(75)	(5%)

When production includes material, labor, and overhead, scrap must include the accumulated cost to the countpoint. Inventory is credited and scrap expense debited, an overhead account. A separate log is needed, as follows:

Scrap Log   Department _____   Date _____
Countpoint: Quantity

		Actual	Standard	Variance	at	Amount	Cause
Job:	1	100	80	20	$ 2	$ 40	Poor material
	2	180	175	5	60	300	Operator error
	3	60	55	5	15	75	Bad die
	4	75	74	1	28	28	Tolerances
	5	44	40	4	18	72	Unknown
	6	92	100	(8)	12	(96)	High standard

Periodic reports can be prepared with dollar and percent limits for individual items. When rejected pieces are reworked, the extra cost is charged to rework labor expense, a separate overhead account. Rework is undertaken as a rule of thumb when the estimated cost of completion is less than the scrap cost to the countpoint. Reworked pieces that are accepted enter into the count of good pieces.

The logs should be reviewed during the shift and recaps prepared promptly for supervisors. The format and degree of detail is a pragmatic choice. Major variances are investigated at once and reported orally as soon as possible.

CONTROLS FOR LABOR

Classification

Total labor is a major cost that embraces earnings and fringe benefits for all employees. Employees are assigned to departments classified as to SGA (period expense) and factory overhead (product cost). Each department has separate expense accounts for types of labor and fringe benefits. Budgets are based on manpower tables, compensation levels, and work plans. SGA budgets are usually fixed in amount and differences between actual and budget are generally small. Large variances are often approved in advance and arise usually because of changes in plans. Accomplishment in quantity and quality of effort relative to goals is obtained by training and supervision. Efficiency in the narrow sense is relevant only at the clerical level.

The classification of departments between SGA, expensed as incurred, and production, charged to product cost at predetermined overhead rates, is a pragmatic choice. Practice varies widely among companies, and within companies at separate plants. The general guideline is to include in factory overhead all expenses necessary for production. There is no effect on expense control--all departments are budgeted. There is no effect on profit planning, either for short-term incremental analysis or for longer-term capital expenditure evaluation.

Finally, cost levels of inventory are higher or lower, but only changes between the opening and ending balances affect period profit. This change is minor in most cases. To illustrate, a shift of overhead from SGA to factory overhead is proposed as follows:

	Present	Proposed
Total Overhead	$1,000	$1,000
SGA	600	500
Factory	400	500
Direct Labor	200	200
Costing Rate	200%	250%

Production and cost of sales are recast with no change in inventory:

	Present	Proposed
Material	$ 400	$ 400
Labor	200	200
Overhead	400	500
	$1,000	$1,100
Inventory Change	0	0
Cost of Sales	$1,000	$1,100

The income statement shows a lower gross margin for the proposal but the same profit:

	Present	Proposed
Sales	$2,500	$2,500
Cost of Sales	1,000	1,100
Gross Margin	1,500	1400
SGA	600	500
Profit	$ 900	$ 900

With no sales all production is in unity and there is no cost of sales. SGA is expensed so the loss is $600 compared to $500 loss for the proposed change.

Organizational responsibility for manufacturing includes some departments usually classified as period expense such as plant management, purchasing, engineering, production scheduling, and quality control. These departments are staffed with salaried people, have fixed budgets, and no traceable relationship of activities to products. All service and production departments are included in factory overhead and charged to inventory through departmental costing rates. Service departments include activities directly supportive of production, such as maintenance, tool room, material handling, and utilities. Production departments work directly on products.

Payroll earnings are calculated for each employee for each period and charged by department and account. Direct labor employees are charged to a payroll clearing account; the cost department determines from time records the distribution for each employee between production, labor, and downtime, an overhead account. Earnings for production time at standard are charged to inventory and credited to payroll clearing. The difference in this account is labor variance, composed of both time efficiency and labor rates analyzed later in this chapter. Factory overhead is analyzed in the next chapter.

Time Efficiency

All direct labor operations are stated in detail on the production process sheets. Standard labor cost is standard time per unit times the standard wage rate, multiplied by good pieces completed at the countpoint. Labor time efficiency is based on both actual and standard time by operation. Total labor earnings are total time at work, by clockcard, at the wage rate for each worker. Total earnings are subdivided between production and downtime, based on details kept on the floor by use of worksheets and trailer cards, the responsibility of workers, supervisors, and timekeepers. Time not spent on production-- downtime--is accounted for by cause: no work schedule, machine down, power out, die not available, no material, wrong setup, company meeting, personal time, training, first-aid.

Total production time is charged to inventory at standard, with debit or credit to labor variance according to time efficiency. Downtime is charged to overhead in a separate account budgeted relative to total time. All indirect labor is charged to separate overhead accounts. Control of direct labor is critical to performance efficiency and must be exercised in real time on the floor by worker and by operator. Both accurate time records and correct piece counts are essential. The periodic accounting totals for total production labor, standard and actual, and for downtime as part of overhead, budget and actual, are financial summaries without control usefulness.

A record for 8 hours, or 480 minutes, at $12 per hour, or $.20 a minute illustrates the details in minutes:

Job A	Actual	Standard	Gain (Loss)	Time Efficiency
Operation 21	100	94	(6)	94%
32	110	121	11	110%
43	132	165	33	125%
	342	380	38	111%
Pay at $.20	$68.40	$76.00	$7.60	

The standard earned of $76.00 is debited to inventory; payroll earning is credited $68.40 and labor variance is credited $7.60.

Total time 480 minutes less 342 for production is 138 downtime, coded by cause. The charge to overhead is $27.60, credited to payroll clearing. The combined total is $96.00 ($68.40 plus $27.60). The allowance for downtime is budgeted at 25% of total time or 120 minutes. The variance is: 138 - 120 = 18 or 15% over budget or $27.60 - 24.00 = $3.60 debit.

Recap:

	Actual	Standard	Gain (Loss)	
Production	342	380	38	Direct Cost
Downtime	138	120	(18)	Overhead
	480	500	20	

The time efficiency output rate of 380/342 = 111% can also be expressed 342/380 = 90%. Both measures conceal the lost minutes for operation 21.

It it enlightening to consider the effect of 20 minutes shifted by workers in the time detail to improve the efficiency rate:

Production	Actual	Standard	Gain (Loss)	
Reported	342	380	+38	= 111%
Actual	362	380	+18	= 105%

The actual efficiency of 105% has been boosted to 111% by the shift of 20 minutes. Standard time is not affected. It is computed from operating time standards in the process sheets and pieces completed. Count accuracy must also be closely controlled. The 20 minute shift also affects downtime:

	Total	Actual	Standard		
Reported	480	- 342 = 138	- 120 = 18	= 15%	
Actual	480	- 362 = 118	- 120 = (2)	(2%)	

Downtime was slightly below budget but was reported at 15% over. Labor time control thus requires the current recording of all time factors for effective control. Time efficiency and downtime must be tracked constantly during the shift to minimize downtime and to clock output rates. Inefficiencies must be resolved ahead of time or corrected as they develop. Review of performance at the close of the shift should confirm the results of actions taken, permit evaluation of reporting

accuracy, and provide guidance on improvements needed.   A shift summary,
or daily labor log, is given for the data reviewed--in minutes, with a
total for all workers:

	Production			Memo	Downtime				Total
	Actual	Std.		Loss	Actual	Std.			Actual
Worker 101	342	380	111%	6	138	120	18	15%	480
Total	3480	3689	106%	98	1320	1200	120	10%	4800

Loss minutes are set out because they are netted in the time
efficiency percent and must be paid for; this is referred to as make-up
pay.   Separate records may be kept for downtime by cause and for each
worker. Also weekly and cumulative totals may be kept for shifts and
departments, and for the plant total.
The standard wage rate is a projected weighted average of employee
time and pay rates. The actual pay averages are usually close to the
standard.   Small variances occur with shifts in actual time by employee.
A larger change would be approved in advance. An example is the use of
higher rate people, temporarily available, for lower rate work.   This is
an opportunity cost: the booked cost of rate variance is less than the
cost of idle time.
When production is paid for with a full incentive plan that pays
workers for all output at standard time earned the credit variance
disappears.   For example, with 100 standard hours at a $12 standard rate,
the charge to inventory is $1,200. With 80 hours worked, assuming actual
and standard are the same, at a rate of $12, earnings are $960. With the
incentive plan, the extra $240, or 25%, is paid to the workers.   Without
the plan it is a credit to labor variance. The purpose is to encourage
higher productivity. The company benefits from higher output and fewer
men for the period: 80 men at 125% equal 100 men at 100%. If 6 standard
hours are earned in 8 hours--75% efficiency--inventory is debited $72 but
the worker is paid $96, with $24 charged to make-up pay, a separate
overhead account. If the incentive is based on the week for which total
standard exceeds actual there is no make-up time:

Day	Standard	Actual	Over	Under
1	10	8	2	
2	8	8	0	
3	6	8		2
4	9	8	1	
5	11	8	3	
Week	44	40	6	2

The incentive rate is 110% (44/40) for the week. If computed daily:

	Standard	Actual	Net	
Incentive	38	32	+6	119%
Make-up	6	8	-2	Overhead
	44	40	+4	

Total pay is 38 plus 8 = 46 hours, 115% of actual. The illustration omits downtime, which is usually paid at the actual rate. Use of weekly totals helps to overcome the possible rigging of time details.

Total labor is planned to meet production schedules geared to sales forecasts, inventory levels, and plant utilization. The labor plan is translated into department head counts by period. For example, a manpower table for one month for the factory is calculated as follows:

	Hours
Scheduled output at standard time	69,000
Actual production time at 115% efficiency	60,000
Downtime at 20%	12,000
Direct labor hours	72,000
Time off	8,000
Total paid time	80,000

Head count:
> 80,000 hours/20 days = 4,000 hours per day
> 4,000/8 hours = 500 men

The relevant output range is 10% plus or minus = 450 to 550 men.

Indirect labor is scheduled at 60% of direct labor: 500 at 60% = 300 men. The range is plus 8% = +24 and minus 5% = -15 or totals of 285 to 324. Recap of headcount:

Direct Labor	450	500	550
Indirect Labor	285	300	324
Total	735	800	874

Manpower tables should be prepared for all departments in the company, by labor category. Periodic reports should compare planned and actual headcounts.

Recording Variances

Inventory is charged with production labor at standard hours and rates, with credit to the labor clearing account. This account is charged with direct labor earnings at actual times and rates. Downtime is also credited to the clearing account and charged to overhead. The balance is labor variance, expensed as incurred. It includes both time efficiency and rate variance, determined separately only by analysis. Marketing may watch time efficiency and rate trends to anticipate changes in product cost standards. The daily labor logs and reports described provide operating control for time efficiency and downtime. Rate variance is usually small and known in advance for any major change such as for pay raises or use of high-rate people in lower-rate work. Periodic accounting reports show total variances as financial amounts.

The entries for the direct labor clearing account for one month are illustrated with hours and a $10 pay rate for both actual and standard:

	Hours	Debit	Credit	
Actual pay	2500	$25,000		CR Payroll Accrual
Downtime	600		$ 6,000	DR Overhead Account
Production at standard	1800		18,000	DR WIP Inventory
Variance	100		1,000	DR Labor Variance
		25,000	25,000	

The analysis is made as follows for production time--1,900 hours (total 2,500 less 600 downtime):

	Actual	Standard	Analysis
Hours	1,900	1,800	100 @ $10 = $1000 DR
Rate	$ 10	$ 10	0
Total	$19,000	$18,000	$1000 DR

For this example rate variance is zero and time efficiency variance is negative $1,000. Time efficiency is 94.7% (18/19). The 100 hours worked in excess of standard are detailed in the daily labor log by worker and operation. A recap of the production hours shows both over and under standard subtotals:

	Actual	Standard		
Over 100%	1200	1260	+ 60	105%
Under 100%	700	540	-160	77%
Total Hours	1900	1800	-100	94.7%

The example is given in reverse form:

	Actual	Standard	Analysis
Hours	1,800	1,900	100 @ $10 = $1,000 CR
Rate	$ 10	$ 10	0
Total	$18,000	$19,000	$1,000 CR

Rate variance is zero and time efficiency variance is 105.6% (19/18). The standard work was achieved with 100 fewer labor hours. There is no make-up pay. No incentive is paid. If incentive is paid total earnings are $18,000 at the incentive rate of 105.6%, or $19,000. In this case the actual pay is $19,000 and there is no variance.

A more realistic example is given:

	Actual	Standard	Analysis
Hours	6,000	5,700	300 @ $10.10 = $3,030 DR
Rate	$ 10.00	$ 10.10	.10 @ 6,000 = 600 CR
	$60,000	$57,570	$2,430 DR

The example in reverse reads:

	Actual	Standard	Analysis
Hours	5,700	6,000	300 @ $10 = $3,000 CR
Rate	$ 10.10	$ 10.00	.10 @ 5,700 = 570 DR
Total	$57,570	$60,000	2,430 CR

The gain in time efficiency of $3,000 is offset by $570 loss from rate variance. If incentive pay applies, time variance is zero: 5,700 hours at 105.26% (6,000/5,700) = 6,000 incentive hours at $10 = $6,000.

In all cases the charge to inventory at standard is the same. Rate variances are usually small and time efficiency is controlled on the floor. Total variance may be very small but conceal large debits and credits. For example:

	Actual	Standard	Analysis
Hours	110	100	10 @ $10 = $100 DR
Rate	$ 9	$ 10	1 @ $110 = 110 CR
Total	$990	$1000	$ 10 CR

For fully automated operations there is no direct labor. All labor is part of overhead and standards are set for manpower levels and average rates for labor cost. Other expenses are budgeted and total overhead is divided by total output to determine unit standard cost. Total output is set at standards for running times and speeds, with allowance for downtime. Control is exercised by constant monitoring of output rates and daily logs of running times and downtime, by cause. The labor goal is to maintain running time and minimize downtime. Labor thus requires no separate control because it is based on the manpower tables.

The Learning Curve

Particular attention to labor time is needed relative to the learning curve (LC). If the LC is actually operative but not recognized in the time standards excessive credits will arise as unit times drop with increased experience. If the LC is included in the standards but does not apply, excess debits will occur because unit times do not drop. Such discrepancies cause errors in the standards debited to inventory as well as in the time efficiency rates.

To illustrate, with an 80% LC, the average unit time drops 80% for each doubling of output:

Units of Output	Unit Avg. Time 80%	Total Time	Increments Time	Output	80% = Avg.
100	1,000	100,000	--	--	--
200	800	160,000	60,000	100	600
400	640	256,000	96,000	200	480
800	512	409,600	153,600	400	384
1600	409.6	655,360	245,760	800	307.2

When new processes are started an initial break-in period is needed to establish operating methods and output capabilities, and to set time standards and LC potential. Assuming that a time standard is set for the first eight units at 512 with an 80% LC the following schedule can be written for unit average time:

Units of Output	Unit Average Time 80%	Percent to 8 Units	Percent to Each Prior Unit
8	512.0	100.00	100.00
9	493.0	96.27	96.27
10	476.5	93.07	96.65
11	462.1	90.25	96.98
12	449.3	87.75	97.23
13	437.9	85.53	97.46
14	427.6	83.52	97.65
15	418.2	81.68	97.80
16 (Double 8)	409.6	80.00	97.94
32 (Double 16)	327.7	64.00	80.00
64 (Double 32)	262.1	51.20	80.00

The average decreases at a progressively lower rate as shown by the last column. Thus, for 16 units the average time is 80% of the time for 8 units--409.6/512.0, but the average time is 97.94% of the time for unit 16--409.6/418.2.

The 80% LC is compared with the 70% LC and the 90% LC to illustrate the degree of variation.

	80% LC		70% LC		90% LC	
	Unit Avg.		Unit Avg.		Unit Avg.	
Units	Time	Percent	Time	Percent	Time	Percent
8	512.0	100.00	343.0	100.00	729.0	100.00
12	449.3	87.75	278.4	81.17	685.4	94.02
16	409.6	80.00	240.1	70.00	656.1	90.00
32	327.7	64.00	168.1	49.00	590.5	81.00
64	262.1	51.20	117.6	34.29	531.5	72.90
128	209.7	40.96	082.4	24.00	478.3	65.61

The 70% LC is 39.3% of 80% LC (82.4/209.7) and the 90% LC is 228.1% (478.3/209.7) for 128 units.

The rate of change becomes increasingly smaller. For 80% LC at a much higher level:

Units	Unit Avg. Time	Percent to 7700	Percent to Prior Amount
7700	.056083	100.000	--
7800	.055850	99.585	99.585
7900	.055622	99.178	99.592
8000	.055397	98.777	99.595

In practice, output is subject to several variables and the effect of experience is uneven. Production should be reviewed regularly for the validity of standards, including the LC. Artificially high time efficiency can boost incentive pay unduly while the reverse situation creates substandard pay. And labor is misstated in product cost standards, together with any applied overhead.

The effect of both high and low LCs on the reporting of time efficiency, on inventory debits, and on payroll is illustrated using the 80% LC as correct. Production is 64 units in 16,774.4 minutes of actual productive time. Average actual pay is $12 per hour or $.20 per minute which is also the standard pay rate so there is no rate variance.

64 Units Produced	70% LC	80% LC	90% LC
1. Standard minutes per unit	117.6	262.1	531.5
2. Total standard minutes for 64 units	7,526.4	16,774.4	34,016.0
3. Actual production time	16,774.4	16,774.4	16,774.4
4. Time efficiency rate (3/2)	222.9%	100.0%	49.3%
5. Pay incentive percent (2/3)	44.9%	100.0%	202.8%
6. Pay at $.20 rate for actual time (3)	$3,354.88	$3,354.88	$3,354.88
7. Pay at $.20 rate for std. time (2)	$1,505.28	$3,354.88	$6,803.20
8. Make-up pay (6-7)	$1,849.60	-	-
9. Incentive pay (7-6)	-	-	$3,448.32
10. Standard cost per unit (7/64 units)	$23.52	$52.42	$106.30

80% LC: Inventory is charged with $3,354.88 ($.20 x 16,774.4), or $52.42 per unit ($3,354.88/64). Time efficiency is 100%.

70% LC: Inventory is charged with the total standard cost of $1,505.28 or $23.52 per unit ($1,505.28/64)--only 44.9% of the correct standard. Actual time is more than double the standard--222.9%. The earned pay of $1,505.28 is short of the minimum $3,354.88 by $1,849.60, make-up pay charged to labor variance.

90% LC: Inventory is charged with the total standard cost of $6,803.20 or $106.30 per unit ($6,803.20/64)--over double the correct amount. Actual time is less than half standard time--49.3%. Unearned incentive pay of $3,448.32 more than doubles earned pay of $3,354.88. Inventory is overstated by the same amount of extra cost, charged to income when the goods are sold.

With a standard cost of $52.42 based on 80% LC product pricing and sales plans are made on a correct basis. If 70% LC is used, rather than 80% LC, the standard cost is only $23.52, seriously misleading pricing and sales planning. The apparent profit margins are eroded by the labor variance of $1,849.60. The labor variance is charged to income as incurred. Presumably the product would be underpriced and attract large sales. Product profits are booked when sales are made. Marketing would show an overstated profit margin for billings. Manufacturing would be charged with the labor variance as incurred, a serious timing mismatch.

If the 90% LC is used, rather than 80% LC, the standard cost is $106.30 per unit, over double the cost of $52.42. Competitive pricing would show no, or little, sales margin. Mark-up pricing would raise the price to a point of little or no demand. Marketing would drop the product from the line unless costs could be cut in half. Potential sales and profits would be lost.

These wide ranges provide dramatic results for illustration. Much narrower ranges can seriously misdirect both profit planning and labor efficiency measurement. This can also occur when the LC applies but is not recognized. This vital information is lost in the accounting reports.

12

Factory Overhead and Product Costs

DEPARTMENTS

All production expenses not direct material and direct labor by definition are indirect, or factory overhead. Budgets are prepared by department and account for comparison with actual expenses. Standard overhead costing rates are established to cost products; totals are debited to inventory and credited to absorbed (or applied) overhead. Differences between actual and absorbed overhead are variances, expensed as incurred and not related to products. Expense variances are the differences between actual expense and the budget amounts allowed based on actual activity. The total variance is subdivided for the amount attributable to variable overhead arising from the difference between actual and standard activity, efficiency variance, and the remainder-- spending variance. These variances are the responsibility of factory supervisors. Volume variances are the differences between the fixed overhead absorbed by actual output and planned fixed overhead based on practical output capacity. Responsibility attaches to higher management levels, determinable only by investigation.

The definition of departments and accounts, based on organizational responsibility and degree of delegation, guides expense control and product costing. Budgets are based on production plans, manpower tables, and input price levels. Variable budgets are used when expenses vary with changing levels of activity to a predictable and controllable extent. Fixed budgets are used when the change in expense is negligible, or when expenses change for other reasons. The overhead costing rate is based on the projected capacity of the plant--achievable output in terms of productive assets, technology, efficiency, product mix, and seasonality. Practical capacity is expressed generally in terms of direct labor dollars or labor hours, or machine hours. The expected high and low output levels define the relevant range on which variable budgets are based. Departmental costing rates include both the budgets for production departments and service departments as allocated to production. The objective is to achieve reasonably accurate product costing differentials by departments, along with the direct costs for material and labor. Each product standard cost is the equivalent of a price quotation by manufacturing to marketing, sometimes referred to as transfer price. Completed production is debited to finished goods at standard and, on shipment, charged to standard cost of sales. The difference between product sales price and standard cost is standard gross margin, a relationship of primary importance. The basic profit plan is for manufacturing to operate at standard for the production required and for marketing to realize its plans for sales, standard gross margins, and budgeted selling expenses. General and administrative departments are also budgeted.

All overhead is divided between period expense--SGA and product cost --and overhead charged to inventory. How overhead is classified is not defined by GAAP and practice varies widely. The most practical answer is to limit factory overhead to the production departments and their directly supporting service departments whose activities are readily traceable to other departments. This helps to ensure relatively accurate product costing differentials, also the primary aim of direct material and direct labor. The product cost differences, not the costing level, are crucial to pricing and sales planning. Expense control is not affected because all departments are budgeted according to plans and activities. Profit can be affected by the overhead charged to inventory but the amount is limited to inventory change for the period, usually inconsequential. Shifting departments from SGA to factory overhead requires arbitrary allocations for product costing. The cost level is higher but the differentials are reduced and less clear. This point is illustrated for three products as presently costed and with some SGA transferred to factory overhead:

Present	A	B	C
Direct material and direct			
labor total	$15	$12	$ 9
Overhead:			
Production--direct	15	10	6
Service--allocated by use	10	6	5
Total cost	40	28	20
Price	100	56	33
Margin	$60	$28	$13
Percent	60%	50%	40%
Difference	-	-10%	-10%
Proposed			
Total cost--above	$40	$28	$20
Add SGA--arbitrary allocation	10	8	6
Proposed cost	50	36	26
Price--above	100	56	33
Margin	$50	$20	$ 7
Percent	50%	36%	21%
Difference	-	-14%	-15%
Percent point drop	10%	14%	19%

Arbitrary costing raises the product cost level and decreases the product margins unevenly, seriously misleading pricing analysis and sales planning.

Service departments include such activities as receiving, inspection, stores, material handling, maintenance, plant engineering, utilities, tool room, and cleaning. The expenses are closely related to production plans and are traceable by type of activity performed to the departments served.

Other departments are better classified as period expense--SGA--even though they are organizationally part of the manufacturing function. Examples of such departments include purchasing, production planning, industrial engineering, quality control, personnel, and cost analysis. These departments are staffed with salaried people and have fixed budgets that are based on plans and policies not directly related to output levels. The expenses are not clearly traceable to production departments and products. Some manufacturing expenses are properly part of factory overhead but are not the responsibility of individual production and service departments; they are grouped in a separate general factory department. Such expenses include supervisors for the departments in factory overhead, depreciation, taxes, insurance, utilities, travel, communications, fees, dues, licenses, royalties, and expensed portions of capital expenditure projects. Department classification is guided by the degree of delegation for expense control. Each account in the general factory department must be allocated on a selected basis.

Each service department is budgeted according to its planned activities in support of production plans. Bases of measurement include number of people, total labor hours, productive labor hours, earnings, machine time, square feet, number of requisitions, number of transactions, and product weight. For example, a tool room serves specific production departments with tools, dies, jigs, and fixtures. It receives, inspects, stores, issues, and repairs. Expenses are predictable within a wide output range and are directly traceable to users. The tools themselves are charged to the production departments as tooling expense. Large tools may be depreciated or amortized. Small tools may be inventoried when purchased and expensed when issued, or charged to expense when purchased. All portable tools should be kept in the tool room and be controlled by requisition.

The maintenance department is often large and complex. Expenses are budgeted both by accounts and by work orders used to control all services supplied. Maintenance labor is classified by type--millwrights, electricians, painters, plumbers, mechanics, riggers, fitters--charged to work orders or to general indirect labor. This procedure is similar to recording direct labor time as productive or downtime. All other expenses are charged to maintenance expense accounts. The total budget for all accounts is divided by the total planned work order labor hours to determine the departmental charge rate per hour. This rate is a cost guide to decisions involving repairs, rebuilding, or replacing equipment. Accountability rests on both expense accounts and work orders. Work orders may be estimated in advance for labor hours and costed at the department rate.

There are three types of work orders:

Standing work orders (S-W/O) are for routine, repetitive tasks that are generally plantwide such as oiling machinery, planned preventive maintenance, checking signal, alarm, and communication systems, changing light bulbs, and minor painting. A separate S-W/O is issued for each activity and charged with actual hours for comparison with budget. Allocation is made to other departments for product costing but not for expense control. Allocation may be applicable to SGA, thus lowering factory overhead.

Expense work orders (E-W/O) are for nonroutine maintenance and repair for buildings, machinery, and equipment, and plant rearrangement. A separate work order is issued for each job with an estimate of labor time, dates to start and complete, location, and description. Labor time is posted daily and progress monitored. All work orders are expensed. Charges to SGA are posted as credits to the maintenance department and as debits to SGA departments in a separate account to identify internal cost transfers. Work orders for the factory are reported by the factory department served to establish joint accountability. The work orders are listed after the departmental home expense totals, called "below the line" reporting. The purpose is to involve both parties in expense control. For costing, budgeted E-W/Os are distributed to other departments based on plans.

A Capital work order (C-W/O) is a work order written for each project containing charges to fixed assets according to the capital expenditure program. All charges are collected on the work order: labor time at the maintenance charge rate, purchases, withdrawals from inventory, and subcontracts. Balances are carried on the balance sheet as fixed assets--projects in progress. On completion the work order is closed out to appropriate fixed asset and expense accounts, closing the capital expenditure control period. The expensed portion may be written off each month to avoid carrying expense as an asset. The expense charges are designated by department, often the general factory department or SGA. Work orders include buildings and building additions, machinery construction, machinery improvement as to life or capacity, or any charge that is capitalized. The distinction between capitalization and expense is often a practical decision, with preference for expense to gain the tax advantage and reduce bookkeeping for fixed assets. Guidance from GAAP is broad at best. Work orders are posted daily for labor time and at least monthly for other charges. Progress is monitored against both budget and calendar time. Estimates of time and costs to complete may be advisable. Overruns may require additional approval. Failure to meet calendar schedules may hamper operational plans.

The work order control system is illustrated for the maintenance department for one month to help clarify a complex but important control system.

Budget summary by type of account:

Labor--all work orders	$40,000
General labor	8,000
Total labor	48,000
Supplies--by account	22,000
Other accounts	10,000
	$80,000

The labor wage rate is $10 and work order hours total 4,000. The charge rate is $80,000 divided by 4,000 hours = $20 per hour.
The budget by work order is:

	Hours	at $20
S-W/O	1,000	$20,000
E-W/O	1,800	36,000
C-W/O	1,200	24,000
	4,000	$80,000

Actual expense is compared with budget by account:

	Hours	Actual	Budget	Expense Over (Under)
All W/O labor	4250	$42,500	$40,000	$2,500
General labor	832	8,320	8,000	320
	5082	$50,820	$48,000	$2,820
Supplies		20,000	22,000	(2,000)
Other		11,180	10,000	1,180
		$82,000	$80,000	$2,000

Comparison by work order is:

		Actual		W/O
	Hours	Charged at $20	Budget	Over (Under)
S-W/O	950	$19,000	$20,000	$(1,000)
E-W/O	1900	38,000	36,000	2,000
C-W/O	1400	28,000	24,000	4,000
	4250	$85,000	$80,000	$5,000

The 250 hours over budget (4,250 - 4,000) at $20 equals $5,000 but actual expenses are only $2,000 over budget, or $3,000 net. (The actual rate of $82,000/4250 hours = $19.294 is not used for analysis.)
The accounting record is:

	Actual	Budget	Over (Under)
Total expense	$82,000	$80,000	$2,000
Less C-W/Os capitalized	28,000	24,000	4,000
Expensed	54,000	56,000	(2,000)
S-W/Os	19,000	20,000	(1,000)
E-W/Os	38,000	36,000	2,000
Subtotal	57,000	56,000	1,000
Expensed Net	$ 3,000	$ 0	$3,000

The C-W/Os are capitalized at $4,000 more than budget and the S-W/Os and E-W/Os in total are $1,000 over budget, creating $3,000 net. The overcharge of $4,000 on C-W/Os is capitalized and subject to control as part of the capital expenditure budget. The maintenance department is responsible for its performance but the overcharges may have other origins. Maintenance alone is responsible for the S-W/Os with a budget credit of $1,000. The E-W/Os with a $2,000 overrun are the joint responsibility of maintenance and the other departments. Work order control rests primarily on labor hours, posted daily and charged at the standard rate of $20, composed of $10 labor and $10 of other department expenses, an internal rate of 100%. As with production labor, the department should keep a daily log of labor hours. The budget allows for $8,000 general labor (like downtime) and $40,000 for all work orders (like production time) or 20%. The actual totals were $8,320 and $42,500. At 20% general labor allowed is $8,500, or $180 more than $8,320.

EXPENSE ACCOUNTS

Departments are defined in terms of organizational responsibility and budgeted by accounts to the extent useful for expense control based on the degree of delegation. Department actual and budget totals are compared and summarized into totals. Each expense account is budgeted in terms of planned amounts needed for the services required. Variability is related to an activity that is based on planned ranges of output--the relevant range. Expense accounts can be cross-totaled for the factory as a matter of information but control is exercised only by department. The periodic accounting reports contain the actual and budget amounts that provide financial summaries but not expense control. The department budget also provide the basis for the allocations needed to determine overhead rates for product costing.

Indirect Material

This account is restricted to materials that would be measured as direct if practical--sandpaper, glue, paint, paper, washers. As part of the overhead rate the expenses enter equally into the cost of all products processed; great care is called for in the classification to minimize costing differentials. The question is pragmatic--the benefit to expense control and product cost relative to the clerical cost. Materiality is the primary criterion. In some cases a department is subdivided into cost centers to improve expense control and refine overhead rates. Or, a department may be subdivided into cost centers for separate overhead rates only. Another consideration is the recording of purchases to inventory and limiting requisitions to current needs. The direct expensing of purchases and the use of large requisitions tend to distort reported expenses relative to actual use. Floor balances should be closely watched. A daily log of requisitions may be needed, including purchases expensed when booked, classified by type of material. The basis for budget amounts should be consonant with the bookkeeping procedures for comparisons to be useful. The account is budgeted as variable with planned production. Significant variations, caused by usage or price, should be spotted quickly, thus anticipating variances in the periodic reports to avoid surprises. This account should not contain supplies, described below.

Direct Labor--Downtime

Direct workers' time on production is measured as standard production labor--a separate cost element, described above. Earnings for time not spent on production are charged to a downtime account. Indirect labor accounts are used for people who do not work on production, described below. Downtime is budgeted relative to planned performance, expressed usually as a percent of total direct labor. The daily labor log, as illustrated in chapter 11, contains the details in hours for each worker for production time, output, and downtime. The causes for downtime should be coded and recapped daily to help keep close control. For example, the daily labor log for a department in total hours:

Direct Labor	Plan	Actual	+/-
Production	800	720	-80
Downtime	200	280	+80
Total	1000	1000	0
Downtime percent to total	20%	28%	
Downtime percent to production	25%	39%	

The shift of 80 hours lowers production time by 10 percent while downtime is increased by 40 percent. Downtime coding is illustrated:

		Budget	Actual	
1.	Time Breaks	30	35	+ 5
2.	Waiting for Work	40	80	+40
3.	Machine Down	30	25	- 5
4.	Setup Delay	50	50	0
5.	Wrong Tools	20	50	+30
6.	Personal	10	20	+10
7.	Co. Meeting	10	0	-10
8.	Union Time	10	20	+10
		200	280	+80

This breakdown highlights codes 2 and 5. Downtime must be monitored and controlled continuously; the daily recap is needed to capture the net result of a large variety of situations on the production floor.

Indirect Labor

Factory employees not assigned to work directly in production are classified by department and account. Budgets are based on manpower tables prepared to define employment levels as headcounts for planned output. For example, if the plans call for 150 direct and 120 indirect workers, the ratio is 80 percent. If direct worker requirements are expected to range from 120 to 180 based on the relevant ranges of production, the manpower table is developed as follows:

Manpower Table--Headcount--Relevant Range

Direct Workers	120	135	150	165	180
Indirect:					
General Factory					
Supervisors	15	15	15	15	15
Clerical	19	20	20	21	22
Inspection	8	9	10	11	13
	42	44	45	47	50

Maintenance	23	24	25	26	27
Tool Room	5	5	5	5	5
Cleaning	15	16	16	17	18
Material Handling	16	18	20	22	24
Store Rooms	4	5	6	7	8
Utilities	3	3	3	3	3
Total Indirect	108	115	120	127	135
Total Factory	228	250	270	292	315
Ratio of Indirect					
to Direct	90%	85%	80%	77%	75%
Headcount Increase:					
Direct	--	15	15	15	15
Indirect	--	7	5	7	8
Total	--	22	20	22	23

The manpower table is used to plan employment and prepare budgets. It shows the degree of variability for indirect relative to direct worker output. In practice, employment policies may moderate layoffs. Budgets should be realistic about both the extent and timing of layoffs and hiring. The control of indirect labor is based on headcount plans, by department and account, supplemented by daily logs of hours as needed. Operating controls should provide adequate information on financial results prior to issuance of the periodic accounting reports. The nature of the activity is the key to both expense control and allocation for product costing. Illustrations were given above for the general factory, tool room, and maintenance departments.

Rework Labor and Scrap

The time of direct workers on production includes time spent on pieces that fail inspection but can be reworked. For example:

Standard Production: 60 pieces at 5 minutes = 300 standard minutes. 50 pieces accepted. 10 pieces are reworked and then accepted.

Actual Time:

50 pieces	240 minutes
10 reworked	30
60 pieces	270
Pay incentive	300/270 = 111%

If the rework is done by a separate work team charged to indirect labor, the direct worker performance would be:

50 pieces at 5 = 250 standard minutes
Pay incentive   250/240 = 104%

If the 30 minutes spent by the direct worker on rework is charged as downtime, rather than being absorbed by the worker, the productivity rate is overstated:

Pay incentive   300/240 = 125%

These distinctions require close floor control for both time recording and piece counts.

When pieces are scrapped they are excluded from the production count. The number of pieces scrapped times the standard cost through the last countpoint is credited to work in process and charged to a separate scrap account in overhead. A daily log of rework and scrap may be needed. Both the record keeping and the physical control of scrap require close control. If product scrap rates vary widely in a department it can be subdivided into cost centers. Scrap can be a separate cost element if necessary.

Setup Labor

Setup time can be an important cost factor requiring close control. It may be performed by direct labor or indirect labor and should be part of the daily labor log. Each setup should have a standard time that is compared with actual. Standard setup cost is a factor in the calculation of the economic lot sizes (ELS) used for production scheduling. Setup labor is charged to a separate overhead account, supported by details of the setups as needed. Setups are the preparation required for a new lot--adjusting machinery; changing tools, dies, jigs, and fixtures; cleaning surfaces; test runs. The budget is based on production plans and the requisite number and type of setups. Comparison of total actual setup cost with budget in the periodic accounting reports can be interpreted only by reference to daily operating controls. If setups are made by the maintenance department an expense work order is used and reported by both departments, as described above.

Setup costs are part of the overhead rate that is applied to all production. If sufficiently material in its effect, cost centers may be used, even for one machine with exceptionally high setup costs. If further refinement is sufficiently important, setup can be a separate cost element.

If marketing demands a change in production schedules to meet a customer request, an extra setup is needed. The extra cost should be estimated and quoted to marketing as a transfer price. If marketing accepts, the charge is made on the books to a separate marketing account and credited to an expense recovery account in factory overhead.

Overtime and Shift Premiums

Pay premiums are the additional rate paid over the regular rate for time worked beyond regular hours, as specified by law, labor contract, or company policy. Premiums are generally either 50 or 100 percent and apply to work beyond shift schedules, to Sundays and holidays, and to second and third shifts. The extra earnings are budgeted as overhead in one or more accounts by department, for direct and indirect labor. The budgeted amounts reflect planned premiums based on work schedules. Unexpected developments causing extra premiums are generally approved ahead of time or are unavoidable in the circumstances. Notation can be made on the daily labor log.

Overtime may be preferable to establishing a second shift or to delayed output. For example, one worker with 48 hours in a week:

Regular pay 48 hours at $10 = $480
Premium pay 8 hours at $ 5 =   40
                                $520

For a special order to which all costs are added, the calculation could be made:

40 hours at $10 = $400
 8 hours at $15 = 120
                  $520

The $520 is charged to inventory and the premium does not have to be segregated.

A power station that is manned around the clock could have scheduled overtime as follows:

365 days at 24 hours =   8760 hours
8760 divided by 4 operators =   2190
Regular hours--50 weeks at 8 hours =   2000
Premium hours   190

Shift premiums may be handled several ways. For example:

		Hours	Regular	Premium	Rate Total	Day Total
Shift 1	7A-- 3P	8	$11.20	$ --	$11.20	$ 89.60
Shift 2	3P-- 11P	8	11.20	1.40	12.60	100.80
Shift 3	11P-- 7A	8	11.20	2.80	14.00	112.00
		24				$302.40

Another example:

		Total Hours	Average Rate	Total
Shift 1	7A-- 4P	9	$11.20	100.80
Shift 2	4P-- 12A	8	12.60	100.80
Shift 3	12A-- 7A	7	14.40	100.80
		24	12.60	302.40

Total pay is equal for all shifts but the hours are scaled. The average hourly rate would be $12.60 for each shift if total hours are equal.

Some industries operate continuously such as refineries and paper mills. For example, a paper mill runs for 360 days and shuts down five days for cleanup. Four crews are scheduled: 360 days at 24 hours = 8,640 divided by 4 = 2,160. All crews earn 2,160 hours of regular pay, plus premium rates for 160 hours. There are no shift premiums because the crews are rotated through eight-hour shifts as follows:

Crew	Shift 1	Shift 2	Shift 3	Total	Days
A	720	720	720	2160	270
B	720	720	720	2160	270
C	720	720	720	2160	270
D	720	720	720	2160	270
	2880	2880	2880	8640	
Days	360	360	360		

Each crew works a ratio of 270/360 days or 3/4. The schedule could be six days work and two days off every eight days, with shift changes every ninety days.

Fringe Benefits

All benefits granted to employees of a monetary nature beyond earnings for time worked (regular pay, incentives, bonuses, commissions, premiums) and included in their payroll earnings are termed fringe benefits. They may be based on law, contract, and company policy. The total amount of fringe benefits relative to earnings is in a wide range, generally 20 to 50 percent, with a median of about 35 percent. Fringe benefits may include social security, unemployment, pensions, medical coverage, sick leave, child care, vacation, personal time, holidays, gifts, educational expenses, outings, use of company recreational facilities, or prizes. Each benefit must be separately budgeted for each location and each employee group. The benefits do not apply evenly throughout the year so the budget totals are divided by 12 for the monthly average. The fringe benefit percent is the total budget divided by the budgeted earnings for each employee group. This percent is applied each month to earnings for debit to a provision for fringe benefit expense and for credit to accrued fringe benefit liability--a clearing account. This clearing account is charged with the accrual for each separate fringe benefit as budgeted, and each account is charged with the actual expense as incurred. Periodic corrections are made through the clearing account to expense. Each department has a separate fringe benefit expense account and actual and budget differ for changes in earnings and changes in the actual benefit expense.

Vacation pay is illustrated for wage earners. Salararied employees take vacation time without book entry. The example is for a 10-man department for 52 weeks with a 40-hour work week (2,080 hours) and a $10 pay rate. The average vacation time is estimated at an average of 104 hours, an accrual rate of 5% (104/2,080).

	HOURS		
	Per Man	10 Men	Amount $10
Week	40	400	$ 4,000
Year	2080	20,800	$208,000
Vacation	104	1,040	$ 10,400

Record for Year by Quarters

	Actual Earnings	Vacation Accrual	Actual Expenses	Accrual Liability Balance
Q1	$ 48,000	$ 2,400	$ 0	$2,400 CR
Q2	52,000	2,600	1,200	1,400 CR
6 months		5,000	1,200	3,800 CR
Q3	60,000	3,000	6,200	3,200 DR
9 months		8,000	7,400	600 CR
Q4	48,000	2,400	3,000	600 DR
Year	$208,000	$10,400	$10,400	$ 0

For this example, actual and budget earnings are equal, and actual and accrued vacation are also equal. In practice, correction can be made at the year-end. It is apparent in the schedule that booking vacation pay as taken, without accrual, would distort quarterly expenses significantly:

	Earnings	Actual Vacation Pay	Percent
Q1	$48,000	$ 0	--
Q2	52,000	1,200	2.3%
Q3	60,000	6,200	10.3%
Q4	48,000	3,000	6.3%
	208,000	$10,400	5.0%

Social security expenses are based on a percentage of earnings up to a yearly maximum. Individual earnings may reach this limit very early in the year, or late in the year, or not at all. The annual expense must be accrued at a budgeted rate of expense to total earnings to provide the same expense rate for all periods, similar to the example for vacations.

Total fringe benefit expense can be handled as a separate overhead expense account or it can be added to the pay rate. This method provides greater accuracy and lowers the overhead rate. An example is given for a production department for one month with $10 pay rate and a 35% fringe benefit rate:

	Earnings	Fringe	Total
Indirect labor	$1,000	$350	$1,350
Direct labor:			
Downtime	200	70	270
	$1,200 A	$420 B	$1,620
Production	800 D	280 C	1,080
Total	$2,000	$700	$2,700
Overhead:			
Indirect labor	$1,000		
Downtime	200	$1,200 A	
Fringe benefits		420 B	
Production fringe		280 C	
		$1,900	
Other expense accounts		540	$2,440 E
Production labor			800 D
Rate			305%

Recast by switching $280 of production fringe:

Total overhead	$2,440 E	
less production fringe	- 280 C	$2,160
Production labor	800 D	
plus fringe	+ 280 C	1,080
Rate		200%

Costing is more accurate with $13.50 rather than $10 charged directly to products:

	200%	305%
Direct	13.50	10.00
Indirect	27.00	30.50
	40.50	40.50

Total cost is not affected but the direct charge is $13.50 rather than $10.00 per hour. Unit cost is also unaffected, but the lower overhead rate creates an illusion of lower expense--for some.

Supplies

Supplies are distinct from indirect material but some items may appear in both categories. For example, paint may be a direct material in some cases and indirect in others, but paint used in maintenance is charged to supplies. Nails may also be either direct or indirect material, or supplies. The classification should be made, by account coding, on the requisitions when items are withdrawn from inventory, and on the purchase order when the item is charged directly. Supplies are budgeted by department and account. Classifications include operating, lubricating, maintenance, plating, repair, cleaning, heat-treating, finishing, packing, testing, shipping, office, data processing, and medical. Each department and account is budgeted in total for the year. Usage may be variable with activity to a large or small extent. Purchases should be charged to inventory and requisitions limited to current needs for accurate measurement and useful budget comparison. Variance can arise from both usage and price difference from budget. Major variances should be investigated at once. A daily log may be needed, coupled with policing of requisitions and floor stocks. Any major discrepancy in the periodic accounting reports should be anticipated. The practice of using a monthly average for an annual budget may cause discrepancies for the short term. Control should be exercised in light of materality and controlled in the circumstances, and after determination of possible recording discrepancies. Pilferage must also be guarded against on a selective basis.

Maintenance

Maintenance work done by a department with department labor is charged to accounts for maintenance labor and maintenance supplies. It may appear in the daily labor log as direct labor downtime or indirect labor. A separate record by machine may also be kept. Maintenance work done by the maintenance department is collected by an expense work order, described above, and reported by the department served as maintenance expense "below the line," that is, after the department's home expense total. The purpose is to establish joint accountability. The work orders are reported by both actual and budget expense based on labor hours and the maintenance charge rate, with a description of the nature of the work done. A particular problem arises with capital expenditure work orders because, in many cases, large amounts are expensed as the work progresses, as specified in the project. The motivation is to reduce taxes by immediate deduction and to minimize the expense of fixed asset records. Limiting considerations are possible disallowance by IRS and lower reported current profit. The project is carried as a fixed asset and the expense portion may be expensed each month or when the project is completed. The charge may be made to the department benefited but it is often debited to the general factory department because of the high level of responsibility for capital expenditures. Charge may also be made to SGA. A separate account should be used because of the unique nature of the charge and because it includes a mix of expense elements. It may be compared with budget but control is part of the capital expenditure program.

Tools

The handling of tools, dies, jigs, and fixtures varies widely. Major items are capitalized and depreciated individually, or grouped by type and life. Smaller items may be grouped and amortized over a rolling period. Minor items may be inventoried and expensed when requisitioned, or expensed as purchased. The criterion is materially relative to expense control and costing. All small tools should be controlled by the tool room, whether or not inventoried. Separate expense accounts should be assigned to the extent needed for clarity. Major expense discrepancies from budget should be detected and reported currently--for example, replacing a large new tool that breaks. The control system must be pragmatic and adapted to needs, but the familiar cry for cost-benefit analysis is easier said than done.

Tools made for customers and charged to them are a product. Costs are collected on a work order and billed on completion. The tool may be delivered or retained for use on customer orders. The overhead rate should exclude company tools not used because the customer's tool is used, if material in amount. The tool room should maintain positive identification of customer tools and restrict their use to customer orders.

When a company must make special tools for an order, the cost is a separate item in the cost estimate. If a customer requires a price quotation on a large quantity, that the tool can produce, but limits the initial order to a fraction of the total, the full tool cost can seriously reduce the profit. Alternatively, the initial order may be charged with its share of tool cost and the balance carried as an asset in deferred charges. This balance may be absorbed by future orders or it may have to be written off--a matter for periodic appraisal.

Utilities

Electricity, gas, water, and steam are often metered only to the entire building. Charges may be split between SGA and the factory office based on estimates. Expenses and liabilities must be accrued because of varying usage and different billing periods. Budgets are based on planned usage and the expenses may vary widely by season and output levels. Utility rates are often complex and reflect levels of total consumption, stand-by charges, night and holiday usage, usage minimums, and various taxes. The plant engineer is responsible for planned usage and budgets, approves bills for payment, and monitors usage. Consumption by department is estimated for expense allocation to determine costing rates. Separate measurement by meter is used only for exceptional cases

where usage is high, variable, and controllable. If the company
generates its own power, a separate department is used and standard rates
established based on budgeted expenses and usage. The standard rate
times actual usage is charged out based on the estimated consumption for
each user.

Discretionary Expenses

Discretionary expenses include travel, entertainment, fees,
stationery, forms, telephone, postage, rentals, conventions, dues,
licenses, subscriptions, and donations. These expenses are a relatively
small part of factory overhead, budgeted as fixed expenses, readily
controlled, and included in the general factory department. Actual and
budget should be close for the year but there could be large monthly
variances, particularly if the monthly budgets are equal. A major
consulting contract would be approved at a high level and might not be in
the budget. The fees could be charged to deferred expense and amortized
over a few years if tangible benefits are predictable.

Fixed Expenses

Fixed expenses include salaries, depreciation, amortization, taxes,
insurance, rentals, lease payments, and royalties. These charges may be
substantial but are readily budgeted and controlled. A major change
would be approved in advance, such as revised depreciation methods or
changes in insurance coverage. These expenses are part of the general
factory department and must be allocated individually to other
departments to determine costing rates. It is worth noting that in
particular situations depreciation may be booked on the basis of units
produced rather than the passage of time. Although the book entry is in
variable form, the expense remains fixed in nature; any depreciation not
absorbed by usage must be taken within the asset's economic life.
Royalties may apply to either SGA or factory overhead, and they may be
fixed or variable. Large amounts may be shown as a separate expense item
in the income statement, either as cost of sales or sales expense.

Summary

Some key points relative to expense control are as follows:
1. Expenses can be controlled only by advance decision and the
exercise of practical judgment during operations relative to the current
circumstances, regardless of budget.
2. Hourly, daily, and cumulative data must be recorded currently at
the scene of action, primarily in quantitative terms, to supplement,
confirm, and augment personal observation.
3. Major changes and significant developments, good and bad, should
be reported up the line promptly to preclude suprises in the accounting
reports, and to afford higher managers the opportunity to intercede.
Estimates, approximations, and possibilities all help convey knowledge
that may be useful to others in ways not known to the communicator.
4. Budget variances that appear in the accounting reports should be
traceable to (articulated with) supporting detail--by period, department,
account, and transaction--to insure system validity. Management queries

must be satisfied with prompt and substantial answers, but approximations
are sufficient in most cases. The general rule applies: 20 percent of
the detail provides 80 percent of the answer.

    5. Planning and budgeting are carried out some months before the new
year, a necessary but challenging process dealing with assumptions about
the unpredictable, and also requiring cooperation among many who prefer
not to commit themselves or to make difficult estimates. The accounting
system is matched to budgeting to insure comparability of format but
there may be major differences in the accrual timing and transaction
handling that distort comparison. The relation to expense control is
loose at best and random to an unknown degree. Accounting results are
financial rather than operational. If the expense control system is
effective there should be no surprises in the accounting reports.

    6. The degree of expense variability is peculiar to each department
and each account. Fully fixed and fully variable expenses are relatively
small, and they are more readily budgeted and controlled in the context
of one year and the relevant range of production. Budgeting of the other
expenses, partially variable, partially fixed, is based on production
plans but the formula determination of the degree of variability is
arbitrary. Actual expenses change in an uneven manner and are subject to
random events.

    Expense variability is illustrated with an example based on five
levels of output and with direct labor and total budget for each level:

Level	Direct Labor	Budget	Rate
1	$ 800	$2,720	340%
2	900	2,835	315%
3	1,000	2,900	290%
4	1,100	3,080	280%
5	1,200	3,120	260%

A variable rate can be arbitrarily derived by the high-low method:

Level 5	$1,200	$3,120	
Level 1	800	2,720	
	400	400	= 100% variable rate

The fixed amount is $1,920:
Level 5 $1,200 at 100% = $1,200 less 3,120 total = $1,920 fixed
Level 1 $ 800 at 100% = $ 800 less 2,720 total = $1,920 fixed

The budget schedule is rewritten:

Level	Direct Labor	Variable @ 100	Fixed	New Total	Total Budget	Change
1	$ 800	$ 800	$1,920	$2,720	$2,720	$ 0
2	900	900	1,920	2,820	2,735	+85
3	1,000	1,000	1,920	2,920	2,900	+20
4	1,100	1,100	1,920	3,020	3,080	-60
5	1,200	1,200	1,920	3,120	3,120	0

Other combinations give different results:

```
Level 2          $  900    $2,835
Level 1             800     2,720
                    100      115 = 115% x $800 = $970
                                       - 2,720 = $1,800 Fixed
Level 3          $1,000    $2,900
Level 2             900     2,835
                    100       65 = 65% x $1000 = $650
                                       - 2900 = $2250 Fixed
Level 4          $1,100    $3,080
Level 3           1,000     2,900
                    100      180 = 180% x $1100 = $1980
                                       - 3080 = $1100 Fixed
Level 5          $1,200    $3,120
Level 4           1,100     3,080
                    100       40 = 40% x $1200 = $480
                                       - 3120 = $2640 Fixed
```

Recap: Levels	Variable Rate	Fixed Expense
5-4	40%	$2640
3-2	65%	2250
5-1	100%	1920
2-1	115%	1800
4-3	180%	1100

These swings illustrate the nonlinear nature of variability and its limitation for expense control. More complex methods establish closer correlation but cloud understanding.

PRODUCT COSTS

The departmental budgets are translated into product costs as follows:

1. Total expenses are budgeted for all departments--home department expenses--and used for expense control. There are no allocations.
2. Planned output for allocation of each production department is expressed as a single activity--production labor hours or dollars, machine hours.
3. The relevant activity base for allocation of each service department is determined--number of employees, square feet, number of requisitions, earnings, hours.
4. Service departments are allocated to all other departments by progressively closing out each one in sequence based on a combination of budget amounts and number of other departments served. Reciprocal analysis may also be used for greater accuracy.
5. All overhead is now assigned to the production departments. This total divided by production capacity is the costing rate.

A simple example with all overhead fixed is presented with totals:

Budget	Service	Production
Home	$2,000	$3,000
Allocated	-2,000	2,000
	0	$5,000
Production labor		$2,000
Costing rate		250%

The accounting entries are made to a factory overhead control account, charged by department and account for all expenses incurred. For example:

Actual expenses		$5,200 DR
Applied at 250% on $1,840 labor		4,600 CR
Variance--underapplied		600 DR
By analysis:		
Expense--actual	$5,200	
Budget	5,000	$ 200 DR
Volume--labor dollars		
Plan	$2000	
Actual	1840	160 at 250% 400 DR
Total		$ 600 DR

Expense variance is reported by department and account. Volume variance can be determined by production departments or for the entire plant.

The allocation of service departments is illustrated with four service (1, 2, 3, 4) and three production (A, B, C) departments, with sequential allocation. The bases used for allocation are omitted as well as the logic of the departmental sequence:

	1	2	3	4	A	B	C	Total
Budgets	$1000	$800	$600	$400	$1500	$1200	$1000	$6500
Allocate #1	-1000	+100	+300	0	+ 200	+ 150	+ 250	0
	0	900	900	400	1700	1350	1250	6500
Allocate #2		- 900	+100	+200	+ 400	+ 100	+ 100	0
		0	1000	600	2100	1450	1350	6500
Allocate #3			-1000	+100	+ 200	+ 400	+ 300	0
			0	700	2300	1850	1650	6500
Allocate #4				-700	+ 200	+ 250	+ 250	0
Total				0	$2500	$2100	$1900	$6500

Output base:

Labor dollars	$500	
Rate per dollar	500%	
Machine hours		105
Rate per hour		$20
Labor hours		190
Rate per hour		$10

With the sequential allocation, there is no charge back--any work done for prior departments is disregarded. Trials with different sequences or reciprocal analysis can be made to ascertain whether changes in the rates are consequential. There is no plant rate because no single output base is expressed.

The purpose is to develop overhead costing rates that provide accuracy in product cost differentials, along with the direct material and direct labor costs. For review and analysis, the allocation schedule illustrated provides a clear trail for the sources of all overhead in a product cost.

The activity base used to express the costing rate is most usefully based on the planned practical capacity for the year. Practical output is based on the plant assets, technology, and efficiency, as related to potential sales volume allowing for seasonality and product mix. The limiting factor in output is a bottleneck point, and this point changes with different plans, except for a fully autonomous operation. Practical capacity requires careful determination but is necessarily an approximation. It can be set for each production department or for the plant as a whole. It reflects the capital expenditure program for the plant and all the facilities and organization in place. With production below capacity, volume variance is generated--unused capacity in dollars of planned fixed expense. This is a positive measurement that guides management in planning and in operating decisions. It is the basis for short-term analyses, such as break-even and incremental. When sales plans press planned capacity to the point of bottleneck costs, it is a signal to increase capacity or the amount of subcontracting. When sales plans indicate substantial unused capacity it is a signal to plan for more sales or less capacity. Volume variance is set out separately in the profit plans and compared with actual each period. The timing of sales, production, and capacity is handled primarily through the capital expenditure plan that covers several years.

An alternative method uses a theoretical capacity concept that disregards practical limitation such as available equipment, current technology, and achievable efficiency. The higher output rate lowers the costing rate and volume variance is higher. The charge to product costs is lower and profit margins are higher. The overstated profit is reduced by the overstated volume variance debit. Sales planning is overly optimistic. A useful index of capacity is lost.

Another approach uses the annual sales plan translated into production schedules. No volume variance is planned. Actual volume variance may be debit or credit. There is no indication of available capacity in the plans, true only in the rare circumstance of full capacity utilization. Otherwise, when sales needs are less than capacity, the costing rate is higher and product margins are lower. Sales planning is pessimistic. Frequently, actual output will exceed plan and cause credit variance, overstating inventories and cost of sales.

In practice, the capacity factor should be carefully developed on a pragmatic basis to serve best the measurement of product costs, inventory valuation, and volume variance. Capacity should be measured for each production department by the factor that best relates overhead to products. Standard production labor in hours or dollars and machine hours are commonly used. Fully autonomous operations have no direct labor and overhead is based on planned operating time. A department may be subdivided into cost centers to obtain more accurate costing rates. Examples are given for overhead costing rates based on standard production labor hours and a plant budget for the three activity levels discussed--sales plan, practical capacity, and theoretical capacity. It is assumed that total actual and budget expenses are equal so there is no expense variance. Volume variance is planned fixed expense only. At product capacity of 1,500 hours the budget is:

	Total	Variable	Fixed
Service	$3,600	$1,200	$2,400
Production	3,900	1,800	2,100
	$7,500	$3,000	$4,500

For expense control the variable rate is $2 per hour ($3,000/1,500) with fixed overhead of $4,500. The costing rate is computed on the basis of three activity levels:

	Capacity	Variable @ $2	Total Fixed	Overhead Total	Fixed Rate	Costing Rate
Sales plan	1200 hrs.	$2,400	$4,500	$6,900	$3.75	$5.75
Practical	1500 hrs.	3,000	4,500	7,500	3.00	5.00
Theoretical	1800 hrs.	3,600	4,500	8,100	2.50	4.50

The variable rate is constant at $2; the total variable overhead varies with hours. The fixed rate varies; the total fixed overhead is constant at $4,500.

Five levels of actual output in standard labor hours are assumed to illustrate the effect of the three rates on volume variance. Only fixed overhead is shown to limit the detail.

ACTUAL LABOR HOURS AT STANDARD

	1200	1300	1400	1500	1600
1200 hours					
Sales plan at $3.75	$4,500	$4,875	$5,250	$5,625	$6,000
Fixed budget	4,500	4,500	4,500	4,500	4,500
Volume variance	0	375 CR	750 CR	1,125 CR	1,500 CR
Percent DR(CR)	0	(8.3%)	(16.7%)	(25.0%)	(33.3%)
1500 hours					
Practical at $3.00	3,600	3,900	4,200	4,500	4,800
Fixed budget	4,500	4,500	4,500	4,500	4,500
Volume variance	900 DR	600 DR	300 DR	0	300 CR
Percent DR(CR)	20.0%	13.3%	6.7%	0	(6.7%)
1800 hours					
Theoretical @ $2.50	3,000	3,250	3,500	3,750	4,000
Fixed budget	4,500	4,500	4,500	4,500	4,500
Volume variance	1,500 DR	1,250 DR	1,000 DR	750 DR	500 DR
Percent DR(CR)	33.3%	27.8%	22.2%	16.7%	11.1%

At 1,200. With the sales plan the full $4,500 is charged to inventory and variance is zero. The unused available capacity of $900 is undisclosed. At practical capacity, $3,600 is costed and $900 is debited to variance. With the theoretical rate only $3,000 is costed and variance is artificially high. If the annual sales plan included volume variance at $900, actual output using the practical rate of $3.00 would show volume variance equal to budget. At the $3.75 rate, the variance would be zero, indicating a gain over budget of $900. At the $2.50 rate, the variance of $1,500 would exceed the budget by $600, offsetting the undercosted products. The intent of the details illustrated is to emphasize the need for careful determination of practical capacity, and the need to translate sales plans into production schedules so that volume variance can be realistically expressed in the profit plan and compared with performance.

At 1,300.   With the $3.00 practical rate variance is $600, and $1,250 with the $2.50 theoretical rate. The sales plan rate of $3.75 overcosts production and creates a volume variance credit.   At closing dates inventory must be written down to eliminate any credit variance. The overstated costs in cost of sales are offset by the volume variance credit.   Product profit margins are understated.   The problem becomes progressively worse with higher output.

At 1,400, 1,500, 1,600.   The sales plan reaches a 33.3 percent overstatement of applied overhead at 1,600 hours, while it is 6.7 percent overstated at the practical rate.   For the theoretical rate there is still underapplied overhead of $500, or 11.1 percent. With the choice of 1,500 hours and the $3.00 rate, the most reasonable results are achieved in the relevant range from 1,200 to 1,600 hours of output. Practical capacity is exceeded rarely and usually for minor amounts.   Falling below that capacity is a question of sales demand. If that is estimated at 1,200 hours, then the profit plan must include $900 for volume variance. This signal encourages sales effort or alternative uses of extra capacity. If it is expected that the actual sales will exceed plan and reach 1,300 hours, then only $600 variance is put in the profit plan. The table helps to visualize the interrelationships that arise with different volume factors for both plans and actual results.

The profit effect of using three fixed costing rates is illustrated:

Capacity	Fixed Overhead	Output Units	FC Per Unit
Sales Plan	$97,500	750	$130
Practical	97,500	975	100
Theoretical	97,500	1300	75

Variable overhead is 100% of labor.

	Sales Plan-- 750 Units	Practical-- 975 Units	Theoretical-- 1300 Units
Standard Product Cost:			
Material	$100	$100	$100
Labor	100	100	100
Overhead:			
Variable	100	100	100
Fixed	130	100	75
Total cost	430	400	375
Price	600	600	600
Margin	$170	$200	$225
Percent to price	28.3%	33.3%	37.5%

If pricing is based on 50% mark-up on cost (33 1/3% of sales):

	Cost	+50%	New Price	Old Price	Change
Sales plan	$430	$215	$645	$600	+$ 45
Practical	400	200	600	600	0
Theoretical	375	187	562	600	- 38

A price increase from $600 to $645 would decrease sales, reducing volume further below the sales plan for the $600 price. A price decrease from $600 to $562 would increase sales beyond practical capacity. With no price changes marketing is guided by misleading margin differentials. The offsetting effect of volume cannot be correctly interpreted because it contains several causes, appears separately from sales margin, cannot be related separately to products, and is based on production while sales margin arises from shipments.

These exercises clarify the effect of the fixed overhead costing rate on profit measurement for both plans and results.

OVERHEAD VARIANCE ANALYSIS

The bookkeeping system collects all actual factory overhead by charges to the control account and applied overhead credits charged to inventory. The account balance is variance, separated by analysis into expense and volume. The expense variance is set out by department and account, comparing budget with actual. These periodic accounting reports are formal summaries for review but should contain no surprises if effective current operating control is exercised, as described above. They serve no control purpose because they appear perhaps some ten to fifteen days after closing and contain transactions for a month. They are part of the financial evaluation of actual compared with plan. Any substantial differences can be traced if required. The volume portion of the book variance balance may be arrived at simply by deducting the computed expense variance, using variable budgets, from total variance. This remainder would be volume variance for the entire plant. Volume variance by production department can also be computed--difference of actual and planned output at the fixed overhead rate.

For example, on the books:

```
Actual debits from records     $7,600 = 1216 actual hours
Applied at capacity rate        6,750 = 1350 standard hours at $5
Total variance debit           $  850
```

The applied overhead is based on a total budget of $7,500 and $1,500 capacity labor hours--a rate of $5 per hour composed of $2 variable and $3 fixed:

```
Plan                              1500 hours
Budget:                      Amount        Rate
Variable                     $3,000        2.00
Fixed                         4,500        3.00
                             $7,500        5.00

Analysis:
Actual expense (1,216 hours)               $7,600
   Applied--1,350 hours at $5               6,750
   Variance--account balance                          $850 DR
By analysis:
Volume:   1500 plan hours
          1350 applied
           150 at $3                                   $450 DR

Expense:
Variable:  1350 standard hours at $2 =     $2,700
Fixed                                       4,500
Budget                                     $7,200
Actual                                     $7,600     $400 DR
```

The standard labor hours of 1,350 required only 1,216 actual hours so time efficiency is 111% and 134 hours have been saved. The budget is recalculated with 1,216 actual hours:

```
Variable--1216 actual hours at $2 =      $2,432
Fixed                                     4,500
Budget                                    6,932
Actual                                    7,600
Spending variance                           668 DR
Efficiency--134 hours at $2                  268 CR
Expense variance total--above               400 DR
```

The labor efficiency gain is enhanced by $268. Spending variance is $668, the basis for expense control.

Another example illustrates the importance of logical analysis:

```
Plan                              1500 hours
Variable                     $3,000      $2.00
Fixed                         4,500       3.00
                             $7,500       5.00
Actual expense (1,400 hours)             $8,000
Applied--1,600 at $5                      8,000        $0
Volume:  1,500 plan hours
         1,600 applied
           100 at $3                                 300 CR
Expense:
Variable 1,600 at $2 =                   $3,200
Fixed                         4,500
Budget                        7,700
Actual                        8,000                  300 DR
Spending variance:
Variable 1,400 at $2 =                    2,800
Fixed                         4,500       7,300
Actual                                    8,000
                                            700 DR
Efficiency:
  1,400 - 1,600 = 200 at $2                  400 CR  300 DR
```

The zero book balance contains $700 of spending variance partly offset by a $400 labor efficiency credit, a $300 net debit.

Consideration of volume variance must recognize the shifting nature of bottlenecks with changing product mix, seasonality, and changing technology and efficiency. Unused capacity that is potentially available for use is not necessarily an indication of poor scheduling or excessive capacity. Productive assets are acquired through the capital expenditure program and the planned usage may be only a fraction of full physical capacity; a machine may be a profitable addition at a scheduled usage of four hours a week even though it could operate for the full shift.

Additions to capacity vary greatly in size and effect on output. With large lead times for capacity expansion and with timing also dependent on sales plans, excess capacity is often in place ahead of need. And delayed expansion can forestall sales growth. The process is illustrated with demand and capacity for several periods in units:

Period	Demand	Capacity	Rate
1	65	100	65%
2	70	100	70%
3	80	100	80%
4	95	100	95%
5	100	100	100%
6	108	150	72%
7	120	150	80%
8	135	150	90%
9	147	150	98%
10	152	190	80%

In period 2 it is projected that added capacity will be needed in period 5. It is not available, and output reaches 100%. In period 6 capacity increases by 50 and sales grow to 108 for a 72% utilization rate. In practice, planning endeavors to balance sales growth and productive capacity over time. The practical capacity rate puts a calculated cost on available capacity for the annual profit plan and measures results against that plan.

MIX AND YIELD VARIANCE

Products made from a formula have a standard cost computed as follows:

Material	Quantity	Standard Price	Total
A	5	$12	$ 60
B	3	20	60
C	2	40	80
	10		200

Average input cost: $200/10 = $20
YIELD: 80% = 8 units = $200/8 = $25 per unit

If a temporary shortage of a material exists and there is a demand for output with a mix variation that produces a useful product, the cost differences for both mix and yield can be calculated. This net amount can be related to the decision to produce now or wait. Hence, the choice is made before the event, either negative to avoid the variance, or positive to achieve a benefit greater than the extra cost. Only the decision to act appears in the records. Mix and yield variance is an opportunity cost relative to taking no action.

An example is based on a batch of 50 units with a change in formula. Price variances are taken at purchase so all material prices are at standard. Waste or spoilage could occur but are omitted here. Labor and overhead are also omitted because they are not affected by the decision.

Material	Quantity	Standard Price	Total	Qty. Formula	Mix Difference	Amount
A	20	$12	$ 240	25	- 5	$-60
B	20	20	400	15	+ 5	+100
C	10	40	400	10	0	0
Actual	50		1040	50	0	+ 40
Formula	50 at $20		1000			
Mix variance loss			40			

There is no need to calculate the variance for each material but it is given for reference. The change in mix can affect yield, and this may be an estimate.

```
Estimated yield:  38 units at $25            = $ 950
Standard yield:  80% of 50 = 40 at $25       = $1000
Yield loss                                        50
Mix loss                                          40
Combined loss                                     90
Recap:  Batch cost 38 units                   $1040
        Formula cost 38 units at $25            950
        Loss                                      90
The book entries are:
        Credit RM and charge WIP              1040
        Debit FG and credit WIP                950
        Debit variance credit WIP               90
```

In the example both variances are debits. Credits can also occur but a net credit is unlikely. Mix and yield variance is a separate account and is part of cost of sales. It is not budgeted because it is not planned. The decision not to run a batch that is off formula does not appear in the records. The variance reported can only be interpreted relative to the alternatives. Possibilities include an order from a valued customer with a preference for absorbing the variance rather than a delay until the right material is available. Another consideration is maintaining output and inventory levels. Also, a customer may be willing to pay more for the batch to obtain prompt delivery; the mix and yield variance could be netted against sales in the reports.

A second example:

Formula:

Material	Quantity	Standard Price	Total
A	6	$ 2	$ 12
B	8	3	24
C	11	4	44
	25		80

Average input cost: $80/25 = $3.20
Yield: 200% = 50 units = $80/50 = $1.60

Batch:

Material	Quantity	Standard Price	Total
A	15	$ 2	$ 30
B	20	3	60
C	15	4	60
Actual	50		150
Formula	50 at $3.20		160
Mix variance gain			$10 CR

Yield:

Estimated: 95 units at $1.60		+152
Standard: 200% of 50 = 100 at $1.60		160
Yield loss		8 DR
Combined gain		2 CR

This batch uses relatively more of the cheaper materials so the resulting product would be inferior to some extent. The price might have to be reduced.

INCOME STATEMENT ILLUSTRATION

The points discussed in part 2 are presented in the format of a periodic accounting report, with classification based on general organization responsibilities.

	Income Statement--Period		
	Actual	Budget	Gain (Loss)
Marketing			
Sales	$10,000	$9,500	$ 500
Standard cost	4,000	3,800	(200)
Standard GM	6,000	5,700	300
Expenses	2,000	1,900	(100)
Sales margin	4,000	3,800	200
Manufacturing			
Cost variances:			
Purchase price	55	30	(25)
Material usage	45	20	(25)
Labor rate	(5)	0	5
Labor time	15	10	(5)
Spending	45	25	(20)
Efficiency	25	15	(10)
	180	100	(80)
Gross margin	3,820	3,700	120
Other Costs			
Mix and yield	30	0	(30)
Warranty	90	70	(20)
Standard revaluations	(10)	(50)	(40)
Inventory adjustments	110	80	(30)
	220	100	(120)
Volume variance	900	750	(150)
	1,120	850	(270)
Gross profit	2,700	2,850	(150)
General expenses	1,400	1,330	(70)
Operating profit	$1,300	$1,520	$(220)
Percent to sales	13%	16%	44%

Income statements based on accrual accounting are clearly meaningful only in general financial terms. Any interpretation for operating control is impractical, largely because of timing. However, the statements should contain no surprises if the information system is functioning effectively. Questions that may arise are traceable to the underlying transactions.

The income statement shows that marketing has increased sales and maintained a 40 percent sales margin as budgeted. Cost variances budgeted at $100 have risen to $180, or 4.5 percent of $4,000 standard cost. Other costs are $120 over the $100 budget. Mix and yield variance and warranty may relate to marketing. Inventory adjustments, which may also relate to marketing, run $30 over budget. The credits for revaluations to standard (inventory debits) are $40 below the $50 budget. The net of the two accounts is budgeted at $30 (80 - 50) but ran $100 (110 - 10), an excess of $70 (40 + 30). Volume variance is far over budget at $900 compared with $750, a 20 percent increase. This amount equals the gross profit shortfall of $150, by coincidence. With shipments per budget a decrease would be indicated. Other factors are involved and careful inquiry is needed. With general expenses $70 over budget, the operating profit is $220 below plan. The incremental loss rate of 44% lowers the profit rate from 16% budget to 13% actual. In practice the results would be analyzed as ROA. For example, assuming that assets were reduced form $5,500 to $5,000:

	Actual	Budget	
Profit	$1300	$1520	-220
Assets	5000	5500	-500
ROA	26.0%	27.6%	- 44%
Percent to sales	13.0%	16.0%	
Turnover	2.0	1.72	

The drop in ROA is relatively modest because of the turnover gain.
This statement in a conventional condensed form can be given as follows:

	Actual	Budget	Gain (Loss)
Sales	$10,000	$9,500	$500
Costs	4,400	4,000	(400)
Gross margin	5,600	5,500	100
Volume variance	900	750	(150)
Gross profit	4,700	4,750	(50)
SGA	3,400	3,230	(170)
Operating profit	$ 1,300	$1,520	$(220)

Many questions attach to both the validity of the budgets, prepared far ahead of time, and to the accounting system, examined in detail in part 3.

PART 3

INFORMATION AND ACCOUNTING SYSTEMS: DESIGNING THE APPARATUS TO MEET CHANGING NEEDS

Introduction:
The Challenge to Management

Accounting has evolved through the centuries in response to changing needs, an ongoing process. Published financial statements are subject to GAAP promulgated by the FASB. Management is responsible for preparing and issuing all financial information. Outside auditors express an opinion on published statements based on an independent examination of the records and the system of accounting control. The opinion includes an exception for anything questionable in the judgment of the auditor. Management is responsible for the information system and the system of internal control including accounting. The systems must comply with the Foreign Corrupt Practices Act (FCPA) which applies to all U.S. corporations regardless of foreign business. Management must give careful and constant attention to these responsibilities to assure both itself and the public of the validity of all financial information.

GAAP does not cover all situations and many are subject to interpretation. There may be wide latitude in application. In particular cases GAAP may have to be disregarded to provide proper handling. Rule makers are subject to constant pressure from those who favor detailed rules, a cookbook approach, and those who prefer statements of principle to be applied by practitioners.

The information system should be designed to meet the needs of all users, as determined by management. To meet both internal and external requirements, and to operate both effectively and efficiently, systems must be based on meticulous study and be constantly monitored and updated. The design should be based on a building block approach so that each block, or datum, can be used or adapted to meet particular needs. External needs are various: statements for stockholders, reports to the SEC, filings with stock exchanges, tax returns, industry association reports, bond indenture disclosures, government agency forms, contractual data, and royalty reports. Internal information needs are geared to personal responsibilities, analyzing alternatives, planning and budgeting, measuring performance, and analyzing results.

Managers need to understand and use constructively a wide range of analytic tools. They must also appreciate and deal with the wide range of measurements that can occur within GAAP. Choices can materially affect the timing of income, and there may be pressure for profit now at

the expense of future profitability. A particular situation arises with
inventory valuation using LIFO (last-in, first-out)--current taxes are
reduced but lower earnings must be reported.   Part 3 provides clear
descriptions and illustrations to guide judgment in the design and
modification of systems to foster effective communications. Management
must take the lead in directing technical people toward purposeful
endeavors and bridging any communication gap.   Technicians should be
encouraged to understand the whole picture and to express themselves
clearly. Good systems are indispensable to good decisions.
        Accounting is an essential tool but not the only one in the
arsenal.   The challenge is to use accounting effectively as part of the
overall information system.   To speak of accounting inadequacies or
limitations is to miss the point. Accounting should, and can, meet all
internal needs that fall within the accounting discipline. Other needs
must look to other disciplines such as forecasting, risk analysis,
economic evaluation, statistics, and the effects of inflation.

>   Despite 6,000 years of accounting history, substantial fric-
>   tion   and   misunderstanding   still   exist   between   accounting
>   departments and users of accounting information.   It   is
>   surprising to the authors that significant numbers of people
>   who enter general management have only a sketchy ability to
>   handle accounting information ... The experience that students
>   have in college ... develops a very different set of skills
>   than the skills which will be required ... [and] produces
>   graduates who are ill-trained ... and thus have excessive
>   self-confidence. (F. Warren McFarlan and James L. McKinney,
>   Corporate Information Systems Management: The Issues Facing
>   Senior Executives [Homewood, Ill.: Irwin, 1983] p. 5.)

        Several relevant statements of another business school professor
are of interest:

>   The accounting system is comprehensive and pervasive ... No
>   transaction involving the disbursement or receipt of cash will
>   go unrecorded ... But despite the known weaknesses of finan-
>   cial numbers for performance measurement, they are vital in
>   any effective management control system ... The financial
>   accounting process provides a formal discipline   for   the
>   production and collection of data. (Robert S. Kaplan,
>   Advanced Management Accounting [Englewood Cliffs, N.J.:
>   Prentice-Hall, 1982] p. 478)

13

Cash and Accrual Accounting

CASH FLOW

A business starts with cash paid in by investors and ends with cash paid out to owners. Only then can a final profit be determined. Interim measurements are estimates subject to error and to assumptions about the future. These truisms are taught early but soon fade into the background. The periodic measurement of financial performance is necessary for both managers and the public. Transactions occur in a continuing stream and relate to future, present, and past events. The relevant data are collected and recorded constantly. At specified times, such as month-ends, the books are closed (no more transactions are entered), account balances are struck, and statements are prepared. Accounting principles apply but management is responsible for their interpretation, and for assumptions about the future that are the basis for valuation.

The distinction between cash accounting and accrual accounting is primary. The dominance of cash in the financial world may contribute to some unfortunate but avoidable confusion. Timing is the difference between accrual and cash recordings. Accruals are necessary to reflect the economic content of transactions in order to measure income for a period and owners' equity (assets less liabilities) at the end of the period. A sale may be made for cash or on account to be paid later, or cash may be paid in advance. All cash transactions are recorded as they occur but accrual accounting, additionally, recognizes the timing of the sale independently of cash timing and matches costs to sales, again independently of cash transactions relative to costs incurred. Accrual accounting is essential to profit measurement, earnings per share, return on equity, and other measures important to the financial community. Cash management is essential to liquidity, a fiscal responsibility which also includes capital structure. Accrual accounting precedes or parallels cash flows and is essential to planning the timing of cash receipts and payments.

For illustration, a retailer opens a store and records cash transactions that are summarized for the first month as follows, with letter codes to the statements prepared later:

	Receipts	Payments
Paid in by owner	$15,0001	
Bank loan at 12%	10,000j	
Cash sales	8,000m	
Goods purchased		$15,000o
Rent--3 months		9,000s
Wages		6,000r
Total	$33,000	$30,000
Payments	30,000	
Cash balance	$ 3,000a	

Other transactions are reviewed to determine the financial situation based on accrual accounting.

ACCRUAL ACCOUNTING

	Month	DR	CR
Sales on credit	$17,000 b-n	Receivables	Sales
Purchases on credit	15,000 e-p	Purchases	Payables
Inventory at month end	20,000 c-q	Inventory	Purchases
Rent--2 months	6,000 d-s	Prepaid	Rent
Accrued expenses	4,900 f-t	Expense	Accrual
Fixtures	30,000 h-k	Fixed Assets	Note Payable
Depreciation--5 years			
Month (1/60)	500 i-u	Depreciation	Accum. Depr.
Interest on note for $30,000			
fixtures at 16%			
$4,800/12	400 g-v	Expense	Accrued Int.
Interest on bank loan			
for $10,000 - 12%			
$1,200/12	100 g-v	Expense	Accrued Int.

These transactions and the cash record are put into a format to provide an orderly display of assets and liabilities, or statement of financial position--the balance sheet:

Current Assets:	Cash	$ 3,000a	
	Receivables	17,000b	
	Inventory	20,000c	
	Prepaid Rent	6,000d	$46,000
Current Liabilities:	Payables	$15,000e	
	Accruals	4,900f	
	Interest	500g	20,400
Net Current Assets			$25,600
Fixtures (pledged)		$30,000h	
less depreciation		500i	$29,500
Net Assets			$55,100
Debt:	Bank Loan	$10,000j	
	Note Payable	30,000k	$40,000
Equity:	Paid In	15,0001	
	Profit--to balance		
	(income statement)	100*	15,100
Capital			$55,100

The balance was achieved by adding $100 profit to equity, supported by an income statement:

Sales:	Cash	$ 8,000m	
	Credit	17,000n	$25,000
Purchases:	Cash	15,000o	
	Credit	15,000p	
		$30,000	
	Inventory	20,000q	
Cost of sales			10,000
Gross profit			15,000
Expenses:	Wages	6,000r	
	Rent (9000 - 6000)	3,000s	
	Expenses	4,900t	
	Depreciation	500u	14,400
Operating profit			600
Interest			500v
Profit (balance sheet)			$ 100*

Income tax is omitted. Wages of $6,000 can be considered to include $2,500 for the owner as the amount he could earn elsewhere. The $100 profit, or $1,200 annualized, is a return of 8 percent on the investment of $15,000, compared with 9 percent yield on AA bonds. Balance sheet items include these expectations: that the receivables of $17,000 will be collected in full without collection expense; that the $20,000 inventory contains no loss items; that the prepaid rent of $6,000 will be recouped by future operations because it is not refundable; that the $30,000 fixtures purchase will be recouped by future operations over five years because salvage value is low; that all liabilities are correctly recorded; that no transactions are unrecorded. These considerations affect valuations and the validity of the equity balance. It is apparent that the $3,000 increase in the cash balance and the $100 accrual profit are entirely different expressions, each with a necessary but distinct purpose.

Changes in the balance sheet for the period are drawn off to disclose changes in financing and investing--a funds statement, or changes in financial position:

Financing			
Equity:			
Profit	$100		
Depreciation	500		
Funds from operations		$ 600	
Paid in		15,000	$15,600
Debt:			
Bank loan		10,000	
Note payable (fixtures)		30,000	$40,000
Total		$55,600	
Investing			
Fixtures (note payable)		$30,000	
Net current assets (per balance sheet)		25,600	
Total		$55,600	

This statement reflects all changes in the balance sheet. The $500 depreciation is a book entry only, added back to profit, and the total outlay for fixtures is an investment of $30,000. Funds from operations are available for investments or dividends, together with changes in debt and equity. The funds statement thus reveals changes in capital structure relative to short-term (net current assets) and long-term (fixed assets) investments. It relates to solvency and liquidity. The change in the cash balance ($3,000) is incidental within the change in net current assets ($25,600) but is central to liquidity and cash management. A record of actual cash transactions leading to the $3,000 balance was given above as the first statement. The critical question is future cash flow. For example, a cash projection for the second month could read:

Cash balance		$3,000
Add: Cash sales	$12,000	
Receivable collections	8,000	20,000
		23,000
Deduct:		
Cash purchases	6,000	
Paid on payables	10,000	
Wages	7,500	
Expenses	4,500	28,000
Deficit		5,000

Payments of $28,000 exceed receipts of $20,000 by $8,000, reducing $3,000 cash to a $5,000 deficit. The owner must plan to add to his investment, or borrow more, or scale back operations to avoid insolvency.

Surprisingly, the FASB requires publication of cash flows for fiscal years ending after July 15, 1988--Statement No. 95. The vote was 4 to 3. It is highly impractical for most companies to draw off cash transactions separately because it is not useful and therefore not provided for by the information system. An alternative presentation is permitted:

Profit	$ 100	
Depreciation	500	$ 600
Increases in:		
Receivables	17,000	
Inventory	20,000	
Prepaid	6,000	
	43,000	
Liabilities	20,400	22,600
Net cash required		22,000
From:		
Bank loan	10,000	
Investment	15,000	25,000
Cash increase		$3,000

Note: Fixtures were acquired with a note for $30,000.

This alternative is simply a different and less definitive format from the funds statement illustrated. In any form, a history of cash flows is of questionable value. It may be of some use to cash managers as a guide to future cash timing.

The statements presented are interrelated and are based on cost, often called historical cost for emphasis. GAAP allows no adjustment for inflation or market values but such revaluations may be made for specified purposes. GAAP does require recognition of expected losses such as from uncollectible accounts and for lost inventory value. Profits can be booked only when realized. The continuation of the business is assumed--the going concern concept. Statements are prepared on the basis of realization and liquidation at current market values if operations are not to be continued--book amounts are not relevant.

The price of publicly traded stock is some combination of expectations for the company, the industry, and the economy. It reflects investor expectations relative to profit and risk, as expressed by the efficient market theory--that prices respond quickly to all available information. The market price of a share of stock can be compared with the book value--stockholder equity divided by number of shares outstanding. But there is no direct connection between the historical costs of accrual accounting and the ever-changing market values driven by world events and psychological swings. Merger possibilities can substantially boost a stock price. In some cases assets with high market values may contribute to a decision to sell if alternative use of the proceeds is attractive. In the case of insolvency leading to bankruptcy, shareholder equity is entirely wiped out. Also, the market value of an asset to be replaced may be a factor in capital expenditure analysis. The net disposal value of the asset is an opportunity cost--the gain foregone to retain the asset. For financial analysis, the net cash proceeds from the sale reduce the acquisition cost of the replacement asset to be acquired.

INFLATION

Inflation (deflation) is the rate and timing of changes in general price levels. Individual prices are, concurrently, changing continually in their interrelationships. These are persistent problems for the individual, the company, and the economy. They affect decisions for both investing and financing. For example, product pricing must consider future input costs, and borrowing involves projection of interest rates. The movement of individual prices must be considered because they are constantly changing regardless of inflation, and its separate effect may be hard to distinguish. Current performance is compared with past projections; current projections become comparable with future performance. Book entries are at cost with prices that differ from projections in varying degrees, a matter for analysis relative to accountability and choices for the future. Financial statements adjusted for inflation have been found to be unrewarding for both management and the public, based on an extensive trial directed by the FASB. No satisfactory way exists to alter the money yardstick to advantage. The two primary adjustment methods are "constant dollars," based on indices of price levels applied to book amounts, and "current costs," based on replacement values without regard to book value. Both methods are complex and lack consensus in application. Attention to the problem varies with the degree of inflation.

A related concept is known as the "maintenance of capital." It is equally complex and sterile. One meaning is the preservation of productive physical capacity and the ability to maintain output regardless of prices. The other meaning is maintenance of dollar capital adjusted for inflation without regard to physical output. These are assumptions of perpetual life, abstract in a world of global competition and the "creative destruction" of capital. Company operations generate continuous liquidation; productive assets are used up, receivables are collected, inventories are sold. All assets convert to cash, liabilities are paid, and owners receive a final cash dividend. The cash cycle is complete. This process is reversed only by investment, made by evaluation of opportunities for profit and risk. With limited investment choices there is gradual asset shrinkage, and dividends are paid to stockholders. With broad investment opportunities cash is needed from debt and equity sources, adding the dimension of financial risk to operating risk. These questions are resolved in the capital expenditure program and the capital structure plan. The rate of investment drives the rate of growth, a major factor in stock valuation, together with risk. The concept of "capital maintenance" is static and not relevant to planning.

Another confusing and misleading idea is called "profit in inventory." Inventory is carried at cost and its profitable sale is planned but can be booked only when realized. The reference is to an inventory cost that is less than its current market price. Hence, the profit is greater on cost than market. For example:

Sale	$100
Cost	40
Profit	60

If the cost has risen by $10 from $40 to $50 currently, the transaction can be rewritten:

Sale	$100
Market price	50
Market profit	50
Cost increase	10
Book profit	60

This translates into saying that profit would be only $50 at market cost but is $60 on historical cost. This does not tell management anything. Any inventory is sold to the best advantage in the current circumstances regardless of assumptions made when purchased. It is known as a sunk cost--the money has been spent. Any purchase is based on current expectations for the future--an investment decision involving profitability and risk. An example is given for a retailer who buys 100 items at $50, total $5,000, with the expectation of realizing a 75% mark-up--$3,750--for total sales of $8,750. The sales plan is:

	Number	Price	Sales	Cost	Markup	Percent
Full price	60	$100	$6,000	$3,000	$3,000	100%
Markdown #1	20	80	1,600	1,000	600	60%
Markdown #2	10	65	650	500	150	30%
Close out	10	50	500	500	0	0
	100		8,750	5,000	3,750	75%

The range of outcomes is estimated as:

Low: $5,000 plus 40% or $2,000 = sales $7,000
High: $5,000 plus 90% or $4,500 = sales $9,500

After the purchase actual sales will be responsive to current conditions. An extreme case would be a market collapse and disposal of the lot below cost, a possibility too remote to include in the risk range. No change in the market price for acquiring these items is relevant to the inventory book cost. A new purchase would be guided by the same criteria as before--a range of selling prices and costs for a probable margin. In practice, retailers maintain full lines to meet demand, and must constantly make decisions on pricing, replenishing stock, and adding and dropping items, along with other factors affecting profit.

CLOSING THE BOOKS

The need for periodic financial statements requires "closing the books," a difficult but inescapable task. It was observed long ago, and many times since, that a closing would be "indefensible" if it were not "indispensable." The closing requires a cut-off date for all transactions--billings, payables, cash, deliveries, shipments, wages, accruals, debt, and dividends. All transactions and book entries must be matched and reconciled so that assets are not overstated or liabilities understated. The closing process must be closely scheduled and regulated by procedures and internal control. There is room for error, miscalculation, and manipulation. Sales may include shipments made in the next period. Purchases may be included in inventory but not in payables. Expense accruals may be omitted. Pressure for profit may encourage "creative accounting." Published quarterly reports call for close attention; monthly closings are often routinized for economy. It is particularly important for management to take responsibility for asset values whose realization depends on the future--collection of receivables, salability of inventory, utilization of fixed assets, validity of asset balances for prepaid expenses, deferred charges, patent rights, and goodwill. All known liabilities must be disclosed with notation of any contingencies.

Accrual accounting is a necessary and valuable tool. It is management's responsibility to provide for an adequate system. The complexities are readily handled by experienced accountants who should be given the means to meet all internal and external needs.

CHART OF ACCOUNTS

All transactions must be coded to provide the required information for both internal and external use. Coding must be made at the source and verified; it supports the the entire information system. The coding of all documents enters into the journals, records, ledgers, reports, and statements.

A uniform chart of accounts with codes and definitions is used throughout the company. The following examples present a chart in

outline, with numbers omitted. One chart defines the entire organization
in terms of responsibility by departments, illustrated for two levels
only:

                    Board of Directors
                    Office of the President
                    Corporate Expenses
                    Finance:
                       Treasury
                       Controller
                       Systems
                       Tax
                       Audit
                    Legal
                    Corporate Relations
                    Research and Development
                    Marketing:
                       Domestic Sales
                       Export Sales
                       Government Sales
                       Advertising and Promotion
                       Market Research
                       Credit and Collection
                       Orders and Distribution
                    Manufacturing:
                       Factory Manager
                       Purchasing
                       Production Control
                       Quality Control
                       Personnel
                       Manufacturing Engineering
                       Industrial Engineering

Additional levels are illustrated for the factory manager:

                    Factory Manager:
                       Production Manager:
                          Superintendents:
                             General Foremen--departments
                       Maintenance
                       Plant Engineering
                       Utilities
                       Tool Room
                       Cleaning
                       Material Control
                       Inspection

     Department expenses are coded for both expense element and
department. The following list of expenses is representative:

Salaries	Freight
Commissions	Depreciation
Premiums	Insurance
Bonuses	Taxes
Welfare	Communications
Fringe	Stationery--Forms
Direct Labor Downtime	Advertising
Postage	Warehousing
Indirect Labor	Utilities
Temporary Help	Bad Debts
Professional Services	Meetings & Exhibitions
Indirect Materials	House Publications
Supplies	Rentals
Travel & Entertainment	Donations
Auto	Licenses
Fees and Dues	

Reporting is by departments, with totals summarized by division. It is also possible to cross-total an account, if needed, such as professional services. All accounts can have subaccounts for added detail as desired for clarity. The chart should be prepared in grid form by department and account with an X to designate accounts not applicable to certain departments.

The chart of accounts for the income statement is stated briefly:

> Revenue:
>   Sales - Service - Rentals
> Cost of Sales:
>   Sales - Service - Rentals
> Revenue Deductions:
>   Freight-out - Returns - Allowances - Discounts
> Variances:
>   Material Price - Usage - Labor - Overhead
> Other Costs:
>   Freight-in - Scrap - Warranty - Royalties - Plant Rearrangement - Project Expenses - Inventory Adjustments - Revaluations
> Selling Expenses
> Administrative Expenses
> Research and Development
> Other Income and Expense:
>   Cash Discounts - Capital Disposal Gain/Loss - Interest - Royalty - Salvage - Casualty - Dividends Received - Accounting Adjustments
> Income Taxes

A chart for the balance sheet is given in brief form:

> Current Assets:
>   Cash - Securities - Receivables - Inventory - Prepaid Expense - Deposits - Claims

Current Liabilities:
    Payables - Accruals - Payroll - Dividends - Taxes -
    Deferred Credits
Fixed Assets - Accumulated Depreciation:
    Land - Buildings - Machinery - Equipment - Capitalized
    Leases - Furniture and Fixtures - Transport - Capital
    Projects in Process
Intangibles - Patents - Goodwill - Franchise
Deferred Charges - Deferred Tax Liability
Debt
Capital Stock
Retained Earnings
Currency Translation Adjustment
Dividends Declared

Additional codes may be used for employees, company products, customers, vendors, agents, material purchased, and fixed assets. Code numbers are also used for capital expenditure projects and expense work orders. The chart may also apply to company subdivisions, divisions, profit centers, locations, sales offices, branches, and warehouses.

This brief presentation demonstrates the need for a comprehensive, logical, and relevant chart of accounts that is observed meticulously and revised promptly to meet changed needs. An accounting manual should provide definitions for the chart of accounts and schedules for closing the books and issuing statements, as well as instructions for asset capitalization, work orders, capital expenditures, billings, payables, inventory valuation, payroll taxes, prepaid and accrued expenses, revision of cost standards, and other pertinent topics. The manual should carry the authority of top management. Internal auditing should provide continual monitoring for compliance. Systems analysts should evaluate all systems for effectiveness and cost. Management should provide close support and guidance.

14

Expenditures:
Expense Timing and Methods

All expenditures are made to acquire something of value--an "asset." Expenditures debited to the balance sheet to accounts such as inventory and fixed assets are said to be "capitalized"--additions to assets. Debits made directly to the income statement are "expensed"--charges to income. "Cost" is a broad term that requires definition in the context of its use. The outlay to acquire a truck, its cost, is charged to fixed assets for the most part, but some of the outlay may be expensed at once. The cost to operate the truck includes depreciation, plus ownership and operating outlays--all expenses for a period. The cost of material purchased for resale is a debit to inventory, charged to cost of sales when sold--an expense. Both the classification of expenditures when made as assets or expense and the method of charging assets to expense, over time or as used, have a direct effect on profit for the period. Practice varies widely. The principle is to match revenue and expense by periods, subject to asset valuation based on estimated future realization.

PRODUCT COSTS AND PERIOD EXPENSES

All expenses are divided between product costs and period expenses. Products are carried in inventory at cost until shipment and billing. The sales and costs are matched to measure product profit margins. Period expenses are charged to expense as incurred without regard to revenue. Product costs are composed of costs measured directly to products (material and labor [prime costs]) and indirect costs (all other production expenses, or factory overhead). All other overhead is period expense by definition, often referred to as selling, general, and administrative expense (SGA). The classification of overhead as product cost or period expense is important; references to overhead must always be specific. A short income statement summarizes the points made:

        Sales - shipments - debit to receivables
        Cost of sales - an expense - credit to inventory cost
        Gross margin - by product
        SGA - all period expenses
        Operating profit

The effect of expense classification and timing on profit is
illustrated with total overhead of $1,200 divided between product cost
and period expense in three different proportions:

	I	II	III
Factory overhead	$400	$600	$800
SGA	800	600	400
	$1200	$1200	$1200

Sales are $2,000. Half the inventory is sold. There is no opening
inventory.

	I	II	III
Debits to inventory:			
Material and Labor	$1400	$1400	$1400
Factory Overhead	400	600	800
	$1800	$2000	$2200
Balance on hand--half	900	1000	1100
Cost of Sales--half	900	1000	1100
Sales	2000	2000	2000
Gross Margin	1100	1000	900
SGA	800	600	400
Operating Profit	$300	$400	$500
Percent to Sales	15%	20%	25%

The shift of $200 from SGA to factory overhead adds $100 to profit, based
on sales of half the inventory.
     If all the inventory is sold the total inventory and SGA costs are
equal at $2,600 and sales double to $4,000. Profit is $1,400 or 35
percent of sales in all cases, assuming SGA is fully fixed.
     The exploration of expenditures as to classification and timing is
presented in the balance of this chapter. The subject is part of the
accounting system, which is part of the information system, all subject
to internal control and audit. Management is responsible for ensuring
the design, installation, and operation of systems that are effective and
efficient. Good data aids good decisions. The investment in systems
work involves accountants, systems analysts, auditors, methods
specialists, and consultants, plus the participation of all managers to
ensure acceptable results. The pay-off is better decisions and more
economical systems and procedures.
     GAAP provides limited guidance in the area of expense timing and
methods. There is a wide range of practice among industries and
companies, and often within a company's divisions and plants. Pressure
for clerical economy may lead to inadequate systems and simplified
procedures that impair expense control and profitability analysis. The
trade-off between cost and benefit is seldom clear. Too much data can
cause an information overload. Lack of data and inaccuracies can
handicap evaluation. Subterranean methods spring up to fill voids at an
unknown cost and with data isolated from the system. Good systems design
should preclude such deviations and achieve minimum cost. System design
must provide for all transactions: billings, receivables, payables,
payrolls, cash, fixed assets, taxes, inventories, debt, dividends, and
stock records. Required published statements include stockholders,

government agencies, SEC, stock exchanges, associations, and tax returns. Any added expense to provide for information needed internally is minimal.

Income taxes have a major impact on profits and may affect decisions on expense timing. An expenditure that is fully expensed at once reduces both profit and tax at once. If the item is capitalized and expensed over time there is a difference for each period. For example, tools costing $12,000 expensed at once would save taxes of $4,800 at a 40% rate, a net expense of $7,200. Or, the tools could be expensed over three years at $4,000 with the following effect on net income:

Year	Expense	Tax	Net	Net-- Expensed	Net Change-- Income
1	$4,000	$1,600	$2,400	$7,200	($4,800)
2	4,000	1,600	2,400	0	2,400
3	4,000	1,600	2,400	0	2,400
	12,000	4,800	7,200	7,200	0

The net effect on taxes saved is:

Year	Amortized	Expensed	Net Gain (Loss)
1	$1,600	$4,800	$3,200
2	1,600	0	(1,600)
3	1,600	. 0	(1,600)
	$4,800	$4,800	0

The net tax saving in year 1 is offset in the next two years by higher taxes--the equivalent of a loan without interest. Total expense net of tax in year 1 of $7,200 less amortization of $2,400 is $4,800 more charged to income, with a $2,400 gain in the following two years. The question of expense timing relative to purchases for inventory and fixed assets also involves the extra clerical cost for asset records. The attraction of lower current taxes is to be weighed against the effect of lower net income and the possibility of reversal by tax audit. This would entail payment of assessed taxes for past periods, plus interest, and the revision of records to the tax bases.

Purchases of materials and supplies may be expensed or charged to inventory and issued by requisition. Material requisitions may be charged directly to material cost--a transfer to work-in-process inventory--or to factory overhead as indirect material expense. All factory overhead is charged to work-in-process at the costing rate, with variances expensed. Supplies may be requisitioned from inventory for factory overhead or for SGA. Purchases charged to inventory are better controlled and better matched to revenue. Costs in finished goods are matched with sales. This route provides better expense control and more accurate product profit margins. Requisitions on inventory for current needs that are charged to SGA match usage with periods more closely than larger purchases charged to expense directly. The procedures followed must be observed in both budgeting and accounting for comparability. Similar considerations apply to fixed assets, prepaid expenses, and deferred charges. The benefits of improved asset control and profit measurement must be weighed against higher clerical expenses.

Inventory Costing Methods

Specific Identification: Articles with high unit cost and specific physical identification are inventoried individually and sold by item. The inventory is composed of specific items with individual costs. Examples include autos, trucks, yachts, pianos, art objects, computers, and machinery.

FIFO--First In, First Out: It is assumed that the first, or oldest, purchase is used first. The inventory consists of the latest purchases. This accords with the physical facts in most cases where specific identity is lacking. An inventory record is illustrated:

Date		Units DR	CR	at	DR	CR	Cumulative Balance
31	Bal.	100a		$8.20	$820		$ 820
8	Buy	40b		8.50	340		1,160
10	Issue		110:				
			100a	8.20		$820	
			10b	8.50		85	
						905	
	Bal.	30					255
15	Buy	60		8.60	516		771
22	Issue		20b	8.50		170	
	Bal	70					601
Totals		200	130		$1,676	$1,075	

Recap		Units		
	Open balance	100	$ 820	
	Buy	40	340	
	Buy	60	516	
		200		$1,676
	Issue	110a & b	905	
	Issue	20b	170	
		130		$1,075
	End balance	70		$ 601

The ending balance is directly determinable by analyses of the ending balance:

Last buy	60	at $8.60	516
Prior buy--balance	10b	at $8.50	85
Inventory	70		$601

Average Cost: Average cost can be determined for each new purchase or periodically. Using the month-end cost average and reworking the first example:

Date		Units	at	
31	Balance	100	$8.20	$820.00
8	Buy	40	8.50	340.00
15	Buy	60	8.60	516.00
Average at month-end		200	8.38	1676.00
10 Issue		110	8.38	921.80
Balance		90	8.38	754.20
22 Issue		20	8.38	167.60
Balance		70	8.38	586.60

If the opening balance average of $8.20 is used for issues, the result is:

	Units	At	
Total Debits	200	$8.38	$1,676
Total Issue	130	8.20	1,066
Balance	70	(8.71)	610

Use of the average for each purchase would produce another result. Practice varies.

LIFO--Last In, First Out: The most recent purchase is assumed to be used first. Inventory contains the oldest purchases. This artificial approach is allowed for tax purposes but the tax code requires that it also be used in published financial statements. With escalating prices the tax saving can be substantial. The inventory value on the balance sheet expresses the lower prices from earlier periods, often far below current cost. Net income to date is equally lower. Revenue each period is charged with the purchase costs most recently incurred, presumably a better matching of income and expense. This method is allowed by GAAP but has no value to management. It is not relevant to decisions, does not deal directly with inflation, and is subject to manipulation by the timing of purchases. The LIFO tax calculation can be made at year-end for tax filing and published statements. The LIFO adjustment requires highly technical, complex, and obscure computations, understood only by some tax specialists and subject to various interpretations. For internal reporting LIFO entries are best incorporated into the tax section so that other values are not distorted.

A brief illustration displays the key relationships.

	With LIFO		Without LIFO	
	Open	End	Open	End
Balance Sheet				
Inventory	$ 50	$ 40	$200	$ 230
Other	750	800	750	800
Total Assets	$800	$840	$950	$1030
Liabilities	$400	$400	$400	$ 400
Equity	400	400	550	550
Net Income	--	40	--	80
	$800	$840	$950	$1030
ROE		$40/400		$80/550
		= 10%		= 14.5%

. Opening inventory is $50 LIFO and $ 200 cost = +$150
. Ending inventory is   40 LIFO and   230 cost = + 190
. Change   -10   +30   = + 40 profit gain
. LIFO equity is lower by the inventory difference of $150.
. Ending inventory with LIFO at $40 is understated by $190 from current cost, as is ending equity at $630 compared with $440.

The inventory transactions illustrated above are repeated using LIFO:

		Units					Cumulative
Date		DR	CR	at	DR	CR	Balance
31	Bal.	100b		$8.20	$820		$ 820
8	Buy	40a		8.50	340		1160
10	Issue		110				
			40a	8.50		$340	
			70b	8.20		574	
						914	
	Bal.	30					246
15	Buy	60c		8.60	516		762
22	Issue		20c	8.60		172	
	Bal	70					590
Totals		200	130		$1676	$1086	

The ending balance is computed for the oldest purchases on hand.

        From: Open Bal   30b at $8.20 $246
        From: 15 Buy   40c at 8.60   344
                               70   590

If all issues are costed only at the month-end the computations are:

        Debits   31 Bal   100b at $8.20 $820
                     8 Buy   40a at 8.50   340
                    15 Buy   60c at 8.60   576
                                 200   1676
        Credits   10 Issue   110:
                                  60c $8.60 $ 576
                                  40a   8.50   340
                                  10b   8.20   82
                                 110   938
                    22 Issue   20b 8.20   164
                                 130   1102
                    Balance   70b 8.20 $ 574

A variety of methods occur in practice.

Standard Cost: Purchases are charged to inventory at the predetermined material prices used for standard product costs. All issues are at the same price. Balances are also at that amount. Accordingly, the quantity records can be kept without dollar entries until month-end when they are made in total. Purchase price variances are expensed when the transaction is recorded. If the standard price is changed, inventory on hand is adjusted and the change is booked in a separate account for purchase price adjustments, companion to the price variance account.

Repeating the example with a $8.20 standard to demonstrate the process:

Date		Units	At	DR	CR	Cumulative Balance
31	Bal	+100	$8.20	$ 820		$ 820
8	Buy	+ 40	8.20	328		1148
10	Issue	-110	8.20		$ 902	246
15	Buy	+ 60	8.20	492		738
22	Issue	- 20	8.20		164	
	Bal.	70	8.20			574
Totals				$1640	$1066	

The entries would be made monthly in practice. Purchase price variances are illustrated:

```
 8  Buy      40 at    $8.50 - 8.20 = .30 = $  12 DR
15  Buy      60 at    $8.60 - 8.20 = .40 =    24 DR
            100                              36 DR
```

If the standard is increased at the month-end to $8.60 the inventory adjustment is $28: 70 units at 8.60 - 8.20 = .40 = $28, added to inventory and credited to purchase price adjustments. Price standards should be reviewed regularly and revised periodically.

Inventory Adjustments: Inventories are significant to both the balance sheet and income statement and should be tightly run and closely monitored. Both accurate records and accurate physical handling are requisite. Physical counts should be kept on a perpetual basis and verified at intervals by independent workers or auditors. Shut-down for full count is expensive and the results are often untrustworthy because of untrained personnel and the difficulty of reconciling physical and book cut-offs. Use of the ABC inventory method is helpful and valuation at standard cost is simple.

Inventories must also be purged promptly for all obsolete, damaged, spoiled, and excessive stocks, physically separated and promptly sold or scrapped. The write-off should be to a separate account which is credited with salvage value. For a tax write-off the items must be physically disposed of.

A further valuation question attaches to good products relative to market values. The valuation rule for all assets is to write-down any loss of value, while a write-up is not allowed because profit cannot be anticipated. For an inventory item the book cost, plus any cost to complete, plus selling expenses, must not exceed expected sales value; any excess is written off. For example, an item with a declining market price each period:

Inventory cost	$100	$100	$100	$100
Cost to complete	80	80	80	80
Selling expense	40	40	40	40
Total cost	120	120	120	120
Market price	200	140	120	100
Margin	80	20	0	- 20

For a similar example the $120 total cost increases and the market price remains at $200:

Total cost	$120	$180	$200	$220
Market price	200	200	200	200
Margin	80	20	0	- 20

The $20 anticipated loss is booked at once rather than being held in inventory to be taken in a subsequent period. No larger write-down is made because that would cause a greater loss currently and a profit subsequently; this is profit manipulation. The write-down presumes a subsequent sale at zero margin.

A debatable rule known as the "lower of cost or market"--LCM--is questionable. Observation in practice is primarily lip service. It embraces the sales value write-down just described and is redundant to that extent. It purports to apply to current purchase prices relative to inventory but its application is either unnecessary or objectionable. The continuation of LCM is habitual, reflecting "conventional wisdom." If considered mandatory for published statements, it should not be reflected in management reports.

Four examples illustrate the possible relationships. LCM terms are in quotation marks and amounts used in the examples are listed:

S--Sales = realizable market value. "Ceiling" $70
S Net--Sales less profit = sales less "normal" profit of $20
                "Floor" $50 ($70 - $20)
M--Market = current cost to replace inventory item $80 - $60 - $40 -$40
C--Cost = book cost of inventory item $85 - $65 - $45 - $55
W/D = Write-down of C = book cost

For the illustration, cost is always over market because a cost below market is never written up to market. For the universal asset valuation rule, cost is written down only to avoid carrying a probable loss in inventory, but never by a larger amount because that would create a larger current loss and a future profit. The LCM rules may give the same result, and thus are redundant, or call for a current loss and future profit, contrary to sound accounting or good logic. These inherent flaws are the basis for ignoring this relic for all practical purposes.

	Example I	Accounting	LCM
Sales	$70	$ 70	$ 70
Sales net	50		
Market	80		
Cost	85	S 70	S 70
Loss (S-C)	-15	0	0
	W/D 15		W/D 15

LCM rule: reduce C 85 to S 70 which is below M 80 and over S net 50. The W/D 15 is booked in the current period as a separate account in cost of sales.   The inventory balance is reduced to $70, a new cost basis for the future. The LCM rule is: Select the middle value of sales - sales net - market; use the lower of that value and cost. In this case the middle value is S70 (50--70--80) and 70 is lower than 85 by $15.   This rule is observable in the subsequent examples.

	Example II	Accounting	LCM
Sales	$70	$ 70	$ 70
S Net	50		
M	60		M 60
C	65	C 65	
Profit (S-C)	5	5	10
		W/D	5

There is no accounting entry--S exceeds C. LC rule: M 60 is the middle value (50-60-70) and 5 below cost, and so it is used. The LCM W/D of 5 currently leads to future profit of 10. Frequently a comparable market value is not available or can only be approximated. Also market values fluctuate irregularly.

	Example III	Accounting	LCM
Sales	$70	$ 70	$ 70
S Net	50		
M	40		
C	45	C 45	C 45
Profit (S--C)	25	25	25

   LCM: S net 50 is the middle value (40-50-70) but over C 45 and so not used. The two results are the same. There is no W/D, even though M 40 is below C 45, because the "floor" at S net 50 is over C 45.

	Example IV	Accounting	LCM
Sales	$70	$ 70	$70
S Net	50		S Net 50
M	40		
C	55	C 55	
Profit (S--C)	15	15	20
		W/D	5

   LCM: S net 50 is the middle value (40-50-70) and under C 55, and so is used. M 40 is below the "floor" and so is not used. LCM calls for a current loss of 5 and a future profit of 20. If cost was 15 higher at C 70 the LCM W/D would be 20, with no accounting W/D because C 70 equals S 70.
   This elaboration supports the point that LCM is either unnecessary (redundant to asset valuation rule) or undesirable (current loss to create future profit). In practice the application of LCM is very broad and limited to any write-down based on the general asset valuation rule. The LCM rule lacks theoretical support.

Fixed Assets and Depreciation

   The decision to charge a purchase to fixed assets or to expense directly rests on several points: size of outlay, economic life, durability, physical control, effect on income, product cost measurement, expense control, tax status, record-keeping expense, and type of asset (land, buildings, machinery, equipment, tools, trucks, lab equipment, furniture, and fixtures). Minimum life may be set at two to three years for capitalization with minimum amounts from $50 to $5,000 or more. All lab equipment subject to breakage is expensed. All fixed assets should carry permanent identification numbers and be controlled by records, whether or not capitalized. Physical counts are desirable periodically. Equipment leased from others should be specifically identified. Equipment leased to others should also be identified and verified periodically with the lessee. Purchases of fixed assets charged to expense should be charged to separate overhead accounts for both factory overhead and SGA. Depreciation is also expensed to separate accounts. Fully depreciated assets in use remain on the books. Fixed assets withdrawn from use should be transferred to a separate account for assets awaiting disposition. Maintenance is capitalized if asset life is extended or capacity enhanced for significant amounts. The tax advantage encourages higher current expense. GAAP provides little guidance. Practice varies widely. The choices are pragmatic. The accounting practices should be echoed in the budgets for comparability. Fixed asset acquisition and disposal is controlled through the capital expenditure program.

Depreciation is simply the allocation of expense over time. It is a noncash item because cash was recognized on acquisition. Depreciation calculations are based on capitalized cost, economic life, and residual value. The method used determines the amount of expense per period. Credit is to accumulated depreciation, offsetting acquisition cost, and debit is to provision for depreciation. Questions of inflation, market value, and replacement cost are considered in the capital expenditure program. Selection of a method of depreciation is a management choice. Faster write-offs (accelerated depreciation) provide greater tax savings currently but net income is lower. If less depreciation (straight line) is taken in the books, book income is higher than taxable income but tax must be provided on the difference to determine net income. The tax provision on the difference is credited to deferred taxes payable; the account is expected to reverse over time.

Several depreciation methods are illustrated.

Usage: Some fixed assets are primarily exhausted by physical use rather than by the passage of time. The depreciation rate is the asset cost divided by the estimated total units of output. This rate needs to be reviewed periodically. If output is low for a period, a minimum depreciation charge may be made to recognize the time loss of value.

Straight Line--SL:

Cost		$90,000 capitalized
Life	8 years	Depreciation $11,250 per year

When the asset is disposed of there may be a gain or loss, taken to a nonoperating section of the income statement. It is some mix of change in market value and correction of booked depreciation. If the asset is fully depreciated there may be a net disposal cost. If the asset is sold at the end of four years for $40,000, the journal entry is:

Accumulated Depreciation	$45,000	
Fixed Asset		$90,000
Cash	40,000	
Loss on Asset Disposal	5,000	

Although some net disposal value may be anticipated at the time of purchase, it is necessarily speculative. It is generally better to depreciate full book value, usually allowable for taxes, and let any gain emerge in the future. For example, if a disposal value of $8,000 is used, the calculation is: $90,000 - 8,000 = 82,000 divided by 8 years = $10,250 per year. At the end of eight years, the net book value is $8,000. The annual depreciation is $1,000 less. If the market value is $5,000, the write-off is $3,000. The practice followed may be based on the method used for the capital expenditure project.

Double Declining Balance (DDB): The annual SL rate is 1/8 or 12.5%; doubled it is 25%. This rate is applied to the net asset balance; a switch to SL is allowable:

Rate 25%	Depreciation	Balance $90,000	Switch to SL	
Year 1	$22,500	$67,500		
2	16,875	50,625		
3	12,656	37,969		
4	9,492	28,477		
5	7,120	21,357		
6	5,339	16,018	$ 7,119	+1,780
7	4,004	12,014	7,119	+3,115
8	3,004	9,010	7,119	+4,115
	80,990			+9,010

DDB results in a $9,010 ending asset balance; this could be considered to be the disposal value. The switch to SL is made when the SL debit exceeds the DDB debit (year 6). In year 5 DDB is 7,120 and SL is $7,119, equal except for rounding. Rates other than double may also be used. For 150% declining balance: 150% of 12.5% = 18.75%.

Sum-of-the-years Digits (SYD): The asset cost is divided by the sum of the years of asset life. The sum of 1 through 8 = 36. By formula: 1 plus 8 = 9 times 8/2 or 4 = 36. Examples:

1 to 10	=	11 x 5 = 55
1 to 16	=	17 x 8 = 136
1 to 18	=	19 x 9 = 171
1 to 20	=	21 x 10 = 210
16 to 20	=	74 (210 - 136) or
		17 + 18 + 19 + 20

The cost of $90,000 divided by 36 is $2,500, the debit for year 8. For year 1 the debit is 8/36 or $20,000:

Year	Rate	Depreciation	Balance
1	8/36	$20,000	$70,000
2	7/36	17,500	52,500
3	6/36	15,000	37,500
4	5/36	12,500	25,000
5	4/36	10,000	15,000
6	3/36	7,500	7,500
7	2/36	5,000	2,500
8	1/36	2,500	0

The annual increments are even and a zero balance is reached.

Financial Method: This method is used for investment analysis and is based solely on actual cash flows and a discount rate.   With no discount rate the calculation is the same as for SL: $90,000/8 = $11,250. For a 10% rate: 10% 8 year f 5.335, and $90,000 divided by f5.335 = $16,870 annuity. The table is:

Year	Annuity	10% of Principal	Principal Reduction	Principal $90,000
1	$16,870	$9,000	$ 7,870	$82,130
2	16,870	8,213	8,657	73,473
3	16,870	7,347	9,523	63,950
4	16,870	6,395	10,475	53,475
5	16,870	5,348	11,522	41,953
6	16,870	4,196	12,674	29,279
7	16,870	2,928	13,942	15,337
8	16,870	1,533	15,337	0
	$134,960	$44,960	$90,000	

This schedule provides a constant 10% yield on the opening balance, reduced by the annuity. The excess of the annuity over the 10% interest amount is a principal reduction, applied to the last column. The principal reduction is the equivalent of depreciation, and it increases from $7,870 to $15,337, almost double and the reverse direction from accelerated methods. The schedule depicts the financial principle that a 10% yield for asset life is also 10% for each period, calculated on the opening balance. The financial method is necessary for investment analysis but is not allowed by GAAP for recording depreciation. Differences between accounting practices and financial methods require reconciliation and are a regrettable source of misunderstanding. Advocates of the financial method for book depreciation have had scant recognition.

The wide differences in the annual depreciation on $90,000 over 8 years are summarized. For each year H (high) and L (low) amounts are noted:

Year	SL	DDB	SYD	Financial	MEMO: Difference High--Low
1	$11,250	$22,500H	$20,000	$ 7,870L	$14,630
2	11,250	16,875	17,500H	8,657L	8,843
3	11,250	12,656	15,000H	9,523L	5,477
4	11,250	9,492L	12,500H	10,475	3,008
5	11,250	7,120L	10,000	11,522H	4,402
6	11,250	7,119L	7,520	12,674H	5,555
7	11,250	7,119	5,000L	13,942H	8,942
8	11,250	7,119	2,500L	15,337H	12,837
	$90,000	$90,000	$90,000	$90,000	

Depreciation is the allocation of cost over time.   There is no theoretical accounting basis for choice but SL is the most logical. The financial method is inherent to discounted cash flow. Cash flows require tax computations based on the depreciation allowances in the tax code; these are complex and changing and are not presented here.   Some acceptable depreciation method must be chosen for the records as part of the measurement of asset value and profit. The basic investment question is always whether to retain the asset for use, sell for the net proceeds, or replace--all part of the capital expenditure program. Book values are not relevant except as a factor in tax analysis. It is also possible to restate assets and depreciation adjusted for inflation if useful for analyses but there are severe practical difficulties as well as theoretical questions.

Major Expenses

The accuracy of profit is improved with the careful measurement of the applicable revenue and expense by period--the core of accrual accounting. Items may be prepaid and taken to expense over time or accrued prior to liability recognition such as for rent, taxes, insurance, supplies, utilities, and payrolls. Revenue may be collected or billed in advance and credited to deferred revenue.

Deferred charges reflect major expenses applicable to future periods such as moving expenses, office supplies, plant rearrangement, consulting studies, and sales promotion materials. All research and development is expensed as incurred, per GAAP, becuase there is no dependable basis for estimating future benefit. The decision to undertake a project may be made with financial analysis based on future gain, and this approach remains applicable throughout project life.

Intangibles may be capitalized and amortized on the basis of estimated remaining value--patents, franchises, goodwill. Goodwill is booked only when purchased and must be amortized within 40 years, per the FASB. Prior to this standard, goodwill could be carried as an asset indefinitely; some balance sheets contain goodwill stated on both bases.

The handling of all these topics needs to be spelled out in the accounting system and carefully reviewed for validity and relevance.

OVERHEAD CLASSIFICATION

Total overhead is classified either as product cost (factory overhead) or period expense (SGA). The choice is crucial to product profit measurement. There is a wide range of viewpoints. Some would include in product cost only direct material and direct labor, with all overhead expensed as incurred because it relates to products only by arbitrary assumptions. At the other extreme, all overhead is considered to be part of cost because all expenses are directed toward future sales. The consensus is to include in product cost all indirect expenses necessary for production--a pragmatic choice. A small minority would include only the variable factory overhead in product cost, mistakenly called "direct costing," and analyzed in chapter 15.

All overhead is defined by department and account, based on assigned responsibility and delegation. Budgets and actual can be compared as a guide to expense control. Product profitability can be studied independently of the classification. The recording of factory overhead as product cost requires the use of production department overhead rates on some basis that best serves in place of direct measurement--labor hours, machine hours, direct labor wages. Also the service departments must be allocated to the production departments in some logical sequence. The upshot is a product cost that is clearly definable for direct material and direct labor, and for overhead by a series of allocations. All excluded overhead is period expense and is not related to products for costing.

Departments are described in four groups to illustrate a scheme for classification:

Factory production--direct work on products:
Machining, heat treating, plating, finishing, welding, stamping, assembly. Departments and accounts are defined to facilitate both expense control and product costing. Departments may be subdivided into cost centers to provide closer overhead costing differentials. For example, a machine shop with a 300% rate might consist of three distinctive machine groups, or cost centers, with rates of 200%, 350% and 600%. The criterion is the significance of the difference in product costs illustrated below.

Factory service--direct support of production:
Maintenance, tool room, material control, utilities, cleaning, plant engineering. Budgets are based on the service to be provided. All service overhead must be allocated to production to arrive at costing rates.

Factory office--general support of production:
Purchasing, production control, industrial engineering, quality control, personnel, cost analysis. Budgets are fixed and relate to plans and policy more than physical output. These activities are better excluded from factory overhead because allocations would be arbitrary and could blur costing differentials. The effect on periodic net income measurement is negligible.

General office--selling, general, and administrative:
These activities are expensed as incurred, together with factory office departments and both are part of SGA. Budgets are fixed. Any product cost relationships are made by analysis for a specific purpose. Activities include all management, financial, legal, accounting, marketing, research, public relations, or other staff functions. General office expense is not allocated. If service is provided by a factory service department, such as maintenance, the charges are collected on a work order. Charge is made to a separate account for internal work with credit to the service department in a separate transfer account. Such entries are made only when deemed relevant for expense control. If marketing requires a change in production schedules to meet a particular customer demand, the extra setup cost may be charged to relieve production of the added expense. This procedure provides marketing with a specific basis for the decision and may help to avoid unwarranted demands. In some cases, the extra costs may be charged to the customer.

PRODUCT COSTS

Material

All materials incorporated into the product or consumed directly in its production are measured directly, as far as practical. If direct measurement is not used the charge is to a separate account in factory

overhead for indirect material, with any desirable subdivisions for
expense control. Indirect material generally lacks the specific control
given to direct material for quantity and price. As part of the overhead
rate, it applies to all products. Indirect material purchases should be
inventoried and requisitions should be limited to amounts needed for
short periods. Some items are used as both indirect material and
supplies and the requisitions should be carefully coded. Reclassification between direct and indirect material should be reviewed periodically. The basis for budgetary expense allowance and the procedures
followed should be consonant. Effective control of usage on the floor
requires daily logs for both indirect material and supplies regardless of
the accounting system. In principle, the preference is for material to
be classified as direct to provide both more accurate product profit
measurement and better expense control.

Labor

Labor is classified by department and by account, either as direct or
indirect relative to production. Direct labor is measured to products
for production time based on time and rate standards. The balance of the
time is charged to overhead as direct labor downtime, coded as to cause
and subject to budget control. Engineering studies help to set all labor
time standards, particularly for production work. Classification of
labor as production rather than downtime is preferable to provide more
accurate costing and better expense control. The question can also arise
relative to classification as direct or indirect labor. Setup time, for
example, may be relatively large or small for different operations and
products. If not measured as direct production time, it is charged to a
separate overhead account. A daily log may be needed to help exercise
control. Time spent on rework and scrap also needs to be carefully
defined and measured. Scrap that is relatively high in amount and
variable among products based on engineered standards may need to be
handled as a separate cost element. When part of overhead it may be
desirable to establish cost centers to derive equitable costing rates.
For automated operations there is no separate direct labor. The work
crews are part of overhead and efficiency is based on output relative to
time and expense, with direct material a separate cost.

Factory Overhead

The overhead costing rate depends on several steps:

> Budget for each expense account based on selected activity for all
> departments
> Allocation of all service expense to production departments
> Output rate based on practical capacity for plant or production
> departments

After definition of all direct material and direct labor, the remaining expenses are budgeted according to planned activity levels--the
relevant range. The budget is expressed as fixed and variable relative
relative to the activity and time period (usually one year). The
specification of time is necessary because in the long run all expenses

are variable, as recognized in financial investment analysis. The relevant range is also a factor because activity outside that range is not planned. Service departments provide assistance to other departments in planned relationships--the basis for both the budget and method of allocation. By allocation all service overhead is added to production overhead to be included in the costing rate. The most practical method is to arrange all service departments in a sequence based on budget size and number of other departments served. Each department is allocated seriatim with no charge back to closed out departments. This limit can be removed by algebraic formulation but the complication may not be worth the difference in results. Direct allocation of all service to production without recognition of service-to-service is generally not sufficiently accurate. The production department activity factor is expressed at the rate of practical capacity to divide into total overhead to get the costing rate.

The allocation process is illustrated in chapter 12. The effect of allocation on product costs is illustrated for three products--K, L, M--first using the following rates for three production departments:

Department	Overhead	Base	Rate
1	$1,150	230 labor hours	$5
2	1,200	$1,200 labor dollars	100%
3	1,250	125 machine hours	$10
	$3,600		

Costs are developed for the products using the departmental overhead rates:

Applied Overhead			K	L	M	Total
Department:						
1 at $5:	K-	130	$650			
	L-	100		$500		
		230				$1150
2 at 100%	L-$	300		300		
	M-	900			$900	
		1200				1200
3 at $10	K-	25	250			
	L-	80		800		
	M-	20				
		125	____	____	200	$1250
Overhead			900	1600	1100	3600
Direct Costs			1600	2400	2400	6400
Total Cost			2500	4000	3500	10000
Sales			6250	8000	6140	20390
Margin			$3750	$4000	$2640	$10390
Percent			60%	50%	43%	51%

An alternative method of overhead allocation (detail omitted) gives this result:

	K	L	M	Total
Change in amount	+$ 136	-$ 320	+$ 184	$ 0
Applied overhead--new	$1036	$1280	1284	3600
Direct costs--above	1600	2400	2400	6400
Total cost	2636	3680	3684	10000
Sales--above	6250	8000	6140	20390
Margin	$3614	$4300	$2456	$10390
Percent	58%	54%	40%	51%
Change in percent	- 2%	+ 4%	- 3%	

The shift in cost differentials produces large differences in the sales margins percents:

```
        K    L
from   60 to 50 = -10%
to     58 to 54 = - 4%
     - 2   + 4   + 6%

        L    M
from   50 to 43 = - 7%
to     54 to 40 = -14%
     + 4 to -3   - 7%

        K    M
from   60 to 43 = -17%
to     58 to 40 = -18%
     - 2   - 3   - 1%
```

These examples illustrate the need to study overhead allocations to select the most useful methods. The accuracy provided by direct costs for material and labor should be closely supported by the relative accuracy of overhead allocation. The product cost standards are used for both inventory valuation and the cost of sales to arrive at the standard sales margin. The differentials among product cost standards are particularly significant in pricing and sales planning. Inaccuracies could contribute to promoting products whose profits are overstated and dropping other products that appear to be unpromising. Mispricing can cause sales shifts in product mix and volume with adverse affect on actual costs and profits. This topic is further developed in the next chapter.

15

Using the Standard
Cost System

The design of a cost system should be guided by three major considerations:

Profit measurement--book record of profit based on GAAP for both internal and external reporting, by period and by product; operating profit, net income, EPS, ROE. Basis for reports to stockholders and SEC, and audited by independent accountants.
Expense control--internal control of the efficiency of operations and the effectiveness of performance based on plans and budgets reflecting individual accountability.
Profitability analysis--internal analysis of business segments, both by individual responsibility and by economic entity, to guide evaluation of profitability, risk, and liquidity relative to goals, strategies, and policies.

The design and operation of the cost system, the accounting system, and the information system requires input from all participants, their acceptance and continuing cooperation, and visible management support at all times. Systems must meet the needs of all users and be relevant to the technological, physical, and competitive situation. Systems have several qualifiers: information for management, accounting requirements, and cost to operate. They are supported by procedures, forms, and methods. Systems are monitored by the overall internal control system including internal auditing.

The cost system specifies the costs charged to inventory and expensed as sold (product costs) and the expenses taken as incurred (period expenses). Product costs include all costs necessary for production material, labor, and overhead. The definition includes both the cost level (how much overhead is included in factory overhead) and product cost differentials. The remaining overhead is period expense--SGA. Production costs are planned to meet sales schedules at achievable levels of efficiency, hence unnecessary and avoidable costs are excluded from inventory and charged to expense as incurred. The planned costs are expressed as standards and deviations from standard are variances.

Direct Material--price and usage variances
Direct Labor--rate and time efficiency variances
Factory Overhead--volume variance based on planned practical
capacity; expense variance based on variable (flexible) budgets
subdivided into spending and efficiency components.

A standard cost system best serves the three major considerations set
forth above and provides the information needed at an economical cost.
It is readily adapted to individual situations and to changing needs. To
provide perspective for the underlying detail described in this chapter,
the basic transactions are illustrated with journal entries posted to
ledger accounts, with dates and amounts omitted.

ILLUSTRATION

Ledger accounts are illustrated without amounts or dates. The
entries are cross-referenced by number.

1. Material purchases:

        DR RM--Inventory
        DR PV--Price Variance
        CR A/P--Accounts Payable

Purchases credited to A/P monthly from purchase journal at actual.
Debit to RM at standard, with balance to PV (DR or CR).

2. Inventory requisitions:

        DR WIP--transfer to work-in process at standard
        DR UV--usage variance for extra usage (or CR)
        DR FOH-- overhead charges for indirect materials and supplies
        CR RM   (entry omitted for purchases charged directly to FOH)

3. Factory payroll:

        DR PRC--payroll clearing account
        CR APR--accrued payroll
        And:
        DR WIP production labor at standard
        DR DLV--direct labor variance
        DR FOH--direct labor downtime and indirect labor
        CR PRC--payroll clearing account

The payroll department calculates the earnings for total time worked
for each worker for each pay period. The total is credited to accrued
payroll and debits are totaled by department. SGA is charged directly.
Factory payrolls are charged to the payroll clearing account and
distributed by the cost department to direct and indirect labor accounts
based on time records. Production labor is charged to WIP at standard
based on piece counts. At month-end any unpaid earnings are a balance in
the accrued payroll account and the payroll clearing account is balanced
to zero.

4. Other overhead expenses:

    DR FOH
    CR (XX) not posted--other debits from prepaid and accrued
    expenses, depreciation accumulations, inventory adjustments,
    deferred charges

5. Applied Overhead:

    DR WIP   CR FOH
    Transfer overhead to inventory at the standard costing rate times
    the activity base.

6. Transfer good production to finished goods inventory:

    DR FG--finished goods   CR WIP
    Write-off scrap--DR FOH--CR WIP

7. Close out balance in FOH:

    DR FOH variance   CR FOH

8. Charge cost of goods sold--CSG--for shipments billed:

    DR CGS   CR FG
    This entry is matched with a credit to sales and a debit to
    receivables; the difference is the product standard gross margin.

    The variances are expensed but are not related to products; expense
control is by responsibility. Payroll clearing and factory overhead
accounts are closed to zero.

Accounts Payable--A/P		Raw Material--RM		Price Variance--PV	
CR	1 RM	DR	1 AP	DR/CR	1 PV
		CR	2 WIP		
			2 UV	Usage Variance - UV	
			2 FOH	DR/CR	2 UV
Accrued Payroll--APR		Work-in-Process--WIP		Direct Labor Variance--DLV	
CR	3 PRC	DR	2 RM	DR	3 PRC
			3 PRC	(rate and efficiency	
			5 FOH	variance by analysis)	
		CR	6 FG		
			6 FOH		

Payroll Clearing--PRC		Finished Goods--FG		Factory Overhead--FOH	
DR	3 APR	DR	6 WIP	DR	2 RM
CR	3 WIP	CR	8 CGS		3 PRC
	3 DLV				4 (XX)
	3 FOH				6 WIP
				CR	5 WIP
					7 FOHV

Cost of Goods Sold--CGS	Factory Overhead--FOH Variance
DR 8 FG	DR 7 FOH (volume, spending, efficiency variances by analysis)

Recap:

Balance Sheet:	Zero Balance:	Charges to Income:
Inventories at standard:		
RM	Payroll clearing	Cost of goods sold
WIP	Factory OH	Variance:
FG		Material--price & usage
Accounts Payable		Direct Labor--rate & efficiency
Accrued Payroll		Factory OH--volume & expense (operating and efficiency)

MATERIAL VARIANCE

All materials needed to make a product are specified in the product design. The quantity required for each material includes process loss. Material price standards are based on current and projected purchase prices including freight and discounts. Material is a major part of total product cost and standards must be kept up to date for the purposes of both expense control and product costing. Some materials are impractical to measure directly to products or the amounts are too small to warrant the expense. They are charged to a separate overhead account for indirect material and become part of the overhead rate applicable to all products. Reclassification between direct and indirect material should be reviewed periodically. With more material direct, product cost is higher and the indirect amount in overhead is smaller. Price and usage variance are usually restricted to direct materials. Indirect material may be charged to inventory and requisitioned, or charged directly to overhead. Some materials have multiple uses, both direct and indirect, such as supplies. All requisitions must be carefully coded by department and account, and quantities should be limited to current needs. Indirect material and supplies are compared with budgets and the differences include both price and usage variances. Effective control may depend on daily logs for selected items.

Price variances are entered in the purchase journal after receipt of the material and its inspection, and approval of the vendor invoice based on a purchase order. Raw material inventory is charged with the actual quantities at standard price and the invoice total is credited to payables. The difference is a debit or credit to purchase price variance, expensed as incurred. The practice of deferring variance until material is issued is counterproductive. Direct materials are frequently used by a number of products and purchase quantities are based on EOQ. Price variances are not identified to products because they are, by definition, avoidable. Standards must be kept current to maintain the validity of the measurements. When the price standard is changed, all inventory is revalued and the difference is credited (charged) to a separate account for inventory adjustment to standard, companion to the price variance account. The standard product cost sheets are also corrected and provide marketing with a revised amount for profit measurement.

A single purchase price standard is needed based on planned purchases and quotation from vendors, and also equalized for freight and discounts. Purchases are booked net of discount. A lost discount is charged to a separate nonoperating account. Freight charges may be prepaid or collect and may be part of the vendor price or separate. The possible combinations are illustrated with a $4.50 standard price net of discounts:

	DR Inventory	
Freight in price:		
Prepaid	$4.50	CR AP standard practice
Collect	4.50	CR AP vendor invoice
		DR AP CR Freight Clearing
		$.50 to pay freight and debit vendor.
Freight not in price:		
Prepaid	$4.50	CR AP $4.00 for material and $.50 for freight
Collect	4.50	CR AP $4.00
		CR Freight Clearing $.50.

The freight clearing account is used to handle timing differences between payable credits and payments. The balance may be debit or credit pending the matching of entries. In practice the account can become messy and require some arbitrary corrections to expense. An expense account for freight-in collects all freight charges for purchases not charged to inventory and other charges. A freight-out account is used for all shipments not charged to customers.

When material is obtained from several vendors a weighted average is found for charging inventory but price variance is measured for each supplier. For example:

Vendor	Planned Purchases	Net Price	Average
A	50	$12.00	$ 6.00
B	30	11.00	3.30
C	20	12.50	2.50
	100		$11.80

The weighted average of $11.80 is used for both inventory and product costs. For all purchases from A at $12.00 charged to inventory at $11.80, there is $.20 debit variance; from B at $11.00 there is $.80 credit variance; from C at $12.50 there is $.70 debit variance. Separate notation can be made in the purchase order log when orders are issued. For example for vendor A:

Purchase order	1000 units at $12.10 =	$12,100
Vendor standard	at $12.00	12,000
Vendor price variance debit	.10	100
Material standard	at $11.80	11,800
Variance from average debit	.20	200
Total variance	$ 30	$ 300

The accounting record accumulates all booked purchases for the period and total variance. Analysis is possible but not productive because it relates to past periods when the purchases were made. The purchase logs and records disclose all pertinent data as it becomes known.

Usage variance is the difference between the material specification and the actual quantity used, at standard price. The quantity required for a production lot is issued by requisition and charged to work-in-process inventory. If extra material is requisitioned because of loss over the standard the charge is to usage variance. If usage is less than standard, the excess is returned to raw material inventory and credited to work-in-process. The entries are recorded and reported periodically in the accounting records but actual control is exercised daily on the floor. Completed units are credited to work-in-process and charged to finished goods at standard. After material is released to the floor the measure of production earned prior to completion is accomplished by a countpoint. For the good pieces completed at the first countpoint the earned labor standard is debited to work-in-process and credited to payroll clearing, and factory overhead is applied. The debit for all material has already been entered but any shortage is charged to material usage. If a full lot is necessary, a new requisition must be issued for additional material and it is charged to usage variance. After the first countpoint work-in-process includes material, labor, and overhead, and spoiled pieces are written off for the cumulative amounts through the last countpoint. The charge is to scrap expense in overhead. Expense control rests on the daily records of scrap by product, operation, and cause, comparing actual with budget. The accounting total of all scrap for a period is not useful for control. Material usage variance and scrap may arise because of defects not determinable at the time material is received. A charge to vendors may be appropriate for the spoiled material, plus labor and overhead. The charges are collected on a work order and credited to scrap recovery.

LABOR VARIANCE

The payroll department computes individual earnings for each pay period and totals for each department. SGA is charged directly by department and account, including factory offices classified as period expense. Factory service departments are also charged in total and by account. These distributions are reviewed by the cost department for further detailing, such as for work orders. Some work orders are for capital expenditure projects in process. Other work orders may support chargebacks to vendors or expense transfers to other departments. These adjustments are made by separate journal entries. The labor earnings for each production department are totaled separately for direct labor and indirect labor. The totals are charged to a labor clearing account. Cost accounting makes the distribution to production labor, a separate cost element, and to overhead accounts for direct labor downtime and for indirect labor. The charges are based on daily time records for each worker. The payroll clearing account is brought to zero by matching the daily credits made by the cost department and the payroll debits made by pay period. Because earnings are paid after the close of the payroll period, accruals to the closing date are made separately for each pay period for the requisite number of days. Pay periods may be weekly, biweekly, semimonthly, or monthly. To illustrate with a 14-day payroll period with payment six days later for the month of Septemter:

ACCRUED PAYROLL LIABILITY

Date		DR	CR	Balance
8/14	New account			$ 0
8/28	14-day payroll		$74,000 (1)	
8/31	3-day accrual		18,000	$92,000
9/1	reverse accrual	$18,000 A		74,000
9/3	pay 8/28	74,000 (1)		0
9/11	14-day payroll		80,000 B(2)	80,000
9/17	pay 9/11	80,000 (2)		0
9/25	14-day payroll		84,000 C	84,000
9/30	5-day accrual		28,000 D	112,000

The September 25 payroll is payable October 1. The $28,000 accrual is reversed October 1. The payroll clearing account entries from the accrued payroll liability account are cross-referenced.

PAYROLL CLEARING ACCOUNT

Date		DR	CR	Balance
8/31				$ 0
9/1	3 days		$18,000 A	
9/11	14 days	$80,000 B		
9/25	14 days	84,000 C		
9/30	5 days	28,000 D		
	30 days	192,000	18,000	174,000

Total earnings for the thirty days of September are $174,000. The cost distribution is made daily but is illustrated in summary for the month in the next schedule. For each entry from the payroll department, the cost department must balance with its daily total distributions so that the account is cleared.

Credits to the payroll clearing account for $174,000 are charged to production labor and overhead as follows:

	CR	Production DR	Overhead DR
Total direct labor	$98,000		
Charge production labor		$83,000	
Charge downtime to overhead			$15,000
Total indirect labor	76,000		
Charge overhead			70,000
Charge work orders:			
Capitalized projects			3,000
Transfer to SGA			2,000
Vendor debit			1,000
			76,000
	174,000	83,000	91,000

The $83,000 production earnings are for the good pieces completed, as measured at countpoints, times the standard time for each product and operation, multiplied by the standard wage rate for the department. This rate may contain an amount for all fringe benefits, and that total is credited to total accrued fringe benefits; otherwise the fringe benefits are charged to overhead. Overtime premiums are charged to overhead. Worker rates are averaged because product cost is not a factor of individual workers. Incentive earnings are included in the pay rate. Because the hourly rate is minimum, productivity below minimum is charged to make-up pay, an overhead account, analyzed later in this section. Each product cost sheet specifies all production labor by department for each operation: standard time per piece, standard rate, total. Labor is totaled by department and overhead added.

An illustration is based on a department for one week of 35 hours and 20 direct laborers.

Plan
```
   Time:  20 men at 35 hours  =  700 hours
          downtime at 20%         140 hours
          production time         560 hours
          plus 15%                 84 hours
          Time efficiency 115% =  644 hours
   Rates: 10 men at $11.00     $110
           6 men at  10.50       63
           4 men at   9.25       37
          20 men               $210
          $210/20 = $10.50 average per hour
          and $10.50/60 = $.175 average per minute
```
Product Cost Sheet--productive labor for one department:
```
      Department:                Standard Minutes
          Operation 1                 150
                    2                   70
                    3                  220
                                       440 at .175 = $77.00
```

Actual Payroll Earnings
```
          Direct labor 720 hours at $10.65 = $7,668
```
Cost Department Record
```
          Downtime 170 hours at $10.65     = $1,810
          Production 550 hours at $10.65    = $5,858
```
Total standard time 605 hours. Incentive rate 605/550 = 110%. The charge to WIP is: 605 standard hours at $10.50 standard rate = $6,353
```
                                        Actual earnings =   5,858
                                             Variance = CR 495
```

Variance is analyzed for efficiency and rate::

	Actual	Standard	Analysis
Hours	550	605	55 at $10.50 = $578 CR
Rate	$10.65	$10.50	$.15 at 550 = 83 DR
	$5,858	6,353	
		5,858	
		495 CR	495 CR

The rate variance reflects a change in the weighted average for hours and rates. In some cases, higher-rate men are assigned to lower-rate work temporarily because of work schedules. Pay hikes also may be a factor prior to recognition in a new standard. Monthly rate variances are usually small and control is exercised daily on the floor. Unusual developments are reported as they occur.

If the earnings include all standard hours earned as an incentive plan the analysis is:

	Actual	Standard	Analysis	
Hours worked	550			
Incentive	55			
Paid	605	605	0	0
Rate	$10.65	$10.50	$.15	605 = 91 DR
	$6,444	$6,353		91 DR

Alternative: Rate $10.50 at 110% = $11.55 times 550 hours = $6,353.

The swing from $495 CR to $91 DR, or $586, is an incentive to achieve higher output. The company benefit is limited to higher output in the period with lower per unit fixed cost.

The time efficiency of 110% is below the planned rate of 115%. Standard hours earned (605) are below plan (644) by 39 hours. This discrepancy is solely a question of scheduling. Changes in schedules in response to changing demand are met by a combination of total hours, downtime, and efficiency.

Downtime and variance must be measured as complements:

	Hours	at $10.65
Worked	720	$7,668
Downtime plan 20%	144	$1,533
Actual downtime	170	$1,810
Excess	26	$ 277 DR

The efficiency gain of $578 is reduced by the extra downtime of $277 to a net of $301. The total downtime of $1,810 is charged to overhead as direct labor downtime. Time records may be manipulated to create the impression of higher time efficiency by charging more hours to downtime and less to production. For example, if time records are altered to shift 55 hours from production to downtime the efficiency rate is artificially inflated.

	Actual Hours		
	Reported	Correct	Standard Hours
Production	550	605	605
Downtime	170	115	144
	720	720	
Time efficiency	605	605	
divided by	550	605	
=	110%	= 100%	

Reported downtime: 170 - 144 = +26 at $10.65 = $277 DR**
Correct downtime: 115 - 144 = -29 at $10.65 = $309 CR*
Swing   55 $586

The idea is to "hide" hours in overhead and show higher time efficiency. The payroll analysis:

CORRECT	Actual	Standard			
Production:					
Hours	605	605	0		0
Rate	$10.65	$10.50	$.15	605 =	91 DR
as given above	6,444	6,353			91 DR
Downtime:					
Hours	115	144	29	10.65	309 CR
Rate	$10.65	$10.65	0	0	0
	1,224	1,533			309 CR*
Net Total	7,668	7,886			218 CR

REPORTED (no incentive)					
	Actual	Standard			
Production		(no change)			
Hours	550	605	55	10.50	578 CR
Rate	$10.65	$10.50	$.15	550	83 DR
as given above	5,858	6,353			495 CR
Downtime:					
Hours	170	144	26	$10.65	277 DR
Rate	$10.65	$10.65	0		0
	1,810	1,533			277 DR**
Net Total	7,668	7,886			218 CR

Recap of Variance:		Correct	Reported	Net
	Production	$ 91 DR	$ 495 CR	$586
	Downtime	309 CR	277 DR	586
		218 CR	218 CR	0

REPORTED (with incentive)					
Production	Actual	Standard			
		(no change)			
Hours	605	605	0		0
Rate	$10.65	$10.50	$.15	605	$ 91 DR
as given above	6,444	6,353			91 DR
Downtime	1,810	1,533			277 DR**
Net Total	8,254	7,886			368 DR

With no incentive pay the time switch does not affect total earnings of $7,668. With incentive pay, total earnings are inflated by $586 to $8,254 because the extra 55 hours in downtime are paid at $10.65. In totals, $1,810 less $1,224 = $586. Correct production pay and reported production pay with incentive are the same in both cases--$6,444. All elements of labor time require close control.

Piece counts are also basic to good records. Actual costs are recorded as incurred. The value of the work done is measured only by piece counts multiplied by product time standards for each operation, times the standard wage rate. Piece counts exclude rework until the piece passes inspection if corrected by the worker. Rework pieces are excluded if passed to a separate salvage crew. Scrap pieces are also excluded from the piece counts. Good pieces at standard amounts are debited to WIP and any excess time is variance. Hence, close measurement is necessary. Work done after a countpoint and before the next count-point is float; labor cost is incurred but standard cost is not booked. This difference is an element in variance that can distort efficiency measurement. Countpoints are located to achieve satisfactory measure-ments. A simple illustration is given for five days and three count-points, and with actual and standard hours equal:

Day	Actual	Countpoint	Float End of Day
1	50		50
2	50	#1 - 100	
	20		20
3	80	#2 - 100	0
4	60	0	60
5	40	#3 - 100	0
	300	300	

With only three countpoints the record of daily efficiency is erratic. With five countpoints the daily record could read:

Day	Actual	Countpoint	Cum Float	Daily Efficiency
1	50	49	1	98%
2	70	70	1	100%
3	80	76	5	95%
4	60	63	2	105%
5	40	42	0	105%
	300	300		100%

In practice, daily efficiency for a department would reflect many operations and time standards with several countpoints. If float is relatively constant, the efficiencies are little mistaken. For example:

	Actual	Standard	Rate	Float
Day 1	10,000	11,000	110%	500
Day 2	10,000	10,800	108%	700
Float correction		+ 200		-200
Day 2 corrected	10,000	11,000	110%	500

For day 2 the drop to 108% arises from the float increase of 200. The cost of more record keeping must be balanced with the gain from better information--the cost/benefit trade-off.

Another factor of labor performance is make-up pay--the worker's earnings in excess of standard hours earned. Only standard labor is charged to inventory and the excess pay is charged to overhead. Control is exercised daily on the floor along with all the other labor factors. For example, the hours for one worker for five days:

Day	Actual	Standard	Make Up	Incentive
1	8	6	2	
2	8	7	1	
3	8	8		
4	8	10		2
5	8	11		3
Week Total	40	42	3	5

On a daily basis the worker is paid for 45 hours--42 standard plus 3 make-up, or 40 actual plus 5 incentive. On a weekly basis, the pay total is based on the standard 42 hours; the 3 make-up hours are absorbed by the 5 incentive hours. Failure to make standard is subject to close control regardless of the pay plan. Workers may shift reports to show below standard hours one day and over the next.

Another example is for five men for one day:

Man	Actual	Standard	Make-Up	Incentive	Pay	Efficiency
1	8	6	2		8	75%
2	8	7	1		8	87%
3	8	8			8	100%
4	8	10		2	10	125%
5	8	11		3	11	137%
Day Total	40	42	3	5	45	112%

The time efficiency for the day is 105% (42/40). Standing alone 105% could be the result of multiple combinations by man. Paid hours are 45, or 112.5% of 40 hours worked because each man is paid individually. With a team pay plan the 105% rate applies to all.

When production is automated all labor is part of overhead and there is no direct labor. Operations are planned for downtime, running time, output rate, and crew size. The crew's job is to keep the operation up and running. An example for one month is based on a fixed budget. Direct material is excluded:

```
Plan:       Six-man crew at $1,500    =          $ 9,000
            Other expenses                         29,400   $38,400
            Cost per day for 20 days                        $ 1,920
            Time:  Total              8 hours
                   Down at 25%        2 hours
                   Run               6 hours at 100 units = 600 units
            Standard:  $1920/600 = $3.20 per unit
Performance for one day:
            Run                       5 hours at 108 units = 540   108%
            Down                      3 hours
            Total                     8 hours
            Actual expenses                        $ 1,860
Debit to inventory:
            540 units at $3.20        =             1,728
            Variance                               $   132  DR
Analysis:
            Efficiency gain:
              Run 540 units - 500 = 40 at $3.20             $128 CR
              There is no rate variance--all labor is part of
            overhead.
            Downtime loss:
              Actual     3
              Plan     - 2 = 1 hour = 100 units at $3.20    $320 DR
            Productivity net                                 192 DR
            Expense:
            Budget                                          $1920
            Actual                                           1860
            Expense variance                                  60 CR
            Total variance                                   132 DR
```

The gain from 108% time efficiency, $128, is lost with excess downtime of $320--a net debit of $192. Total variance booked for accounting provides only a net financial outcome. Effective control requires constant tracking of output efficiencies and downtime by cause throughout the shift. A monthly report of expense variance is usually sufficient. Direct material usage should also be logged as it occurs.

THE LEARNING CURVE

Increased labor productivity gained from the efficiency of repetitive operations lowers unit costs progressively--the learning curve (LC), also known as the experience curve when referring to all related costs. The LC is applicable in several circumstances: production measurement, product costing, capital expenditure analysis, and vendor price negotiations. If the LC affects the production process but is not incorporated into the labor standards, misleading credit variances arise, or debit variances are less. If standards include the LC effect beyond what is attainable, misleading debit variances arise. Careful application of the LC is required but many other factors affect productivity and the LC effect is not constant. The LC is analyzed in chapters 4 and 11. This section analyzes measurement of labor time efficiency and the accounting entries.

The LC time for any quantity and any LC rate can be taken from tables or calculated.

Quantity	Unit 80% LC Average	Total Time	Time & Qty Increments
1	10,000	10,000	
2 double	8,000	16,000	6,000/1 = 6,000
3	7,021	21,063	5,063
4 double	6,400	25,600	4,537
			9,600/2 = 4,800
5	5,956	29,780	4,180
6	5,617	33,702	3,922
7	5,345	37,415	3,713
8 double	5,120	40,960	3,545
			15,360/4 = 3,840
9	4,930	44,370	3,410
10	4,765	47,650	3,280
11	4,621	50,831	3,181
12	4,493	53,916	3,085
13	4,379	56,927	3,011
14	4,276	59,864	2,937
15	4,182	62,730	2,866
16 double	4,096	65,536	2,806
			24,576/8 = 3,072

An example for 80% LC illustrates the comparison of actual production time in minutes with total standard time for 8 units set at 40,960:

Quantity	Actual Time	80% LC Standard Time Increments	Rates
1	9,901	10,000	101%
2	5,825	6,000	103%
3	5,166	5,063	98%
4	4,280	4,537	106%
5	3,870	4,180	108%
6	3,735	3,922	105%
7	3,345	3,713	111%
8	3,223	3,545	110%
	39,345	40,960	104%

The rates range from 98% to 111% with an average of 104% through 8 units. There is no practical way to cost out the effect of elements other than the LC on productivity. Hence, time efficiencies are necessarily approximation, particularly for the short run.

The effect of several LCs is compared:

Quantity	Unit LC 90%	Increment	Unit LC 80%	Increment	Unit LC 70%	Increment
1	10,000	10,000	10,000	10,000	10,000	10,000
2	9,000	8,000	8,000	6,000	7,000	4,000
4	8,100	7,200	6,400	4,800	4,800	2,800
8	7,290	6,480	5,120	3,840	3,430	1,960
16	6,561	5,832	4,096	3,072	2,401	1,372
Percent Range at 16	160%		100%		59%	
Actual Time 16	4,096		4,096		4,096	
Variance Time	-2,465 CR		0		+1,695 DR	

This table shows the need for careful selection of a realistic LC and revisions as needed to provide useful time measurements.

Also important for continuing operations is the determination of the correct location of output on the LC. As more experience is gained the rate of time decrease is constant but the amount of time is progressively less. For example, if 64 units are to be made:

Quantity	Unit 80% LC	Increment	Make 64 Units	
1	10,000.00			
16	4,096.00	3,072		
32	3,276.80	2,458		
64	2,621.44	1,966	1966	125%
128	2,097.15	1,573	1573	100%
256	1,677.72	1,258	1258	80%
512	1,342.18	1,007		
1024	1,073.74	805		

For 64 units to be made the choice depends on the experience point reached to date. If Q128 is applicable, choice of Q64 is too high by 25% and choice of Q256 is too low by 20%.

The labor standard used for time measurement is also the basis for product cost charges to inventory based on the LC appplied to the quantity made. Shipments are credited to inventory and charged to cost of sales at the average for all units. Thus, there is necessarily a debit balance. The account reaches zero only when all units are produced and shipped. If the LC used is a poor choice, labor variances will show the difference. However, large variances indicate over- or undercosting of the product, distorting inventory balances and product margins.

An example is given to illustrate the entries to an inventory account using 80% LC for 16 units at 4,096 for all shipments expressed in time only for clarity:

	Production		Shipments at 4,096		Balances	
Period	Units	80% LC	Units	Total	Units	Time
1	2	16,000	0	0	2	16,000
2	2	9,600	1	4,096		
Cum	4	25,600	1	4,096	3	21,504
3	0	0	2	8,192		
Cum	4	25,600	3	12,288	1	13,312
4	6	22,050	2	8,192		
Cum	10	47,650	5	20,480	5	27,170
5	0	0	5	20,480		
Cum	10	47,650	10	40,960	0	6,690
6	6	17,886	5	20,480		
Cum	16	65,536	15	61,440	1	4,096

All shipments are credited at 4,096. The debits are at the 80% LC average time. The first 2 units are carried in inventory at 16,000 (10,000 + 6,000), an 8,000 average. Unit 16 is produced at 4,096 and remains in inventory at 4,096. At the first cum 4 the inventory balance is 21,504 for 3 units and at the second cum 4, one item in inventory has a balance of 13,312. At cum 10, the balance of 5 units at 27,170 averages 5,434 and at cum 10 with a quantity balance of zero the time balance is 6,690. Necessarily all debits and credits must be based on the same LC. If production is cancelled at cum 10 with the balance of 5 units at 27,170 there is a write-off of 6,690 (27,170 - 20,480). At cum 10, with no inventory balance, the time balance of 6,690 must be written off. Inventory balances based on a LC require careful evaluation to provide acceptable valuations for the balance sheet and charges to income. If production continues for four more units the example can be extended to a zero unit balance:

Production:			Shipments:		
	Cum 16	65,536		Cum 15	61,440
	17	4,017		5	20,480
	18	3,944			
	19	3,875			
	20	3,812			
		81,184		20	81,920
				Balance	736 CR

The 736 credit balance is the difference of debits for the added 4 units at 15,648 less 16,384 credit for 4 units shipped at 4,096. The charge to cost is too high by 4.5 percent (736/16,384).

The time factors can be expressed in dollars as follows:

Hourly wage rate	$12	
Plus fringe at 25%	3	$15
Overhead at 300%		45
Cost per hour		$60
Cost per minute		$ 1

This schedule permits reading all time factors in the example as minutes and dollars.

Factors that disrupt the learning curve must be recognized and corrections made. If the LC is set too low, the standard labor cost is too low and both profit margins and labor variance will be high. Marketing is encouraged to sell with an inflated standard profit margin. With a high LC the product profit margins are understated and sales are discouraged or the product is dropped. These effects are obscured by accounting. Analysis must weigh all relevant factors to evaluate results.

FACTORY OVERHEAD

All production costs other than direct material and direct labor are factory overhead. All charges are coded by department and account to establish accountability based on the organization structure and degree of delegation, referred to as responsibility accounting. All transactions are the responsibiltiy of someone. Delegation determines the degree of control, and expenses reported in a department are controllable by that department. The term underlined uncontrollable expenses is best avoided; all expenses are controllable by someone. Budgets and reports must be consonant to assure correct measurement. Expense accounts are also defined to clarify expense control.

The charges to overhead arise from several sources: withdrawals from inventory, accounts payable, accrued and prepaid expenses, and depreciation allowances. The charge to work-in-process inventory for overhead is an amount based on the planned overhead rate times the the activity base. The actual expense total less the credit for applied overhead is overhead variance, debit or credit.

Flexible Budgets

Overhead variance contains several important factors that are determinable only by analysis:

Volume--the amount of budgeted fixed expense not absorbed because
    actual volume was less than planned volume. Relates to plant
    capacity, sales volume, and productivity.
Expense--the difference between actual and budgeted expense, by
    department and account.
Efficiency--variable expense attributable to difference between
    actual and standard production labor. Relates to labor performance.
Spending--actual expense less budget based on actual production
    labor. Relates to control of expenses.

Department budgets are prepared by account and relative to the performance responsibility for a given range of activities, known as the relevant range. The budget period of one year is also an important parameter. Both the level of expense and degree of variability relate to periods and output ranges. Expenses are estimated for each department and account and the amount of change in expenses relative to volume is estimated. These calculations are made by the manufacturing personnel directly involved, assisted by engineers and accountants. The perspective is based on planned operations and achievable efficiency-- neither a tight nor loose budget. Reference to past performance is of limited value. The budget is expressed as flexible, or variable, to the extent that expenses are found to vary with volume. With little or no variation, it is a fixed budget.

Effective expense control can only be exercised on the floor as events occur, with the help of labor logs, manning tables, and records of scrap and material usage. Monthly reports provide a needed financial summary but the comparison of actual with budget requires a close understanding of the budgetary process. The following points should be noted.

The actual expenses incurred may not be closely measured by the accounting system: purchases for use over several months charged directly to expense; inventory requisitions that provide supplies for several months; inadequate use of prepaid and accrued expenses; late time recording due to procedural delays; expense timing of tools and fixed assets; loose distinction between direct material, direct labor, and overhead; handling of work orders relative to expense timing and accountability; errors in recording. Differences arising from such sources can be traced back to bookkeeping procedures and undermine confidence in the system. With unsupportable facts or inappropriate recording, accountability evaporates; opinion and fiction hold sway.

Monthly budgets are often expressed as one-twelfth of a year but actual expenses may vary because of seasonality or random events. The degree of expense variability is arbitrary at best and the flexible budget may not relate closely to the facts. The actual expenses on the floor each day may be guided by considerations of expediency or urgency not reflected in the budget. There is also the knotty question of exercising foresight in changing expense levels currently relative to uncertain expectations, particularly for labor.

Changed conditions may lead to policy decisions affecting expense levels for such activities as capital expenditures, maintenance, training, systems, audit, research, fringe benefits, or other discretionary areas.

Variances must be considered as a general guide to performance measurement that can be interpreted only by detailed knowledge of all the circumstances. Effective daily control and communication should preclude any surprises in the accounting results. Monthly variances are primarily financial measures, historical and statistical summations of a multitude of details.

As a practical matter expense variability is measured relative to a single activity base but in fact many factors are involved. Recognition of several factors by correlation analysis can produce a greater degree of accuracy on paper but may be of limited practical usefulness. The patterns of expense are highly diverse. Some accounts are fully fixed or fully variable. The balance varies with time and volume, and other factors, in a variety of patterns. The expression of a flexible budget as a formula--fixed expense plus variable based on a single volume factor --is arbitrary.

The overhead costing rate is based on a selected basis of capacity. Practical capacity is the output that can be achieved based on planned facilities, technology, efficiency, seasonality, product mix, run sizes, learning curve, and without extraneous interruptions. Practical capacity often hinges on bottleneck operations that may differ with changed conditions and are hard to predict accurately.

Analysis of a budget for flexibility is illustrated with the individual expense accounts grouped into three categories with the account detail omitted:

	Volume--Direct Labor Hours (DLH)			
	900	1000	1200	1500
Fully variable	$450	$500	$600	$750
Variable rate	.50	.50	.50	.50
Fully fixed	1800	1800	1800	1800
Fixed rate	2.00	1.80	1.50	1.20
Mixed	2070	2200	2400	2520
Mixed rate	2.30	2.20	2.00	1.68
Total expense	4320	4500	4800	5070
Total rate	4.80	4.50	4.00	3.38

This table shows the results of a budget process using specific volume levels based on direct labor hours, with fully variable expenses at a constant rate $.50, and fully fixed expenses at a constant total of $1,800. The expenses are individually budgeted as the allowable amount at that volume. The degree of change for the accounts in mixed expenses varies but is condensed into the total and the overhead rate declines more slowly than the rate of volume increase.

The budget schedule is restated to derive the relationships of total variable and fixed expenses:

DLH	Total Expense	Increments Hours	Amount	Total Variable Rate
900	$4,320			
1000	4,500	100	$180	$1.80
1200	4,800	200	300	1.50
1500	5,070	300	270	.90
		600	$750	

Using the DLH 1200 line with the $1.50 variable rate:

DLH	Variable at $1.50 a	Total Expense	Balance Fixed	Fully Fixed	Mixed Fixed
900	$1,350	$4,320	2,970	$1,800	$1,170
1000	1,500	4,500	3,000	1,800	1,200
1200	1,800 b	4,800 c	3,000 d	1,800 e	1,200f
1500	2,250	5,070	2,820	1,800	1,020

The budget formula at DLH 1200 is: Fixed $3,000 plus $1.50 variable for the department total, or:

	1200 DLH Budget	Rates Variable	Rates Fixed	Variable Expense	Fixed Expense
Fully variable	$ 600	$.50		$ 600	
Fully fixed	1,800		$1.50		$1800 e
Mixed	2,400	1.00	1.00	1200	1200 f
	4,800 c	1.50 a	2.50	$1800 b	3000 d

The product costing rate depends on the determination of practical capacity. The full rate range for the budget is from $3.38 to $4.80 per DLH. At 1200 DLH the costing rate is:

Plan Expenses:	Amount	1200 DLH Rate:
Variable	$1800b	$1.50a
Fixed	3000d	2.50
	$4800a	$4.00

The $4.00 rate is used to debit WIP inventory and credit applied overhead expense, and it is also the product cost standard.

Variance Analysis

Actual overhead for a period is $5,000, actual DLH are 1,240. Standard DLH are 1,100. The applied overhead is 1,100 hours at the $4 costing rate, or $4,400 charged to WIP with a variance of $600.

Recap: Debit to overhead control--actual expenses $5,000
        (actual DLH 1240)
        Credit to overhead control--1100 at $4   4,400
        (standard DLH 1100)
        Variance debit--book balance   600

The variance is analyzed as follows:

```
Expense:
    Actual (1240 DLH)                                    $5,000
    Budget--Variable 1100 at $1.50      $1,650
            Fixed                        3,000            4,650
    Total expense debit                                          350 DR
    Efficiency:  Actual DLH              1,240
                 Standard DLH            1,100
                 Variable only at $1.50    140             210 DR
    Spending:    Budget--
                 Variable 1240 at $1.50                   1,860
                 Fixed                                    3,000
                 Allowed                                  4,860
                 Total actual                             5,000
                                                           140 DR
                                                           350 DR
```

Volume:
    Plan   1200
    Standard   1100
                    ‾‾‾‾‾
                    100 DR at $2.50   250 DR
                                                                       ‾‾‾‾‾‾
                                                                       600 DR

    The $350 expense variance includes $210 for variable expense due to excess labor and $140 for overspending. Failure to use 100 hours of productive capacity has a cost of $250 fixed expense. The actual 1,240 hours are 140 hours over standard and are not recognized for volume analysis. By definition these variance hours are avoidable and are considered not irrelevant to future planning.

    The costing rate depends on the capacity chosen:

Volume--Direct Labor Hours

	900	1000	1200	1500
Variable at $1.50	$1350	1500	1800	2250
Fixed	3000	3000	3000	3000
Total	4350	4500	4800	5250
Costing rate	4.83	4.50	4.00	3.50
Fixed rate	3.33	3.00	2.50	2.00

Volume variance is recalculated for each level of DLH.

	900	1000	1200	1500
Plan	900	1000	1200	1500
Standard	1100	1100	1100	1100
Variance hours	200 CR	100 CR	100 DR	400 DR
Fixed costing rate	$3.33	$3.00	$2.50	$2.00
Variance	666 CR	300 CR	250 DR	800 DR

    The selection of a practical capacity is essential for product costing, used for both inventory valuation and product profit margin measurement. It also designates the capacity in place ready for use. The cost of using otherwise idle capacity is the basis for analyzing short-term decisions. Excess capacity arises in planning production to meet sales plans. It is recognized in capital expenditure planning and for estimating lead times for sales growth. Expected volume variance can be included in the financial plan for comparison with the actual amount realized. Causes for differences can be investigated for major deviation but the analysis is often complex and individual responsibilities are not evident. The most practical approach may be to subtract the total expense variance calculated from the budgets from total book variance to determine volume variance. Plantwide analysis is often sufficient.

Another example of variance analysis:

		Plan 1,200 DLH	
	Variable	$1,080	$ .90
	Fixed	2,520	2.10
		3,600	3.00
Actual (1,150 DLH)		$3,750	
Applied 1,250 at DLH at $3		3,750	
Variance total			0
Expense:			
Variable--1,250 at .90	$1,125		
Fixed	2,520	$3,645	
Actual		3,750	105 DR
Efficiency:			
Actual DLH	1,150		
Std DLH	1,250		
	100 CR at .90	90 CR	
Spending:			
Budget--V 1,150 at .90	1,035		
Fixed	2,520		
	3,555		
Actual	3,750	195 DR	
		105 DR	
Volume:			
Plan	1,200		
Standard	1,250		
	50 CR at 2.10	105 CR	

The total variance is zero. Expense variance of $105 is offset by the $105 volume credit. Labor efficiency creates a $90 credit and spending variance is $195. Analysis based on variable expense budgets is necessary to derive the significant findings--expenses over budget $195 and volume over plan $105. Such results should be in line with expectations based on effective operational controls and good communication of significant developments.

Seasonal Volume Variance

All variances are expensed as incurred but volume variance may be adjusted for seasonality. The practice of budgeting total fixed expense for a year and assigning one-twelfth to each month is valid only when monthly operations are planned for the same level. For example, for $24,000 annual fixed expense and 6,000 DLH the annual rate is $4. A seasonal production pattern would distort the results:

Quarter	Fixed Budget		Planned DLH	At $4 Rate	Volume Variance
I	$6000	1/12	500	$2000	$4000 DR
II	6000	4/12	2000	8000	2000 CR
III	6000	5/12	2500	10000	4000 CR
IV	6000	2/12	1000	4000	2000 DR
	24000		6000	24000	0

Volume variance would seriously distort quarterly profits. Volume variance alternatively can be taken to a clearing account on the balance sheet and included with inventory. The clearing account would read:

Quarter	Entry	Cum
I	4,000 DR	4,000 DR
II	2,900 CR	2,000 DR
III	4,000 CR	2,000 CR
IV	2,000 DR	0

The QI balance of $4,000 is the cost of facilities to be used later in the year. At the end of QIII there is a credit balance, reduced to zero at year-end. This schedule simply reconciles the output plans for seasonal factors and arbitrary expense allocations. The same result could be obtained by allocation of fixed expenses on the seasonal pattern. Seasonality is a major factor in many industries. The seasonality adjustment is essential for matching revenue and expense. For example, assuming gross profit of 40% in seasonal sales and excluding expense variances, without seasonal volume adjustment:

Quarter	Sales	40% Profit	Vol. Var.	Profit	%
I	10	$ 4	$ 4 DR	$ 0	0
II	40	16	2 CR	18	45
III	50	20	4 CR	24	48
IV	20	8	2 DR	6	30
	120	48	0	48	40

With seasonal volume adjustment, profit is 40% on sales for all quarters. With volume variance expensed evenly each quarter, the profit percent ranges from zero to 48%.

For another example, a plant in the north might be closed down for the first quarter, so no fixed expenses apply to production. If output in Q2 is for half a year, the charge is for six months. The clearing account balance is part of inventory valuation, and it may need correction during the year for changed conditions.

The actual DLH each quarter and for the year will vary from plan in differing degrees. The bookkeeping is illustrated:

Q	Plan DLH	Actual DLH	Over (Under)	At $4 To Income	Cum
I	500	400	(100)	$ 400 CR	$ 400 CR
II	2000	2200	200	800 DR	400 DR
III	2500	2800	300	1200 DR	1600 DR
IV	1000	800	(200)	800 CR	800 DR
	6000	6200	200	$ 800 DR	

The balance sheet clearing account always clears. The deviations are taken to income, signaling a departure from plan. The validity of the plan should be reviewed quarterly and recast if necessary to avoid a large adjustment at year-end. Any expense variances are taken as incurred as part of total expense variance. Volume variance is limited to planned and budgeted fixed expenses. The seasonal adjustment provides a better matching of revenue and expense.

Costing Rates

The definition of departments for expense responsibility also provides a basis for departmental costing rates. Flexible expense budgets are a guide to expense control. The assumption of a volume factor translates total fixed expense into a rate, added to the variable rate for a total rate. This is the costing rate used to determine overhead in standard product costs. Overhead costing, equally important to direct material and labor costing, deserves close attention because of the significance of standard product costs in pricing and profitability analysis. The department rates based on responsibility accounting may need refinement for product costing by subdivision into departmental cost centers. A separate cost center may be needed for even a single machine. These distinctions arise when an expense in a department is controllable in total by budget but unevenly related to products in the department rate. Examples include indirect materials, setup, scrap, inspection, and fixed charges.

For example, a plant is analyzed for three departments with rates based on DLH.

		Departments		
	Plant	1	2	3
Indirect materials	$ 1,500	$ 700	$ 800	$ 0
Setup	2,500	1,500	400	600
Scrap	2,000	800	1,200	0
Inspection	1,500	0	600	900
All other	7,500	3,000	3,000	1,500
Total expense	$15,000	$6,000	$6,000	$3,000
DLH	1,000	300	400	300
Rate per hour	$ 15.00	$20.00	$15.00	$10.00

The use of the departmental rates could materially affect product costs. The differentials among product costs are critical to valid analysis: the general cost level for all products is relatively unimportant. Use of the departments for expense control also is desirable but the plant budget may be sufficient. In rare cases the application of the department rates may have little effect on product costs; this can occur if all products have about the same time in each department. Also, if the department rate differences are small the plant rate may be acceptable. The subject of expense control and product costing calls for close analysis. More accurate product costing can contribute significantly to profit improvement.

An example is based on three departments with DLH rates of $20, $15, and $10, and a plant rate of $15, as above. Products A, B, and C are processed, as follows, in DLH:

Product	Total	Dept. 1	Dept. 2	Dept. 3
A	200	180	0	20
B	300	120	180	0
C	500	0	220	280
Total Hours	1000	300	400	300

Applying rates to DLH, overhead dollars are:

Plant	at $15	at $20	at $15	at $10	Department Cross Total	Over (Under)
A	$ 3000	$3600	$ 0	$ 200	$3800	$ 800
B	4500	2400	2700	0	5100	600
C	7500	0	3300	2800	6100	(1400)
	15000	6000	6000	3000	15000	0

The example is continued by adding direct labor at $10 per hour and amounts for direct material, then analyzing the product price-cost relationships:

Department Rates	A	B	C	Total
Overhead--above	$ 3800	$ 5100	$ 6100	$15000
DL at $10	2000	3000	5000	10000
Add material	3200	3900	3900	11000
Product cost	9000	12000	15000	36000
Sales	12300	17100	24600	54000
GM	3300	5100	9600	18000
Percent to sales	26.8%	29.8%	39.0%	33.3%
Plant Rates				
Overhead--above	$ 3000	$ 4500	$ 7500	$15000
DL at $10	2000	3000	5000	10000
Add material	3200	3900	3900	11000
Product cost	8200	11400	16400	36000
Sales	12300	17100	24600	54000
GM	4100	5700	8200	18000
Percent to sales	33.3%	33.3%	33.3%	33.3%

These are substantial differences. If target pricing is based on cost plus 50% on product costs with department rates:

	Cost	+50%	New Price	Old Price	Old Price Low (High)	% to Old Price
A	$ 9,000	$ 4,500	$13,500	$12,300	$1,200	9.8%
B	12,000	6,000	18,000	17,100	900	5.3%
C	15,000	7,500	22,500	24,600	(2,100)	(8.5%)
	36,000	18,000	54,000	54,000	0	

The effect of price on sales, costs, and profit depends on sales elasticity and other factors entering into pricing policy.

For products A and B current prices are low compared with target prices; A would have to increase 9.8% and B 5.3%. This would lower sales volume to some extent. Product C's price would be less by 8.5%, and sales volume should increase. The changes in sales dollars depend on the degree of demand elasticity. Changes in volume also affect costs relative to variable and fixed cost components. In turn, any changes in assets would be a factor in calculating incremental ROAs. There is a strong tendency for underpriced products (A, B) to attract higher sales while C would have lower sales. Target pricing would shift both total volume and the relative volume among the products and departments.

The effect on product profit differences is magnified if selling expenses are included at 20% of sales:

Department Rates:	A	B	C	Total
Sales	$12,300	$17,100	$24,600	$54,000
Cost	9,000	12,000	15,000	36,000
GM	3,300	5,100	9,600	18,000
Expenses at 20%	2,460	3,420	4,920	10,800
Sales margin	$ 840	$ 1,680	$ 4,680	$ 7,200
Percent to sales	6.8%	9.8%	19.0%	13.3%

For example, comparing C to B: 19.0% - 9.8% = 9.2 or 9.2/9.8 = 94%
and at the GM rates: 39.0% = 29.8% = 9.2 or 9.2/29.8 = 31%

With the plant rate all products have a 33.3% GM or 13.3% after 20% for selling expenses.

Product pricing policy is necessarily pragmatic but careful and continual analysis of price-cost-asset relationships can yield rich results.

Separate attention should be given to factory overhead applicable to material. This is particularly essential when purchased goods are resold without processing. This situation is analyzed in chapter 6.

VARIABLE COSTING

Standard costs include all factory overhead to accord with GAAP as required by the SEC and IRS. An alternate method is to exclude fixed overhead from product costs in order to measure margins based on variable costs only: direct material, direct labor, and variable overhead. This method is called variable costing, as contrasted with full costing, to provide information for short-term decisions, similar to marginal and incremental analysis. This system has mistakenly acquired the designation "direct costing," which it is not. Variable costing can be recognized on the books concurrent with the required full costing if considered useful. However, the elimination of fixed costs also eliminates their relationship to product costs. Product costing without fixed costs can distort pricing and profit measurements and have serious long-term consequences. It is better to use full costs in the records and reports and to prepare separate analyses for variable costing as needed.

Variable costing is illustrated with two service and three production departments. Variable and fixed costs are given and allocations are made without the supporting details.

Overhead	Service		Production			Total
	A	B	1	2	3	
Direct:						
Variable	$100	$200	$300[1]	$400	$500	$1500
Fixed	400	500	500[2]	400	300	2100
	500	700	800[3]	800	800	3600

Allocation:

Variable	-100	-200	+120[1]	+ 90	+ 90	0
Fixed	-400	-500	+200[2]	+600	+100	0
	-500	-700	+320[3]	+690	+190	0
Total	0	0	1120	1490	990	3600

Recap:

	1	2	3	Total
Variable--direct and indirect	$420[1]	$ 490	$590	$1500
Fixed--direct and indirect	700[2]	1000	400	2100
Total	1120[3]	1490	990	3600

Overhead Rates:

				Memo
DLH	200	500	100	800
Variable rate	$2.10[1]	$ .98	$5.90	(1.88)
Fixed rate	3.50[2]	2.00	4.00	(2.62)
Full rate	5.60[3]	2.98	9.90	(4.50)

Note that the variable rate includes both direct and indirect overhead, as does the fixed rate. There are large differences within the departmental rates for both variable and fixed. The direct overhead for department 1 is $800 (300 + 500) and allocated (indirect) costs are $320 (120 + 200), for a total of $1,120. With 200 DLH the rates are $4.00 direct, $1.60 indirect and $5.60 total but these rates are not relevant in variable costing. Only the department variable rates are used for product costing: $2.10 - $.98 - $5.90. The total fixed overhead of $2,100 is expensed as incurred without product identity. The omission of fixed overhead, both direct and indirect, from product costs necessarily causes both lower cost levels and distortions in product cost differentials. Variable costs are considered to be the equivalent of cash outlays and a higher price is said to contribute to profit by recovery of fixed overhead.

The effect of using variable costs is illustrated with four examples, all based on the following data:

Selling price		$9	
Costs:			
Variable--material & labor			
& overhead		3	$6 Variable cost margin
Fixed:			
Total	$400		
Units	100	4	4 Fixed cost
Full cost		7	2 Full cost margin

Volume variance is based on 100 units. The full cost margin is $2 (9-7). The variable cost margin is $6 (9-3).

Example 1   Start-up and shutdown operations
    A   Start-up--no sales:

	Units	Full	Variable
Sales	0	$ 0	$ 0
Produce	100	700	300
Inventory	100	700	300
Cost	0	0	0
GM		0	0
Volume variance (100 - 100)		0	
Fixed OH			400
Profit (Loss) A		0	(400)

B	Shutdown--no production		
	Units	Full	Variable
Sales	100	$900	$900
Produce	0	0	0
Cost	100	700	300
GM	100	200	600
Volume variance (100 - 100)		0	
Fixed OH			0
Profit B		200	600
Combined A̅ & B		200	200

Example 2 Constant Sales--Varying Production:

Units	Year 1	Year 2	Year 3	Total
Sales	100	100	100	300
Production	100	70	120	290
Open balance	60	60	30	60
End balance	60	30	50	50
Change	0	-30	+ 20	- 10
Full Cost				
Sales	$900	$900	$900	$2700
Cost	700	700	700	2100
GM	200	200	200	600
Volume variance:				
100-100 = 0	0			0
100- 70 = 30 DR		(120)		(120)
100-120 = 20 CR			80	80
Profit	200	80	280	560
Variable Cost				
Sales	$900	$900	$900	$2700
Cost	300	300	300	900
GM	600	600	600	1800
Fixed OH	400	400	400	1200
Profit	200	200	200	600
Profit change	0	+120	- 80	+ 40

The profit change and volume variance are equal. The profit change is also the change in inventory.

Unit Change	0	-30	+20	- 10
at $4	0	+ $120	- $80	+ 40

Example 3 Varying Sales--Constant Production:

Units	Year 1	Year 2	Year 3	Total
Sales	100	130	80	310
Production	100	100	100	300
Open balance	60	60	30	60
End balance	60	30	50	50
Change	0	-30	+20	-10
Full Cost				
Sales	$900	$1170	$720	$2790
Cost	700	910	560	2170
GM	200	260	160	620
Volume variance (100-100)	0	0	0	0
Profit	200	260	160	620

Variable Cost

Sales	$900	$1170	$720	$2790
Cost	300	390	240	930
GM	600	780	480	1860
Fixed OH	400	400	400	1200
Profit	200	380	80	660
Profit change	0	+120	- 80	+ 40

Change in inventory:

Unit change	0	- 30	+ 20	- 10
at $4	0	+ $120	- $80	+ 40

Example 4 Varying Sales--Varying Production:

Units	Year 1	Year 2	Year 3	Total
Sales	100	130	80	310
Production	100	70	120	290
Open balance	60	60	0	60
End balance	60	0	40	40
Change	0	- 60	+ 40	- 20

Full Cost

Sales	$900	$1170	$720	$2790
Cost	700	910	560	2170
GM	200	260	160	620

Volume variance:

100-100 = 0	0			0
100- 70 = 30 DR		(120)		(120)
100-120 = 20 CR			80	80
Profit	200	140	240	580

Variable Cost

Sales	$900	$1170	$720	$2790
Cost	300	390	240	930
GM	600	780	480	1860
Fixed OH	400	400	400	1200
Profit	200	380	80	660
Profit change	0	+240	-160	+ 80

Change in inventory:

Unit change	0	- 60	+ 40	- 20
at $4	0	+240	-160	+ 80

Recap: Balance Sheet Inventory Balances by Year

Ending	Year 1	Year 2	Year 3	Total
Units	60	0	40	40
Full	$420	0	$280	$280
Variable	180	0	120	120
Difference	240	0	160	160

Opening				
Units	60	60	0	60
Full	$420	$420	0	$420
Variable	180	180	0	180
Difference	240	240	0	240

Change	0	+240	-160	+ 80

In practice, variable costing analysis off the books may be useful for studying the contribution of individual products within a product line when fixed cost allocation below the product line would be arbitrary and misleading.

16

Production Methods

The physical production process can be described in three categories that relate to product costing:

Job Order--A separate production order is issued for each batch or run for a specified quantity, either a custom design or for stock. A job order may be for a part to be processed further on another job order or for finished stock. Orders are kept separate on the production floor.

Continuous Process--The flow of output is continuous from start to finish and stops only for a shutdown. The end product may be finished goods or processed further on job orders.

Joint Products--A single material is processed to the split-off point where separate products emerge, not obtainable by any other method. The distinction is inherent in nature; it is not related to common costs which are individual and allocable. The joint products may be salable at the split-off point or they may be processed further individually.

Production costs for all methods are charged to work-in-process inventory, completed goods are transferred to finished goods, and shipments are charged to cost of sales. The balance in the work-in-process inventory account is supported by production on the floor. Costing may be at actual or standard. Output is based on completion of operations as measured at countpoints located on the production floor to keep float at an acceptable level. Float is the work done after one countpoint and before the next. Actual cost has been incurred but credit is booked only at the next countpoint; the difference appears as variance.

JOB ORDERS

A job order issued by production control authorizes the withdrawal of materials from inventory by requisition and the scheduling of labor operations. These steps are based on product operation sheets that contain the specifications established by design and manufacturing engineers.

The specifications are expressed in dollars on the product cost sheets used for inventory valuation. The information system embraces the full cycle from design through production, sale, and collection.

All material requisitions are charged to job orders. The material balance in work-in-process is supported by the material on job orders in process. Direct labor for production time is charged to job orders from daily time records, supporting the labor balance in the work-in-process account. These debits are balanced to the charges in the payroll clearing account from the payroll department. Overhead is applied to job orders when they are transferred to finished goods, and to the orders in process at the end of the period. At closing, all job orders in process are listed and should agree with the inventory balance in total and by cost element. Finished goods are supported by items in stock identified by product. All inventories are supported by perpetual records and subject to periodic physical count. Evaluation of inventories for marketable value should also be reviewed for possible markdown. These steps are part of the internal control system.

Job orders include dates and amounts, all materials, labor charges by operation, applied overhead, opening and closing balances, credits and transfers, and totals to date and on completion. Job orders can be tracked for timely progress related to completion schedules and for costs incurred relative to estimates. Cost overruns that exceed sales amounts require timely write-off. With a standard cost system all entries are at standard, with variances expensed as incurred. Variances are subject to operational expense control separate from job order identification. With actual costs, all material and labor are charged, plus applied overhead at the predetermined rate. Charges to job orders can be subdivided as to actual and variance for reference. For custom work priced on a cost estimate the actual cost record is useful for reference in the future for similar bids. The cost estimates are a guide to actual performance and to revisions indicated for other work. Actual costs can be monitored and projected as the work progresses. For example, if half the total labor estimate has been incurred but the work is only 40 percent along, a new estimate should be made.

An example is given:

Job Order ____	Start Date ____		Completion Date ____	Estimate Date ____	
			Projected	Bid	
	To Date	To Complete	Total	Estimate	Over
Materials by item:					
(all)	$1,600	$ 640	$2,240	$2,000	$ 240
Labor by operation:					
1	600	0	600	450	150
2	300	100	400	375	25
3	400	400	800	700	100
4	0	700	700	600	100
	1,300	1,200	2,500	2,125	375
Direct costs	2,900	1,840	4,740	4,125	615

Applied overhead					
on labor at 100%	$1,300	$1,200	$2,500	$2,125	$ 375
Total	4,200	3,040	7,240	6,250	990
Recap	Bid Est.	New Est.	Over		
Material	$2,000	$2,240	+ 240		
Labor	2,125	2,500	+ 375		
Overhead	2,125	2,500	+ 375		
	$6,250	$7,240	+ 990		
Mark-up (20% on bid)	1,250	260	- 990		
Price	7,500	7,500	0		

The mark-up is estimated to drop from $1,250 to $260, or to a markup of $260/7240 = 3.6%. A new estimate may be made and the work yet to be done may be reviewed for possible savings.

A repeat job estimated on the basis of the cost estimates could read:

Material	$2,240
Labor	2,500
Overhead	2,500
	$7,240
Mark-up 20%	1,448
Price	8,688
Old price	7,500
Increase	$1,188 = 15.8%

When a cost estimate projects a total in excess of selling price, the difference is credited to inventory and charged to cost of sales as a provision for loss. When the job is completed and billed, the margin is booked based on the final costs, and there may be some deviation from the loss estimate. Some jobs will come in under the cost estimate but profits are booked only when realized. Estimating the amounts of completion costs can range from a brief desk review to extended and complex projections requiring network analysis such as CPM and PERT. For major long-term construction contracts interim recordings of sales and profit are allowable on the basis of estimating total costs for the completed contract and the percentage of work accomplished to date. This method is known as percentage-of-completion as contrasted with the completed contract method with billing made in full when the work is done.

CONTINUOUS PROCESS

Production runs in a continuous flow. The flows may be departmentalized for both expense control and product costing. The output for a department may proceed by continuous flow through the next department or become finished goods. Continuous flow output may also be completed by job order. Charges are made by department for material, labor, and overhead. Labor and overhead are a combined charge designated as CC for conversion cost. Unit cost is the total amount charged divided by the number of units completed. If work-in-process charges are $10,000 for 2,000 units completed, the unit cost is $5. Actual or standard costs may be used but only a standard cost system provides practical cost control and valid unit costs. The CC incurred must be related to the number of

units processed to determine unit costs. At each closing total units are
the sum of completed units plus the degree of work done on units in
process, known as equivalent units. Illustration:

Physical # of Units	Percentage of Completion	Equivalent Units
1,000	100%	1,000
1,250	80%	1,000
2,000	50%	1,000
3,333	30%	1,000
10,000	10%	1,000
1,000	100%	1,000
1,000	80%	800
1,000	50%	500
1,000	30%	300
1,000	10%	100

Work flows through the departments to finished goods and the cost is
cumulative from the issuance of material to finished goods.   The amounts
in inventory must be calculated each month: opening inventory--plus
charges for material and CC and from prior departments--less costs
transferred but = ending inventory. The cost calculation must also take
account of any lost units.   The costing process is illustrated for B
without amounts:

```
Open inventory:
            from A
            by B
                        Total
Charges:
            from A
            by B
                        Total       Total
Transfers to C          Total
Balance--End inventory:
            from A
            by B
                        Total       Total
```

An example is given based on standard costs.   Actual costs and
variances are omitted.   Two departments are used--A and B--and two time
periods--P1 and P2.   All material is issued to A.   Lost units are
omitted. The physical units are illustrated first without dollars.

		A		B
P1	Open	0		0
	Add M	+100	from A	+60
	to B	- 60	to FG	-40
	Balance	+ 40		+20
P2	Add M	+160	from A	150
		+200		170
	to B	-150	to FG	130
	Balance	50		40

The physical units are restated as equivalent units to correspond with the costs incurred and to determine unit costs. Equivalent units--EU--are the total of transferred units plus the percentage of completion for units on hand. Material is complete for both units transferred out and for the ending balance.

Material EU:	A	B
P1	60 + 40 = 100	40 + 20 = 60
P2	150 + 50 = 200	130 + 40 = 170

EU for CC is a percentage of units on hand, ranging from zero to 100%, based on floor estimates, plus units transferred out:

CC EU:		A		B
P1 Transferred out		60		40
On hand	40 at 25%	10	20 at 50%	10
EU		70		50
P2 Transferred out		150		130
On hand	50 at 60%	30	40 at 75%	30
EU		180		160

The costs incurred by A in P1 are material $600 and CC $840 = $1,440. The calculations are made as follows:

			A	P1
I.	Physical units:			
		Open	0	
		Add	100	100
		to B	60	
		End (25% CC)	40	100
II.	EU			
		M	60 + 40 =	100
		CC	60 + 10 =	70
III.	Costs:			

			Total	EU	Unit
		M	$ 600	100	$ 6
		CC	840	70	12
		Total	$1440		$18
IV.	To B		$1080	60	18
	Balance:				
		M	$ 240	40	6
		CC	120	10	12
			360		18
		Total	$1440		

This model keeps all amounts, EU, and units in separate columns for clarity. The unit costs found in III reflect the matching of costs incurred with work done. The transfer to B is found by multiplying 60 units at $18. The ending balance is costed separately for M and CC. III and IV balance to prove the accuracy of the calculations. The ending balance is the opening balance for P2.

In P2 for A the costs incurred are M = $960 and CC $2,040 = $3,000.

<pre>
                               A   P2
  I. Physical units:
                    Open   40
                    Add   160   200
                    to B   150
                    End (60% CC)   50   200

 II. EU
                              M   150 + 50 = 200
                              CC   150 + 30 = 180

III. Costs: Balance   Add
                  P1   P2   =   Total   EU   Unit
           M $240 $ 960 $1200   200 $ 6
           CC   120   2040   2160   180   12
                 $360 $3000 $3360 $18

 IV. To B $2700   150   18
      Balance:
                      M $ 300   50   6
                      CC   360   30   12
                                        660   18
                                      $3360
</pre>

The ending balance is the opening balance for P3, not given. B receives transfers from A and adds no material. CC for P1 is $1,000 and for P2 it is $3,000. Completed units are transferred to finished goods.

<pre>
                               B   P1
  I. Physical units:
                    Open   0
                    from A   60   60
                    to FG   40
                    End (50% CC)   20   60

 II. EU
                              M   40 + 20 =   60
                              CC   40 + 10 =   50

III. Costs
                                     Total   EU   Unit
                      from A $1080   60 $18
                      CC   1000   50   20
                      total $2080 $38

 IV. To FG $1520   40   38
      Balance:
      from   A $ 360   20   18
                  B   200   10   20
                                       560   38
                  total   2080
</pre>

		B	P2	
I.	Physical units:			
	Open		20	
	from A		150	170
	to FG		130	
	End (75% CC)		40	170

II. EU

		M	130 + 40 = 170
		CC	130 + 30 = 160

III. Costs:

	Balance P1 +	Add P2 =	Total	EU	Unit
from A	$360	$2700	$3060	170	$18
CC	200	3000	3200	160	20
	$560	$5700	$6260		$38

		Total	EU	Unit
IV.	To FG	$4940	130	38
	Balance:			
	from A	$ 720	40	18
	B	600	30	20
		$1320		38
		$6260		

These illustrations use standard costs:

A:	M	$ 6
	CC	12
	to B	18
B:	from A	18
	CC	20
	to FG	38

The actual costs and variances are omitted. If actual costs are introduced and run through the models, unit costs fluctuate and the basis for expense control is lost.

Several other factors are described briefly. If more material is added in B with no change in the number of units, unit cost increases proportionately. If no material is added but the nature of the process doubles the number of units, unit costs are halved. The model provides a logical guide for changes. When there are units lost in the process, adjustment can be made as follows: Assume that in B-P2 the 130 units sent to FG at $38, or $4,940, are only 110 units, with 20 units lost:

B-P2

		Total	EU	Unit
IV.	To FG	$4180	110	$38
	Lost	760	20	38
	Subtotal	$4940	130	38
	Balance:			
	from A	$ 720	40	18
	B	600	30	20
		1320		38
		6260		

The $760 loss is charged to overhead, or it can be a separate expense element in cost of sales.

   If lost units are provided for in the standard, the unit value is adjusted upwards and there is no write-off for the lost units. For B-P2 if 17 lost units are planned:

   I. Physical units:
            Open   20
            from A   150   170
            to FG   113
            Lost   17
            End (75% CC)   40   170

  II. EU
                          M   113 + 40 = 153
                          CC   113 + 30 = 143

 III. Costs: Balance   Add
                 P1   +   P2   =   Total   EU   Unit
        from A $360 $2200 $3060   153 $20.00
        CC   200   3000   3200   143   22.38
                 $560 $5700 $6260 $42.38

  IV. To FG $4789   113   42.38
       Balance:
       from   A $ 800   40 $20.00
               B   671   30   22.38
                                        $1471 $42.38
                                        $6260

   Unit cost increases from $38.00 to $42.38 because the loss of units is a necessary cost. If more than 17 units are lost, the extra units are costed at $42.38. If fewer units are lost, the reduction in units is credited to cost at $42.38.

   The process costs in a department can be considered to be the equivalent of costs for a job order. Job order accounting is based on countpoints designed to keep float at a minimum. Process cost accounting uses estimates of completion to account for float. Such estimates may be imprecise but a large degree of error is tolerable because the effect on the large volume processed is negligible. With large steady flows it may be practical to assume a 50% completion rate.

JOINT PRODUCTS

   If a single material is processed to a point where separate products emerge as a fact of nature they are joint products. Costs incurred to that point, the split-off point, are indivisible. Assignment of the process cost total to the emergent products is necessarily arbitrary, done only to serve a defined purpose. The market value of the products in total less their joint cost is the margin; there is no separate margin for each product. Example:

Joint Products	Quantity	Price	Market Value
A	100	$ 6	$ 600
B	60	15	900
C	250	2	500
Total			$2,000
Joint costs			1,200
Margin--40%			$ 800

If all products are sold in the period the record is that given. If there are no sales the inventory is $1,200 total. With partial sales it is necessary to make some arbitrary allocation to measure product costs individually. Because management authorizes the process with the prospect of 40% margin in total, it is logical to establish each product cost to provide a 40% margin. This result is accomplished as follows:

Product	Qty.	Price	Market	Ratio	Allocated Cost	Margin	%
A	100	$ 6	$ 600	30%	$ 360	$240	40%
B	60	15	900	45%	540	360	40%
C	250	2	500	25%	300	200	40%
			$2,000	100%	$1,200	$800	40%

The allocation of the joint cost in the ratio of market value provides a uniform 40%. Unit product costs are:

	Quantity	Allocated Cost	Per Unit
A	100	$ 360	$3.60
B	60	540	9.00
C	250	300	1.20
		$1,200	

With partial sales in a period:

	Qty.	Price	Sales	Cost Unit	Total	Margin	%
A	50	$ 6	$300	$3.60	$180	$120	40%
B	10	15	150	9.00	90	60	40%
C	250	2	500	1.20	300	200	40%
			$950		$570	$380	40%

The inventory is:

	Make	Sell	Balance	Unit Cost	Total
A	100	50	50	$3.60	$180
B	60	10	50	9.00	450
C	250	250	0	1.20	0
					$630

Inventory of $630 plus cost of sales of $570 = $1,200 joint costs. The income statement would read:

```
Sales
A                  300
B                  150
C                  500      $ 950
Joint Cost                    570
Margin--40%                   380
```

The examples are given based on plan. Actual sales prices could vary
and show a margin over or under the 40% plan. The allocated unit product
costs would not be adjusted unless a need for write-down arises.
It frequently happens that an unwanted joint product arises in the
process unavoidably, called a by-product.   Two disposal situations are
possible:

        Net disposal cost--added to joint cost
        Net disposal gain--deducted from joint cost

To illustrate with the example given, C is a by-product with $500
disposal value less $125 disposal cost, or $375 net credit. The net
joint cost is $1,200 - 375 = $825.

	Qty.	Price	Market	Ratio	Cost	Margin	%
A	100	$ 6	$ 600	40%	$330	$270	45%
B	60	$15	900	60%	495	405	45%
			1,500		825	675	45%

The $375 net disposal value is debited to an inventory account.
Alternatively, if the disposal of C is a loss of $300, joint cost
rises to $1,500 and there is no margin. Classification of products as
joint or by-products can change over time. In each case, the decision is
made on the basis of the planned results. The only satisfactory method
for management is cost allocations based on relative market values.
A joint product may be processed beyond the split-off point.   The
measurement question is whether the added sales value exceeds the added
cost to provide added margin. The allocated joint cost is not relevant--
it is the same for either choice. The marketing question involves many
factors including demand elasticity and competition.
The example used above is restated in terms of unit amounts:

	40%			Projected Increments			Combined			
	Price	Cost	Margin	Price	Cost	Margin	Price	Cost	Margin	%
A	$6.00	$3.60	$2.40	$1.50	$1.20	$.30	$7.50	$4.80	$2.70	36%
B	15.00	9.00	6.00	3.00	3.00	0	18.00	12.00	6.00	33%
C	2.00	1.20	.80	1.00	1.20	(.20)	3.00	2.40	.60	20%

A Incremental margin gain of $.30 on sales price increase of $1.50, or
   20%. Percent drop from 40% to 36%.
B No incremental margin gain. Percent drops from 40% to 33%.
C Negative margin increment. Percent drops from 40% to 20%.

Changing market conditions and processing costs warrant close
attention to incremental analysis with the possibility of higher dollar

margins. The choices made are translated into the sales plans, remember-
ing that the output ratio for joint products is fixed. Assuming that A
and B are to be processed further but not C, the schedule is:

				Cost				Increment	
	Qty	Price	Mkt.	at	Total	Margin	%	Mkt.	Margin
A	100	$7.50	$750	$4.80	$480	$270	36%	$150	$30
B	60	18.00	1080	12.00	720	360	33%	180	0
C	250	2.00	500	1.20	300	200	40%	0	0
			2330		1500	830	36%		
Prior			2000		1200	800	40%		
Gain			330		300	30	9%	330	30

This schedule becomes the sales plan for comparison with actual results.
    Some joint products have no market at the split-off point and must be
processed further. In order to determine a market value ratio at the
split-off point so that the joint costs can be allocated it is necessary
to determine a derived value by deducting the necessary processing costs
from the known sales.   This is the equivalent of the illustration given
for B with incremental price and cost equal at $3.00.   An example is
given for products D, E, and F. D has no market at the split-off point
but sells for $800 after added costs of $160 for a derived market value
of $640, used to allocate joint costs of $500:

	Actual	Less Process	Net		Allocated	Add	Cost		
	Mkt.	Cost	Mkt.	Ratio	Costs	Back	Total	Margin	
D	$800	$160	$640	51.2	$256	$160	$416	$384	48.0%
E	500	0	500	40.0	200	0	200	300	60.0%
F	110	0	110	8.8	44	0	44	66	60.0%
	1410	160	1250	100.0	500	160	660	750	53.2%

    If D could be sold at the derived price of $640 with the allocated
cost of $256, the margin would be $384, or 60%, equal to E and F.
Incremental analysis can also be applied to the schedule shown. D can
also be analyzed as follows: E and F have sales of $610 (500 + 160) -
deduct joint costs of $500 = $110 margin without D. Any sales price for
D over the necessary incremental cost of $160 adds to the total gain.   D
price $800 - 160 = 640 + 110 = $750 total margin.

Appendix:
Present Value Tables

Table 1   Present Value of $1

Years Hence	1%	2%	4%	6%	8%	10%	12%	14%	15%	16%	18%	20%	22%	24%	25%	26%	28%	30%	35%	40%	45%	50%
1	0.990	0.980	0.962	0.943	0.926	0.909	0.893	0.877	0.870	0.862	0.847	0.833	0.820	0.806	0.800	0.794	0.781	0.769	0.741	0.714	0.690	0.667
2	0.980	0.961	0.925	0.890	0.857	0.826	0.797	0.769	0.756	0.743	0.718	0.694	0.672	0.650	0.640	0.630	0.610	0.592	0.549	0.510	0.476	0.444
3	0.971	0.942	0.889	0.840	0.794	0.751	0.712	0.675	0.658	0.641	0.609	0.579	0.551	0.524	0.512	0.500	0.477	0.455	0.406	0.364	0.328	0.296
4	0.961	0.924	0.855	0.792	0.735	0.683	0.636	0.592	0.572	0.552	0.516	0.482	0.451	0.423	0.410	0.397	0.373	0.350	0.301	0.260	0.226	0.198
5	0.951	0.906	0.822	0.747	0.681	0.621	0.567	0.519	0.497	0.476	0.437	0.402	0.370	0.341	0.328	0.315	0.291	0.269	0.223	0.186	0.156	0.132
6	0.942	0.888	0.790	0.705	0.630	0.564	0.507	0.456	0.432	0.410	0.370	0.335	0.303	0.275	0.262	0.250	0.227	0.207	0.165	0.133	0.108	0.088
7	0.933	0.871	0.760	0.665	0.583	0.513	0.452	0.400	0.376	0.354	0.314	0.279	0.249	0.222	0.210	0.198	0.178	0.159	0.122	0.095	0.074	0.059
8	0.923	0.853	0.731	0.627	0.540	0.467	0.404	0.351	0.327	0.305	0.266	0.233	0.204	0.179	0.168	0.157	0.139	0.123	0.091	0.068	0.051	0.039
9	0.914	0.837	0.703	0.592	0.500	0.424	0.361	0.308	0.284	0.263	0.225	0.194	0.167	0.144	0.134	0.125	0.108	0.094	0.067	0.048	0.035	0.026
10	0.905	0.820	0.676	0.558	0.463	0.386	0.322	0.270	0.247	0.227	0.191	0.162	0.137	0.116	0.107	0.099	0.085	0.073	0.050	0.035	0.024	0.017
11	0.896	0.804	0.650	0.527	0.429	0.350	0.287	0.237	0.215	0.195	0.162	0.135	0.112	0.094	0.086	0.079	0.066	0.056	0.037	0.025	0.017	0.012
12	0.887	0.788	0.625	0.497	0.397	0.319	0.257	0.208	0.187	0.168	0.137	0.112	0.092	0.076	0.069	0.062	0.052	0.043	0.027	0.018	0.012	0.008
13	0.879	0.773	0.601	0.469	0.368	0.290	0.229	0.182	0.163	0.145	0.116	0.093	0.075	0.061	0.055	0.050	0.040	0.033	0.020	0.013	0.008	0.005
14	0.870	0.758	0.577	0.442	0.340	0.263	0.205	0.160	0.141	0.125	0.099	0.078	0.062	0.049	0.044	0.039	0.032	0.025	0.015	0.009	0.006	0.003
15	0.861	0.743	0.555	0.417	0.315	0.239	0.183	0.140	0.123	0.108	0.084	0.065	0.051	0.040	0.035	0.031	0.025	0.020	0.011	0.006	0.004	0.002
16	0.853	0.728	0.534	0.394	0.292	0.218	0.163	0.123	0.107	0.093	0.071	0.054	0.042	0.032	0.028	0.025	0.019	0.015	0.008	0.005	0.003	0.002
17	0.844	0.714	0.513	0.371	0.270	0.198	0.146	0.108	0.093	0.080	0.060	0.045	0.034	0.026	0.023	0.020	0.015	0.012	0.006	0.003	0.002	0.001
18	0.836	0.700	0.494	0.350	0.250	0.180	0.130	0.095	0.081	0.069	0.051	0.038	0.028	0.021	0.018	0.016	0.012	0.009	0.005	0.002	0.001	0.001
19	0.828	0.686	0.475	0.331	0.232	0.164	0.116	0.083	0.070	0.060	0.043	0.031	0.023	0.017	0.014	0.012	0.009	0.007	0.003	0.002	0.001	
20	0.820	0.673	0.456	0.312	0.215	0.149	0.104	0.073	0.061	0.051	0.037	0.026	0.019	0.014	0.012	0.010	0.007	0.005	0.002	0.001	0.001	
21	0.811	0.660	0.439	0.294	0.199	0.135	0.093	0.064	0.053	0.044	0.031	0.022	0.015	0.011	0.009	0.008	0.006	0.004	0.002			
22	0.803	0.647	0.422	0.278	0.184	0.123	0.083	0.056	0.046	0.038	0.026	0.018	0.013	0.009	0.007	0.006	0.004	0.003	0.001			
23	0.795	0.634	0.406	0.262	0.170	0.112	0.074	0.049	0.040	0.033	0.022	0.015	0.010	0.007	0.006	0.005	0.003	0.002	0.001			
24	0.788	0.622	0.390	0.247	0.158	0.102	0.066	0.043	0.035	0.028	0.019	0.013	0.008	0.006	0.005	0.004	0.003	0.002	0.001			
25	0.780	0.610	0.375	0.233	0.146	0.092	0.059	0.038	0.030	0.024	0.016	0.010	0.007	0.005	0.004	0.003	0.002	0.001	0.001			
26	0.772	0.598	0.361	0.220	0.135	0.084	0.053	0.033	0.026	0.021	0.014	0.009	0.006	0.004	0.003	0.002	0.002	0.001				
27	0.764	0.586	0.347	0.207	0.125	0.076	0.047	0.029	0.023	0.018	0.011	0.007	0.005	0.003	0.002	0.002	0.001	0.001				
28	0.757	0.574	0.333	0.196	0.116	0.069	0.042	0.026	0.020	0.016	0.010	0.006	0.004	0.002	0.002	0.002	0.001	0.001				
29	0.749	0.563	0.321	0.185	0.107	0.063	0.037	0.022	0.017	0.014	0.008	0.005	0.003	0.002	0.002	0.001	0.001					
30	0.742	0.552	0.308	0.174	0.099	0.057	0.033	0.020	0.015	0.012	0.007	0.004	0.003	0.002	0.001	0.001	0.001					
40	0.672	0.453	0.208	0.097	0.046	0.022	0.011	0.005	0.004	0.003	0.001	0.001										
50	0.608	0.372	0.141	0.054	0.021	0.009	0.003	0.001	0.001	0.001												

374

Table 2 Present Value of an Annuity of $1

Years (N)	1%	2%	4%	6%	8%	10%	12%	14%	15%	16%	18%	20%	22%	24%	25%	26%	28%	30%	35%	40%	45%	50%
1	0.990	0.980	0.962	0.943	0.926	0.909	0.893	0.877	0.870	0.862	0.847	0.833	0.820	0.806	0.800	0.794	0.781	0.769	0.741	0.714	0.690	0.667
2	1.970	1.942	1.886	1.833	1.783	1.736	1.690	1.647	1.626	1.605	1.566	1.528	1.492	1.457	1.440	1.424	1.392	1.361	1.289	1.224	1.165	1.111
3	2.941	2.884	2.775	2.673	2.577	2.487	2.402	2.322	2.283	2.246	2.174	2.106	2.042	1.981	1.952	1.923	1.868	1.816	1.696	1.589	1.493	1.407
4	3.902	3.808	3.630	3.465	3.312	3.170	3.037	2.914	2.855	2.798	2.690	2.589	2.494	2.404	2.362	2.320	2.241	2.166	1.997	1.849	1.720	1.605
5	4.853	4.713	4.452	4.212	3.993	3.791	3.605	3.433	3.352	3.274	3.127	2.991	2.864	2.745	2.689	2.635	2.532	2.436	2.220	2.035	1.876	1.737
6	5.795	5.601	5.242	4.917	4.623	4.355	4.111	3.889	3.784	3.685	3.498	3.326	3.167	3.020	2.951	2.885	2.759	2.643	2.385	2.168	1.983	1.824
7	6.728	6.472	6.002	5.582	5.206	4.868	4.564	4.288	4.160	4.039	3.812	3.605	3.416	3.242	3.161	3.083	2.937	2.802	2.508	2.263	2.057	1.883
8	7.652	7.325	6.733	6.210	5.747	5.335	4.968	4.639	4.487	4.344	4.078	3.837	3.619	3.421	3.329	3.241	3.076	2.925	2.598	2.331	2.108	1.922
9	8.566	8.162	7.435	6.802	6.247	5.759	5.328	4.946	4.772	4.607	4.303	4.031	3.786	3.566	3.463	3.366	3.184	3.019	2.665	2.379	2.144	1.948
10	9.471	8.983	8.111	7.360	6.710	6.145	5.650	5.216	5.019	4.833	4.494	4.192	3.923	3.682	3.571	3.465	3.269	3.092	2.715	2.414	2.168	1.965
11	10.368	9.787	8.760	7.887	7.139	6.495	5.937	5.453	5.234	5.029	4.656	4.327	4.035	3.776	3.656	3.544	3.335	3.147	2.757	2.438	2.185	1.977
12	11.255	10.575	9.385	8.384	7.536	6.814	6.194	5.660	5.421	5.197	4.793	4.439	4.127	3.851	3.725	3.606	3.387	3.190	2.779	2.456	2.196	1.985
13	12.134	11.343	9.986	8.853	7.904	7.103	6.424	5.842	5.583	5.342	4.910	4.533	4.203	3.912	3.780	3.656	3.427	3.223	2.799	2.468	2.204	1.990
14	13.004	12.106	10.563	9.295	8.244	7.367	6.628	6.002	5.724	5.468	5.008	4.611	4.265	3.962	3.824	3.695	3.459	3.249	2.814	2.477	2.210	1.993
15	13.865	12.849	11.118	9.712	8.559	7.606	6.811	6.142	5.847	5.575	5.092	4.675	4.315	4.001	3.859	3.726	3.483	3.268	2.825	2.484	2.214	1.995
16	14.718	13.578	11.652	10.106	8.851	7.824	6.974	6.265	5.954	5.669	5.162	4.730	4.357	4.033	3.887	3.751	3.503	3.283	2.834	2.489	2.216	1.997
17	15.562	14.292	12.166	10.477	9.122	8.022	7.120	6.373	6.047	5.749	5.222	4.775	4.391	4.059	3.910	3.771	3.518	3.295	2.840	2.492	2.218	1.998
18	16.398	14.992	12.659	10.828	9.372	8.201	7.250	6.467	6.128	5.818	5.273	4.812	4.419	4.080	3.928	3.786	3.529	3.304	2.844	2.494	2.219	1.999
19	17.226	15.678	13.134	11.158	9.604	8.365	7.366	6.550	6.198	5.877	5.316	4.844	4.442	4.097	3.942	3.799	3.539	3.311	2.848	2.496	2.220	1.999
20	18.046	16.351	13.590	11.470	9.818	8.514	7.469	6.623	6.259	5.929	5.353	4.870	4.460	4.110	3.954	3.808	3.546	3.316	2.850	2.497	2.221	1.999
21	18.857	17.011	14.029	11.764	10.017	8.649	7.562	6.687	6.312	5.973	5.384	4.891	4.476	4.121	3.963	3.816	3.551	3.320	2.852	2.498	2.221	2.000
22	19.660	17.658	14.451	12.042	10.201	8.772	7.645	6.743	6.359	6.011	5.410	4.909	4.488	4.130	3.970	3.822	3.556	3.323	2.853	2.498	2.222	2.000
23	20.456	18.292	14.857	12.303	10.371	8.883	7.718	6.792	6.399	6.044	5.432	4.925	4.499	4.137	3.976	3.827	3.559	3.325	2.854	2.499	2.222	2.000
24	21.243	18.914	15.247	12.550	10.529	8.985	7.784	6.835	6.434	6.073	5.451	4.937	4.507	4.143	3.981	3.831	3.562	3.327	2.855	2.499	2.222	2.000
25	22.023	19.523	15.622	12.783	10.675	9.077	7.843	6.873	6.464	6.097	5.467	4.948	4.514	4.147	3.985	3.834	3.564	3.329	2.856	2.499	2.222	2.000
26	22.795	20.121	15.983	13.003	10.810	9.161	7.896	6.906	6.491	6.118	5.480	4.956	4.520	4.151	3.988	3.837	3.566	3.330	2.856	2.500	2.222	2.000
27	23.560	20.707	16.330	13.211	10.935	9.237	7.943	6.935	6.514	6.136	5.492	4.964	4.524	4.154	3.990	3.839	3.567	3.331	2.856	2.500	2.222	2.000
28	24.316	21.281	16.663	13.406	11.051	9.307	7.984	6.961	6.534	6.152	5.502	4.970	4.528	4.157	3.992	3.840	3.568	3.331	2.857	2.500	2.222	2.000
29	25.066	21.844	16.984	13.591	11.158	9.370	8.022	6.983	6.551	6.166	5.510	4.975	4.531	4.159	3.994	3.841	3.569	3.332	2.857	2.500	2.222	2.000
30	25.808	22.396	17.292	13.765	11.258	9.427	8.055	7.003	6.566	6.177	5.517	4.979	4.534	4.160	3.995	3.842	3.569	3.332	2.857	2.500	2.222	2.000
40	32.835	27.355	19.793	15.046	11.925	9.779	8.244	7.105	6.642	6.234	5.548	4.997	4.544	4.166	3.999	3.846	3.571	3.333	2.857	2.500	2.222	2.000
50	39.196	31.424	21.482	15.762	12.234	9.915	8.304	7.133	6.661	6.246	5.554	4.999	4.545	4.167	4.000	3.846	3.571	3.333	2.857	2.500	2.222	2.000

375

Index

Purchase of a company, 83-87

Rate of return, investors, 114-16
Receivables, 11-12, 41-46
Refunding a bond issue, 91-93
Return of assets (ROA), 13, 151-52,
    172-73
Return on equity (ROE), 13, 24-26
Returns and allowances, 232-33
Risk, 4-5, 102-116
Risk and return guidelines, 126-27
Risk indicators, 119-127

Safety stocks, 38-41
Sales deductions, 232-35
Sales discounts, 235
Sales expense, 184-90, 236-38
Sales order log, 231-32
Sales plans, 180-84
Sales reports, 238
Salvage value, 63-67
Shenkir, William, G., xv
Standard cost elements, 132-35
Standard deviation, 119-21
Standard product cost detail, 147-49
Stock valuation, 114-16
Stockholder Equity, 23-26
Storage charges, 187-88
"Sustainable Earnings Growth Rate," 26
Systems design, 331-34

Tax measurement, 6
Tools, 286

Uneven cash flows, 67-70
Units sold, industry analysis, 220-22,
    244-46

Variable costing, 67-70
Vernon, John M., 29
Volcker, Paul A., 3
Volume of production, 137-40

Wertz, Kenneth L., 29
Williams, Harold M., 224
Work orders, 276-78

About the Author

SHERMAN L. LEWIS is a former professor of accounting and finance. He was the directing partner for Management Advisory Services at an international accounting firm, a principal at a major consulting firm, and a corporate controller. Lewis is the author of *Evaluating Corporate Investment and Financing Opportunities* (Quorum Books, 1986).